Sexualities and Popular Culture

8

FOUNDATIONS OF POPULAR CULTURE

Series Editor: GARTH S. JOWETT
University of Houston

The study of popular culture has now become a widely accepted part of the modern academic curriculum. This increasing interest has spawned a great deal of important research in recent years, and the field of "cultural studies" in its many forms is now one of the most dynamic and exciting in modern academia. Each volume in the **Foundations of Popular Culture** series will introduce a specific issue fundamental to the study of popular culture, and the authors have been given the charge to write with clarity and precision and to examine the subject systematically. The editorial objective is to provide an important series of "building block" volumes that can stand by themselves or be used in combination to provide a thorough and accessible grounding in the field of cultural studies.

1. **The Production of Culture: Media and the Urban Arts**
   by **Diana Crane**

2. **Popular Culture Genres: Theories and Texts**
   by **Arthur Asa Berger**

3. **Rock Formation: Music, Technology, and Mass Communication**
   by **Steve Jones**

4. **Cultural Criticism: A Primer of Key Concepts**
   by **Arthur Asa Berger**

5. **Advertising and Popular Culture**
   by **Jib Fowles**

6. **Sexualities and Popular Culture**
   by **Carl B. Holmberg**

Sexualities and Popular Culture

Carl B. Holmberg

Foundations of Popular Culture

6

SAGE Publications
International Educational and Professional Publisher
Thousand Oaks   London   New Delhi

For information:

SAGE Publications, Inc.
2455 Teller Road
Thousand Oaks, California 91320
E-mail: order@sagepub.com

SAGE Publications Ltd.
6 Bonhill Street
London EC2A 4PU
United Kingdom

SAGE Publications India Pvt. Ltd.
M-32 Market
Greater Kailash I
New Delhi 110 048 India

Printed in the United States of America

Library of Congress Cataloging-in-Publication Data

Holmberg, Carl Bryan.
    Sexualities and popular culture / by Carl B. Holmberg.
        p.   cm. — (Foundations of popular culture; v. 6)
    Includes bibliographical references and index.
    ISBN 0-7619-0350-X (cloth: alk. paper).   ISBN 0-7619-0351-8
    (pbk.: alk. paper)
    1. Sex in popular culture   I. Title.   II. Series.
    HQ23.H723   1998
    306.7—dc21   97-45333

This book is printed on acid-free paper.

98 99 00 01 02 03 10 9 8 7 6 5 4 3 2 1

Acquiring Editor:	Margaret H. Seawell
Editorial Assistant:	Renée Piernot
Production Editor:	Sherrise M. Purdum
Production Assistant:	Denise Santoyo
Typesetter/Designer:	Janelle LeMaster
Print Buyer:	Anna Chin

For Lily Holmberg and Erin Holmberg,
who thought a copy of *Our Bodies, Ourselves*
as a Christmas present was a mighty strange gift—
then wore it out over the next few months.

Contents

Series Editor's Introduction

Human sexuality is by its very nature and function a major (some say 'the' major) part of almost every facet of our lives. We cannot escape dealing with "sex" in its many manifestations as we proceed through our lives; we are conceived by sexual activities; we choose our spouses and therefore our familial structures largely because of sexual attraction; we clothe and otherwise adorn ourselves because of conscious and unconscious sexual urges; and ultimately we leave our genes behind and therefore our mark on history because of our sexual activities.

No one doubts the role that sexual activities play in our society and culture, and yet the issue of "sex and popular culture" has not received much in the way of systematic examination across the full spectrum of our sexual practices. Carl Holmberg goes a long way toward dealing with this problem in this provocative, innovative, and eminently entertaining study. Rising to my challenge as the series editor to make the material "accessible," he has provided the reader with a fascinating and intellectually sound introduction to a complex subject. Clearly, no one volume can cover every nuance of this vast subject, but Dr. Holmberg's wide-ranging and informed examination provides an important base upon which to build more detailed work on specific topics.

In this seminal work, Carl Holmberg traces the history of "sex and popular culture" by both using and evaluating a range of pertinent disciplinary approaches. This technique illuminates the intricate ways in which the subject of "sex" is woven into the very fabric of our culture and society. Literature, anthropology, history, communication studies, sociology, psychology, mythology, and even zoology are all incorporated into his study of the subject. The result is a wide-ranging tour de force that is likely to inform, provoke, and delight readers while also suggesting many avenues for further research. I am grateful to Carl for accepting the challenge to undertake the writing of this complex volume; all of his hard work has paid off in the creation of an important introduction to a fundamental part of popular culture studies.

—GARTH S. JOWETT
Series Editor

Acknowledgments

I gratefully acknowledge and thank publishers who have permitted the incorporation of previously published scholarly articles and who also helped me improve these pieces:

Felicia Campbell and *The Popular Culture Review* for "Parties as Sound Rituals: An Audeography," 3:2 (1992), 67-75.

Dennis Hall and *Studies in Popular Culture* for "Clive Barker's Poetics: The Rhetorical Nature of Horror and Human Experience," 14:2 (1992), 85-95.

Richard Schneider and *The Harvard Gay and Lesbian Review* for "Hey Butch, Your Slip(page) Is Showing! The New Language of Self-Presentation and the Paradoxes of the He/art," 3:3 (1996), 25-27.

Thanks to Sara Irwin, Anissa Ma, and The Royal Ontario Museum, Toronto, Canada, for their assistance and advice about Chinese ivory figurines as well as the selection of a representative photograph.

Various persons who work at the television show *Days of Our Lives,* Corday Productions, and NBC were quite gracious in helping me select a photograph. They include Nancy Lewis, Greg Meng, Michael Feeney, John Paschal, and Griffin Meyer. Thanks so much. Picture of Marlena (Deidre Hall) and John (Drake Hogestyn) courtesy of John Paschal.

David Hampshire at Instructional Media Services at Bowling Green State University produced glossy photos quickly and patiently. Thank you.

The cover concept was designed by Julie Scott. Nice work, as usual. I shall never forget her participation in the first graduate seminar I offered through the Department of Popular Culture. Blessed be.

The staff at Sage Publications also deserves accolades. Many readers would otherwise never see many of the following names: Sophy Craze, Kassie Gavrilis, Janelle LeMaster, Jennifer Morgan, Renée Piernot, Sherrise Purdum, Margaret Seawell, and, of course, series editor Garth Jowett. Thanks for the laughter as well as the elbow grease.

Bernice Aguilar manages the Department of Popular Culture's business and clerical matters so well that I was able to meet deadlines on time. *Muchas gracias.*

To all the clients and students who made the workshops on sex and popular culture memorable and touching for all of us: Way to go! Your voice is here, too.

Finally, although any number of mentors truly speak through the text and scholarly apparatus of this monograph and deserve mention, one group merits utmost praise. My colleagues in the Department of Popular Culture at Bowling Green State University have been the most supportive, helpful, and considerate colleagues I've known throughout my professional career. I wish I could say I have worked as closely with others in the popular culture studies movement as I have with them. Many thanks for taking me in and nurturing me through rough times: Ray Browne, Chris Geist, Marilyn Motz, Jack Nachbar, Angela Nelson, and Jack Santino. Without you, nothing.

Introduction

Before you read the main part of the book, I would appreciate a favor from you. Please read the following statements instead of skipping them, as we all so often do, because in this case, they may alert you to textual features crucial to the approaches taken and to be presented. Some of it may also be amusing.

The Use of Examples

At any given example of a popular culture artifact, event, or experience, particularly those mentioned in early chapters, readers may understandably desire a more complete interpretation of that example, especially if they are knowledgeable about it or familiar with it. To do so would digress from the concepts currently being explicated, however, and cannot always be pursued because of limitations imposed on the book's length. In addition, the examples, after all, are employed to illustrate a point, not to present each example beyond that topical domain. Readers should keep in mind that the opening chapters are not as artifactually oriented as they are focused to present conventional vocabulary, topics, and issues prevalent in culture studies and gender studies. Some of the examples mentioned early do indeed appear later in the narrative; later chapters are more artifactually oriented as well as more thorough in exploring alternative angles concerning examples. Alas, some do not reappear later in the text. Further explications of them must wait for others or myself to render a more extended interpretation.

On Provocative Language

Although any word choice about body parts and their sexual connotations and activities other than scientific nomenclature may be objectionable to some constituencies, colloquial use is often more correctly the language level that exhibits the norms inscribed in popular culture artifacts, events, and experiences. Some language, customs, and habits admittedly evoke discomfort sometimes. Discomfort is not necessarily a justification for avoidance, censorship, or standardization of the language, customs, and habits of everyday peoples and the arts they treasure. If discomfort is an infallible sign of pornography, then most classroom seating for students in public and private schools is pornographic, as are many sports in which discomfort is to be overcome. For that matter, many math and foreign language classes would probably need to be censored for all the discomfort they promulgate.

It is unfortunate that some readers may be offended by candid disclosure and interpretation of sexualities in popular culture. Considering that sexuality is one of the core experiences of being human, and considering that in some cultures, the discussion and kind nurturance of sexuality is closeted to the point of never explaining sex's ways to children, let alone adults, it occurs to me, among many others, that access to information and dialogue about sexualities is more important than not offending someone. I have taken great strides to offer a diversity of perspectives on sexual practices so as not to offend by omission everyone or anyone in particular. I have no intention to offend anyone by reporting phenomena found in everyday culture. Unfortunately, too many people seem to think that research is not on the same level as everyday life. Research is itself offensive if it appears in everyday life, and if it actually acknowledges the raciness that may occur in everyday life, it is perceived to push credulity. It is entirely unfortunate that the two are conceived so they may not meet. I, myself, do not think that way. Research can be fun and interesting, not dry and boring. I will do my best not to be provocative, however. Believe me, the opportunities for word play have been rather tempting, but I have restrained myself. I affirm, however, that I feel committed to exploring diversity, which, to be honest, can itself be provocative.

A truly free society does not stifle the statement of diversity, particularly when diversity sometimes can only speak in its own words, words that are chosen and used so as not to reflect standard and conventional norms. A truly free society does not deny access to information that potentially enables all citizens to participate better in that society in the sense of being and remaining healthy. A truly free society allows and encourages freedom of expression over parochial control and insular censorship.

Thus, I choose not to censor language used by various cultures and subcultures nor to substitute scientific jargon. Insider language is the language of popular culture and reveals norms and values that so-called professionals and proper wording smother. So-called polite language may all too often be alien to a cultural scene and thus must be treated suspiciously as an imposition of outsiders, of colonization by outsider norms, if you will. Insider language— emically studied—will be shown deference instead of the potentially serious belittlement and expurgation imposed by the etically determined imperialism of standardization or clinical politesse.

Other Word Use

Readers familiar with either gender studies or cultural studies may be aware that the same word or phrase works differently in different disciplines. All readers should alert themselves to the following uses employed in this book:

1. Whenever possible, I have chosen to employ the word *performance* instead of the word *behavior.* Although they may be interchangeable to some people, they are not always, and actually, there is a world of difference between them. Performance indicates a sort of dramatism, that individuals and groups are aware of scenes, scripts, action, and proper or improper performance of them. That is different from behaviorism, which uses the word *behavior* to indicate unthinking, automatic responses. Performance includes motivations and interpretive perspectives, particularly the rhetorical awareness that specific situations hold their own exigencies, which evoke a series of alternative actions for communicating in and about that situation.

2. Similarly, the word *place* will be employed whenever many cultural researchers might use the word *space. Space* is a materially biased word that suggests that problems and answers to them may be found only in a physical sense. In contrast, *place* can indicate material space, but it also may indicate mental, spiritual, or symbolic phenomena. *Place* also derives from the rhetorical tradition that in its full is not inclined to reduce everything to matter, physical science, and quantification.

3. Readers ought to beware that common, even everyday, words may have technical meanings in popular culture studies. *Everyday life* will be explained early on as a crucial concept. For now, however, it is enough to relay that the

terms *historic* and *historical* will be applied as a technical differentiation. *Historic* will be used to indicate the sense of a momentous event; *historical* will indicate anything in the record of history.

Problems with "Review of the Literature"

Although literature reviews may be standard operating procedure in many scholarly studies, the custom is rendered unworkable or at best cumbersome in the study of popular culture and sex. Unlike other areas of inquiry, there is no literature about sex and popular culture that has developed through time the way Western philosophy or science have and that therefore may be traced for significant developments in its public interactions between commentators. I also must caution that the literature review tradition, in the guise of rehearsing great lights of scholarship, too often sets research agendas that exclude, or at least overcontrol, diversity. This assumption is indeed problematic at the very least in late modern North America, in which voices about sex, gender, race, ethnicity, class, and sexual orientation have never before been raised but now are setting new research agendas that reflect the glories and vicissitudes of sex, gender, race, ethnicity, class, and sexual orientation. The nature of sex and popular culture has proved to be quite dramatically diverse and has been so all along, in everyday life, historical and present, and contemporaneously in the scant but growing number of commentaries about sex and everyday life, although until recently such diversity was ignored or at best did not receive public acknowledgment and discussion. Hence, research literature will be incorporated by topic or issue as appropriate but not set aside in one heap to honor it. Certain areas do overlap and inform each other, however, as witnessed by the example of Chapter 4, in which women's studies, gay/lesbian studies, and men's studies will be shown to share certain research agendas as well as herald more unique trajectories.

A Curious Scholarly Fashion

I have intentionally chosen to employ the phrase *late modern* instead of the word *postmodern* and its related terms. Although *postmodernism* enjoys a fashionable coinage and does indicate related modes of inquiry and writing representative of cutting edge research and commentary found mostly in the last thirty years, the term itself is problematic. Literally, it means "after the modern." To me, that is quite odd because many of the so-called postmodernists do not accept received traditions, the notion of chronological development, or linearity itself, for that matter. I note with interest that even Jameson seems to believe that Western culture has not moved beyond "late capitalism." Yet moving to something new Western culture seems to be doing. Although I incorporate some "postmodern" writers and viewpoints, I do not pretend to maintain that postmodernism speaks for all or most of the peoples of the world. Postmodernism does create places of understanding and interpretation that other modes of inquiry and writing do not easily afford. But although I am cognizant of and respect numerous contemporary and historical commentaries about sex and culture, I do not valorize one of them or maintain that there is one and only one proper scholarly tradition about sexualities and popular culture, let alone anything. Imperialism and dominance by any other names are still imperialism and dominance.

Some postmodernists and their fans may therefore not take a fancy to my reportage concerning classic Western sources such as Aristotle, among others. I refer to them as formative of culture, not the be-all and end-all of culture. Ignoring them, then, popular culture itself must be ignored: Popular culture—in the West, anyway—carries their influence, and although popular culture may be understood without them, I suppose, one way to understand popular culture—not the whole way, not all the ways—is to recognize their influence. Then again, I do not limit myself to them, to postmoderns, or to Western cultures. An African proverb says it best. "One han no fit tie bundu." One hand cannot tie a bundle. One tradition cannot speak for all. If we really are in a "postmodern" sort of way with the interpenetration of cultures and cultural levels, then limiting ourselves to one nation, one culture, one period, and one set of literature would not be very postmodern.

1

Popular Culture

Common word use and misrepresentations of the terms *culture, culture studies,* and *popular culture* may easily confuse even the most serious person who wants to understand and interpret culture, let alone popular culture. If nothing else, our notions of culture and what is popular are riddled with class assumptions, that is, assumptions associated with particular social classes and their perceived hierarchy. Often, the word *culture* denotes excellent learning, fine arts, the sciences, and the finest of leadership. To be cultured, thus, means to be upper-class or high-class. In turn, high-class indicates advanced competence, mastery, and expertise—and here is where the assumption of equating culture with high-class breaks down, collapses, and becomes nonsensical, particularly in an ostensibly free, democratic society.

Artifacts, experiences, and events that are well done can emerge from all classes, all societies, and all cultures. They are not limited to one class, let alone to the received traditions of a ruling class in one nation state or of an overarching Zeitgeist such as Western culture or Eastern culture. Laborers who tool machinery to precise tolerances of measurement may be perceived by some people who for whatever reason want to distance themselves from common laborers as "low" class, yet their work is not something many others could do; it is high quality. There is no reason to belittle laborers for high-quality work because their profession is blue-collar, just as there is no reason to pose culture as only what owners and rich people do or have. Furthermore, there is culture in producing the machinery and among the various persons who produce them. The same goes for making sound recordings, films, books, plays, and advertisements.

Thus, the notion that culture means only what elitists, snobs, and aristocrats do and the standards of taste that occur as rulers "do" culture is simply not useful or accurate. At best, it misleads that all culture must conform to one and only one set of cultural norms. It cannot explain, for instance, the cachet that French cooking has among many North Americans who assume it to be high-class when the bulk of so-called haute cuisine is peasant in its origins and practice.

Similarly, what is popular is not always a question of mass production—that a lot of products, ideas, and experiences are consumed by many people and are hence "popular." That is like taking a majority vote to determine what is popular, a procedure that ignores what subcultures and other cultures prefer as popular by focusing on one and only one "winner." For example, a folktale may be popular in a small community and not elsewhere. Would that mean the folktale is not popular? Certainly not. John Fiske also warns that predefining popular culture is, at best, dicey, particularly with regard to mass production:

> The object of analysis, then, and the basis of a theory of everyday life is not the products, the system that distributes them, or the consumer information, but the concrete specific uses they are put to, the individual acts of consumption-production, the creativities produced from the commodities. (37)

This confirms Fiske's observation that popular culture is not a fixed category but fluid, dependent on communities and not experts' predefinitions. "The popular can also be characterized by its fluidity. One person may, at different times, form cultural allegiances with different, not to say contradictory, social groups as he or she moves through the social formation" (30). Not only that, specifically looking into what ostensibly is a "culture" does not mean one will find the popular. This is why popular culture is such an elusive concept; it cannot be firmly located in its texts or in its readers. One cannot go, for instance, to working-class Hispanic women and guarantee to find popular culture among them. Cultural forces and social categories do not always match so precisely (45). Thus, needed is a definition of popular culture that does not predefine what popular culture is.

Popularity refers to the habits of a community that shares interests and preferences, sometimes avidly, sometimes not, yet repeatedly. The use of a bitter-tasting medication may not be popular in the sense of "tastes good," but it may be common in a community because it is held to be effective despite the bitter taste. Popularity may well vary through time and across different terrains with their innately variant ecological resources and possibilities. One does not assume there to be the same herbal remedies in Lapland as in Belize because the flora in each terrain is different, yet both indeed have herbal remedies. The phenomenon of communities living their preferences repeatedly persists despite the realm of variation.

Culture grows people in communities. A community may be an ethnicity, race, neighborhood, family, class, or group oriented to artifacts and events its constituents find fascinating, or even dull. Each of these communities may overlap, intersect, or dwell with the others. A community is also an *interpretive* community. Discussing reading as a constitutive act, Stanley Fish argues,

> It is interpretive communities, rather than either the text or the reader, that produce meanings and are responsible for the emergence of formal features. Interpretive communities are made up of those who share interpretive strategies not for reading but for writing texts, for constituting their properties. (14)

Thus, a culture as a community may be identified not just geographically or physically but for its interpretive habits: All Monopoly players do not physically know each other yet share common rules, courtesies, strategies, folklore, and methods for playing Monopoly. New players come into the community and become acculturated. Monopoly communities grow people. What is popular is what is habitually shared and how the sharing occurs. This definition of popular culture does not limit popular culture to particular artifacts or to the commodification process itself. It includes them but acknowledges the fluidity through which communities determine what is popular on an ad hoc basis. By not predefining popular culture, the definition meets Fiske's criterion for defining popular culture.

That said, however, some, and perhaps most, interpretive communities are *sexualized* interpretive communities. They may be sexualized by gender. For instance, Radway reports that the readers of popular romance novels are mostly women, age twenty-five to forty-five. Unlike Douglas, who observed that women who read romances enjoy the titillation of "seeing themselves, not necessarily as they are, but as some men would like to see them: illogical, innocent, magnetized by male sexuality and brutality" ("Soft-Porn Culture" 28), Radway discovered that some women found reading romances as a way of opposing sexist stereotypes of women "because the women use it to thwart common cultural expectations and to supply gratification ordinarily ruled out by the way the culture structures their lives" (211). In part consciously applying Fish's construct of interpretive communities, Radway also reports numerous interpretive strategies common to romance readers.

Sexualized interpretive communities are not always circumscribed by gender or by written texts. One interpretive culture found in gay male culture involves those men who use variously colored bandanas to announce their sexual interests overtly to other men sharing the same interpretive strategies yet who keep these announcements covert to outsiders, who merely see a bandana. The color coding and the placement of the bandana on the body can be extremely elaborate and, until the last ten years or so, varied from locale to locale. The fashion objects serve as openers to conversation and thus enable people who might not otherwise identify each other as sharing mutual interests that nurture them—that is, the same culture.

Although "popular culture" is whatever grows people while communities share mutual interests repeatedly, generate them, and learn new ones, interpretive strategies are also communication strategies. As Fish comments, "those who participate in this communication do so confidently rather than provisionally . . . while their confidence has its source in a set of beliefs, those beliefs are not individual-specific or idiosyncratic but communal and conventional" (321). A community sharing mutual interests necessarily involves the means of and rituals for communicating and sharing those interests. Thus, the study of popular culture necessarily will involve the communication norms and media for growing people in a community. Communication and media need to be understood alongside popular culture, not as a separate endeavor, not as something with no interest in popular culture, and certainly not as an afterthought to popular culture and its consideration.

The Culture Wars

Some critics disparage the study of popular culture, however, claiming that the study of popular novels, film, music, and the like dilutes school curricula and lowers educational standards by exploring diversity (Bloom; Hirsch). Hirsch, particularly fond of calling diversity "fragmentation" and then equating diversity with illiteracy (144), never really considers that there are many types of literacy because there are so many media to "read," each with its own demands of literacy, not just one. Instead, critics such as Hirsch argue that common culture, not diversity, should be the focus of public and private schooling. Thus, any sort of diversity orientation in education, such as the study of popular culture—as if diversity were engraved in stone for all time, for all cultures in exactly the same way—either is of little value or corrupts society by damaging not literacy, but *cultural* literacy.

Cultural literacy means knowing a set of terms common to the American people, as listed in an appendix to Hirsch's book, which apparently is a remedy for declining education. Hirsch feels that "the literate culture necessary for reading" (114) will make better learners and better citizens. Lynne Cheney similarly assumes that indeed there is one truth and that relativism cannot get at it, particularly basing curricula on or including multiculturalism, feminism, and ethnicity (44). Cheney's policy leadership of the National Endowment of the Humanities, which excluded diversity critical of common culture, is consistent with this view. Oddly enough, then, Bloom, Hirsch, and Cheney do not appear to know the *common* and traditional name for this procedure of assembling a list and then requiring people to know it. At least, they should follow their own procedures. It derives from Christian culture. Core teachings are customarily called the *canon*. Canon is basic information and doctrine everyone must know and acknowledge to be considered a true Christian. Other religions make similar assumptions for learning and proving one's orthodoxy. Thus, their true argument lies in *canonical* culture—that only it ought to be taught instead of diversity, instead of investigating popular culture, if not exclusively, mostly. Canonical culture is limited to those received historical versions of great deeds written by winners of wars and other controversies, artifacts made by great men, and knowledge determined to be valuable by ruling experts who are schooled in the doctrines of canon. The points of view of minorities and other cultures are presumably irrelevant or less significant, hence not worthy of inclusion in curricula or classroom experience. Worse still, they allegedly corrupt education.

Case in point: Allan Bloom is particularly weighted in the canonicity of privilege. *The Closing of the American Mind* prefaces his assumptions: As a teacher, he is privileged; the craft of teaching requires knowing students' "hungers" and "what they can digest." The teacher is in a unique position to influence unshaped souls and "spy out and elicit those hungers" (19). Yet oddly enough, by the close of the "Preface," Bloom addresses the nature of the students he has in mind.

> A word about my "sample" in this study. It consists of thousands of students of comparatively high intelligence, materially and spiritually free to do pretty much what they want with the few years of college they are privileged to have—in short, the kind of young persons who populate the twenty or thirty best universities. (22)

In the spirit of being a liberally educated person myself, "who is able to resist the easy and preferred answers, not because he is obstinate but because he knows others worthy of consideration" (21), I am not only alarmed at the repetition of the word *privileged* but also shocked that Bloom actually contradicts the subtitle of his own book, "how higher education has failed democracy and impoverished the souls of today's students." Students at "the twenty or thirty best universities" are not exactly representative of North American college and university students or of American culture, for that matter, and certainly not of the world's universities.

Is Bloom *so* privileged that he is unconcerned and perhaps professionally unfamiliar with the millions of students who *must* go to university, who *must* pay their own way, who *must* be constrained in their material and spiritual freedom, just to make ends meet *and* get a degree? The ones who arrive to class exhausted from full- or part-time jobs, not because they partied all night, not because they have been discussing the glories of Plato until dawn in their pursuit of material and spiritual freedom? As a teacher, I have not privileged myself to work with and mostly think about only the best students because democracy is about working with *all* peoples. Some of the "best" students I have known I met when they were C-to-failing students because their other professors saw them as intellectual trash and mostly gave their attention to the "best." I don't stand for that and expect "the best" from *everyone*. Let's face it, the closing of the American mind lies in the insistence of working with only the best clients, fooling ourselves in the self-perpetuating orgy of privilege. Forget about the millions who never go to college but who still contribute to American culture. The true enemies of an open society are the ones whose minds are already closed inside their own elitism (Popper).

Canonicity is a bad habit. Perhaps that is why Bloom, Hirsch, Cheney, and others like themselves avoid the word like the plague so as not to alert anyone that their agenda is about indoctrination, not freedom. Canonical approaches give the impression that there is one correct version of history, one correct way to interpret life, artifacts, and people. Throughout Western and other cultures, this has meant that the artifacts to be analyzed and interpreted are those determined traditionally by male experts, in Western literature, for instance, works by Melville, Conrad, Hawthorne, Chaucer, and Shakespeare and the historical and literary commentaries penned mostly by men. Yet the very mention of Shakespeare itself falsifies this rather limited canonical point of view: Shakespeare was "popular" in his own lifetime.

Canonical critics of popular culturally based studies seem to assume a nineteenth-century vision of culture and its transference. They might do well to read and seriously consider what one of the foremost interpreters of culture, Clifford Geertz, has to say about unitary cultural approaches.

> Once upon a time, not so very long ago, when the West was a good deal more sure of itself, of what it was, and what it wasn't, the concept of culture had a firm design and a definite edge. At first, global and evolutionary, it simply marked the West,

rational, historical, progressive, devotional, off from the Non-West, superstitious, static, archaic, magical. Later, when, for a host of reasons, ethical, political, and wistfully scientific, this seemed too crude, and too candid, the need for a more exact, more celebratory representation of the world elsewhere came into being, and the concept shifted to the life-way-of-a-people form familiar to us now. Islands, tribes, communities, nations, civilizations . . . eventually classes, regions, ethnic groups, minorities, youth (in South Africa, even races, in India, even sects) . . . had cultures: manners of doing things, distinct and characteristic. (*After the Fact* 42).

Geertz's choice opening phrase "Once upon a time" is a classic marker that indicates that the former interpretation of culture as Western-and-only-Western culture was or is a fairy tale. Geertz observes not only that there is more than one culture ("culture*s*") but also that there are numerous ways to realize cultures, such as tribes, communities, classes, and ethnic groups. Geertz also acknowledges that this reformulation has been under attack since its inception: "This notion came under attack virtually as soon as it was articulated; the clearer the articulation, the more intense the attack" (42). Hence, it is not surprising that the study of popular culture and its incorporation into education are under attack in what has been called "the culture wars." Attacks on the study of the life of everyday people are no small matters and deserve further articulations that the people can read and judge for themselves.

Critics who level canonical and other elitist claims against popular culture studies ignore the many advantages of studying popular culture as well as the realities of diversity, multiculturalism, and training citizens to consider alternatives, weigh them, and honor genuine, heartfelt differences between individuals and between peoples. Because these critics' arguments have already made them money and have been well read and discussed (Lovett-Graff 100-101), I address some of the positive educational and social advantages for studying popular culture in a free society and a diverse world. These critics' publications have been *popular*—which on *their* own terms, because their publications are not in themselves canonical, ought to be dismissed as merely popular. Instead, it is more honest and decent to say that there are people agendas just as important and as valuable as canonical points of view, people agendas that do not often get considered by policymakers keen on restricting the free interplay of sharing knowledge about everyday lives, if that is advantageous to themselves and their affiliations. Finally, popular culture certainly is influenced and in no small way created by canonical ideas, teachings, liberations, and restrictions. Popular culture studies do not necessarily avoid the canonical, but they approach the canonical with a strong sense of the positive values of interpreting everyday life and people.

Reasons to Study Popular,
Noncanonical Culture

First of all, in contrast to the impression garnered from canonical views, there is no such thing as monolithic culture. North American culture is North American cultures. Although a monolithic North American culture would be simpler and easier for canonical understanding to be taught and learned, it would stifle the free diversity of choice and lifestyle that many early European Americans sought in leaving Europe, let alone be inaccurate. There are various regions, classes, ethnicities, races, levels of education, and personal interests, as well as local communities of secular, sacred, and sexual interest. Each of these overlap, interpenetrate, and coinfluence the others, sometimes in obvious ways, sometimes in barely noticeable yet subtly powerful manners. Indeed, with canonical viewpoints having set the conceptual agenda for seeing ourselves and our world for at least the past two thousand years in national and community groupings, even the voices of diversity that criticize canonicity often seem to buy into the notion that culture is indeed monolithic. Culture is not monolithic in North America, despite various mass media and consumerism influences, nor is it monolithic in, say, China. China itself includes numerous recognizable subcultures. Although they are interrelated, they are by no means the same. In addition, there are at least sixty-seven million indigenous people in China (Mander 354). Suddenly, any presumption of a monolithic nation and culture becomes suspect at best. *It is advantageous to study popular culture and noncanonical cultures because they more accurately reflect the daily life of the vast majority of the peoples of the world.*

Second, there is no universal or rigidified canon unless the people accept it as so—and that acceptance and its ramifications and consequences would change eventually as the nature of people changes. Canon as forever fixed is a fiction. It lends another shady impression that after familiarity with canonical culture, there really is nothing more to become familiar with. Thus, there are plenteous educational assumptions that once students have mastered an or-dained curriculum, students are educated. Unfortunately, many people with diplomas do not easily appear to be educated, particularly for a democratic society and a diverse, intercultural world. The long-standing traditional learning approaches invented by rich, aristocratic, blue-blooded, churchy men are some-thing current critics of culture and canonical points of view call *patriarchy* (Berry). Patriarchy is the orientation to life received or inherited from ancestors that growing numbers of voices in the late twentieth century claim to be male-dominant. Although patriarchy will be discussed at length later, at this point I acknowledge that indeed what some commentators call patriarchy does at least trivialize other views and experiences of culture. Yet there are canons, traditions in occupations, regions, countries, and so on, that coexist. *It is advantageous to study popular and noncanonical culture because education and learning do not and should not stop when one has covered all the bases of a dictated curriculum.* Diversity *is;* it is a real-world cultural phenomenon. Living that diversity is the ultimate curriculum. Life is education that never really concludes.

A third observation reveals another advantage in studying popular culture: *Much of what is canonical was once popular.* Shakespeare has already been mentioned. Bach used drinking songs in some of his works, and a major portion of his music was composed for Sunday church and a local congregation—not for large concert halls. Many Greek tragedies and comedies were initially performed at annual Athenian festivals, which awarded prizes to that year's best of the competition; the festivals were heavily attended by the people—in those days, admittedly, men. But certainly not all of them were the calibre of Aristophanes, Plato, or Pericles. Bocaccio, Chaucer, and Petrarch, among others, popularized their vernacular language in some of their works so well that their local Italian and Middle English set the norms for later Italian and English. Just because the work of an artist, writer, critic, or performer stands the test of time and is acclaimed as high quality does not mean it never was—nor still is—"popular." *Perhaps it is only human nature and self-interest to label the cultural phenomena of honoring and celebrating great works and creators as the best of culture, thus awarding themselves—the acclaimers—a higher status than mere common mortals.* It still sets a hierarchy of elitism.

What some interpretive researchers such as anthropologists, ethnographers, and folklorists call the *emic* point of view is exactly the point of view of everyday life, as the people who live it perceive and conceive their everyday life. Instead of researchers imposing their own class, gender, racial, ethnic, and cultural values on the cultures they study, they strive to describe and interpret cultures and then verify their findings strictly with values employed by the people they study. They know that their own "expert" baggage is an *etic* point of view that well may lead them to notice things differently or incorrectly compared with the persons they study. Some cultures may never accept their point of view about their own culture. Hence, a new realization emerges: *The fourth advantage of studying cultures in noncanonical, emic manners lies in the reality that many individuals and groups may never have bought into canonical interpretations of themselves anyway. Diverse interpretations of individuals' own culture and of other cultures may shed understanding about themselves and others, thus improving the chances of enhancing life by learning, thinking, and acting through another's point of view.*

Canonical critics sometimes ignore that we are surrounded by and constantly bombarded by popular culture. If nothing else, we spend great amounts of money and time consuming culture; we ought to know how to do so wisely. Canonical admonitions that encourage us not to engage popular culture, which issue from the privileged, are then perhaps self-serving fuel for the rest of us to consume uncritically the popular events and artifacts many elitists themselves produced or caused to be produced. Luddites such as Hirsch and Bloom must admit that some rather prestigious culture observers admitted to their canon do not agree with them. Aristotle observed that animals have tooth and claw to defend themselves, yet humans also have language. He asked, why would a person *not* want to develop language and critical skills to be able to defend oneself from alluring yet inaccurate and potentially harmful ploys (*Art of Rhetoric* 13)? If one expands Aristotle's question beyond speaking and listening of an oral tradition to all communication media, there are certainly many instances when advertisers, salespersons, friends, families, journalists, and politicians share apparently compelling messages for their audiences to consume, many of which are not at all necessarily good for those audiences. *Therefore, citizens ought to be literate in as many media as possible so they may more easily detect subterfuge and exploitation; this long-standing advice constitutes the fifth advantage for pursuing popular culture seriously.* Those saying to ignore popular culture are saying to ignore daily life, not to examine it; Socrates recommended just the opposite—he said the unexamined life is not worth living. Those saying to focus on the canonical are saying to focus on experts' assessments instead of direct and heady interaction with popular culture and each other.

Sixth, some popular culture is rich, serious, and touching in our lifetime—not fifty to a hundred years from now—as may be proclaimed by some canonical experts at that time. The elitist argument to wait to study popular culture seems to rest on the notion that when an important event occurs, when some popular culture phenomenon hits the scene, we are so immersed in it we cannot observe and interpret it objectively. Only time will tell. Yet it is a historical fact that Beethoven, let alone other artists, was acclaimed in his own lifetime—so much for waiting for future objectivity. Culture affects us during our lifetime; it is not something insignificant to be left for discussion after we can no longer participate in that discussion. Culture should be shared, discussed, criticized, enhanced, or trashed as communities determine their mutualities. *The sixth advantage of studying popular culture resides in recognizing the enrich-*

ments that occur in our lives and that emerge as new forms and formats during our lives. Computer and telecommunication culture did not exist as it does now just twenty years ago. Are we to wait fifty or more years to assess what is happening now? Certainly not.

These six rationales for studying culture and popular culture were implicit in the origins of popular culture studies and their subsequent development. Indeed, the origin of popular culture studies was not an isolated phenomenon. Many "canonical" research disciplines contemporaneous to the origins of popular culture studies were already actively departing from exclusively canonical views. Culture studies were and are in themselves a cultural phenomenon.

Origins and Subsequent Development
of Popular Culture Studies

The entire conception of human performance as sexual has also undergone numerous transformations in Western culture in the last hundred years since the end of the nineteenth century, particularly as regarded by medical experts, researchers, and scholars. Before Krafft-Ebing's major publication on sexology in the late nineteenth century, *Psychopathia Sexualis,* medical science did not view certain human activities as necessarily sexual in their motivation and cause. Yet by the 1905 publication of Sigmund Freud's *Three Essays on the Theory of Sexuality,* not only were there already more than two hundred classifications of behaviors as sex-related, but all of them were considered to be mental disorders. Although science was then thought to be objective and untainted by cultural values, sexology and psychology largely confirmed the restricted roles of gender and sex prescribed contemporaneously by religious traditions, thus reinforcing the canonical prescriptions for performing sexuality.

As scientists began to research sexuality more carefully, the concepts of sex and gender modified as they were reported to the public by means of a variety of periodicals (Bailey). Consequently, norms for romance and dating changed in North America in the early twentieth century, from more strictly family-monitored rituals of introduction and courtship to the more fluid, socially monitored "dating the field." By the time of the so-called sexual revolution heralded by magazines such as *Playboy* in the mid-twentieth century, the locus of formulating conceptions of sex and gender had shifted from medical experts to social scientists to journalists and always had been conceptualized by people themselves.

The "sexual revolution" was not an isolated cultural phenomenon. A number of new liberation movements were already under way. Not only did the human rights movements of African Americans, women, gay men, and lesbians fuel the mood of the times, but traditional academic disciplines were already entertaining more purely descriptive modes for human performance rather than merely focusing on prescriptive modes for explaining human behavior.

Folklorists began more frequently to understand folk culture not from the *etic,* or outsider's, desire to collect, say, folktales, but to document and understand how the stories were and are used by people in their everyday life. Ethnographers inside of anthropology began to study the everyday patterns of common people strictly from the point of view of those people, the *emic,* or insider's, perspective (Geertz, *Interpretation* 14). Psychologists began to consider their clients' self-reports at least as seriously as their expert body of literature; thus, humanistic psychology rose in opposition to or as an extension of Freudian psychotherapy and the behaviorist inclination to avoid anything about a person except physical behaviors that can be observed. Historians were particularly challenged by the Vietnam War. Their long-standing research habit had been to wait until sufficient time had passed before seriously considering the events and issues related to a period or event; thus, they were methodologically restrained from explaining and interpreting Americans dying overseas, the napalming of nonmilitary populaces, and honest democratic dissent. In addition, their basic problem revolved around whether to study the great deeds of leaders and captains of industry or to study the everyday life of people expected to fight and support the war.

Each of these academic areas hotly debated the utility and appropriateness of canonical research versus the new manners. Eventually, black studies emerged, as did women's studies and gay/lesbian studies. These became, respectively, ethnic studies and gender studies. The canonical traditions eventually included the alternative methods and perspectives. Hence, folklore, ethnography, and organizational communication studies began to research what now is called occupational culture—the everyday life of people at work and of business culture.

Popular Culture Studies

The term *popular culture* was popularized by Ray B. Browne. A member of the English Department at Bowling Green State University in Ohio, Browne specialized in American literature and folklore. He was particularly interested in how Shakespeare was performed in frontier North America. Compared with explicating Elizabethan word use, character development, and theatrical staging and acting, frontier research was not seen as canonical. Prompted to take a new direction, Browne began a department of popular culture as well as regional, national, and eventually international professional organizations for the study of popular culture for interpreting the everyday realities of people's lives.

Early formulations and definitions of popular culture focused on the new, noncanonical emphasis. Four interrelated areas constituted Browne's original formulation: (1) popular mythologies such as beliefs, values, superstitions, and actual myths; (2) popular artifacts such as product packaging, architecture, toys, and icons and logos; (3) popular arts such as *Little Women,* rock and roll, and film; and (4) popular rituals such as parades, the Olympics, concerts, holidays, and festivals (Nachbar, Weiser, & Wright 6-8). While these four served as definitive road signs for the subject matter of popular culture studies, other elaborations informed the early conception and practice of research in the discipline.

Browne rearticulated popular culture as a real-world spectrum of cultural phenomena to be located in the form of diagrams (Nachbar et al. 14). One poses popular culture as spanning the entire spectrum of elite, mass, and folk cultures. Elite culture is what blue bloods and rich people do in their everyday life, which includes the production of mass-marketed artifacts and diversions. Mass culture includes these artifacts and diversions but also the everyday life situations of purchasing, using, and moving on to new interests on a large population basis. Folk culture includes the face-to-face interactions of a small, localized community and their stories, lore, traditions, artifacts, and modes of interaction.

Although this second formulation indicates that popular culture spans all three areas, many later observers limit popular culture to mass culture. This restriction is unfortunate for at least two reasons. (1) "Mass" culture too often is limited to those phenomena that are mechanically and electrically distributed among the people. Hence, media studies tend to focus on books, newspapers, radio, film, and television—as if that covers everything. It does not. Indigenous cultures rely most heavily, if not exclusively, on oral tradition as their medium for sharing culture. Media researchers frequently ignore other media of culture communication, such as letter writing, logic, rhetoric, billboards, posters, comic books, telegraph, and so on. (2) Conceptually, the assumptions of the diagram are as misleading as they are accurate. Popular culture may be studied for its aesthetic impact in real-world populations with little or no regard to production, commodification, and distribution. Furthermore, the categories too often collapse. Local bands in many geographical areas play the versions of mass-promoted songs such as "Louie, Louie," but in their own version, a "cover." If a band hypes it up with its own words, particularly including specific persons in its immediate audience, the song, once marketed by owners of record companies (elite, to make money) and played over the airwaves and sometimes in movies (mass), now is suddenly local, personal, and specific in nature (folk). Although the three categories articulate three areas along a conceptual spectrum, they are not always mutually exclusive in real-world circumstances.

Other early participants in the movement such as Russell Nye formulated different conceptualizations of popular culture. Focusing on popular art, Nye maintained that it is "aimed at the majority," "adaptable to mass production," and directed to an audience with loosely defined standards (4) as opposed to elite art, which is aimed at the few, with fewer, more exclusive artifacts and strict standards. Unfortunately, this sort of vision is additionally flawed because it uses the "elite" as a foil to define the popular. Perhaps it is wiser to conceive the popular as itself, rather than in opposition to something else—much like the conception offered in this book. Furthermore, majority conceptions often fail to recognize diversity and minority views; not all popular culture is mass-produced, and many popular audiences have clearly defined, exacting standards of the art and artists they favor.

The study of popular culture should allow, if not encourage, the consideration of communities repeatedly employing similar conscious and unconscious means of nurturing their participants. Growing and nurturing people in community are similar to what some academics call socialization and acculturation. They may be similar, but they are not the same. The distinction between cultural activities controlled by policy or law and cultural activities that communities favor despite policies and laws is important: Traditionally speaking, the terms *socialization* and *acculturation* are employed by specialists in fields that promote etic or outsider visions of a culture, particularly among many sociologists and some etically informed anthropologists. Ordinarily, the two terms do not appear to have technical meaning, but for some researchers, they do. In the case of sexualities and popular culture—by these experts' definition—socialization and acculturation are to be seen as norms, rules, and habits for normalizing, and thus implicitly controlling, sexuality. In this sense, not merely is culture conceived as something that orders and organizes sexuality, culture is the primary means of keeping people "cultured." If individuals step outside the bounds of sexual norms, they can be considered as uncultured, not really approvable, and most likely only too ready for cultural sanction. More realistically, sexualities and popular culture are not limited to controlling factors such as "official," "legal," or majority auspices for conveying culture, nor to received norms of conduct dictated by experts. Each culture allows emic individuality as well as community; even then, community norms are not always lived universally throughout that community in the same manner. To understand popular culture, therefore, the emic interpretation of sexual events and artifacts must be embraced if the interpretation itself is not to become rigidified and alien to that which we desire to understand, namely, to sexualities as they occur to the persons for whom they occur, not as they are "supposed" to occur. The terms *socialization* and *acculturation* set prescriptive parameters for understanding; popular culture studies seek to be descriptive—and descriptive from the point of view of the people who live and breathe popular culture.

In sum, popular culture includes the human activities, languages, and artifacts that grow and nourish people in communities and that generate observable, describable interest about its events and artifacts, within a community and *between communities*. Communication of popular culture between communities has gathered interest for many constituencies in the late modern period, judging by the plethora of publications about influences between cultures via popular culture. Actually, cross-cultural influence has occurred for ages, for example, between citified and nomadic communities in ancient Greece (Holmberg "Dialectical"), between Genghis Khan's conquerors and conquered, and between Western culture and Middle Eastern culture via the Crusades, shipping, and the Renaissance. Yet in each of these historical situations, one cultural point of view, and its inherent descriptive powers to describe the situation, has emerged and tended to be remembered and recounted more often than others— that of the culture that dominated its cross-cultural scene: city culture over nomadic culture in Attic Athens; mobile militarism over local customs in the Mongolian Empire; and, initially at least, Italian aristocratic, bourgeois, and Roman Catholicized control of trade during the Renaissance.

The dominance inherent to traditional narratives for describing culture with its accompanying univocal biases is instructive for late modern commentators who live in a milieu of rampant poaching of images, sounds, beliefs, customs, and even foods from other cultures, as well as the influences between peoples from differing communities as they meet and interact. The commentators who interpret popular culture and its poaching and influence across cultures might do well to avoid the singular, dominant, point of view inscribed in previous cultural narratives. For instance, although popular culture is frequently taken to identify with or be mostly generated by American culture, to assume so is to par take of the timeworn habit of dominance to communicate and describe cross-cultural phenomena. For the purposes of *Sexualities and Popular Culture,* therefore, I will assume six descriptive parameters that can begin to ameliorate the habit of narrative dominance in culture studies and to permit and encourage diversity:

1. If popular culture speaks to anyone in this world, it does so at least in part through the communities that nurture the person. Few persons interpret anything from a simple point of view that is identical to their neighbors'; most people may interpret any phenomenon variously on a cultural level (social, lawful, religious observance), a family level (duties, habits) and a personal level (self-discipline, musical preferences, hobbies). They may combine any of these levels, and others, and vary their weighting by whim or choice at any given moment of interpretation. "American culture" is more diverse and less monolithic than some commentators and detractors of popular culture claim. When popular culture speaks, more than one culture's view speaks. Popular culture texts are "open," not closed, texts (Eco, *Open*), meaning that there is no such thing as one and only one correct interpretation of popular culture.

2. Therefore, it is necessary to explore popular culture *qua* popular culture and not as an outgrowth of or adjunct to American culture studies. Ineluctably, the North American spin on popular culture is not insignificant, unimportant, or summarily dismissible. The North American spin does not yarn all popular culture, however; perhaps this helps to explain the current penchant in culture studies to derive its nomenclature, methods, and interpretative power from French poststructuralism. Thus, although *Sexualities and Popular Culture* will unavoidably reflect an emphasis on North American experience, the text will also display a commitment to explore popular culture in other cultures as well as North American subcultures, some of which do dismiss, ignore, or at least resist the dizzying spin of mainstream American culture. As will be seen, other cultures have vastly influenced American culture's dynamics of sexualities and popular culture.

3. Culture is by nature diverse. Common sense alone recognizes that there are culture*s*, not just one culture. Therefore, the apparently simple word *culture* is not so simple in the real world. Not that narrative descriptions should be complicated, but narrative descriptions need to embody and embrace the diversities they attempt to communicate.

4. Sex is itself a diverse location of human interest. Phenomena, artifacts, events, language, images, sounds, music, gesture, fashion, rituals public and private, daily habits, and more can be and are sexualized, gendered, and oriented diversely, within a culture, across cultures. If there were one and only one manner in which popular culture has historically and is contemporaneously sexualized, there would perhaps be little interest in the topic of sexualities and

popular culture, even for market-smart entrepreneurs, because there would be no diversity of target markets to research or influence. Sexualities as diverse are a given, if for nothing else, this book.

5. The notion of community employed in the present book to define culture is advantageous in that it removes and avoids boundaries between the formerly misleading deifications of "high" and "elite" culture and the demonization of "low" and "popular" culture. In the United States, opera is commonly taken to be an epitome of high culture, but in Italy, people on the streets know their opera and share it avidly.

6. Finally, culture is also diverse in that it does not tidily cut up human experience as do academic departments in universities. Culture is diverse in the sense that it is most usually interdisciplinary, with more than one sort of cultural phenomenon concurrent with others at any given moment or continuing in an individual's life. Tattoos, body piercing, grungy clothing, and androgynous looks and habits are not separate disciplines for many people in real life; they are one and inform each other. Thus, I will not pretend to carve up everyday life for the sake of specialists who limit themselves to areas of inquiry that they feign to relate to the rest of life. Although many later chapters focus on thematically chosen topics, such as sexualities and horror, these chapters will posit various perspectives in an interdisciplinary manner. Insistence on limitations for the study of sexualities and popular culture in one book to literature or film, for instance, is a sign of dominant, canonical thinking. Interdisciplinarity more mimetically reflects the diversity of culture although it is vastly underexplored and much maligned.

Even more unexplored in culture studies is communication, particularly how media work. Popular culture *communicates* and relates. It is time to describe *how* so that the contextualization of popular culture events and artifacts in everyday life can be articulated as communicative matrices of mutual desire.

2

Communication and Media

Communication studies has undergone transformations in its theories and methods, much like other research disciplines, yielding a consequential diversity of useful, interpretive strategies that can illuminate popular culture events and artifacts. Communication studies embrace a number of areas, such as speech, theater, speech pathology, linguistics, semantics, rhetoric, interpersonal communication, and philosophy. Two broadly conceived definitions of communication, however, are widely assumed throughout the spectrum of communication studies. A long-standing and most historically discussed definition renders communication as message sending and reception. An equally venerable definition, yet less discussed until the late modern period, relegates communication as the patterns of relationships between communicators, particularly those that are influenced by the types of media the communicators share; sometimes, this alternative perspective on communication emphasizes media as formative of content, humanness, and culture.

Communication as Message
Sending and Reception

With a renewed emphasis on empiricism and materialism, many sciences and social sciences in the earlier twentieth century shared a sense of new discovery about communication. Since Descartes' earlier formulation of two human substances, mind and body, later physical philosophers had been searching for an explanation of how a substance that is material and a qualitatively different substance that is immaterial could communicate with one another. By the twentieth century, language arts and sciences had once again moved center stage in Western philosophy. Thus, the search was on for explaining language, communication, and the connection between mind and matter. Reformulating communication as "cybernetics," for instance, researchers such as Wiener formulated scientifically sounding terms to describe both the material communication of machines, particularly early calculators or computers, and human communication *by the same terms*. Using the same terms served to demonstrate the likenesses between human and material communication.

Communication had to have a material source or initiation point of the communication. It also was defined to have a sender apparatus for transferring the content of the communication. The content was usually called the message or signal. Naturally, there needed to be an equivalent receiver apparatus located at a physical destination. Later, sender and receiver were accorded more precise terms, being renamed as encoder and decoder, respectively. The concept of coding was significant because it recognized that message formulation and interpretation involved symbolic or cultural codes for communication to succeed. Thus, Schramm added what he called "field of experience" to one of his communication models to indicate the sum total of experience a communicator brings to any communication interaction (6). Despite how elaborate communicological models later became, all the material models of message transfer have included three necessary components: (1) the location of signal formulation, such as a human who transforms thoughts or desires into words, gestures, or some physical means of symbolism; (2) the medium of transmission, such as air vibration for vocal sounds and light for gestures; and (3) the location of signal deformulation, such as a human who transforms physical symbols into thoughts and desires.

Although these sorts of formulations of communication seemed to be an entirely fresh approach, they had been well known for quite a while, just not elaborated in the same manner. Aristotle's conception was basically the same, threefold model. He had observed communicators at assembly, at court, and in the agora and discerned that speakers deliver speeches to audiences. The threefold pattern has been used to understand human communication for no less than two thousand years: (1) speaker, (2) speech, and (3) audience. The terms Aristotle instituted in *The Art of Rhetoric* were imitated later in various forms. In scientific method, the threefold description has stood the test of time. Scientists and social scientists still employ it, whether or not they are aware of or acknowledge the description's history.

Within the Western rhetorical tradition, however, and recently in the twentieth century with the development of alternatives to canonical traditions, drawbacks to the threefold model of communication have been noted. One of the more obvious criticisms of the model observes that communication between communicators is simultaneous; the models seem to indicate that communication occurs in only one direction at a time. Indeed, the Western, male-dominant system of rhetoric inculcates dominance in its very model of communication, especially considering that only recently has education—which was largely education of language arts—been opened to women, and then, not universally in all countries. Greco-Roman education and its Western descendants have been boy and man exclusive (Clark). The remedy for this unidirectional problem in theory and practice has been, simply, the notion of turn taking, such as the formal turn taking common to judicial deliberation and legislative debate. Turn taking alone, however, does not describe that communication occurs between communicators, even when the presumptive audience or receiver appears not to be sending messages like the speaker. Thus, some twentieth-century communication theorists added a feedback loop in their models to indicate both turn taking and simultaneity of communication, which, considering that Wiener much earlier formulated feedback as an important material component of communication (113-136), seems like an idea too long in the making for communication studies.

Another and related criticism of the models led to a new area for communication studies. Often, more than one medium or type of message sending and reception happens at any one moment. A speaker may employ gestures. A receiver consciously or unconsciously displays body language—hence, the invention of the term *nonverbal communication,* although to be honest, posture and gesture had been called "delivery" by rhetoricians and actors for thousands of years. Delivery supports or enhances the transferred message. Yet again to be honest, nonverbals may occur by habit or unconsciously. The threefold model still emphasizes unidirectionality and quite possibly ought to be considered an artifact of canonical, high culture.

Despite good theory-building intentions, simultaneity inscribes a major problematic of communication theory itself that is gendered. In the past thirty years or so, numerous voices, many to be incorporated in later chapters, have increasingly stated concerns about entrenched systems of dominance that enforce and perpetuate male privilege and ways of thinking, ways that disable other and diverse thought patterns. Even unidirectional models of communication that incorporate turn taking and feedback still include the material assumptions of dominance; at any given temporal or conceptual moment, one communicator is the focus of the obvious message sending, controlling it. Communication theorists have yet to address that simultaneity itself suggests alternative possibilities of nondominance, or adominance, in communication and its theories. The further assumption, derived from more than two thousand years of rhetorical theory and practice, that one source, one communicator, currently or ultimately prevails in a communication interaction is itself an inscription of dominance that reinforces decision making as a primary and continuing act of dominance. One speaker to another or one speaker over many is unidirectional persuasion. Persuasion and its combative stance of winning is the dynamic of dominance. Communication theory tends to promote these vectors as merely descriptions of communication. They are not. Culture influences people. They are formations of consciousness and human action. The very canonical understanding of communication, its base concepts, and its systemic assumptions promote dominance, and particularly, dominance of the message and its content. Thus is communication theory biased by gender.

There are certain advantages, however, to the threefold model. The threefold model is particularly useful for discerning and remedying communication problems. Because there are three components to the model, there are three types of communication problems: (1) faulty formulation (e.g., confusion, gum in the mouth, and orofacial anomalies); (2) interception or interference (something independent of the speaker and audience overpowers the message); and (3) faulty interpretation (e.g., hearing impairment, preoccupation, and lack of familiarity with the language). Any of these sorts of communication problems are properly labeled communication breakdowns.

The threefold communication model is laden with significant critical assumptions that demonstrate its limits: (1) Communication works in one direction; (2) communicators must share a material medium in which messages transfer; if communicators do not share a physical medium, they cannot communicate; (3) therefore, a communication problem is automatically defined as a "breakdown" of something physical; that is, communication is fundamentally a material process; thus Descartes' mind-body dichotomy is sidestepped by defining everything as body, ignoring the mind as formative to communication; and (4) communication is neutral, as in, "I'm just relaying the message" or "Don't slay the herald for the message." In other words, the medium/media employed for any given transmission generates no message value in and of itself.

Fortunately, there is one strong area for understanding communication that encompasses diverse concepts for theorizing communication. In one way or another, these theorists share one concept or an emphasis on it, focusing on the concept of the medium of the communication and the relationships the medium generates as formative of humanness and human consciousness. The majority of these theorists contribute to communication theory from outside the traditions of communication studies.

Communication as Relationship and Medium/Media

When Marshall McLuhan suggested in the 1967 publication *The Medium Is the Massage* that ships, stagecoaches, and trains are media for communication (72-75), he signaled an already occurring shift in communication studies to define communication more as media and relationships. His suggestion underscored perhaps another criticism about the threefold communication definition, that *all* means of physical transference inherently contain communicative power, even when message sending and reception does not appear to be intended or involved at all. The distribution of products by ships, stagecoaches, and trains transfers whole symbol systems, such as clothing, foodstuffs, and tools. Not only do a sense of fashion, eating habits, and types of work, art, or craft become transferred, but the level of quality of particular pieces of clothing, food preparation, and tooling also relays levels of technology. Thus, modes of conveyance are media of communication, and a culture's goods are media that transfer messages about their source culture. Thus, one may interpret, or decode, a culture by investigating its artifacts, just as popular culture researchers were rapidly beginning to do contemporaneously with McLuhan's observation.

Earlier, Edmund Carpenter noted that media forms or shapes human consciousness. For instance, in archaic or prehistoric cultures, the oral tradition is the main medium of communication. Communication tends to be "polysynthetic" or merged as one. Words are not separate entities; they flow one into another. The archaic mode of consciousness reflects the polysynthesis of language habits and conceptions: everything is one. Hence, historical and contemporary aboriginals depict themselves as immersed in the foliage of the world. Carpenter then describes a significant change both in the major medium of communication and the consciousness humans have about themselves. The inception of writing invested a sense of authority to the writing communicator. A written story most properly is read in the manner the writer writes, that is, from start to finish. If a reader is to read, he or she must conform to the linearity of the writing. In turn, the writer is rendered an authority who dictates not just the content of communication but how it is to be decoded. The author is an *autho*rity.

Carpenter's observations also include newspapers, film, and television, but suffice it to say he is not the only researcher to observe the formative nature of a particular medium of communication and that medium's influence on its users. Ong noted that writing did not become universal in its use or influence overnight, yet the shift from listening to seeing was reflected in early Western writers such as Plato and Aristotle, whose concepts of knowledge and knowing are largely bound to vision and the written word (*Presence of the Word*).

Some of the earliest writing in linear A and linear B ancient Greek was written with no breaks between words and sentences, that is, it was inscribed in an archaic, polysynthetic manner. Later, with the separation of author and audience, words became separate.

Historically, in the West, developments in writing and subsequent media for communication influenced human consciousness. For instance, in the Middle Ages, a new development in writing emerged as letter writing, *ars dictaminis* (Baldwin). Letters not only transferred messages but like Paul's earlier letters to incipient Christian communities, influenced congregations to discipline themselves and adhere to ways presumably acknowledged by Jesus, his apostles, and later bishops of the Church. In other words, letters helped establish and maintain orthodoxy. *Ortho* literally means "straight," and thus orthodoxy means straight seeming. Although countless images in the ancient world had cautioned believers to remain on the narrow or straight path, now believers could literally do so by adhering to the written word. It should not escape the late modern interpreter of culture that writing was also a fixable medium of communication that could flawlessly be delivered miles away. Hence, in no small way, orthodoxy was enabled by the same apparent characteristics of writing, that it was linear and to be followed, and that it could give the appearance of one, correct meaning.

Oral tradition did not disappear in the Middle Ages; tales were still shared among common folk, apparently bawdy ones at times, but writing was so influential in the ruling classes that some orality became transformed to the strictures of writing. Sermonizing set new standards for oral communication. Perhaps guided in part by Augustine's *On Christian Doctrine,* sermonizing emphasized orthodoxy, and numerous Church assemblages sought to standardize Christian liturgy.

The medieval developments in communication media affect us today, particularly with regard to sexualities and popular culture. Norms for performing one's sexuality are straight and narrow, from no sexual sharing with another until marriage, to monogamy enforced by a church hierarchy, to gender roles for male and female, and to the underscoring of sexuality's ultimate forbearance by a church, the production of children. Many of these Old World traditions that were transferred to the Americas by European immigrants were initially quite evident and still may be observed at the end of the twentieth century, such as older women wearing black like nuns, either because they have not borne children or because their husbands are dead and they cannot or will not remarry. Wearing black is not merely a cultural custom, it is a sexualized custom, originally shaped by adherence to orthodoxy and the hierarchies, sacred, secular, sexual, or unsexual, that orthodoxy generates. As McLuhan jibed, "a piazza for everything and everything in its piazza" (53), meaning that under the older order of writing and its innate hierarchization of consciousness, all persons knew their place, their role, and now it can be said they knew their sexual place and role.

It is perhaps then no accident that the advent of the age of revolution in the West was the advent of pamphleteering, broadsides, and newspapers. Under the former type of writing, an audience was rendered a passive follower to the writer.

With the new newspaper writing, the audience was rendered active and in control of the medium and its messages. A reader need not read each page from start to finish before proceeding to the next page nor read each column in the same manner. Furthermore, although previously the custom had been to put information in a chronological manner, now information became organized differently, from eye-catching and generally already known information to the bottom of a column where more specific information may usually be found. Newspaper writing also eventuated into the lurid reportage of scandals, peccadillos, and private lives, including what hitherto had been private sex. It took a good two hundred years or so for the initial revolutions against monarchies to give way to the revolutions of other disenfranchised or oppressed groups, such as women, African Americans, and gays. Journalistic or newspaper types of written media have proved to be signal in generating group solidarity as well as informing each group's individuals about the group's common cause.

Although radio returned to audiality, it did so not for an entire, archaic tribe but instead for families and smaller groups, in their homes. The shrieks of endangered women in broadcasts such as *The Inner Sanctum* and *The Witch's Tale* helped to reinforce the by then "orthodox" female gender stereotype of weakness and panic while the calm, deep voice of the male narrator reinforced the mainstream male stereotype of strength and rationality.

Film was and is multimedia. It conveys visual images and initially included writing to fill in the blanks of the current plot. Early, silent film also included the live production of music to enhance the screen story. By the late twentieth century, the multimedia nature of film has blossomed into color, soundtrack, and source music; sound effects; special effects; and more, all in one premeditated package. Yet all film cast on a large screen shares one medium that impressively shapes consciousness: spectacle. The hugeness of images literally makes the characters and screen actions larger than life, so much so that by the close of the twentieth century, Baudrillard and others have been prompted to observe how the huge perfections of the silver screen have transformed America into a realm of hyperreality, with North Americans' obsessions to reproduce screen perfections in their daily lives. Indeed, as sexualized, breast implants, muscles, swiftness, bigness, cosmetics, and even fashion and automobiles are hyperreal outcomes of film's centrality in twentieth-century American popular culture as medium of communication *par deluxe.*

Television reintroduced intimacy while employing many film conventions for screen images. Hence, soap operas specialize in extreme close-up shots of character's faces. On the one hand, the image can more easily be seen on a smaller screen. On the other hand, subtle feelings can be shown to convey a particular character's feeling (Timberg 166). The advent of MTV, however, demonstrated other characteristics of the televisual medium. First of all, sexual images in "music videos" are ubiquitous. Sexiness, partial or full nudity, and scenes of sex acts attract attention—not that this was unknown to publishing prior to MTV. Getting the audience's attention with sexy images and then interspersing the music videos with advertisements that employ the same sorts of images and production values, however, demonstrate that television programming—in North American, commercially sponsored television, anyway—is the constructed ad for an ad. The program brings attention to the commercial sponsor and, in the case of telecast music videos, not just to themselves as ads for compact discs (CDs), records, tapes, and videotapes (Kinder 234-235). Thus, even television is a medium that may be used to control or shape human consciousness.

Just as oral tradition did not disappear once writing appeared but could be transformed to the qualities of written media, so too written media and its qualities did not disappear and indeed influenced the consciousness-forming capabilities of subsequent media. That media that emerged in the West subsequent to early writing have often retained the authorial control of audience passivity is not inconsequential. Deleuze and Guattari characterize representations in various media as "despotic" or oppressive because they are still so heavily influenced by the early, authorial written medium. They credit McLuhan's observation of the shift from the cultural epoch largely influenced by writing to a new media order, "What exactly is meant when someone announces the collapse of the 'Gutenberg galaxy'? . . . not only is writing adapted to money as the general equivalent, but the specific functions of money in capitalism went by way of writing and printing" (240). Deleuze and Guattari further characterize the heavy influence of written culture in late modern times as "despotic representation" that emphasizes the signifier or message content. They then suggest, however, that McLuhan recognized a new age of culture governed by a new medium of electric flows innate to electronic media. Thus, at least two "postmodern" authors recognize media as important for theorizing culture because media are formative of cultural consciousness. Western history and its progression of new media and new ways to influence consciousness are not the model for the world; other cultures have not developed media in the same order as the West (Holmberg, "Rhetoric of Media"). It should be clear, however, that regardless of culture, the main media of communication employed will influence the consciousness of individuals and groups in that culture.

While McLuhan, Carpenter, Ong, and others were reformulating communication as media, a growing number of psychologists were also reformulating their understanding of mental illness and therapy. Carl Rogers emphasized relationships, noting that the therapist needs to approach the client as an equal, as a helper and facilitator, to more clearly read the client's "messages." Paul Watzlawick went further to suggest that in the therapy of some persons with schizophrenia, the therapist might better imitate the client's language use, get inside the client's world, and thus better enable the client (*Language of Change*). Both Rogers and Watzlawick emphasize an emic approach, or trying to understand a client and the client's illness from the client's point of view and not just from the therapist's expert, etic point of view.

Watzlawick, Beavin, and Jackson, however, noted that relationships themselves are the cause of bad communication and mental illness (*Pragmatics*). Watzlawick et al. articulate, then develop, Gregory Bateson's anthropological work on culture groups communicating across cultures, what Bateson called "schismogenesis," or the origins and handling of differences between culture groups. However the new formulation is applied to interpersonal relationships, Watzlawick, Beavin, and Jackson note that relationships may be either healthy or sick and that, therefore, if an individual is ill, the relationship needs to be healed, not just the individual. *The Pragmatics of Human Communication* then concludes with an extended interpretation of Edward Albee's play *Who's Afraid of Virginia Woolf?* employing their reformulation of Bateson's theory and observations of schismogenesis. In many ways, their analysis demonstrates that not all human behavior is gendered.

The definition of communication as media and relationships is also laden with critical assumptions: (1) The relationship between communicators, particularly the media they share to communicate, is the communication, not just the content of the messages transferred; another way of saying this is the relationship between communicators is as important, or more important, than message "content"; (2) communication always occurs on many levels simultaneously and in both or all directions of shared relationships; (3) a communication problem is properly conceived as a sickness, illness, or pathology to which each of the communicators contributes, thus calling for dyadic or family therapy to heal a relationship; and (4) communication is inherently "loaded"; its meanings and influence on how individuals think and act are not at all neutral.

Both definitions of communication help to locate aspects of sex in popular culture.

Sex as Communication and Media

In advertising, it is clear that "sex sells." Thus, individual ads may be studied for the sorts of images they convey, for their message sending. Many researchers of advertising, however, combine both definitions of communication, noting if not emphasizing the consciousness-forming aspects of ads as media. Goffman presents and analyzes scores of visual images used in advertising, noting received stereotypes, but then placing these stereotypes in the cultural context of ritualization.

> From the perspective of ritual, then, what is the difference between the scenes depicted in advertisements and scenes from actual life? One answer might be "hyper-ritualization." The standardization, exaggeration and simplification that characterize rituals in general are in commercial posings found to an extended degree. . . . A commercial photograph is a ritualization of social ideals. . . . When a man in real life lights a cigarette for a woman . . . this little interpersonal ritual, may be no more an actual reflection of the relationship between the sexes than is the couple pictured in the cigarette ad a representative couple. (*Gender* 84)

Goffman also employs the definition of communication of relationships, both about the images themselves with a viewer and about the presumed roles between pictured persons.

Brown notes images of femaleness but then discusses the cultural impact of stereotypes of beauty (Goldstein 163-177). Providing fictive points of view of various cultural icons such as Vladimir Nabokov and Anne Rice, Paglia runs through a variety of issues concerning the use of children in advertising, including historical examples, moral and legal viewpoints, and the reluctance of some fathers even to touch their children (*Vamps* 146-159).

The observation and interpretation of commercial advertisements that cover far more than their message-sending aspects can hardly be construed as a communication-as-message-sending-and-reception paradigm. Nor do these commentators and others discuss ads as forms of turn taking. These illustrations, however, involve researchers discussing artifacts, ads, which may be viewed again and again. Although the ads and their descriptions are clearly sexualized, that is, involving sex, they are not sex, at least not quite the same as "having" sex with another, or with oneself.

Descriptions of ads are one thing. Descriptions of sexual communicators are another; they necessarily involve numerous experiential levels that are quite real and evocative to the communicators. Ads reflect sexualities and sexual norms but in physical embodiment are not sex in and of themselves. A kiss is not unidirectional, nor is it turn taking. A kiss is a simultaneous mutual feedback loop by way of encouragements and endearments. It is multimedia, but not just verbal and nonverbal; all senses may be involved. Then again, a kiss defines relationship, molds consciousness of the kissers, may involve creativity, and may lead the kissers into further sexual explorations of one another.

As Pronger puts it, an embrace may convey sympathy; it works as a sign, but it is moreover "the physical embodiment of sympathy, an incarnation" (44). Sex as communicative, as a medium of communication, includes embodiment, incarnation. One may possess sexual signs, but one *participates* in sexual communion (Nelson 35). The act of participating in sex may well endow the participant with a transformed sense of self. Pleasure involves a distinct sense of happiness and, in its more intense moments, self-transcendence. In the climax of sexual communion, orgasmic pleasure can reach the heights of ecstasy in which the body-self feels profoundly unified, taken out of itself into another, yet intensely itself. There is self-abandonment, a willingness to risk the depths of experience (Nelson 87). Many people report they feel most alive and human not just during orgasm but in a variety of sexual pursuits. Thus limiting research about sex and communication to ads sometimes does not permit the evocation of the wholeness, the affirmation, the transcendence of sex as it is communicative and a medium of communication itself.

The Common Sensibles

Yet admittedly, there is still a scholarly need, call it, to render descriptions of sexually evocative artifacts and events in a reliable, repeatable manner to

TABLE 2.1 A Matrix of the Common Sensibles

Senses	Common Sensibles	Received Terms
sight	Sights	icons
sound	Sounds	audes
touch	Touches	(hauphes)
taste	Tastes	(geusis)
smell	Smells, Aromas	(osmes)

ensure a semblance of completeness. Once again, instead of letting researchers determine what one is to pay attention to in sex research, why not let experience dictate what is involved? Yes, there is message sending, yes, consciousness forming, but the kiss example suggests another avenue, what Kant called the "common sensibles" (*Critique*). Although Immanuel Kant is frequently perceived as old hat, if not just another representative of canonical culture, it should be noted that Kant also did not buy received tradition. He rejected scholarly cant for lived experience and what we call common sense. Of course, as the adage goes, common sense is not all that common.

Kant's premise was deceptively simple. The basis of morals may be found in the common sensibles, in the everyday experiences of sight, sound, touch, taste, and smell. The matrix in Table 2.1 articulates Kant's observations but also acknowledges, in the right-hand column, the sorts of terminology common in popular culture studies, or in the case of terms similarly derived from Greek, uncommon in almost any study.

These terms indicate the commonplace experiences that are the living feel of sexuality and that are embedded in artifacts that convey sexuality. As a whole, the matrix suggests no less than two avenues down which to stroll: (1) What examples of each of the common sensibles might be familiar to us? and (2) why have cultural studies emphasized sights or icons almost to the exclusion of the other four common sensibles?

Examples of the Common Sensibles as Sexualized

Briefly, let me suggest some examples of sexualized common sensibles. *Esquire* magazine pioneered the publication of naughty cartoons for the masses. Early issues included no less than thirty cartoons each. One particular cartoon, however, illustrates a Sight or icon quite strikingly. The frame is set on a tropical beach. A voluptuous blonde woman in a string bikini writhes fetchingly as she leans against a palm tree. The caption? A male photographer says to her, "Now in this next shot, we'd like to get across the superiority of Marton Motor Oil!"

There is no oil in sight (June 1949, Vol. 31, 133). Note how the sexualized image of a woman sells oil. Such exploitative, almost pinup sexual objects in their iconage, these Sights have been legion in automobile ads in general until quite recently.

The Sounds of the thumping beat in heavy metal rock, disco, progressive, and alternative music are frequently reported to be major characteristics of the music. The rate of the beat is signal. On the one hand, it may often produce a euphoria through its hypnagogic repetition (Harner 64-67), and, on the other hand, the rapidity mimics the pulse of sexual intercourse. Boom, boom, boom, boom.

Many people are aroused by touch, particularly Touches of beards, hair, cleanly shaven skin, skin, or fabric. Touches of hardness and paradoxical, simultaneous softness are often included in sexual fantasies, for example, "I figured he wanted me to feel up his arms, so I started rubbing all the hard muscle under the silky, sweat-slick skin" (Mick Tyler 17). Television ads for shampoo and hair conditioner not only show models Touching hair but emphasize that the treated hair feels great. Understandably then, skin lotions hawk Touches of dry skin by comparing them to alligators and lobsters.

Fans of *Days of Our Lives* are familiar with a continuing food ritual between the characters Marlena, Roman, and John. As part of foreplay, they dip fresh strawberries into chocolate and feed each other seductively, savoring the flavors as they savor each other. Although the television medium does not convey Tastes per se, the imaging is so consistent and well done that Taste is evoked in the audience.

Smells or Aromas are a multibillion-dollar-a-year portion of the cosmetics industry in their production of perfumes and colognes. As included in numerous stories and experiences, however, other sexually evocative Aromas include sweat, body odor, fresh laundry, cooking smells, and poppers, an illegal substance that has its own peculiar, model airplane glue smell that is reported to spread a warmth through the body.

Of course, these sensibles may be commingled, sometimes one doing the work of another, a phenomenon called *synaesthesia*. Clive Barker embeds synaesthesia in the short story "The Book of Blood" (*Books of Blood: Volume One*) to uncover that things are not what they appeared to be and to cue both the characters and the reader that something out of the ordinary was happening. Dr. Mary Florescu was a psychic researcher and had finally found an authentic psychic, Simon Neal, whom she installed at a psychically active spot, the attic at Number 65, Tollington Place. All her professional career, Dr. Florescu had looked outside herself—like a good scientist—for objective confirmation of parapsychological phenomena. Verging on triumph, she turned inside to herself, paying attention for once to her subjective experience and ironically discovered not only that Simon Neal was a fake but also that she herself was psychic and that Number 65, Tollington Place was a crossroads for the violently dead.

While waiting for the latest results, she toyed with her loose wedding ring. "Through the tips of her index finger and thumb she seemed almost to taste the sour metal as she touched it. It was a curious sensation, an illusion of some kind" (6). As her thoughts turn to Simon's body, the synaesthesia intensifies, and she is startled to notice that a halo of light appeared around her assistant's head, making her feel giddy: "Seeing the halo on him, feeling new sensations waking in her, coursing through her." Quite soon the synaesthesia expanded; she could hear the voice of the desk at which she sat; the world opened and her senses were thrown into ecstasy. Her senses had become "a system of senses" that could pierce to the heart of anything. The synaesthesia then went beyond wood and gold and discovered a crack between this world of the living and the otherworld of the dead and in "her head she heard voices that came from no living mouth" (7).

She then saw Simon through the ceiling above her in the attic. Instead of his channeling messages from the otherworld, the boy was masturbating, and she herself was in a sympathetic state of sexual ecstasy, the synaesthesia now joining her sense arousal to his sexual arousal. But then she realized another Sight, "the lie in him, the absence of power where she'd thought there had been something wonderful."

At the greatest intensity of synaesthetized sexual arousal, Mary Florescu knew she had been betrayed and felt outrage. Yet she is not the only outraged participant in the scene. The violently dead had been outraged that Simon had lied for them and not told their stories properly. Both Mary's sexualized outrage and the dead's outrage merge and conspire as an agony of feeling.

Now it was done. The lies were told, the tricks were played, and the people on the highway, sick beyond death of being misrepresented and mocked, were buzzing at the crack in the wall, and demanding satisfaction.

That crack *she* had opened: *she* had unknowingly fingered and fumbled at, unlocking it by slow degrees. Her desire for the boy had done that: her endless thoughts of him, her frustration, her heat and her disgust at her heat had pulled the crack wider. Of all the powers that made the system manifest, love, and its companion, passion, and their companion, loss, were the most potent. Here she was, an embodiment of all three. Loving, and wanting, and sensing acutely the impossibility of the former two. Wrapped up in an agony of feeling which she had denied herself, believing she loved the boy simply as her Go-Between. (7-8 all italics Barker's).

Dr. Florescu finally recognized that her feelings were sexual, that she "wanted him now, deep inside her." Her self-admission opened the highways of the dead entirely, and she was horrified to witness their revenge: writing their stories by means of broken glass shards on every surface of Simon's body. "He was to be their page, their book, the vessel for their autobiographies. A book of blood. A book made of blood. A book written in blood" (11). Mary's sexual desire for Simon eventually empowers his salvation but not soon enough to prevent his entire body from becoming one flowing tattoo of hieroglyphics that told the tales of the dead, her tactile and visible proof of the otherworld.

Synaesthesia may function as the senses combining simultaneously. In the film based on D. H. Lawrence's original novel, *Women in Love,* there is a dining scene, often recalled by fans of the movie as "the fig scene." The man at the head of the table regales the others about the erotics of eating a raw fig as he eats it.

The Iconic Connection

The bulk of popular culture scholarship focuses on visuality, particularly of icons and iconography. Little attention is paid to the other common sensibles as now it will. Even then, however, few commentators approach the fundamental workings of icons. These workings may or may not suggest how the other common sensibles work.

Originally, an icon was a stylized image of Christ or saints employed in Eastern Orthodox Catholic communities. The icon as an image itself is not only a representation of someone considered to be holy—a "sign"—but the object, the image, is in itself taken to be sacred. Thus, in the language of Tillich and others, it is foremost a symbol of holiness that reaches beyond the icon itself and is invested with sacrality beyond itself; it is not just a representational sign (*Systematic*). Thus, in popular culture studies, an icon is an image that carries a set, if not system, of assumptions behind it, a sacral aura that calls to mind other images, concepts, memories, and feelings identified with the image.

Thus, Anne Rice has the scholar David explain the significance of holy images and icons to the vampire Lestat.

"You understand the fundamental principle of an icon, don't you?" David asked.
"Inspired by God."
"Not made by hands," said David. "Supposedly directly imprinted upon the background material by God Himself."
"You mean like Jesus' face was imprinted on Veronica's veil?"

"Exactly. All icons fundamentally were the work of God. A revelation in material form. And sometimes a new icon could be made from another simply by pressing a new cloth to the original, and a magic transfer would occur." (*Memnoch* 100)

Thus, if researchers, journalists, or everyday conversationalists were to call the artist Madonna Ciccone (Madonna) a cultural icon, they may not be saying just that she is a striking image but that as a culture, we have invested her with a sacred status that any of her images carry. Claims that images of Elvis Presley magically heal people through the transference of sight or touch are legion. Cultural icons are thus venerated to the point that the human beings who are/were the iconed image are felt to do no wrong—or if they do, like the offspring of a mortal and a divinity, they are automatically forgivable, beyond the rules and laws of mere mortals.

David's explanation of the workings of an icon is important as crux of the novel *Memnoch, the Devil* and, ultimately, involves sex and sensuality. Like Pronger and Nelson earlier, it is Memnoch's contention that sex and orgasm give knowledge of Heaven's joy and therefore are not automatically bad or sinful. Yet for ages, God has maintained that humans are merely part of Nature and deserve no special assistance to reach Heaven—that indeed sex and sensuality are natural stumbling blocks. Memnoch thoroughly disagreed with God, maintaining that self-conscious sexuality is not merely survival for humans; it is divine. With God's approval, Memnoch took human form to experience what it is like to be human, to see if he could prove his point. Memnoch later reports the major discovery of his participant-observation ethnography to his would-be acolyte, Lestat.

"In the orgasm, as my seed had gone into the woman, I had felt an ecstasy that was like the joy of Heaven. I had felt it and felt it only in connection with the body that lay beneath me, and for one split second or less than that I had known, known, known that men were not part of Nature, no they were better, they belonged with God and with us!" (234)

Of course, Lestat agrees with the basic point of view that sensuality is not something to be punished, as he converses with Memnoch.

"You've told me the story of Creation and the Passion, of Your Way and His Way, you've described how you oppose Him on Earth, and I can imagine the ramifications of the opposition—we are both sensualists, we are both believers in the wisdom of the flesh."

"Amen to that." (302)

By the end of the novel, Lestat himself has come into possession of Veronica's veil, and on giving it to Dora, she flees and begins sharing the veil at St. Patrick's cathedral in New York City. Lines blocks long queue up for one sight of the veil; miracles occur; a true icon redeems both sensualists and ascetics. In other words, one can be a sensualist and still get into Heaven. People just needed a little inspiration to see things as they really are.

Clearly, both Madonna and Elvis sexualized their performances, Madonna with black lace, sometimes leather, often miming sexual acts onstage; Elvis with his gyrations that earned him the nickname "Elvis the Pelvis." Both performers broke public norms for gesture, fashion, and sexuality. They are venerated by fans for having done just that, for conveying images of transgression that sanctify sex and sensuality. What about the other common sensibles, however, as media for sexual communication and perhaps its sanctification?

In *Plaisirs d'Amour,* Elizabeth Nash acknowledges not only that sexuality involves more than just vision but also that it is not easy to write the other four senses.

> Sex is the only human activity which excites and engages all the senses: that is why it is so pleasurable, just as Nature intended it should be. (Nature in her generosity also compensates those who do not have a particular faculty by increasing the power or the senses that remain to a degree hard to imagine.) The fact that sex keeps our entire sensory quintet busy creates certain problems for the writer. What is the best way to approach the subject? (9)

Although Nash's work is more an erotic handbook than cultural interpretation, the professed difficulty in writing about the other senses indicates the cultural comfort most of us have learned in describing the visible and the discomfort in describing the rest.

Sights particularly are "high" culture or cultured—that is, sacred. Sacred images are often placed above our heads so we must look up at them, inscribing a sense of high and low in the very act of Sight. Sounds, particularly as sacred music, may convey a sense of high culture, yet we have far fewer descriptive methods than we do, say, for poetry and literature. Tellingly, except for a few voices in the wilderness, music is seen as a lesser art than literature and oratory. Given that sexual groans and encouragements are not exactly biblical material, it is no wonder less copy has been published on sounds and culture, or *audeography.*

In comparison with Sight and Sound, Scent, Touch, and Taste are frequently considered to be base, lowly, and not suitable for the cultured and polite chitchat. That is, Scent, Touch, and Taste are secular, if not animalistic. Sight is higher and a sign of divinity (God is, after all, light). The others are sensual.

The common sensibles may be employed as a fundamental framework for the study of popular culture, and there is no reason to sanctify Vision by excessive research about icons, which is a sign of received culture that deifies Sights when clearly there are other common sensibles available. As Nelson cautions, however, "feelings, then are neither antirational nor irrational" (31); they are not automatically sanctified or demonized. The present text proposes to explore all the common sensibles as evocative of those moments when we feel most human yet most divine. Nothing is as simple as merely running through each of the common sensibles to understand humanness or human culture, however. Everyday experience is not always amenable to the cookie cutters of frugal scholars. Thus, each of the common sensibles will be encountered as combined with other commonplace experiences, such as movement, action, and the fulfillment of desire. Clearly, Sound will be covered in the chapter on popular music, although it would be foolish to think that one chapter would cover everything about Sound as a common sensible as far as sex is concerned. Touch will relate to sports and gesture, although it certainly is not limited to either. Taste emerges with regard to sex toys, particularly food as aphrodisiac, but taste also comes into play with horror artifacts and sex manuals. Aroma permeates culture as the osmosis of sex toys, horror, and sex manuals, but it should always be remembered that sex is, in and of itself, a medium of communication. It may be conveyed by other media and yet, ultimately, sex is a medium unto itself.

3

Popular Culture Studies

Popular culture studies have frequently investigated the perennial topics of icons, myth, stereotypes, rites, and ritual and interpretive communities and have applied them as descriptive and explanatory concepts for elucidating other popular culture phenomena. More recently, issues concerning literacy and cultural literacy have become prevalent. As a movement, people and groups in popular culture studies have also come to grapple with issues concerning not just what to study but also the diversity of methods and approaches for studying popular culture. Each of these areas informs the study of sexualities and popular culture, and yet some of them need to be amplified because of the nature of sex as communication and of communication that conveys sex.

Myth

The term *myth* is a cognate of Attic Greek *muthos* (μυθοσ). *Muthos* was an all-purpose word, variously meaning tale, story, history, lore, and roughly what we call myth. The original word literally meant "mouth," and that goes a long way to underscore the basis of myth in oral tradition. In the late twentieth century however, the word *myth* is often used to imply a fiction, a falsity.

Truth and falsity tend to be norms of thinking endemic to science, whereas utility tends to create norms of technology. Myth is often judged by scientific norms and thus dismissed as bunk. Actually, myth is the first technology. It is more something that is useful or unuseful than truthful or untruthful. Myth is neither true nor false because it is treated, lived in everyday life, as if it *were* true. For instance, in many public forums, I have asked for a show of hands in answer to the question, "Who here believes that vampires really exist?" Usually, less than ten percent raise their hands. Immediately, I ask a follow-up, "Who knows the defenses and remedies against vampires?" Almost everyone present raises a hand, to which I say, "That's the utility of myth; we act as if it were true, just in case."

Myths and their narrative structures help people make sense of their lives regardless of truth. Their structures set up what I call *mythic expectation.* Mythic expectation is the human ability to discern a variety of trajectories or consequences to a myth, especially when only a small part of the myth is present in any artifact or event. The conscious recognition of the presence of a myth in the experience of a popular culture artifact or event, as well as the unconscious activation of that mythic expectation by artifacts and events, cues us to process information in channelized, formulaic manners, most commonly called archetypes (Jung) but sometimes forms or mythemes (Lévi-Strauss 204, 211).

Perhaps one of the simplest ways to invoke mythic expectation is to begin storytelling with the phrase, "Once upon a time . . . " This cue generates a commonly accepted mythic expectation in most Western audiences that a fairy tale will follow. Other cues are more clearly, inherently sexual. For instance, if a male and a female meet in a story, a number of mythic expectations present themselves, logically and experientially. The two may ignore each other, yet in a heterosexually sanctioned context, the appearance of a protagonist at the beginning of a story activates the expectation that sooner or later, another protagonist of the opposite sex will also appear, and the two persons will meet and interact. A further expectation usually insinuates itself: The two of them will become romantically or sexually involved, if not married. They may further become the basis of a family unit, replete with children and the social status associated with successfully bearing and caring for a family with the means, possessions, and attitudes to support them.

Traditionally speaking, in modern, bourgeois culture, this more complex myth of the nuclear family lends an aura of personal, economic, and social success to couples who bear and support offspring. Consider the beautiful homes and families depicted in the television shows *Father Knows Best, Leave It to Beaver,* and *Ozzie and Harriet.* The Currier and Ives lithographs that frequently display a similar scenario affirm that the myth of the nuclear family had popular coinage almost a century prior to the advent of nationally broadcast television. Images of the family therefore traditionally have required predictable ingredients in the family's mythic complex, pattern, or as some call it, archetype. The archetype includes a male-female couple, presumed married, preferably with at least a boy child and a girl child, all depicted in nice clothing of the period and in a domestic setting, such as a drawing room, dining room, or porch, or pursuing some family outing.

Related to the myth of the nuclear family is the myth of romantic love. Romantic love activates the idea that there is someone in the world just right for each person and that there ought to be a courtship that may be characterized as "romantic." Numerous examples abound, from stories of medieval chivalry to *Romeo and Juliet,* both the novel and movie *Love Story,* and countless romance novels.

Couples and families in the late twentieth century, however, have established new images and myths of the family. Television shows such as *The Brady Bunch* show what happens when two formerly married persons and their children become one family. *One Day at a Time* presents a divorced woman and her two daughters making it on their own as well as a financially viable woman and mother. *Cybill, Sisters, Who's the Boss,* and *Alice* each explores variations of the single-parent family and new roles and images of working women and domestic men. Thus, at the conclusion of the twentieth century, in North America at least, the "nuclear family" no longer universally requires a married couple of opposite sexes who bear and manage a family. It was inevitable, perhaps, that these two visions of "family" would come to loggerheads, and they did in the much publicized controversy between the story line of the sitcom *Murphy Brown* and Vice President Dan Quayle, who insisted that anything less than the entire mythic complex of the nuclear family—such as single parenthood—is bad. Hence, he targeted Murphy Brown, a woman character of celebrity status as a national newscaster on the sitcom who bears and raises a child as a single parent.

A Brief Diversion Concerning Stereotypes

A stereotype is commonly conceived as a set of characteristics that are true about any representative of a group. Stereotyping thus works in the following manner: One encounters an individual, say, a child, and on recognizing the individual as a child, imputes that child's individuality with stereotyped characteristics of children, such as childishness, a proclivity to play, a short attention span, smallness in size compared with adults, and so on. The problem with attributing these characteristics to an individual child, however, is the possibility that the child may not be playful, may be quite attentive, and may be tall compared with other children of the same age.

A stereotype is thus a shorthand caricature of a group that is mythically invoked on encountering someone who appears to be a representative of the caricatured group. A stereotype works by mythic expectation. Naturally, various groups view stereotypes of themselves to be at best inadequate for locating their common characteristics, let alone individual characteristics, and at worst so offensive that they consider the stereotypes to be a defamation and violation of their human rights.

One further ingredient in stereotyping is often missed, however: For individuals to become acculturated, they must associate their experiences into groups, if for nothing else, for example, to communicate the desire for food to others. The concept of food is a stereotype. Conceptualization is stereotyping. Thus, the offensiveness of racial, ethnic, class, geographical origin, gender, and sexually oriented stereotypes can be more precisely located: It is not the stereotyping itself that is offensive, it is leaving the stereotype unquestioned and unthinking; it is letting the stereotype do the thinking. Stereotyping is a human activity for experience.

A stereotype is a set of symbols that also has a separate and independent existence from the individual human or group it is purported to represent, in a book, a poster—or in hate graffiti. When individuals or groups employ the stereotype and experience the stereotyped person or group only as the simplified stereotype, dismissing all other considerations, then the individuals or groups are blinded to active thinking and prevented from engaging the fullness of the individual or group they stereotype. It is as if they see only their stereotype and not the person or group as they really are. Stereotypes also marginalize the person or group they represent, meaning they endow the stereotyped human with the status of little, less, or no importance to the majority of a larger group such as a nation or culture. This marginalization also reinforces the hierarchical status of the stereotyper as more important—and supposedly inherently so—than the stereotyped. Stereotypes thus form consciousness as a type of communication medium. The very reality that stereotyping separates the stereotyper from those stereotyped indicates how stereotypes shape consciousness. The separate existence of a stereotype from the humans represented by a stereotype mimics the barrier the stereotyper assumes as difference from the stereotyped human.

Being stereotyped is not usually that much fun, either. One particular use of stereotyping can be quite alarming—its incorporation into propaganda. Nazi propaganda stereotyped Jews, Poles, Gypsies, homosexuals, and other racial and ethnic communities as causes of Germany's woes since the First World War and as scapegoats to escalate the fervor against these groups their propaganda produced (K. Burke, *Grammar* 264-268). Thus, the prevalence or frequency of stereotypes in a narrative, advertisement, or political theory suggests the possibility that these media may well communicate and operate as propaganda. As an example of sexual stereotypes, statistically, many women are still paid less then men with the same job and years of experience at that job; women are stereotyped as of less value for their work. A blonde female may easily be perceived as the stereotypical "dumb blonde." An African American male may easily be typed as sexually insatiable, with a huge penis. None of these stereotypes are true in all or even most cases.

Sexualized Stereotypes Derived from Myth

Some stereotypes of femaleness and maleness have existed for at least ten thousand years as myths that generate mythic expectations of maleness and femaleness. Although it is currently fashionable to attribute recognition of many of these stereotypes to the rise of later modern feminism and gay liberation—and to attribute them to the modern rise of male chauvinism—the mythic expectation about the performance of gender is embedded in numerous myths from hundreds of cultures, not just Western cultures and not just in the past three hundred years. The issue is not so much whether these stereotypes are right or wrong, innate or acquired—although those are serious and important issues that will be taken up later. Instead, their mythic expectations evoke and activate humans as open texts with multiple interpretations.

The vast majority of ancient, historical, and contemporary indigenous peoples experience the earth as a living, spiritual being who is recognized as fundamentally female. Frequently she is called Earth Mother. Earth Mother provides for her people, usually called The People, as many indigenous groups' names for themselves translate as The People. In this archaic sense, Earth Mother is a Nurturer. Early archaeological evidence shows Earth as a voluptuous, fecund female, like the so-called Venus of Willendorf. Yet two other manifestations of Earth Mother are important to The People.

In her wisdom, Earth Mother sometimes realizes that a major catastrophe will befall The People, one so cosmic that even Earth Mother cannot prevent it. Yet she can help The People survive the disaster. Earth Mother accomplishes her protection by visiting incrementally more serious problems on her people to toughen them. In this second case, Earth Mother is not a sweet, kindly mother.

She is a Tempter/Temptress, a witch, a crone. Plague, crop failure, and invasion all toughen The People.

Later in the development of the mythic pantheon of the Earth Mother, a new woman surfaces. After the disasters have been survived, with fewer people remaining, women must be able to do everything—and everything well, including hunting. Indeed, many indigenous cultures base chief and shamanic status according to natural ability, not biological sex. Enter the Huntress who can hunt and compete as well or better than any man, such as Atalanta or Artemis.

Each of the three manifestations of the Earth Mother—nurturer, temptress, and huntress—subsequently have modeled stereotypes of women. Thus, some classes, ethnicities, and communities have understood that the "complete" or "successful" woman particularly is a nurturer, that is, in an industrial-age narrow way, she is a devoted, giving wife who is a mother, cook, seamstress, and house manager whose domain is inside the home. In other cases, women who object to this restrictive role or who violate what has commonly been accepted as the mainstream images and norms of the "proper" woman are often considered "bad," "lewd," "pushy," and "manipulative." The spectrum of this set of womanly images covers pinup "girls," prostitutes, and strippers, while also including conniving individuals such as Cinderella's stepfamily, entrepreneurs such as Mae West, and rivals for the heart of a man already ostensibly committed to someone else, such as the Joan Collins role of Alexis in the television series *Dynasty*. The advent of late modern feminism certainly influenced the increasing number of female roles of huntress-like leads in television. Although susceptible to moderate emotional experiences, Mrs. Brady of *The Brady Bunch*, Jaimie Somers from *The Bionic Woman*, and Angela on *Who's the Boss* are most usually presented as more than competent, level-headed, and logical as well as courageous and successful in situations.

The Mary Tyler Moore Show featured all three Earth Mother stereotypes. During the first episode, Mary Richards was depicted as a single woman who had recently decided not to marry, who had moved to Minneapolis and was looking for employment. Mary is a huntress, keen on making it in a man's world on her own, which she does. Eventually, however, a new character enters the series, Sue Ellen, the woman in charge of the domestic features and cooking shows. Sue Ellen is the temptress in disguise as the nurturer, particularly cued by her sexual innuendoes to Murray. Finally, Georgette appears on the scene, a classic nurturer who is so calm and supportive she can even manage and placate Ted. By the conclusion of the series, all three stereotypes of women populate the show. Each of the aspects presents what may be considered a limiting vision of femaleness, yet the message of the show is clear; each of these types of persons exists and has her ways in the world. A series of televised Enjoli perfume commercials went further in suggesting that a complete woman is able to perform all three stereotypes. The song lyrics ran, "I can bring home the bacon [huntress], fry it up in a pan [nurturer] . . . and never ever let you forget you're a man [temptress]."

Mythic expectation among ancient peoples also correlated another mythic complex: If the Earth under our feet is female, then the sky above our heads is male. Earth Mother, meet Sky Father. Sky Father is known for his shine, the sweat of his efforts, especially the flash of his sword, spear or lightning, armor. Sky Father keeps the sky in order and travels considerably. One day, he touches down to Earth. He likes this part of the sky. He catches a glimpse of Earth Mother, and she, he, and the rest are history. One way or another, they woo each other, make love, and raise a sexual ruckus. The sky thunders, and the earth shakes in ecstasy. The People are sore afraid. After what seems to be an age of lovemaking, the sky and earth settle down. Sky Father and Earth Mother share ritual smoke, talk, and then get back to work. Sky Father returns to the Sky, and Earth Mother checks on her People.

An age later, a child is born from their union, usually a son or sons, and is considered one of The People. The Son shows characteristics of both parents. He is strong, courageous, and quick like his Father and caring and helpful like his Mother. He is neither sky nor earth; he is either both or something in between, endowed with a liminal status during which he must prove his worthiness. Thus, Son is liminally invested with probationary status.

One day, a new and strange problem surfaces. Earth Mother is not well. Son cheers her up, administers healing of The People, and Earth Mother gets better. Too soon, however, she is ill once again, more ill than the first time. Eventually, it becomes clear that she is dying. No matter what Son does, nothing works. Sooner or later, Earth Mother, another deity, or one of The People tells Son there is only one remedy to save Earth Mother—Son must go on a quest for a medicinal herb, a talisman, or a prayer. Dutifully, Son takes off.

Son suffers all sorts of privation, hunger, pain, and suffering—much like The People being toughened by Temptress. He may suffer alone, maybe not, but he suffers. Sometimes, he never completes the quest and dies thinking he has failed. His heart breaks. Sometimes, he succeeds in acquiring the mystical remedy but does not make it home. Other times, he arrives home only to find that on administration, the remedy does not work; again, he dies thinking he has failed. His heart breaks. Sometimes, he makes it all the way home, only to find Mom has just died or that he is too late. Once again, he dies a failure from a broken heart if not suicide by his own sword or spear.

On his death, his blood flows on the dirt. The blood heals the Earth. Earth Mother gets better yet mourns the loss of her Son. The People mourn the loss, too. The following spring or growing season, at the spot the Son had died, a new grain grows aplenty, providing a new source of food for The People. Miraculously, one of the stalks of grain is the reborn Son, returned to His People, who name him King of The People. Son now becomes the Corn King.

Interpretation

All three dramatis personae of the Earth Mother, Sky Father, and Corn King mythic complex set trajectories for performing gender. Earth Mother is a nurturer with emphasis on her breasts and fecundity; she can also be a witch and a competitor in hard times. Some people find the first two stereotypes objectionable because they codify prescriptions of what a woman "should" be, a nurturer, and what she too often is perceived to be instead, a witch who causes trouble. Others find the huntress objectionable because she is perceived to be "mannish." All three manifestations yield stereotypes originally associated with divinities. As human standards, the stereotypes are impossible to achieve because humans are perceived not to be fully divine.

In comparison, Sky Father is known by his equipment. Clearly, the shine from a sword, spear, shield, or chariot identifies Sky Father with a phallic tool of power, life, and death. Hence, men are supposed to be physically powerful and are supposed to be masters of weapons, tools, and gear. Men are caretakers; poor caretakers are poor men. Furthermore, his "weapon" had better be in tip-top shape—and big. His head is up in the clouds; he is not down to Earth; he is not inclined to set up home in one place for long. He's a wandering salesman. Moreover, sometimes the shine is attributed to the work he does. He exerts effort and sweats. He works. He also impregnates. The stereotype of the remote male who often keeps to himself who provides, protects, and impregnates has also been existent for thousands of years and not just in Western cultures (Abbott). This later informs the tough warrior stereotype. Numerous voices in the men's movement find this stereotype objectionable (Dolce).

There is another set of mythic expectations for males, however—the Corn King's. He saves by suffering. Nothing is too much to expect of him; no privation or sacrifice is too much. To be a man, he must suffer and suffer without complaint, even unto death, particularly for a woman or women. Then, through the miracles of deity, he is reborn, thus adding one further wrinkle to the entire mythic complex—rebirth and resurrection. Male sacrifice brings new life. To be a male, he must be prepared to go on quests, and it is his lot in life to suffer.

Derring-do may be appealing to some persons, but the suffering is a clear sign of a culture that habitually abuses males (Kammer). The Corn King myth furthermore posits the "good boy" who is obedient and respectful of his culture's norms. If the boy—or man—is not an obedient conformer, he may well be considered to be deviant (Reid). In its entirety, the Earth Mother, Sky Father, and Corn King mythic complex inscribes a cosmic set of mythic expectations: birth, life, death, and rebirth. This archetype includes cyclical patterns, such as the four seasons.

Three trajectories have guided the acculturation of females in biological sex for thousands of years—nurturing, tempting, and hunting. Women, of course, are not limited to these mythic norms, yet they have been imprinted generation after generation with these three main alternatives, creating a sense that these are essential and natural. Similarly, for males in biological sex, two trajectories have guided the acculturation of males for thousands of years—the protector/provider/impregnator and the suffering servant who does not live for himself but all or mostly for others. The three female trajectories complete and compete with each other, creating identity concerns about the proper performance of femaleness in many cultures. The two male trajectories fundamentally contradict one another: A proper male remains aloof yet studies himself in potency; he is not really much of a family man. Or, a proper male is a terminal family man who lives for his family and not for himself. Naturally, both sets of trajectories create a cultural context in which one of the trajectories can become a norm to the exclusion of the others or can create serious contradictions in individuals' lives.

Other myths may support these stereotypes of masculinity and femininity. For instance, the myth of human perfectibility is a common assumption in many cultures—that with learning, experience, and discipline, an individual can improve himself or herself. The ancient Greeks particularly applied this mythic expectation to men who were to be both physically beautiful and morally good. In late modern culture, however, the influence of the myth can be seen in the fitness craze in North America, in the ability to transform the body by plastic surgery, and in the verve with which various constituencies ornament their bodies by clothing fashions that are deemed to create a look or good image for themselves.

The myth of material success informs the myth of human perfectibility by rendering all personal goals as a commodity one can work for and purchase. Individuals are considered unsuccessful if they do not consume quality products and services. For instance, a man or woman without a shiny car is not as successful as a man or woman who does have a shiny car. Persons who do not continuously and actively improve their looks by reasonable means available for sale are considered if not failures, a waste.

The myth of eternal youth ordains that youthfulness and its vitality are preferable to aging. Thus, to be "successful," one must look young. Advertisers make fortunes by selling youth to people who appear to believe largely in the myths of material success and human perfectibility.

Even myths that do not seem to have a direct connection to sexuality, body image, and personhood can seriously affect people sexually. For instance, one mythic group may be called the in/out group, by which interiors of buildings are valorized as safe and secure and the out-of-doors is noted as problematic and perhaps dangerous. Numerous generations have been schooled by fairy tales that caution that away from home is unsafe. This myth has so ingrained itself that despite criminological statistics, many people think they are safer from assault and date rape at home, in their rooms, although attacks most frequently happen indoors, usually in familiar surroundings, not outdoors (Holmberg & MacDonald).

Sexualized Stereotypes that Endow Mythic Glamor

After centuries of aristocratic, divine, and militaristic stereotypes predominant for modeling maleness and femaleness, a new mythic complex began to overlay the Western mythic tradition, namely, Romanticism and the noble savage. The basic concepts of Romanticism may be found in the Neoclassical period, during which the relationships of ruler and ruled were hotly discussed. As soon as Hobbes, Locke, and eventually Rousseau posited a "golden age" during which men were independent and naturally moral and that government therefore corrupted natural innocence, it was possible also to posit the noble savage, a being who was wise and good, whom society could only inhibit and harm. It is also no accident that the Neoclassical period, just prior to the Romantic period, was rife with reports from explorers who observed indigenous populations and reported their halcyon existence; these reports affirmed the sense of a golden age and noble savages. The beginning of a new mythic complex, however, was inhibited by the European tradition in that the vision of natural goodness, close to the earth, was mostly male coded. Noble savages were men. Men made social contracts. Although this was not and is not entirely true (Mander 217), a new tradition arose that glorified nature, being close to the earth, and the common and everyday. The older tradition had emphasized reaching for heavenly, heroic deeds, the out-of-the-ordinary, and the special. Thus, eventually Goethe pens *The Sorrows of Young Werther,* a prototypically New Age guy who is emotive and in touch with his feelings. Eventually, in her first novel *Frankenstein,* Mary Shelley lambastes the over-self-indulgent, aristocratic male—Victor Von Frankenstein—and counters him with the tragic monster who is quite clearly portrayed as a noble savage. Although I have characterized the initial acquaintance with the concept of noble savage to fiction writers, not only did initial reports from explorers fuel early formulations, but also anthropologists of the eighteenth and nineteenth centuries subsequently matter-of-factly attributed savages (so-called by them) with primitive sexual urges compared with civilized peoples (Kinsman 27).

In retrospect, the noble savage has become a norm of masculinity, particularly blue-collar, working-class manliness. As Bronski has commented concerning American literature, "Male bonding usually occurs between a white man and a 'noble savage,' the idealized male companion who, because of race and ethnicity, is portrayed as primitive and therefore 'natural' " (15). Bronski exemplifies the observation with, among others, Natty Bumpo and Chingachgook in *The Last of the Mohicans,* Ishmael and Queequeg in Melville's *Moby Dick,* and Huck Finn and Jim (15). For the most part, the white character has been sullied or inhibited by acculturation in his society; his growing relationship with a noble savage reveals a greater variety of aspects to himself, thus ennobling him.

Of course, later in the twentieth century, the noble savage who earlier had clearly emerged from the indigenous golden state of wilderness was joined by blue-collar, working-class types who are good with their hands, strong and muscular, perhaps dangerous seeming, and clever. Although some of these working-class noble savages crop up in gay novels, such as dark, earthy Frankie Olivieri in Holleran's *Dancer from the Dance,* a more focal, main character appears in Helprin's novel, *Winter's Tale,* Peter Lake. Peter Lake was raised by near-aboriginals (persons of some European origins who had gone back to nature) near Manhattan, then became both a machinist and master thief. Breaking into what he took to be an unoccupied mansion, he encounters Beverly Penn, civilized, playing the piano. They immediately fall for one another, and each, the savage and the civilized, informs the other not just in love but in other sorts of goodness (117-120).

Blue-collar, earthy men are frequently portrayed as the ultimate sex partner: Herb Ritts' photograph "Fred with Tires" wears greasy overalls, grips oversize tires in an auto shop, and is slick with smudged desire, looking right at the viewer. The Village People dress in various working-class costumes that exhibit noble savagery: a cowboy and a worker wearing their equipment close to the groin; a motorcycle cop wearing black leather boots and carrying a big stick. A jockstrap can be seen under the construction worker's torn jeans. For that matter, athletes in general are imagined as earthy forces of nature, they sweat so much. Lucky Vanous, the Diet Coke-swilling "construction worker," seems to manage most of these butch, blue-collar images in the 1995 Lucky Vanous Calendar. Catalogs such as *International Male, Sport Europa,* let alone *Sears* and *J. C. Penney,* include butch numbers in their sales pitches.

It is perhaps wise to recognize that not all pairings of "civilized" and "savage" persons can be credited to the influence of the literary traditions of the West. Culture studies must not privilege popular artifacts and events as the sole etiology of human pairings and interest. Some pairings may well stem from psychological needs and their management, uninformed by literary tradition. Referring to homosexuals who already have same-sex orientation and proclivities in common, Tripp observes as a psychologist that although a great many homosexual men and women choose partners from "backgrounds very like their own,"

> it is not unusual to find homosexual relationships in which . . . chasms are bridged with ease. Sometimes the contrast between partners is enormous: the man of letters and a stevedore, a newscaster and a Japanese chef, the professional man and a construction worker, a biochemist and a truck driver. It is as if a fundamental rapport between same-sex partners not only permits them to hurdle huge social distances but often to be especially stimulated by them. (158)

It should also be noted that Tripp's observations do not falsify the literary—and lived—premise that differences between an alleged civilized and the alleged primitive bring out the noble in either person.

Naturally, journalists are aware of the noble savage stereotypes. The *Toledo Blade* once featured an article on the sex appeal of United Parcel Service (UPS) delivery men. Not blue-collar, but "brown collar" because of the uniform they wear, "Brown collar fantasies have spilled over into books, plays, television shows, and rock songs. In the new movie, *Boys on the Side,* Drew Barrymore's character remarks on the sex appeal of men in uniforms—'especially UPS uniforms.' " As the *Blade* article attests, a song by a group called The Bobs, "Drive by Love," tells of a romance between a Fotomat clerk and a UPS driver with the refrain, "I can't get that driver out of my head/He honks his horn and my face turns red." With a phone number that spells 1-800-PICK-UPS, the sexualization of the working man is underlined (Frank C12).

Not all noble savage, sexualized stereotypes are flattering, however. Some are extremely racist and blatantly negative. Bogle's landmark study of black stereotypes gets right to the point while discussing D. W. Griffith's *The Birth of a Nation.*

> Pure black bucks . . . are always big, baadddd [*sic*] nigger, oversexed and savage, violent and frenzied as they lust for white flesh. . . . Griffith played on the myth of the Negro's high-powered sexuality, then articulated the great white fear that every black man longs for a white woman. Underlying the fear was the assumption that the white woman was the ultimate in female desirability, herself a symbol of white pride, power, and beauty. Consequently, when Lillian Gish, the frailest, purest of all screen heroines, was attacked by the character Lynch—when he put his big black arms around this pale beauty—audiences literally panicked. (13-14)

Herbert Samuels attributes the origins of the African (American) "bestial instinct" to

> 16th century accounts of West Africa that . . . were replete with images of the lewd, lascivious, brutal black man. The sexual attributes that were embodied by the word "bestial" had a greater impact on the Elizabethan English than they would have today because of the popular belief in demon possession. (Bullough & Bullough 507)

Because Africans were universally taken to be heathens, they were more likely to be possessed of superhuman sexuality. Samuels also maintains that the oversexed stereotypes of Africans preexisted English contact (508). Griffith's film thus articulates a long-standing stereotype for the first time on screen.

Whatever the origins, this sort of unflattering, degrading depiction is not limited to silent film. *The Great White Hope,* the *Fly* series, *Blacula,* and numerous other examples repeat the stereotype like a theme with variation. Sidney Poitier kisses a blind white girl in *A Patch of Blue* (1965) but is otherwise nonsexualized. Hollywood still appears at times to be aware of the stereotype, both for its fascination—and hence bigger box office—and for its racist ramifications. *The Pelican Brief* cast Denzel Washington and Julia Roberts in the leading male and female roles. As tempting as sexualizing on screen plot developments may be for Hollywood, the film miraculously steers clear of any sexual innuendo between the two of them. Perhaps that is natural; Roberts' character can trust no one, and any breech of sexuality might falsify that characterization. Then again, maybe not: Roberts' character began the movie with an existing affair with her teacher, whom she trusted.

That the "black buck" stereotype still alarms North Americans is patently obvious in the murders of Nicole Brown and Ron Goldman, the white Bronco car chase of O. J. Simpson, the charge of murder, the trial, and the eventual verdicts. A black man and a white woman, formerly married, then divorced, with allegations of abuse, were plainly fascinating for television viewers who followed the details of the black buck and allegations that verified the stereotype, all the while professing shock at the first black man to break into broadcast sports journalism. The entire stereotypification was apparently even more fascinating for media moguls and televisual, yellow journalists; they cashed in on oodles of airtime under the guise of business-as-usual reportage. Coverage that extensive, that explicit, had never before been attempted. As a continuing event that galvanized a nation, if not the world, the shame of the whole media spectacle—the playing on the black buck stereotype while feigning its lack of presence at all—was almost universally unmentioned for its exploitation of a racist stereotype. Most assuredly in everyday life, the issue of a black man with a white woman surfaced frequently and indeed drove the attention to any media coverage. It was the first time in North American history, too, that the professional journalists highlighted a seamy side of celebrity life as much as did the tabloid journalists whose magazines are sold at grocery store checkout counters.

Some stereotypes are extremely sexist and negative in the sense that persons are presumed not to be in control of themselves sexually. These stereotypes are the classic nymphomaniac and the much lesser known satyr. Carol Groneman has traced the medical pathologization of nymphomania in the nineteenth century as far back as Hippocrates and other Greeks who classified certain sexual performances as maladies of "insane love—accompanied by symptoms of uncontrolled sexuality and/or pining away for love" (343). Although the Renaissance apparently recognized that female sexual desire was "normal," fundamental "belief in female irrationality continued to inform the medical discussion of nymphomania into the nineteenth century" (345). Thus, even moderate signs of a woman enjoying, let alone seeking, sexual love quickly became a suspicious sign of an out-of-control, sex-crazed female. Consequently, popular culture became rife with "the insatiable sexuality of women, devouring, depraved, diseased. It conjures up an aggressively sexual female who both terrifies and titillates men" (337).

In contrast, during the same period, satyriasis—male nymphomania—was considered less frequent and less dangerous to the public. It is perhaps no accident, however, that for years *Playboy* magazine has published cartoons of frolicking nymphs and satyrs. Groneman then isolates the source of the female stereotype: "Men's nature—unlike women's—was never primarily defined by their genitalia" (352). The last conclusion is perhaps as true in centering the stereotyping of women as sexually dangerous on female genitals as it is untrue in claiming men have never been primarily defined by their genitals. If nothing else, the "black buck" stereotype suggests an alternative conclusion. Satyrs—insatiable males—are, however, perhaps more envied for their excess, although the differences between Don Juan, Casanova, and *Alfie* are not as certain as, say, some people's admiration for Hugh Hefner, Wilt Chamberlain, or the ubiquitous captain of the football team who populates teen horror novels such as *Cheerleaders* and countless movies.

The gay man is subject to numerous stereotypes, one which clearly centers on male genitals and their insatiability. According to Pronger, the "homosexual monster myth paints a dismal picture of homosexuality, one that has worked its way through the culture and has been enshrined not only in a multitude of sociocultural institutions . . . but in the minds of most people" (77). Citing United Press International reports of crimes of "homosexual rage," Kirk and Madsen ponder the impression such word choice creates, "as though this were a specific kind of rage, a particularly *sordid* rage. Such crimes-*qua*-media events seal and re-seal the reputation of gays as sex fiends of the first order" (47). Furthermore, by rehearsing the equation of homosexuality as *only* sexuality, the stereotype encourages "little appreciation that homosexuality is also about love, intimacy and romance" (51). In other words, the stereotype blinds true thinking and interpretation of individuals. Hocquenghem also finds this emphasis on the penis and its satisfaction as equation of gays and madness: "Sex is reduced to the penis. . . . Thus the homosexual becomes a subject who dreams of being an object, in his mad desire for the one and only component object, the penis" (120).

Then again, perhaps an even more widespread stereotype of gay men prompts many people to identify them as sissies, fags, and feminine—men who talk with lisps and flutter limp wrists, such as Bronson Pinchot's sales clerk's character in *Beverly Hills Cop*. Of course, in an *All in the Family* sitcom episode, Archie Bunker was horrified to discover that one of the roughest, toughest football players he drank beer with was gay. The interplay of "manly" ways and "nelly" ways is sometimes a social drama of stereotype management; one of the strategies some guys/gays have developed consciously to resist or fight the nelly stereotype has been the cultivation of butchness (Holmberg, "Hey"). As Alex Karras's character, Squash, says in the film *Victor/Victoria,* "Listen, if you didn't want the guys to call you queer, you became a rough, tough, son-of-a-bitchin' football player." Stereotypes may be unrealistic, but they have impact in everyday life. They affect individuals and groups negatively, forcing them to conform to a social norm or be construed as violating it.

Men in general, however, are quite subject to genital-centered stereotyping. Perhaps guided by the myth of the Sky Father, men are supposed to have a big penis, or at least an adequate one. Greg Perry confesses that he is "hung like a hamster" and until recently, other people's reactions to his size have been highly problematic and embarrassing (Harding 41). With folklore such as "it's not the size of the boat; it's the motion on the ocean," it is no wonder that men's penis size—real or perceived—can stigmatize them. Not only that, but if a man is not acting confidently, he "lacks balls." So much for Groneman's "men's nature—unlike women's—was never primarily defined by their genitalia."

Homosexual women, lesbians, are also frequently stereotyped as dour, humorless, mannish women who enjoy doing guy things. Women athletes are frequently taken to be lesbians, so much so that

> the "female athlete" role represents a microcosm of a larger process—that of capitalizing on lesbiphobic attitudes to limit, suppress, and control *all* women regardless of their athletic performance *or* their affectational preference. . . . As the twentieth century draws to a close, the team sport playing female athlete, the "tomboy," is still the most blatant representation of woman stepping out of her ordained gendex [*sic*] role. However, not far behind her is the "aggressive CEO," the "too-tough cop," the "assertive and independent professor," the "defiant single mother," the "questioning student." None of these women, regardless of their actual affectational preference, are immune from lesbiphobic attacks. (Peper 205, emphasis Peper's)

As Katz reports, a "dike" is a "female homosexual, especially if aggressive or masculine" (*Gay/Lesbian* 576), and a "bull-dike" "wears mannish clothes and is in other ways aggressively masculine" (574). Russo affirms that the mannish stereotype extends to film, the "presentation of lesbianism as an alien state of being emerged much more strongly in the Fifties in hard female characters who were seen as bitter reminders of the fate of women who tried to perform male roles." Women characters in movies such as *Young Man with a Horn, All About Eve,* and *Caged* "shared unstated lesbian feelings and murderous impulses" (99-100). Whether a woman otherwise dresses or acts mannishly, a lesbian is still often depicted as doing things in the stereotypic, male dominant, violent manner. Marcia Brady's admirer, Noreen, in *The Brady Bunch Movie,* decks a sexually harassing lad, which is all the more stereotypically striking because the nelly guy friend who is also interested in Marcia is reluctant to get physical. When Marcia discovers the lout laid out on the floor, she automatically attributes the feat to the boy, not the girl, ironically, oblivious to the girl's passion for her.

Then again, there are hyperfeminine women stereotypes, particularly attributed to Asians. In many pornographic movies, the Asian woman is paradoxically submissive yet knowledgeable about sex in ways that make European American women look rather cold by comparison. Asian men in gay pornography are almost always submissive and are rarely penetrators or "tops."

In all these cases, stereotyped sexual capabilities are mythic in their attribution. Statistically speaking, big African American males are not seething noble savages; few women are sex-crazed nymphos; few men are on the make one hundred percent of the time; few gays are naturally nelly; few lesbians are always mannish. To stereotype is to endow the person stereotyped with mythic excess, something to which many a human may aspire but few come by naturally.

Ritual

The origins of magic and ritual are as archaic as they are late modern; some semblance of one rarely occurs without the other. The basic concept of magic involves powers to affect the material and spiritual worlds, powers that are not ordinary, not available to everyone in the same way. Some prehistoric and historical indigenous peoples recognize signs by which they may identify some children as manifesting a greater innate ability for such magic (Kalweit 75-93). Those who display strong inherent magic, however, may be trained to control and direct it; similarly, those with lesser power may also learn to develop what magic they can access. In both cases, rituals, or codified, proven procedures, enhance natural ability.

As artifacts of the oral tradition, rites and rituals are formulaic, following archetypal patterns, and may be passed from generation to generation in basically the same oral form. Rites hold and convey their own mythic expectations, particularly to produce some desired effect. In this sense, natural magic gets channeled into formulaic performance and becomes sympathetic magic. Sympathetic magic assumes that the symbolic rehearsal of producing an effect in ritual form, if performed well or correctly, will produce an effect in the material or spiritual world. Symbolic rehearsals may include cleansing participants and the place of ritual from impurities, singing, praying, dancing, paintings on cave walls or in sand, and so on.

The difference between individual, innate, and natural ability and shared, ritualized, and formulaic performance developed through trial and error through countless generations inscribes cultural trajectories that live among peoples to this day. Both individual ability and rituals for communally accessing magic are focal points of a culture. A culture has an interest to identify its people's talents, not just magical knacks, but a culture also intensifies its attention to that magic by focusing on individuals to train them and on individuals who, once trained, in turn become ritual fulcrums as leaders of rituals that may not be for training of talented individuals, such as birth, coupling, and death rituals. These rituals are rites of passage from one area of human existence to another. All rites and rituals then carry and convey cultural identity.

The cultural habits embedded in the ritual performance of selfhood and social grouping do not die away when a culture abandons pure archaic lifestyle. Just as the adoption of new media does not erase old media, so too, new cultural habits do not completely erase former shared performances. They may change, however, even to the point of losing their original—or *ab*original—interpretation, with new ones assigned from the point of view of the new cultural habits. Many folklore valences associated with rites of passage were originally highly sexualized and formalized for indigenous or agrarian peoples.

Industrial and now late modern cultures still retain cultural forms but attribute different meanings to them. By the mid-twentieth century in the West, the "honeymoon" was a time immediately following the marriage ceremony, a time for the couple to leave their immediate community, have time for themselves, rest, get accustomed to one another—and make love, presumably for the first time, without interruptions from family, friends, bosses, or coworkers. Yet well into the twentieth century, these defining features of honeymoons were overshadowed by other cultural habits, ones more residual from agrarian lifestyles. For instance, shivarees were expected events in rural communities right after wedding hoopla. The bride and groom were taken to a place prepared for their wedding night, again presumably their first full sexual encounter, but then they were constantly detained from consummation by pranks and serenading perpetrated by friends, family, and neighbors. Notice that the newly wedded pair did not immediately depart for some glamorous trip. In rural communities, the newlyweds had only the one night or a few at most to get it on; there was no trip; they were needed to help with chores.

Indeed, there were special chores newlyweds could and should perform. The newlywed ritual of "carrying her over the threshold" was one of those magical chores. In earlier times, especially when the best grain had been carefully retained for the next year's planting, the newlyweds were expected to bless the grain to ensure its fertility. Instead of going to a prepared house or cottage to await a shivaree, they went to the place where the grain was stored. The granary customarily had one, half-open door. The lower, closed half was spanned by a board or boards that kept the grain from spilling out, called the threshold, because it held the thresh, the grain. The new husband lifted his wife over the threshold, and both entered the granary where they made love as often as possible to imbue the grain with their sexual vitality. Now that is crossing the threshold, a rite of passage during which the newlyweds are in a magical place and time, endowed with mythic power and during which they are not their former selves nor their new, mundane, workaday selves. Turner (*Forest* 93-111) and Van Gennep call this ritualized place and time *liminality,* a time in between other areas of life. Others might call it a rite of reversal (Nachbar et al. 245).

Yet the honeymoon involves an even earlier, mythic connection to the seasons and the cosmos. In ancient Celtic culture, the June or Mead moon was also called the honey moon because that was the time during which it was first safe to collect honey from beehives—enough time had elapsed since winter for the bees to build up an excess of honey that could be tapped without endangering the bees' amount of food (Campanelli). Basically, the honeymoon was a natural period that involved less work, thus new couples could be spared from their chores temporarily; by superstition, however, May was considered an unlucky month to wed, it being the month the Goddess and God wedded. May was their month, not to be intruded on or imitated by mere mortals, but June, a reflection of sacred May, was taken as an appropriate time to wed as a homage to the two major earth spirits.

In late modern, postindustrial Western culture, new rituals have emerged as definitive for signifying one's connection to and social standing in a particular community. New rituals have become crucial in the late modern period for no few reasons. Macroscopically, large industries and groups of people desire to make more money or have more people think and act as they do—or both. Thus, some groups take on those impositions but make them their own in a unique sort of way, what Fiske calls "excorporation" (15). For instance, Adolf Hitler made homosexuals in concentration camps wear a pink triangle for easy identification of their "crime." Ironically, numerous persons who were homosexuals did not enter concentration camps. In the latter part of the twentieth century, some homosexuals have taken that mainstream imposition—a pink triangle that marks one a criminal, a concentration camper, a sexual outlaw—and now wear them as logos on shirts, pins, badges on baseball caps, and car window and bumper stickers. They do this freely as a way of detoxifying the icon, of absorbing it into their lives, not as a mark of shame but as a mark of pride. The pink triangle icon also memorializes the atrocities committed on homosexuals by a mainstream culture that wanted everyone to be the same—or die.

Despite fears that current North American culture not only has locked North Americans into a consumer vision but also is quickly exporting its concomitant values all over the globe (also known as the new world order and globalization), people in North America and in communities around the globe pick and choose what interests them and do not always accept the baby with the bathwater that carries postindustrialism's wastes and pollution. Some North Americans regularly perform a rite I call a *rite of deconstruction.* A rite of reversal involves a temporary, liminal time and space. A rite of deconstruction, however, not merely temporarily reverses the usual and the everyday but transforms individuals and groups on a continuing basis. The Xerox rep who wears a dress-for-success business suit by day changes into ska or reggae threads after arriving home. Then, off to a bar or party where the transformed rep will find Caribbean music and like-minded souls. Persons who opt for a tattoo or some form of body piercing clearly make a permanent deconstruction of their former normality. Depending on the nature of the tattoo—how large it is, its location on the body, its colors, whether it tends to signify a particular subcultural community or some image truly unique—the tattoo may be visible in everyday life, presenting all sorts of potential changes in relationships to family, friends, and employers. But it also may create an instant identity with others who are tattooed or pierced.

Cultural Literacy

Historically, thousands of cultures have existed. They can be studied and are studied, particularly older civilizations. The persons who perform these studies are most frequently taken as researchers of Culture with a capital *C.* Having performed and communicated their research for hundreds of years, they have become accustomed to employ certain tactics for communicating and understanding one another. In their sense, literacy begins with the nuts and bolts of reading and writing but then continues into modes of logic and modes of presentation.

In North America in the twentieth century, reading and writing are still taken as a basic human acquisition. The world that produced basic literacy, however, has demonstrably changed. Except for reading the numbers and letters when dialing or punching a telephone, reading is not a necessary part of the literacy of phone communication at all. Same for radio. Film and television have presented a vast array of new conventions for crafting communication, and audiences have learned the literacy of reading the films by noticing lighting, staging, makeup, the film score, the acting, the action, the color, and so on. Thus, cultural literacy is much more involved than the simples of reading and writing the written word.

The cultural literacy of the written word also involves one other significant feature: Reading and writing were/are simple, so simple that once learned, a person can use implements other than pen or pencil on surfaces other than paper. Consider graffiti. Furthermore, if one's implement broke, it was/is an easy matter to fix it or replace it oneself. But who can fix a television? Not everyone. More curious, no less than ninety percent of the images, messages, and news presented on television are unidirectional. Although opportunities for interactive television appear to be increasing, there really is no instant feedback such as one can encounter in an everyday conversation around a table. This additional feature of the cultural literacy of television has preempted the political process envisioned by the signers of the U.S. Constitution. One of the most hotly contested debates centered on elected representatives having to face their constituents as often as possible—face-to-face. All sorts of compromises were made, and only half of Congress was assigned short terms of 2 years, the House of Representatives. Given that recognition of the fundamental need for face-to-face meetings, television has mostly destroyed it. The cultural literacy to be found in the Constitution requires and assumes face-to-face meetings, give-and-take. Television gives. The elected persons have production staffs craft their messages to their constituencies. Getting access back to the elected person does not work in the same way at all. The cultural literacy of television is largely a mirror of the received, canonical tradition, signified by its unidirectionality (Holmberg, "Stray").

Thus, it has become crucial to familiarize each other in the panoply of cultural literacy featured endemically in each popular culture event and artifact. If one is to be a knowledgeable person, even citizen, reading and writing are not enough. Once again, critics who maintain that only canonical culture is worthy of educational curricula commit the closing of the diversity of discourse by limiting people to the cultural literacy of the written word. The world has moved on, not erasing the written word but placing it in new media literacies.

A good deal of performance art, photography as well as writing, is currently being done about the human body. Countless images of sexy bodies populate the airwaves, periodicals, and billboards. Some of them are scantily clad. Some of them are carefully dressed. Whatever the sexiness is, in and of itself, it is used to sell a product or service, indeed is hoped to be identified with the product or service. One would be ill-advised only to read this writing uncritically. Tattoos, piercing, and other forms of body art are also writings on the body. They cannot be read simply as the written word.

In other words, cultural literacy is cultural literacie*s*. There no longer exist one and only one medium and its literacy. Perhaps that never was true, a myth of the ruling class that monopolized control over the written word, even to the point of conscientiously keeping others illiterate. Late modern literacies are complex and diverse in their media demand that issue from their media features, yet they are learned rapidly, frequently by millions of persons worldwide who envision not only the intended uses of new media, new fashions, and new customs but also ways to adapt them to their own desires and pleasures.

Popular Culture Studies

Maligned by arbiters of canonical culture, the study of popular culture also entails its own cultural literacy. While many other academic disciplines or intellectual movements maintain canonical norms, popular culture studies have begun to deconstruct timeworn assumptions not just of what to study but also how to study and present it.

In communication studies, for instance, research methods cluster into two forms, quantitative and qualitative. Although some individuals may place rhetorical studies in either camp—depending on whether they quantify something or criticize it—the rift between the two is palpable. There is a usually unstated hierarchy between them, that quantitative approaches are superior to qualitative modes, that a qualitative study cannot be as definitive as a quantified study.

I find this presumption of difference and opposition quite absurd. Given that we live in a business-driven culture, it is only natural that the Urtext of business—quantification—be a norm for all research. Yet that inscribes a hierarchy of dominance that is inhibitive if not exclusionary to other sorts of research and thinking. I remember when I first began the ethnography of social gatherings. My field notes were loaded with tidbits about the presence of alcohol at most gatherings. I began to search for research on alcohol and parties and, to my surprise, literally found thousands of journal articles on alcohol— and almost every single one of them presented alcohol as a problem for the social welfare and health systems. All of them used quantification. There was no research about social bonding. There was no research about particular beverages that are consumed only at particular holidays. There was no research about the uses of alcohol and other beverages, for that matter, for socializing. Only the misuses were researched. Even then, there were no self-reports of alcoholics, their families, or their friends, no studies of winos. But apparently a considerable amount of private and public money had been poured into the quantitative research machine.

Thus, I prefer to consider popular culture studies as situated differently from the oversimplistic banalities the quantitative-qualitative dichotomy poses. I shall assume a different word, therefore, to locate it: interpretive. Popular culture studies are interpretive studies. They may use social scientific methods but are not limited to them, nor will they usually be employed alone. Popular culture studies are often humanities oriented in approach but again are not limited to critical modes of inquiry, nor will they always be employed unaided by social scientific modes. *Interpretive* means both and more. Perhaps Jack Santino says it best:

> The study of popular culture involves the use of methodologies from both the humanities and the social sciences in the effort to interpret expressive cultural forms, specifically those that are widely disseminated in a group (that is, that are popular) as part of dynamic social intercourse. . . .
>
> Popular culture scholars study these created, expressive and artistic materials as their primary data, much as literary scholars take the novel or the sonnet as their primary data. In this way Popular Culture Studies is within the tradition of the humanities. However, Popular Culture Studies differs from traditional humanities studies in that it recognizes that everything has a history and takes place in a context. Further, scholars of popular culture recognize the existence of alternative systems of aesthetics which guide the creation of popular materials and the evaluation of those materials by an audience. (32)

With Santino's commodious yet specific interdisciplinary vision of the study of popular culture in mind, one that includes the artistic in context and the everyday audiences who interpret the artistic, I proceed into the body of *Sexualities and Popular Culture:* Sex and its cultural and artistic portrayals are actively interpreted by numerous sexualized and/or gendered communities but most particularly as active communicators and commentators about sex, gender, and orientation in the latter half of the twentieth century, by the women's movement, the gay/lesbian movement, and the nascent men's movement.

4

Sex, Gender, and Sexual Orientation

TV Guide is the most circulated magazine in North American history. An issue a week graces grocery store checkout lines, and millions of copies are delivered at home on a subscription basis. Arguably, the images that *TV Guide* has employed through the years reflect American culture as well as influence it in turn. In 1957 and 1958, "family" images abounded: The debut ad for *The Donna Reed Show* featured a family shot; *Leave It to Beaver* consistently pictured the family, as did *The Adventures of Ozzie and Harriet* promos. The casts of *The Real McCoys* and *Father Knows Best* smiled, smiled, smiled. A Grace Kelly special was billed as a family entertainment, and, of course, any Disney show was family from the word go. Twenty years later, in 1976, families were still advertised, but there were fewer such shows. *The Waltons,* perhaps like *The Real McCoys,* most frequently smiled in *TV Guide* promos. In contrast, *All in the Family*'s Archie and Edith Bunker look upset. *One Day at a Time*'s Bonnie Franklin looks angry and upset. There is a decided difference in depictions after only a score of years.

The product ads are perhaps more revealing of change. In the 1950s, housewives had headaches and need aspirin, especially when they must cook and watch children at the same time; images of women are claustrophobic (24 May 1958, 3; 21 June 1958, 3). Women gossip over the fence (15 Feb. 1958, A-23); women do decor (15 Nov. 1958, A-81). Not only do men not wash dishes—they watch TV (15 Feb. 1958, A-43), they explain TV to their daughter (5 Oct. 1957, unpag.), and they take pictures (15 Nov. 1958, 14-15). Boys, not girls, sell *TV Guide* subscriptions (7 Sept. 1957, A-28; 14 June 1958, A-29). All these images of active males contrast with images employed twenty years later, as in a new show broadcast in 1976 that starred three women in action adventure, *Charlie's*

59

Angels (25 Sept. 1976, A-102), and although *The Bionic Woman* is faster than a speeding bullet, she always seems to have Steve Austin on her mind (10 Jan. 1976, A-79).

Something happened between the mid-1950s and the mid 1970s. It is accurate and also misleading to claim that the late modern women's liberation was the proximal cause of these visible changes. Other liberation movements were already well under way. The Vietnam War brought many new images of men, women, and children to the American public. The rapid availability of the birth control pill signaled new freedom to explore sexuality without long-term commitment between heterosexual partners. Other revolutions in fitness, nutrition, consumer trends, literature, art, film, and leisure activities all conspired in the change. Clearly, however, late modern feminism charged the mix with concerns about stereotyping women and about control over their own bodies, particularly sex and child bearing. Led by feminism, the mix began a revolution in the conceptualization of biological sex and its performance as sexuality, as gender.

The words we use and the habits we perform are particularly complicated concerning sex. Few cultures agree on the same norms. Internally, few cultures abide by strict codes without experimentation beyond the codes, in action, thought, or passion. Even the way we talk about sex is fraught with honest issues that concern discussing sex publicly, reading about activities we barely can imagine ourselves doing, and selecting what about sex truly speaks our bodies, minds, and spirits. Thus, I would like to develop a taxonomy of terms about sex that reflects recent developments in culture studies about sex and that will be applied throughout this book.

Sex, Sexuality, and Gender

Sex refers to biological sex for plants, animals, and humans. *Sexuality* refers to the learned, culturally inscribed values, meanings, symbols, habits, and rituals that humans live and experience alone and with other humans. The term *sexualities* refers to the many cultures of sexuality, not just one. Indeed, there are many cultural norms for sexualities and their acculturation, historically, geographically, and contemporaneously. The title *Sexualities and Popular Culture* therefore indicates the ultimate emphasis on the cultural interpretation and understanding of a variety of sexualities as "a sign, a symbol and a means of our call to communication and communion" (Nelson 18).

As it was in 1957, it is still tempting to assume that one's birth sex automatically endows one with cultural ways to perform that biological sex, that is, that one's sexuality is the same as one's biological sex. It is tempting to accept this uncritically because if nothing else, life might be simpler—if it ever worked that way in all cultures, for all persons, and in mostly the same way regardless of place or time or social conditions, which, guided by numerous sources, apparently it did not. It does not now, and it certainly did not in the 1950s in North America. Of course, it could be opined that one's sexuality—or gender— is supposed to correspond to one's biological sex and that if it does not, one should strive to make it so to conform. On the one hand, the basic assumption of the fundamental identity between an individual's sex and his or her gender sets a descriptive norm that some people apply in all cases of sex and gender not only as if that were only natural but also as if it were the *only* natural way. On the other hand, however, the assumption that everyone *should* conform to his or her biological sex is actually a prescriptive norm that impresses a moral imperative that better conformity to that norm equates to a better person, whereas poor performance or violation of the prescriptive code sets one up for correction, censure, and even punishment. Correction, censure, and punishment are not descriptive; they are prescriptive and clearly display the easy shift from describing an alleged, natural link between biological sex and its social performance to what Gayle Rubin calls the mandatory, compulsory performance to be applied in all cases whether the linkage is true or not ("Traffic"). Moral imperatives are not descriptive norms. Both the assumptions that biological sex and its performance are the same and natural and that therefore everyone's sex and gender performance should and will conform may be called *essentialist* positions.

The notion that gender is inborn has been challenged strongly in the last forty years of the twentieth century in North America. The challengers to sexual essentialism consider sexuality to be constructed socially. Sex roles and gender are not inborn and automatic. Not long after 1957, the late modern women's movement burgeoned after the publication of Betty Friedan's 1963 *The Feminine Mystique,* along with other early late-modern, feminist publications. Friedan acknowledges feminist predecessors such as Mary Wollstonecraft, Elizabeth Cady Stanton, Julia Ward Howe, and Margaret Sanger. Friedan also observes that none of these women fit the stereotypes of feminists as "embittered, sex-starved spinsters . . . castrating, unsexed non-women who burned with such envy for the male organ that they wanted to take it away from all men, or destroy them, demanding rights only because they lacked the power to love as women" (75-76) because they embraced marriage but all the same "fought for a chance for woman to fulfill herself, not in relation to man, but as an individual" (76). Friedan frequently posits feminist concerns as criticisms of popular culture media, such as magazines like *McCall's* (31-34) that promotes images of women as domestic heroines content to stay at home and do allegedly womanly things.

Womanly things fundamentally were presumed to be innate. Any woman who tried to be other than that essentialist vision of womanhood was doomed. The entire essentialist complex and stereotypes of woman as feminine Friedan calls "the feminine mystique."

> The mistake, says the mystique, the root of women's troubles in the past is that women envied men, women tried to be like men, instead of accepting their own nature, which can find fulfillment only in sexual passivity, male domination, and nurturing maternal love. (39-40)

The dint of the feminine mystique is so ubiquitous that it is promoted not only by magazines but also by "television, movies, and books that popularize psychological half-truths, and by parents, teachers and counselors" (71).

The signal features of Friedan's book include the recognition of earlier women who long ago set the feminist agenda of issues, concerns, and action. What was found to be objectionable about essentializing women in the early nineteenth century was still so by the early 1960s. The message was clear: The fundamental essentialist assumptions of the femininity of women had not been seriously challenged to overturn them in daily life and in the life of the shared culture, particularly its communication media that produces images and expectations of women. *The Feminine Mystique* was an overt challenge that stated feminist concerns. It was a sensation.

Barely a year before publication of *The Feminine Mystique*, another book also was a publishing sensation, but it covertly embedded feminist concerns of liberation and self-determination: *Sex and the Single Girl* by Helen Gurley Brown. Although perhaps some, if not many, later modern feminists may not credit *Sex and the Single Girl* as a feminist text, it cannot be seriously argued that it was not influential in promulgating images and expectations of women to be or become independent persons. Brown makes it clear that a woman has the option to explore variety in self-presentation—a "petite brunette is gamine but serious-minded" (7). Notice how Brown suggests a woman may be sexualized but also intelligent. Furthermore, despite the book's title, the single girl does not have to bed a man or be promiscuous to be The Girl. "Being The Girl doesn't necessarily mean you are sleeping with him, although you may be" (9).

By her own self-identification, The Girl need not be a looker. In many ways, *Sex and the Single Girl* partakes of an important ingredient in liberation movements: encouraging self-esteem in the face of oppression. In this sense, Gloria Steinem's more recent *Revolution from Within* continues the need to address self-esteem.

After Friedan's and Brown's initial books, overt and covert as they may be, the growing number of publications concerning women's oppression was pivotal in challenging essentialist norms about women and popularizing a liberated series of views about women. The movement liberated some women and men from the burden of assuming received, essentialist, rigid sex roles, from what was then and now called "sexism." Sexism involves assumptions believed by men and women and how those beliefs permeate everyday life.

In 1969, Roszak and Roszak itemized rigid sex role assumptions about women, bemoaning that "men—even educated, politically radical men" continue to rehearse "the ancient litany of lies", or sexism: (1) "Women really are born cooks and bottle washers." (2) "Women really do find their whole fulfillment in the joys of child rearing . . . Those who don't are obviously abnormal." (3) "Women really prefer to be social subordinates." (4) "Women have already been allowed more than enough opportunities to get ahead. If they don't use them, it's their fault." (5) "Women are making steady progress as it is." (6) Women are actually lucky to be women. "They've got it soft. . . . It's no fun being boss big shot." (7) Women must wait for class, race, and national problems to be solved, which in turn will resolve women problems. "Impatience is a sign of selfishness and divides the movement" (x). That was 1969. Although there is a greater diversity of feminist voices at the turn of the millennium, some 30 years later, the "ancient litany of lies" has not disappeared. Recent voices, however, have developed new strategies for destabilizing that litany.

For instance, Sedgwick (1990) reminds late moderns that sex and gender have perhaps always been challenging if not potentially disruptive of strictly defined sexual practices and assumptions.

- Even identical genital acts mean very different things to different people.
- To some people, the nimbus of "the sexual" seems scarcely to extend beyond the boundaries of discrete genital acts; to others, it enfolds them loosely or floats virtually free of them.
- Sexuality makes up a large share of the self-perceived identity of some people, a small share of others'. . . .
- For some people, the preference for a certain sexual object, act, role, zone, or scenario is so immemorial and durable that it can only be experienced as innate; for others, it appears to come late or to feel aleatory or discretionary. . . .

- For some people, sexuality provides a needed space of heightened discovery and cognitive hyperstimulation. For others, sexuality provides a needed space of routinized habituation and cognitive hiatus. . . .
- Some people, homo-, hetero-, and bisexual, experience their sexuality as deeply embedded in a matrix of gender meanings and gender differentials. Others of each sexuality do not. (*Epistemology* 25-26)

Quite plainly, Sedgwick bases these observations on personal experience that naturally varies from person to person. It is also clear that an individual, say, who spends little time thinking about sex, who is satisfied with mundane routine, could easily not only not identify with someone who lives and performs sex for self-discovery and hyperstimulation but also might well find that person's beliefs and activities repugnant, if not alien or foreign to what the individual perceives that his or her own culture approves.

As personal experience, neither of the differentiae Sedgwick suggests is right or wrong—until one aspect is postulated as a cultural norm to the exclusion of the other contrasting aspect or to the realm of variation in between. These differentiae may also and do vary within an identifiable culture and between cultures. Although the more ecstatic performance of sexuality could be designated Dionysian and the more restricted, Apollonian (Evans, *God* 192-193; Nietzsche), this differentiation too would be muddled: Those whose personal experience of sexuality is extremely ascetic may indeed report experiencing something similar if not almost identical to sexual ecstasy. Saint Theresa "remembered that one day, on her knees before the altar, she had felt such unearthly bliss that she thought God himself had descended into her" (Bataille 224). Those who persistently value thrill may report the occasional walk on the unwild side, commonly nowadays called "vanilla sex" (Califia 177).

The foregoing ruminations extrapolated from Sedgwick's formulations strictly outline sex as sexual performance. Except for the last item, they do not mention whether the participants are male or female, masculine or feminine. Clearly, Sedgwick edited these parameters from the picture. Also edited were same-sex parameters, thus destabilizing each differential area as oppositionally male or female, heterosexual or homosexual.

The Late Modern Women's Movement

It is no small measure of misogyny and homophobia that in everyday life, as noted by me ethnographically, many people, males and females, dismissed the women's movement and particularly various leaders of the National Organization for Women (NOW) because the detractors attributed women's dissatisfaction not to their being women but to the assumption that they were lesbians. By stereotype, lesbians are just not fun people, always serious and grim; as stereotypically homosexual, they certainly could never be satisfied with anything because they are deviants. That is how threatened and perhaps desperate some detractors were (and are) so they would not seriously have to entertain feminism, the power of women, and the simple legal affirmation of equal rights. That is pretty much how stereotyping works to prevent true thinking. The logic, if it may be called that, runs something such as this: (1) Women voice their concern; (2) the women are not acting like women; (3) women who do not act like women are lesbians; (4) therefore, the reason for their voiced concerns has nothing to do with their being women; it has to do with their being lesbian; (5) because the women who voice concerns about equal rights are lesbians, they do not speak for all women and certainly cannot be taken seriously. The proponents are suspect as to their motivations, if not sexuality; therefore, the whole women's movement phenomenon is dismissible. This sort of basis for rejection of the women's movement circulates an interesting irony that if dissent equals lesbianness, gayness, or queerness, then the founders of the United States must be suspect as to their orientation, presumably not to each other but to the British who would essentialistically attribute their dissent to sexual deviance—if indeed dissent and sexual deviance are inborn, innate, and automatically connected, a stunning bit of logic not applied to the founding "fathers," only to late modern, dissenting women.

The vectoring of women with sexual variety remains problematic, such as when the National Endowment for the Arts rescinded funding to four artists in 1990, subsequently dubbed the NEA Four (Duggan & Hunter 27). Three of them were lesbians, but one, Karen Finley, was/is not. It was this heterosexual woman's performance art, however, that was attacked vehemently, particularly with regard to sexual deviance implicit in alleged insertion of yams in her body and other allegations that were not true—but well circulated among the threatened funders. Strangely, however, "the issues were oddly understood as being about gay rights, artistic freedom or civil liberties, but not feminism" (3). Finley's "sensitivity toward 'lower class' women" (Juno & Vale 42) undoubtedly further threatens funders from the upper class. The lesbian performance artist, Holly Hughes, received less press in comparison. In other words, it is not enough to attack a woman as a woman—such is impolite if not politically incorrect. But to attack her as if she were a lesbian is certifiably righteous and apparently acceptable in mainstream culture. Ironically, the attackers attributed transgressive orientation where it did not exist.

Earlier, in 1977, Phyllis Schlafly offered at face value an alternative voice as a woman about the empowerment of women. Not even a close reading, however, affirms that she transformed the publicly unvoiced persuasive attack of feminist women as lesbians to dismiss their concerns into the public vilification of feminist women to attack and dismiss their concerns because they were associated with lesbians, if not lesbians themselves. *Power of the Positive Woman* celebrated the alleged negativism of the women's liberationist and proposed that women did not really have it so bad at all. With regard to reproductive rights however, Schlafly highlighted lesbianism: "If . . . the ultimate goal of women's liberation is independence from men and the avoidance of pregnancy and its consequences, then lesbianism is logically the highest form of women's liberation" (12). Notably, both appendixes to the book feature supposedly previously undisclosed pictures of NOW rallies and the platform of NOW, and in both cases Schlafly clearly marks lesbianism as what NOW was really about. As such, Schlafly's works are sometimes taken as prima facie examples of sexism and homophobia.

Terminologies and Later Developments

It can be seen that certain terminology and concepts existed early in the late modern women's movement, terms such as *domination* and *self-definition*. Early press exposure and public awareness centered on issues of sexism, male chauvinism, and patriarchy. The term *patriarchy* is now loaded with tons of pejorative baggage and perhaps sometimes close to stereotyping all men. An interesting substitution might be the word "patrilocality" or perhaps better, "patricentrism." As a generic term, patricentric indicates that there are other possibilities for some cultures to organize by men but without dominant hierarchy. "By using the suffix 'centric' rather than 'archal,' we move from the idea of dominion or rule to that of cultural integrity" (Berry 139). Likewise, the term *matriarchal* also becomes suspect in that it posits a seemingly fixed hierarchy that may not have occurred historically or prehistorically. Instead, in some aboriginal, indigenous communities, responsibilities for various social functions shifted by season and as need arose and were not fixed (Evans, *God* 88-90; Mander 225-236). Berry does admit, however, that the term *patriarchy* does indeed locate "the deepest and most destructive level of determination in the Western perception of reality and value" (141).

I suggest a word group even less charged with any sort of destructive association—"androlocal," or man-located. There is no indication of centeredness or hierarchy, concepts that are alien to many of the world's peoples anyway. Furthermore, androlocal deletes issues of impregnating women entirely; there are no "fathers" (patri) or mothers (matrae), nor are woman and children implicit possessions consequent of impregnation. A woman or women will need to suggest a similar word group to denote woman-located concepts that also display no gendered or heterosexual dominance, hierarchy, or hegemony. I shall employ the term *androlocal* whenever appropriate to destabilize the uncritical presumption that all men are dominant, want it that way, or are incapable of conceiving human relationships in any other way than male-dominant.

A term often related to patriarchy, borrowed from political science, is *hegemony,* a term closely aligned with *dominance* but signifying a sense of perpetuating rule. Hegemony's "bases are the relations of ruling class morality, sex and gender, the gender division of labor, family and kinship, State policies and sexual policing, and it relies not only on consent, legitimation, and 'common sense,' but also uses moments of denial, silencing and coercion" (Kinsman 33). Thus, to say that the cultural system of male dominance is hegemonic goes a bit further than the term *patriarchy* by noting that it is a self-perpetuating, self-enforcing series of interrelated phenomena and social performances. Taken together, these basic terminologies that have fairly consistently been applied to articulate feminism were later adopted—and furthered—in showing sexism to be heterosexism, the oppression of any other sort of sexual performance other than mainstream, conventional, and stereotyped male/female roles.

The core issue for late modern feminism, however, perhaps was always equal rights—as it was in women's suffrage earlier in the twentieth century—and thus the late modern women's movement supported the Equal Rights Amendment (ERA). Yet one issue emerged that was clearly centered on being a woman: women's reproductive rights. *Our Bodies, Ourselves* (Boston Women's Health Book Collective) expands the issue of a woman's body rights to the panoply of medical and ethical issues facing women in the late modern period.

One of the most significant contributions of late modern feminism grew from a series of observations that sexism and the marginalization of women occur not just in sexual and traditionally gendered circumstances but also during those occasions and everyday life events apparently not charged with sex and gender. As Sedgwick aptly remarks,

The second and perhaps even greater heuristic leap of feminism has been the recognition that categories of gender and, hence, oppression of gender can have a structuring force for nodes of thought, for axes of cultural discrimination, whose thematic subject isn't explicitly gendered at all. (*Epistemology* 34)

Sedgwick then suggests that what are taken to be everyday, ordinary conceptual relationships for explaining or defending most anything are fraught with gender hierarchy, such as "culture as opposed to nature, public as opposed to private, mind as opposed to body, activity as opposed to passivity." In each pairing, the first term is usually identified with male, the second with female. One need only cite the cultural convention that men's place is outside at work and women's is in the home to verify the gendrification of public and private. These sorts of pairings are enshrined in men cooking at the barbecue and women in the kitchen. Noting that patrilocal ways permeate society is indeed a conceptual advance over earlier late modern feminist theory. As a conceptual move, it has opened the theoretic playing field and also acknowledges, implicitly, that men can be victims of sexism too—because it occurs even when men and women are not thinking sex and gender.

Once again, although it is tempting to think that all feminists think alike and maintain the same points of view, reasoning, or passion, there are many feminisms. If nothing else, feminism has developed through time and does not remain unchanged and unchanging. Although pundits such as Rush Limbaugh calculatedly toss all feminists in the same corner, calling them "femiNazis," the act of reducing all feminists to the same set of assumptions is far closer to fascism than any of the various feminisms. There are strict separatists who prefer to live in community with other women and without men (Bunch 174-195). There are angry "wymmin" performance artists who actively deconstruct not just male hegemony but also many feminist assumptions (Juno & Vale). Women who raise children often work for reproductive rights in their communities and are no less feminists than those who write and expound their feminisms.

African American feminists also have contributed insights and experiences about women's liberation. Issues of community and class are not second thoughts but primary focuses. Betty Powell has developed what may be described as an Afrocentric (Asante) teaching strategy. She begins by introducing herself with a personal statement. "I am Betty Powell, and I am very good at teaching, but I'd like to be better at tennis." Then each person present is invited to make a self-introduction with Powell reminding the students to participate as if they had to remember all the other students personally, acknowledging that "dealing with difference" with an "initial appreciation of who each person" is works by being able to say "that's so-and-so and that's what they do." Later exercises emphasize sharing autobiography, how topics they cover in class were first learned in their actual, everyday lives, "who they learned it from, where they were in terms of family, environment, neighborhood, schooling." Powell then reports, "The variations . . . for a Jewish kid growing up in Brighton or a black kid growing up in Crown Heights are also great. Seeing that our experiences are very different, yet the same, is something I consider vital" (Bunch 263).

Black feminists remind us that prevalent images of black women derive almost exclusively from slavery. Yet these stereotypes work duplicitously, attaching essentialistic qualities and continuing to justify oppression. As Patricia Hill Collins warns,

> From the mammies, Jezebels, and breeder women of slavery to the smiling Aunt Jemimas on pancake mix boxes, ubiquitous Black prostitutes, and ever-present welfare mothers of contemporary popular culture, the nexus of negative stereotypical images applied to African-American women has been fundamental to Black women's oppression. (7)

Because of these images, black women are not perceived as feminist activists. bell hooks, among others, shows the lie of the situation by documenting black women feminists who were politically active more than a century ago.

> Nineteenth century black women were more aware of sexist oppression than any other female group in American society have ever been. Not only were they the female group most victimized by sexist discrimination and sexist oppression, their powerlessness was such that resistance on their part could rarely take the form of organized collective action. The nineteenth century women's rights movement could have provided a forum for black women to address their grievances, but white female racism barred them from full participation in the movement. (*A'int* 161)

Thus, black women have suffered the indignities of slavery, racism, and sexism from those who ostensibly are fellow feminists.

Black feminist contributions are then perhaps all the more significant. Collins observes that black women's intellectual thought

> can best be viewed as subjugated knowledge. The suppression of Black women's efforts for self-definition in traditional sites of knowledge production has led African-American women to use alternative sites such as music, literature, daily

conversations, and everyday behavior as important locations for articulating the core themes of a Black feminist consciousness. (202)

Thus, Collins articulates the two main alternatives by which ideas, assertions, and beliefs are validated: (1) "institutions, paradigms and other elements" controlled by elite white men and through which "scholars, publishers, and other experts represent specific interests and credentialing processes" that are exclusionary both to women and particularly black women (203-206); and (2) "rather than emphasizing how a Black women's standpoint and its accompanying epistemology are different from those in Afrocentric and feminist analyses, I use Black women's experiences to examine points of contact between the two," a procedure that challenges exclusionary practices and the assumptions that all "real" knowledge is scientific and "built" piece-by-piece only by experts (207). Collins' conceptualization clearly demarcates itself from an oppressive, elitist, canonical approach.

For instance, the dialogue assumes "connectedness rather than separation" as "an essential component of the knowledge validation process" (207). Dialogue and its centrality to culture and community derive from African oral tradition. In turn, the call-and-response communication patterns found in black churches, singing, and gaming also derive from African roots and endured the centuries of slavery.

Dialogue does not mean an absence of criticism, yet black feminist criticism is problematic because dialogue otherwise is not the norm. "Given the pervasive anti-feminism in popular culture," relates bell hooks in *Talking Back,* "in black subculture, a feminist critique might simply be aggressively dismissed" (135). hooks discusses the merits and demerits of Spike Lee's film *She's Gotta Have It,* noting her initial reluctance to see it, but having been encouraged by numerous black woman scholars and friends so she can discuss whether the film portrays liberated black women, hooks relents. Although applauding the soulfulness of the movie, from a feminist perspective, she still found it problematic. The lead female protagonist, Nola Darling, projects "a stereotypical sexist notion of a sexually assertive woman—she is not in fact liberated" (136). The real main characters in the film are men; they talk more; the script employs them as narrators. "The narrators are male and the story is a male-centered, male-biased patriarchal tale" (137). This male-centeredness appears, for instance, in the inclusion of a rape scene in which Jaime demands of Nola, "Whose pussy is this?" She is passive, not independent, and her answer is "yours," thus perpetuating black women as victims of sexist colonization and slavery of their bodies to men.

The advent of the global village also sets the stage for women from other cultures to contribute to the current dialogues of sex, gender, and sexual orientation. Noting that feminist scholarship has tended to fall into two categories, white and black, Angharad N. Valdivia shows that binary oppositions as the way to formulate thinking does not reflect the world at large and its multiculturalism.

> Thus we have issues set in "black and white" frameworks. We have rich or poor, male or female, masculine or feminine, gay or straight, rational or irrational, local or global, nature or culture, multicultural or monocultural. In this process, issues of diversity are fitted into a preexisting framework of analysis foregrounded by binary oppositions. (12)

Valdivia suggests that "undermining the binary opposition" is the very basis of all feminist activity (13).

Indeed, binary opposition seems to have been embraced uncritically by some feminists. Carol Gilligan persuasively demonstrates how language use not only is gendered but also works to perpetuate men as dominant and women as submissive. In other words, men/boys use language differently than do women/girls. Gilligan's perspective is not alone (Roman, Juhasz, & Miller). In a field study of the "structures and procedures used by a group of urban black children to constitute their social world in the midst of moment-to-moment talk as they played on the street" (1), however, Marjorie Goodwin found ample evidence that girls and boys employ the same language strategies (285). For instance, although Gilligan maintains that females are not as likely to dominate talk or to negotiate, Goodwin found that preadolescent girls construct "accusation utterances of considerable sophistication" and that the ritual of "he-said-she-said" can last several days, and in some cases, weeks, with the girl as dominant, lead negotiator (219).

Other women's voices contribute to understanding the diversity of women's liberation, such as Winona LaDuke's Native American activism that is as much environmental, holding the Earth sacred, as it is feminist and Native American. Many other women from around the world speak from spiritual traditions grounded in Earth. Of particular interest are women who celebrate their bodies despite not adhering to prevalent norms of skinniness. Their wisdom will speak later in the book when body image is considered.

Perhaps, then, feminism never was monolithic, but now it can flourish as multicultural. Assuming sameness among a group of persons, or at best an oppositional, simplistic difference of only two points of view—in this case, among feminist women—is just another example of the North American proclivity to stereotype individuals and groups to avoid having to think about them.

Ending sexism is certainly not even the only issue into which the women's movement puts its energies. The women's movement is diverse, complex, and well on its way to providing female-gendered and nongendered theories and observations of cultures.

The Other Sexism: Heterosexism

Women as a group have not been the only targets of mean-spirited stereotypes and oppressive domination. Consider the following film depictions: (1) The costume designer in the film *The Broadway Melody* (1929) acts like a sissy and fusses over all sorts of situations; (2) the word *lavender* was frequently mentioned in early twentieth century talkies as a code word for "boys who were 'that way' "; (3) eventually the word *pansy* was forbidden by censors as unsuitable for any audience; and (4) the actor Franklin Pangborn appears in *Only Yesterday* (1933), window shopping during the stock market crash with a friend.

> "I *say,* Thomas," Pangborn enunciates, stopping suddenly at the window. "Look! That heavenly blue against that mauve curtain. Doesn't it excite you? That kind of blue just *does* something to me." The juxtaposition of their flighty, inconsequential chatter with images of businessmen about to leap from office windows serves to place the two homosexuals in the position of women who play bridge while their husbands run the world. (Russo 37-42; emphasis Russo's)

Lesbians have not been exempt from stereotyping in cinema either. A nightclub owner warns her brother about the kind of women he has been seeing, and his reply confirms her concern while blithely demonstrating how dense her brother really is, "Oh, don't worry, Sis, this one's different. Wears a tuxedo" (Russo 44).

One of the most famous stereotyping of gays goes relatively unremarked by Russo, however. Using a photograph of the Cowardly Lion to get his arguments going, Russo quotes the Cowardly Lion's lyrics, "Oh, it's sad, believe me, missy, when you're born to be a sissy, without the vim and voive" (2-3). He does not mention how negative the character was, or, that an audience familiar with *the* gay stereotype—mostly adults in 1939 and not most children—would have taken Lahr's character as a queer: He whines; he cries; he sulks; he emotes; he even flares a limp-wristed forepaw, all with a Bronx—or at least a New York City—accent, too. Telling, very telling. This imaging of a gay male as automatically cowardly, flaming, and unmanly still feeds the "don't ask/don't tell" policy in the U.S. armed forces. A gay could not possibly possess the fortitude to do his duty and fight or kill, or so the stereotype dictates. If nothing else, the Cowardly Lion is clearly unmasculine, "not a lion but a mou-wuss," with the "wuss" an inescapable self-identification. Among the numerous negative film roles Russo covers, however, he also does not mention that the Cowardly Lion eventually is credited by the Wizard as having common sense, something superior to courage. Hence, at least one cinematized gay stereotype is redeemed on screen—but, admittedly, only after being the butt of homophobic humor.

When screen images were not making light of homosexuals, either the sexual subterfuge was edited to deletion, as in the *Spartacus* (1960) bath scene between Tony Curtis and Laurence Olivier (Russo 119), or the sexual subterfuge was hyped to the level of horror, as in *Vampyres* (1974) with its hitchhiking lesbian vampires. Russo otherwise aptly demonstrates that any male or female who regularly performs his or her sexuality in relationship to the same sex was stereotyped as deviant, mentally ill of health, frivolous, unreliable, or dangerous. Even in the last decade of the second millennium C.E., these stereotypes and fears of gay men and lesbians still abound. It has become customary within the gay and lesbian communities to call these stereotypes and fears *homophobia,* or the fear of queer, the dread of being physically near visibly gay men and lesbians or even be exposed to them in artistic images of various sorts. Yet even the term *homophobia* is contested because its initial conceptualization and common use "closets" or hides what is really going on. Although it rather accurately conveys panic some people show on being made aware of someone presumed to be gay, it attributes the panic to a mental, psychological state.

It merely individualizes and privatizes gay oppression and obscures the social relations that organize it. It reduces homophobia to a mental illness, detaching it from its social context and reproducing all the problems of psychological definitions. I therefore prefer to use the term "heterosexism," relating the practices of heterosexual hegemony to institutional and social settings and to sex and gender relations. In this context homophobia can be seen as a particularly virulent personal response organized by heterosexist discourse and practice. (Kinsman 28-29)

Kinsman's reformulation of homophobia as heterosexism is a conceptual application of feminist terminologies in noting a system of oppression as hegemonic, that is, as culturally policed, enforced, and perpetuated. Thus, gay and lesbian stereotypes have been challenged, however, just as sexist stereotypes have been challenged, except in this situation, it is not necessarily male sexism and patrilocality that is found wanting, it is the entire system of heterosexuality that is called to question.

It has become a fashion to declare the riots at the Stonewall Inn in Greenwich Village in 1969 as the true beginning of the gay and lesbian movement for human rights. Perhaps the idea of drag queens fighting back at police harassment plays into the stereotypes of gay men as dismissible, laughable, conjuring for some people stunning images, at once comic and tragic. The Stonewall Rebellion was no laughing matter, nor is that numerous men and women had already begun the struggle for equal and fair treatment by the police, in courts, in employment, and in their communities decades before the Stonewall Rebellion.

Although many people—essentialists—apparently naturally assume that being born a woman and subsequently acting like one is not a personal choice and, likewise, that being born a man and subsequently acting like one is not a personal choice, the same people illogically assume that persons who are gay or lesbian actually choose their sexual orientation—that they are not born with their sense of desire and personhood. Although essentialist assumptions of sex and gender themselves have been challenged, many gay men and lesbians report they were born that way, that their orientation was not initially socially constructed (Duberman, *Cures*). It is perhaps no accident that numerous facts and fallacies of sexuality and its cultural performance collide and transform one another.

The concept of homosexuality is a relatively late addition to the Western history of ideas in at least three senses: (1) The word itself is barely a hundred years old; (2) only in the last forty years has it begun to indicate exclusive sexual relationships with the same sex; and (3) as indicative of same-sex relations in general, exclusive or otherwise, sometimes the term has carried a pejorative meaning that stigmatizes or pathologizes homosexuals and homosexuality.

That the word itself is only a hundred years old is demonstrable in the older tradition of sexology in which the actual naming of same-sex desire and activity appeared to be problematic, if not difficult. Same-sex activity was called "inversion" (Krafft-Ebing), and the term itself appears as early as 1882 in France (Karlen 187), although some claim that Havelock Ellis was the first to use the term in 1897 (Katz, *Invention* 55). Later, the term *homosexual* was invented by Charles Gilbert Chaddock (Halperin, *One Hundred Years* 15), or earlier, in 1869, by a physician, one Dr. Benkert under the pseudonym K. M. Kertbeny (Katz, *Gay/Lesbian* 153; Lauritsen & Thorstad 6). Curiously, the *Oxford English Dictionary* does not even list the term *homosexual* and its derivatives.

The word has only more recently indicated—for some individuals and groups—exclusive same-sex activity. In various Western societies and subcultures, same-sex relationships were not considered exclusive for all persons, nor was a man always stigmatized if he engaged in same-sex performances. George Chauncey details the variations of homosexuality extant in the turn of the nineteenth to the twentieth century in *Gay New York*. Remarkably, among the working class, as long as a man acted like a man and was dominant and the penetrator, even with another man, he was treated as if he were heterosexual. In contrast, middle-class reformers were horrified by the social and sexual interactions of "fairies" (effeminate men who were stigmatized and many times still are) and "normal" men. "So long as they maintained a masculine demeanor and played (or claimed to play) only the 'masculine,' or insertive role in the sexual encounter . . . neither they, the fairies, nor the working-class public considered *them* to be queer" (66; emphasis Chauncey's). A similar situation still exists in Latino cultures in which the macho man is considered manly (Carrier in Herdt 202-224). Homosexuality unstigmatized by one's culture can be illustrated—and documented—from many of the world's present and historical cultures (Dover; Duberman, *About Time;* Tripp 63ff).

Of course, by the mid-twentieth century, many gay men and lesbians knew they had been stigmatized to the point of considering themselves freaks, and, according to Martin Duberman, World War II as a historical event precipitated orientation movements, preceding the Stonewall Rebellion by a number of decades.

> During World War II many men and women who had grown up in rural areas or small towns and had regarded themselves as singular freaks, discovered in military service legions of others who shared their sexual orientation. The experiences and bonding that followed led many gay men and lesbians to decide, after the war, against returning to their hometowns and in favor of settling down in one of the subcultural enclaves that existed in large cities, and particularly on the two coasts. (*Stonewall* 76)

The Mattachine Society was founded by Harry Hay and others in 1950 in Los Angeles and maintained that "gays were a legitimate minority living within a hostile mainstream culture. They further argued that most gays had internalized the society's negative judgment of them as 'sick,' and that such 'false consciousness' had to be challenged" (77).

Early on, the Mattachine Society was highly radical; many of its founders were avowed communists and socialists. Because of the growing political climate of communist and gay witch-hunting and because of new members, the group quickly became more conservative in its self-concept and activities. "The newcomers were primarily interested in winning acceptance on the mainstream's own terms" (*Stonewall* 77). Later, a group of women founded the Daughters of Bilitis in 1955 to meet social needs, end the isolation of lesbians, and promote education and legal reform. These two groups and others were particularly interested in what in the late twentieth century has been called "human rights" and equality before the law and in social custom for gays and lesbians.

Despite Duberman's and others' afterthought of declaring these early gay and lesbian human rights groups conservative in comparison, perhaps, to groups such as ACT UP and Queer Nation, not all the gay men and lesbians in the United States saw Mattachine or Bilitis as conservative at all. For instance, a chapter of Mattachine was organized in Toledo, Ohio, in the late 1960s, but within a year, they abandoned the name and the association, in part because, as one member has reported, "We didn't think of ourselves as radical at all." So, they began their own group, Personal Rights Organization, that sponsored meetings, a newsletter, educational sessions, a local phone service, bail bonding for those who found themselves entrapped by the police, and socializing. Their story is yet unwritten and will certainly supplement the narratives of gay and lesbian human rights organizations that have almost exclusively focused on the doings of groups on the West and East coasts of the United States. The relatively greater anonymity of the large, coastal, urban centers was not enjoyed in other regions such as small cities, suburbs, and rural areas. Thus, gay men and lesbians in these other areas necessarily adopted association strategies and human rights activities more suitable for hometown America where publicly being gay or lesbian could quickly earn them not just notoriety and verbal harassment but violent physical attack and the immediate and permanent loss of careers and housing.

The Stonewall Rebellion in 1969 still is seen as a watershed moment in the gay and lesbian human rights movements, but the record must include that in Prussia, Britain, and other countries, homosexuals had banded together in the face of homophobia more than a century earlier. "Stonewall, we said, in a sense marks the 100th anniversary of the gay liberation struggle. In the late 1860s, a new penal code was proposed for Prussia that added homosexual acts (among males) to the category of crimes" (Lauritsen & Thorstad 6). Various reactions, particularly from physicians and scientists, eventuated in the beginnings of group action. The criminalization of homosexuality set the stage for the historic inevitability of the Stonewall Riot.

Then again, laws criminalizing homosexuality are not always uniformly enforced. As John D'Emilio reports, arrests of homosexuals in New York City tended to increase during mayoral campaigns. The dates of June 27-28, 1969 (the riot happened at night and involves events that spanned midnight), occurred just after John Lindsay lost his political party's primary; stepping up arrests could make him look good. But other factors intensified the situation: a new precinct commanding officer who wanted to show his muscle, the many young and nonwhite patrons of the Stonewall Inn (231), and, perhaps quizzically to some people, the funeral of Judy Garland that Friday the 27th. Garland was already a favorite of gays for many reasons, and some of the crowd was mourning and not in the mood to be harassed (DiLallo & Krumholtz 222).

Two detectives initiated the raid of the Stonewall Inn and released patrons one by one to the street. A crowd gathered outside and jeered the arrest of "the bartender, the Stonewall's bouncer, and three drag queens" (D'Emilio 231). When police arrested the last of the patrons, a lesbian, she put up a struggle. As the *Village Voice* reported,

> "The scene became explosive. Limp wrists were forgotten. Beer cans and bottles were heaved at the windows and a rain of coins descended on the cops. . . . Almost by signal the crowd erupted into cobblestone and bottle heaving. . . . From nowhere came an uprooted parking meter—used as a battering ram on the Stonewall door. (D'Emilio 232)

Then the bar was torched. The shaken police officers received reinforcements, but the event did not go away.

> "Rioting continued far into the night. . . . people leading charges against rows of uniformed police officers. . . .
> By the following night, graffiti calling for 'Gay Power' had appeared along Christopher Street. . . .
> After the second night of disturbances, the anger that had erupted in the street fighting was channeled into intense discussion of what many had begun to memorialize as the first gay riot in history. (D'Emilio 232)

Within only a few days, already existent homophile organizations such as the New York Mattachine Society remobilized. By the end of July, new groups formed in the city. Not long after, similar groups with more radical, confrontational politics sprang up around the country.

D'Emilio elsewhere reports two aspects of the movement that are significant for understanding the movement: (1) "Coming out" became a way to end personal isolation and relinquish invisibility, making individuals more vulnerable to attack and therefore "personally invested in the success of the movement," all leading to more gathering spots, publications, and communication between gays and lesbians formerly unknown to each other; and (2) a lesbian movement emerged when previously lesbians "were but a small fraction of the tiny homophile movement. The almost simultaneous birth of women's liberation and gay liberation propelled large numbers of lesbians into liberation politics." Lesbian-feminism "pushed the analysis of sexism and heterosexism beyond where either the women's or gay movement ventured and so cogently related the two systems of oppression" (Duberman, Vicinus, & Chauncey 466-467). Feminism provided a place where lesbians could safely come out. Unlike other spots in the country, however, San Francisco became a liberated place for gay men and lesbians to pursue their own, self-identified needs, where they could take advantage of many of the new groups and services in the Bay Area, as well as burgeoning gay and lesbian residential areas.

Political activism early focused on defeating harassment of gays and for the overthrow of patriarchy. Although other issues were important, they were all eventually eclipsed by AIDS. The homophobia of the scientific community showed clearly when the malady was initially called "the gay disease" (Shilts). Eventually, the name changed, both because of protest from the lesbian and gay communities and because outside the United States, AIDS was rampant more exclusively in heterosexual populations. The name was inappropriate. Lack of funding for AIDS research, lack of government-sponsored education programs, and the alarming death rate of the disease called up new organizations, such as ACT UP, Queer Nation, the Gay Men's Health Crisis, and numerous other groups that raised public awareness, raised money, and sponsored services for those having AIDS, those who were HIV positive, and their families.

Perhaps the most stunning public relations activity and fund-raiser has been the Names Project that initiated and sponsored the AIDS Memorial Quilt, or, as is usually said in everyday life, the Quilt. Persons who desired to memorialize a friend, relative, or lover who had died of AIDS-related causes were invited to make a quilt square. The initial 1,920 squares were first assembled together on the Mall in Washington, D.C., on October 11, 1987, covering an area larger than a football field. After this event, smaller groupings of Quilt Squares circulated around North America, raising money for AIDS-related causes, providing mourning opportunities for those unable to attend the Washington event, and significantly demonstrating in local communities the poignancy of the love shown the dead individuals, many of whom were women and children and most of whom were responsible, tax-paying citizens who had the same sorts of pastimes and passions as many others. Touching Sights and Sounds of individ-

QUILT
Book of Remembrance?

ual lives testified the common humanity of persons with AIDS and their families. Later incarnations of the Quilt demonstrated that AIDS was not a homosexual disease.

Intermission: The Intromission of Men's Inner Mission

As the gay rights movements progressed from simple rebellion to ideological salvos and political action, one fairy tale caught the attention of feminists: Cinderella. Women were declared victims of the "Cinderella complex":

> Personal, psychological dependency—the deep wish to be taken care of by others—is the chief force holding women down today. I call this "The Cinderella Complex"—a network of largely repressed attitudes and fears that keeps women in a kind of half-light, retreating from the full use of their minds and creativity. Like Cinderella, women today are still waiting for something external to transform their lives. (Dowling 21)

"Today" was 1981. Huang Mei, among many others, finds Cinderella modeled in numerous literary stories as "the ever-present passive and innocent heroine" (vii).

Introducing a collection of woman-positive fairy tales from around the world, Rosemary Minard relates how "a young mother protested" at a preschool parents meeting "against the reading of 'traditional fairy tales' to the children," such as Cinderella. After the meeting, Minard found herself agreeing about "the unsuitability of the fairy tale heroines." Cinderella

> certainly didn't show much gumption by meekly accepting the abuse of her stepmother and stepsisters. . . . But for the most part female characters, if they are not witches or fairies or wicked stepmothers, are insipid beauties waiting passively for Prince Charming. (vii-viii)

In turn, Jane Yolen contests feminist condemnations of Cinderella as mistargeted.

> Cinderella is not to blame. Not the real, the true Cinderella. Ms. Minard should focus her sights on the mass-market Cinderella. She does not recognize the old

Ash-girl for the tough, resilient heroine. The wrong Cinderella has gone to the American ball. (297)

Minard's concerns are not limited to mass-market Cinderella but also criticize Snow White and Sleeping Beauty—themselves confectioned by Disney into mass-market, passive heroines—as well as the heroines of various fairy tales such as Red Riding Hood and Goldilocks. Minard, however, does not appear to be familiar with the more plucky versions of Cinderella that would be at home with the woman-positive tales she relates. Yolen does agree with one of Minard's basic assumptions, however, that "fairy tales, as all stories for children, acculturate young readers and listeners" (297). In other words, a sexist text, particularly such a favorite, oft-repeated one, can perpetuate sexism.

Indeed, Cinderella is the personification of women's oppression by male dominance. The gender order implicit in the tale almost perfectly inscribes the panoply of negative stereotypes of women. Cinderella lives with two stepsisters and a stepmother. With no man around, the stepmother runs things and plainly favors her own offspring and not the child of another woman. The stepsisters are bitchy. The stepmother is witchy. Cinderella performs all the scullery chores and yet is even economically oppressed in that she wears rags while the rest wear finery. Then, to top it off, the local royalty decides to marry off the son and command the kingdom's women to attend a grand ball so he can check them all out to choose a mate. Cinderella is prevented from attending by her family until a fairy godmother shows up to remedy the situation. Cindy attends the ball in style and sparks fly only between the Prince and her. But then she must flee at midnight or show herself as a ragamuffin because all her finery will return to its unmagical, ashen, tattered state. Eventually, the prince locates her despite her lowly state by placing her tiny slipper on her tiniest of feet. Happily ever after.

Except the stepmother is to be feared, quite plainly, because she is mean and domineering. Stereotype: Older unmarried or divorced women are mannish and therefore bad, let alone remarried women who plainly marry for their pleasure, comfort, and money as Cindy's stepmother's cushy existence attests. Except the stepsisters are to be feared and reviled because they are vain, competitive suck-ups. Stereotype: Young women have few things on their minds, if they have minds at all. They are grasping, conniving, and venal and will not be satisfied until they win a man who will spoil them more rotten. Except the fairy godmother comes in, waves her magic wand, and then splits. Stereotype: Some women mean well, but help as they may, they really have no commitment, not even to other women. Except Cinderella shares her stepsisters' millennial desire to have a man set things right in her life. Stereotype: A woman's place may be low, in the kitchen, on the floor, scrubbing constantly, but she can aspire to greater glory in relationship to a man. Woman is defined by man. And never forget, a good woman is pure, innocent, unpushy, and obedient.

Except—lapsing into an intromissive, personal narrative momentarily and because sometimes personal narrative is as instructive as scholarly prose—remembering hearing the tale as a boy, watching Disney's version dutifully, I wondered why the prince was so disinteresting and why Cinderella found him so fascinating, what had happened to Cinderella's father, and what kind of prince dropped everything to fit a slipper on a foot? No one could answer my questions. My questions did not follow the gist and facts of the story and were cavalierly dismissed, but now I can affirm that not all of Yolen's "listeners" accept fairy tales uncritically, especially children.

Thus, except, once more, with all the attention paid to Cinderella and her family and their mutual oppressions, the prince is left unrecognized, uninterpreted, and basically a villain of the piece. Stereotype: Men are remote. Stereotype: Men are supposed to marry to rightly perform their manhood. Stereotype: Men order women around. Stereotype: Men are strong and silent. Stereotype: Men are truly satisfied only by dressed up, mysterious but beautiful women.

The prince does not get asked if he wants to marry; it is his job. In some versions of the tale, he appears to be rather reluctant about the whole affair. The prince is decked out in military garb—no freedom to choose threads that suit his individuality there. The prince says almost nothing. When he does find a suitable woman, and only the one most lovely, most magical, and most innocent, he goes off the deep end, out of control, head over heels, and moves heaven and earth until he gets his way. Sudden turnaround: Men are so unpredictable, daring, and dominant.

For that matter, we hear nothing of Cinderella's father. What happened to him? What about the stepmother's man who fathered her two daughters? Looks as if we have a black widow going there. The king himself is in the plight of the gene pool. With only one son, the lineage must be continued. And in the mid- and late twentieth century, life imitates art in the British royal family, except they have not lived happily ever after.

Enter the men's movement. A latecomer among the gender/sexual liberation movements, the men's movement initially was rather subdued because men, as a group, are stereotyped as always privileged, always in control, always better off. Speaking up means a man is not a man. Because of their presumed villainy, at first they did not dare speak, or speak loudly. Yet the other liberation movements of the twentieth century—and not only the gender/sexual movements—have succeeded in conveying their well-taken observations, concerns, and issues among many men, so much so that some men realized that they too were being stereotyped and that they too were victims of male dominance and systemic prejudice that ordains how they are to behave, feel, relate, provide, impregnate, and protect.

Most men were out in the lobby, however, not main players at center stage in the discussions, debates, and dialogues of sex, gender, and orientation—like concert goers during intermission, waiting for the show to continue without their input—except for applause or surly disapprobation. Their growing awareness about the gendered and sexualized freedom of others spawned an inner mission, to find themselves on their own terms, undefined by others. Men, formerly take-it-on-the-chin, strong, silent types, began to voice concerns they share with other liberation movements, as well as concerns that are almost uniquely their own.

The intermission is over. The remote prince and the formerly presumed dead fathers have found their voices. We may truly live in a liberated time when the alternative, protesting questions of boys and men about fabled boys and men are no longer so easily dismissed. As Robert Bly has aptly put it,

> We are living at an important and fruitful moment now, for it is clear to men that the images of adult manhood given by the popular culture are worn out; a man can no longer depend on them. By the time a man is thirty-five he knows that the images of the right man, the tough man, the true man which he received in high school do not work in life. Such a man is open to new visions of what a man is or could be. (ix)
>
> We have defective mythologies that ignore masculine depth of feeling, assign men a place in the sky instead of earth, teach obedience to the wrong powers, work to keep men boys, and entangle both men and women in systems of industrial dominance that exclude both matriarchy and patriarchy. (x)

The Men's Movement

Just as the women's and the gay liberation/human rights movements are not monolithic, so too the men's movement is highly diverse while sharing common concerns both among men and with women and gays. That being said, it is unquestionable that the many strands of the men's movement share a common knot: the oppression of women and men as stereotyped in gender and sexuality. As Mann says,

Men suffer in the patriarchal society. It is important to keep in mind that it is not men per se being criticized here, but the system in which we all, men and women, collude. The patriarchal system oppresses women severely—by definition it exerts power over women—but it is by its nature a system of domination, so we must expose where patriarchy oppresses men. (xix)

Some female feminists agree. Susan Bordo maintains,

It is indeed senseless to view men as the enemy: to do so would be to ignore, not only power differences in the racial, class, and sexual situations of men, but the fact that most men, equally with women, find themselves embedded and implicated in institutions and practices that they as individuals did not create and do not control— and that they frequently feel tyrannized by. (*Unbearable* 28)

Bordo then notes that there are good sources about men's issues that carefully explore this enmeshment but that they are too often overshadowed by best-sellers that tend to focus mostly on reclaiming masculinity. Thus the diversity in the men's movement is recognized and will continue to develop and be understood by insiders and outsiders variously. Each segment specializes in ascertaining how men are oppressed.

The two largest segments of the men's movement are usually identified as the "mythopoetic branch" and the "profeminist/gay affirmative branch." Other segments include men interested in men's rights, particularly the rights of divorced fathers, and addiction and recovery groups limited to men only. Addiction and recovery groups are not unique to men or the men's movement, and certainly they share many of the support strategies found in numerous other addiction and recovery groups.

The men's rights groups tend to be active in pursuing legal matters that have made men less equal, such as in divorce and child custody, and they monitor male bashing in the media and work to decrease the sexual harassment of men. They may stereotypically be easily dismissed as bitter men, but the physical abuse of men by their spouses is a vastly underreported crime because of the very stereotype that posits men as the ones who are violent, that men always know how to defend themselves—they would be laughed at. Thus Ellis Cose admits, "For some people, the very idea that a woman could terrorize a man is so inconceivable as to be laughable" (208), but then he documents numerous cases (202-237). He reports that a men's safe house received thirty-five men in seven months, most of whom claimed to have been assaulted by women (210). He concludes,

> If we cling to the belief that women are incapable of violence or that only the men
> in abusive relationships are troubled, we will not see the problem for what it is, and
> we will find it difficult to give many of the men and women who are ensnared in
> violent unions the kind of help they need. (237)

Cose's example clarifies the record about men in troubling relationships and presents not an extreme, but a balanced commentary. Ellie Wymard also presents narratives from and commentary about "divorced fathers and sexual politics" in *Men on Divorce* (77-94).

The profeminist/gay affirmative branch is the oldest group in the men's movement, having grown beside the beginnings of the late modern women's liberation movement in the 1970s. Formerly self-identified as "men's liberation," this group is now increasingly identified as "changing men" because they oppose domestic violence and patriarchy and are most keen on developing or changing themselves and the received attitudes about manhood that initially acculturated them. The mythopoetics engage in "a freewheeling exploration of male spirituality and male psychology" and encourage each other "to delve into their psyches by reintroducing them to literature, mythology, and art" (Harding xiii). Their outlook stems more from the 1980s and a sincere interest in men's understanding themselves from a male perspective.

Although not as long-standing a segment, the mythopoetics have captured more public and journalistic attention. Because they often begin their gatherings with drumming, locate special gatherings in rustic areas, and tell stories, particularly folktales (hence, "mythopoetic"), they have been stereotyped as throwbacks to primitive maleness, if not a suspicious sort of patriarchy. Some people have taken the activities of mythopoetics as an "increasingly common spectacle of men with no apparent disadvantage claiming victim status" who are, therefore, "whiners" (Cose 71). The television comedy *Murphy Brown* aired episode 79 on September 30, 1991, featuring a retreat with a Robert Bly-like leader that the men of the news staff enthusiastically attended. Murphy jeered at them as whiners and as pursuing something rather fraudulent, if not sexist, crashed the retreat as the only woman there, and ended up drumming and discussing her poor relationship with her father like the rest.

Although the Murphy Brown episode is unusual in that it demonstrated stereotypes about men and the men's movement, it also demonstrated that the stereotypes are just that, errors of oversimplification. Men go on retreat with other men—and without women around—so as not to be victimized or influenced by the stereotypes. Supposedly, men shun cooking and cleaning up; at hundreds of retreats for years now, men have done that work exclusively. They often discuss their relationships with their fathers, or lack of relationship, but they do so to suggest strategies and interventions for improving that relationship, if possible. They also share issues they face in their everyday lives so they can better manage them when they return home and to work—issues such as manhood itself; its meaning; mentoring or guiding other men; intimacy with other people, including other men; feelings; work; male bashing; and sexual harassment. Some of these issues, such as being able to express one's feelings, were originally suggested as important by feminists. Issues about one's father, fathering, and male spirituality are more self-generated by men, among men, for men.

One image of manhood with which many men can identify immediately because of their upbringing and fascination with competitive sports is the warrior. This image runs through various mythopoetic texts and gatherings as a leitmotif of manhood. The changing men decry the warrior imagery as one of the main sources of violence perpetrated by men and the perpetuation of male dominance, and thus changing men are most critical of mythopoetics because of the warrior images. Bly unabashedly discusses recovering the "inner warrior" (146-179) yet emphasizes the nonaggressive nature of this warrior. Changing men perhaps do not closely read mythopoetics such as Bly. Then again, the common image of warrior is fairly aggressive, and it conjures images of violence. The discussion of warrior nature at mythopoetic gatherings must not be read, however, as enthusiastic endorsement or final and lasting identification with the warrior. Increasingly, the discussion of warrior nature functions as a way to move beyond war images. Sam Keen offers numerous other models of manhood in *Fire in the Belly,* from hunter and planter to self-made man and psychological man (88-111). Although mentioning the warrior model, he rejects it, striving to move "beyond the myth of war and the warrior psyche" (113-122). He suggests heroic journey as opposed to war images.

The warrior model, however, is ubiquitous in writings about men and men's issues, as a topic to be covered but more insistently, as something men must deal with as masculinity gets rethought at the end of the twentieth century. For instance, having published frequently in the periodical *Changing Men,* Michael Messner and Donald Sabo have compiled their works in *Sex, Violence and Power in Sports: Rethinking Masculinity.* They observe that the "way athletes are taught to regard their bodies as machines and weapons with which to annihilate opponents often results in their using violence against their own bodies" (95). Although numerous men increasingly protest being stereotyped as violent, the issue of violence and sometimes its relationship to war and the warrior pepper texts about and for men as diverse as Farmer's *The Wounded*

Male and Mazis' *The Trickster, Magician and Grieving Man: Reconnecting Men with Earth.* Books such as Abbott's *Boyhood, Growing Up Male: A Multicultural Anthology,* a collection of personal narratives from around the world, attest to the widely held expectations that boys become tough, competitive, and potentially deadly men. The issue of man-as-warrior will not go away soon because it has become so problematic, deserves to be examined, and needs alternatives.

Equally important is the realization how the warrior oppression of men creates the auspices of racism. For instance, Messner and Sabo observe,

> Ironically, although many young black males are attracted to sports as a milieu in which they can find respect, to succeed in sports they must become intimidating, aggressive, and violent. Television images—like that of Jack Tatum "exploding" Darryl Stingley—become symbolic "proof" of the racist belief that black males are naturally more violent and aggressive. Their marginalization as men—signified by their engaging in the very violence that makes them such attractive spectacles— contributes to the construction of culturally dominant (white, upper- and middle-class) masculinity. (98)

Ellis Cose confirms how this sort of imaging happens in everyday life. "The ideal of manhood that is prevalent in many black inner-city communities reflects, if in a sometimes inflated manner, ideals loosed upon the culture generally" (68-69).

Although any number of constituencies may be understandably impatient that the warrior myth be subdued and eradicated from maleness as soon as possible, Arthur Evans reminds everyone that military, male dominance emerged no later than 3,000 years ago: "From about 4500 B.C. to about 1200 B.C., it was apparent that a stunning change had occurred in European life: the patriarchal revolution" (*God* 87). Previously, "widespread cultural uniformity throughout Europe and Western Asia" was marked by goddess worship and societies in which women "appear to have had a generally high status" (84). They lived in relative plenty and had no need for war. Once invaders plundered the stable cultures, merged with them, and spread their ways, however,

> the religious and sexual solidarity of men was also transformed. Since the way for a society to survive and flourish was to win on the battlefield, the ideal man was now one who was trained and ready to fight and kill other men. In general other men became the objects against which a man continually tested and proved his own manhood through bravado, competition in sports and fighting. . . . Any quality conventionally associated with women, such as emotional sensitivity and vulnerability, was looked down upon and ridiculed. (87)

This "quantum leap" in human history engendered a historically and multicul- turally pervasive model of manhood that will not easily change with so many generations of conditioning behind it. That a growing number of men address this and other men's issues is no cause for more cries of sexism. Yet the response from feminist women to the men's movement is at best, mixed. The range runs from suspicious encouragement (Robinson in Kramarae & Spender 438-447) to outright hostility. As a well-known, feminist film scholar related—while specifi- cally asking that her name not be used—at a women's studies conference, she recommended Sam Keen's *Fire in the Belly* and was promptly booed.

Common Grounds

Although some, if not many, lesbians would not place themselves under the same ideological umbrella as gay men (Bunch 196), a number of gay men have embraced basic tenets of feminism, particularly antiviolence against women and children as evidenced in numerous issues of *Changing Men.* Although certainly there are issues that distance feminists, lesbians, and gays from one another, one issue and its related concerns span all three groups and have become concerns of the men's movement too: human rights. Call them women's rights, gay rights, lesbian rights, or men's rights, all four move- ments overlap each other in their concerns about equality, discrimination, stereotyping, and sexual harassment. Differences will remain about how to win and secure human rights, not just between these groups but inside each, but for the first time, members of each group are considering the concerns of the others, working on them, incorporating ideas, and benefiting from the newly emergent dialogue about sex, gender, and sexual orientation.

Reluctance between perceived groups to cross over and read and talk with one another is counterproductive. There is much to be learned. The problem with the various pockets of gender studies resides in the lack of cross reading among them. I suppose that because we have been reading men's generated prose for millennia, it is understandable that many women want to address themselves exclusively in texts generated by women and particularly by those women who have generated and/or have been privy to women's theories. Perhaps cautious cross reading would challenge the straight men I see in bookstores and libraries who studiously avoid standing near women's studies books, let alone picking one up and browsing it. Then again, it isn't just gender studies, it's gay/lesbian studies, too. Although it appears that some feminist theorists read some lesbian and gay theories and that some gay men embrace many tenets of feminism, there are still too many folks, male and female, straight, gay, bi, or try, who would not be caught dead at Borders or Barnes and Noble, standing in front of the gay/lesbian studies and fiction sections. Then again, understandably, some gay men and lesbians want to read only their own literature and theory.

The sexualized, gendered, and orientational concerns for human rights translate into the everyday performance and presentation of self. Instead of perpetuating a dominantly exclusive norm for reading, we might be better off as browsers and cross readers, all the time remaining aware of lurking problems. As bell hooks claims, the struggle for liberation has significance only if its fundamental goal is "the liberation of all people" (*A'int* 13). There is much to learn.

5

Over the Edge:
Taboos and Sexualized, Transgressive
Interpretive Communities

Taboo frees human conscience to explore safe and secure action on the stages
of life, yet everywhere people are chained to the very taboos that set them free.
Many explanations of taboo are offered by those who talk about them, while
the rest of the people recognize the surface of taboo, that it is, that it works, that
one takes risks in courting taboo. Taboo is nothing simple. It certainly is varied
in the way the term alone can be applied. The anthology *Forbidden Fruits:
Taboos and Tabooism in Culture* covers a gamut of conceptualizations, from
customs such as not touching oil paintings, breaking architectural conventions,
and ideological taboos of female beauty to blood taboos in film and detective
stories, adolescent sexuality, and why loggers can't cry. Some of these extended
interpretations seem to equate at times superstition and taboo and, at other
times, flaunt tradition with taboo. Although the points are well taken, a classic
source and a "postmodern" source may help locate and focus the scope of taboos
and their permeation of cultures without limiting the application of taboo to the
sorts of cultural events and artifacts featured in *Forbidden Fruits*. The two main
sources I shall draw on will be Frazer's *Golden Bough* and Bataille's *Erotism*.
Although both exhibit their flaws—particularly Frazer's elitism and Bataille's
latent sexism—they at least convey the locus of taboo without the stunning,
theoretical, near Baroque thrills of Freud's *Totem and Taboo*. Currently, expli-
cation of Freud's faults are fashionable. Freud often serves as whipping boy to
late modern writers, and their reinterpretations and excoriations are now legion.
The current book on sexualities and popular culture acknowledges the merit of

these critiques, and I find Freud's original texts to be as instructive as the later interpretations, no better, no worse. Nevertheless, I do not plan to employ Freud's psychologisms, neither as a cookie cutter to emulate nor as an Occam's razor to smelt in the rusty foundries of "postmodernism." After all, the plan for this book is to survey sexualities and popular culture, not to list, summarize, and interpret all or most of the current voices on Freud. That is entirely another—and different—book.

Taboos: A Primer

Both Frazer's examples of taboos and the apparent definition of taboos he applies are close to *Forbidden Fruits*'s eclecticism. Acknowledging that he had originally applied the concept of taboo to the superstitions of "the black and brown races of the Pacific," Frazer quickly realized that taboo applied to "savages elsewhere" and to "the civilised [sic] races of antiquity." In general, the concept could apply to all cultures and to "all the various sides or elements of it which we describe as religious, social, political, moral and economic" (Vol. III, v-vi) and is not limited to superstition.

Basically, Frazer observes that taboo originates in kingly, priestly functions, noting the fundamental identity of a ruler with creation, that whatever the ruler does, even the slightest gesture, has a magical effect on nature and other humans. Therefore, it is the duty of every ruler and priest to avoid upsetting "the established order of nature" (Vol. III, 2). Similar assumptions about personal influence over nature and the world of spirits abound, however, particularly about the soul and taboos for keeping it in the body during life and managing souls after death (26-100). There are tabooed acts, such as interacting with strangers, dangerous eating and drinking, the evil eye from facial exposure, and so on. There are tabooed persons, including the king, mourners, menstruating women, warriors, murderers, hunters, and fishers. Interestingly, all tabooed persons deal out life and death.

Hence, Frazer defines taboo in relationship to tabooed persons.

> To seclude these persons from the rest of the world so that the dreaded spiritual danger shall neither reach them, nor spread from them, is the object of the taboos which they have to observe . . . to preserve the spiritual force with which these persons are charged. (Vol. III, 224)

Some of these persons are characterized by their holiness, others by their uncleanness. In either case, they must be protected from pollution and from polluting others; their holiness must be protected and kept from indiscriminately sanctifying others (thus potentially becoming polluted). Frazer's *Golden Bough* is a valuable source of information concerning taboos in Western and non-Western cultures, contemporaneous and historical to his writing. The examples alone are varied and illustrate that although many customs in their exact observance are not shared from culture to culture, their basic workings are quite common.

Perhaps subdued from commenting because of academic traditions common in the West almost a hundred years ago, however, Frazer does not suggest how taboos may function erotically nor how the flirtation with sexualized taboos may actually define cultures and subcultures. By only slightly reinterpreting the origins of taboo (and notably without polemicizing either Frazer or Freud), Bataille's *Erotism* provides both the observations of how taboos may function erotically and eventually how pursuing taboo may identify a culture or subculture.

Bataille locates the origin of taboo not in protecting spirit but in the avoidance of violence. From Bataille's perspective, any violence, intended or accidental, is a transgression of natural order, or at least the living order, because violence can cause death, and therefore, particularly in human interactions, transgression is to be avoided. Taboos inhibit violence but, more important, were originated to habitualize the daily avoidance of transgression. To this point, Bataille's conceptualization is similar to Frazer's observations and interpretation of taboo in the management of both life and death, the spirit in this world and of the dead spirit in the otherworld. In a practical vein, avoiding violence prevents the circumstances through which spirits become unruly and dangerous, not just for the individual but for the family and possibly the entire community.

Bataille amplifies this conceptualization of taboo with the additionally compelling human experience of the fascination with and attraction to tabooed persons, events, things, and symbols. Taboo prohibits but also tantalizes people about what is forbidden. In turn, the experience of getting close to taboo and even violating taboo and thus embodying transgression can be erotic. Taboos prohibit yet invite, but because they become everyday norms of behavior, their transgressive violation is frequently all the more invited during certain situations, celebrations, and feasts. Like some natural mechanism, taboos bind people to prevent transgression but also periodically release the bonds and set people free to visit the thrills of transgression. One of Bataille's examples clearly shows conceptual linkage to Frazer's work.

In the Sandwich Islands the people on learning of the king's death commit all the acts looked on as criminal in ordinary times: they set buildings on fire, they loot and they murder, while women are expected to prostitute themselves publicly. . . .

In the Fiji Islands the consequences are even more clearly defined. The death of the chief gives the signal for pillage, subject tribes invade the capital and indulge in every form of brigandage and depredation. (66)

Such rites of reversal are not limited to the Fiji islands but are implicit in old Hawaii and in Brazilian carnival (Bullough & Bullough 214). Clearly, in Bataille's example, the personage of the king is aligned with the forces of nature and society; when the king dies, nature and society are disrupted and thus may temporarily be transgressed with relative impunity. Bataille then takes one further step in understanding taboo and culture.

Religion is the moving force behind the breaking of taboos. Now, religion is founded on feelings of terror and awe, indeed it can hardly be thought of without them. . . . In universal religions like Christianity and Buddhism terror and nausea are a prelude to bursts of burning spiritual activity. Founded as it is on a reaffirmation of the primary taboos, this spiritual life yet implies a celebration, that is, the transgression, not the observation, of the law. (69)

Bataille maintains a fundamental assumption throughout the exegesis of taboo: that violating taboo, that transgressing taboo, can be sensual, erotic, and heightening of sexual experience. This observation is not to be dismissed as philosophic opinion or anthropological observation of other cultures. Some psychologists confirm that "taboos and personally held restrictions do not always inhibit sex—that they may, in fact, enormously intensify it. . . . A taboo that successfully restrains the activity of many people acts as a special incitement for many others" (Tripp 102-103). Bataille quite soundly suggests numerous consequences of religion's "encouragements" of transgression, from sacrifice as a suspension of murder taboos to the direct apprehension of the erotic in death with all of death's laden taboos of corpses and placations of dead spirits.

Disrespect for the earthly remains of the dead is a common cultural phenomenon; sex with corpses, necrophilia, is the stuff of horror stories, the transgression is so tabooed, as in Clive Barker's "Sex, Death and Starshine," in which sex between two characters leads the man into ecstatic horror on his realization that the woman is dead (*Books: Volume One* 122-171). Avoidance of menstruating women is a show of respect for and fear of the internal violence causing the blood flow (Bataille 53-54), as in Clive Barker's "Rawhead Rex," in which a demon is repulsed by a pagan Earth Mother effigy of menstruation (*Books: Volume Three* 39-123). Sex with children is also carefully tabooed and managed in many cultures, not just implicitly in the form of incest taboos (Bataille 51-53) but in maturation rites of passage (Tripp 64-65), as the many transgressions overt and implicit in Clive Barker's "Pig Blood Blues" attest that something sexual has transpired between the dead Hennessy, a lad, and the head of a reform school, a woman (*Books: Volume One* 81-121). These three almost universal taboos are mentioned in passing here not because they hold little interest in themselves but because the three appear among live interpretive communities, communities that live on the edge of taboo; they will be explored variously in a bit.

Taboos demarcate the edge of a culture's domain of permissible performance of selfhood and community; taboos are borders. An edge, however, suggests a place individuals, pairs, and groups can teeter before going over the edge and transgressing that border, if indeed they ever go over the edge. Individuals "on edge" may be characterized as consciously or unconsciously intensified in their awareness of themselves, others, and the situations in which they find themselves. "On edge" begins to describe the appeal Bataille calls the fascination of transgression. Approaching the edge of taboo intensifies feelings and even a sense of the sacred; hence, playing on edge arouses many people, not just physically, but spiritually—and many people seek mutual transgressive interests with like-minded people repeatedly to nurture and grow themselves and others, in this case, in sexualized interpretive communities that explore taboos.

Sexualized Interpretive Communities and Taboos

Some sexualized interpretive communities explore the boundaries here called taboos, push them, even at times relish in them. Before I move to perhaps what many mainstream persons in North America might consider outlaw *transgressively* sexualized interpretive communities, such as sadomasochistic (S/M) culture, drag queens, and others, I will observe that many sexualized interpretive communities ostensibly are not transgressive in their nature, or at least mainstream culture does not perceive their transgression of taboo to be transgressive or sexual at all. These cultures themselves promote prohibitions of transgressing taboo. They undoubtedly favor themselves with a self-description of normalcy. I also suggest that the appearance of sexual extremity in what a participant in a culture of sexualized normalcy perceives as the transgression of taboos is charged with the norms nonmembers and nonparticipants of those groups carry into their experience of persons and groups outside their own culture.

To illustrate, if one were an ultra-Orthodox Jew living in certain neighborhoods in Jerusalem at the end of the twentieth century, one would be unsurprised by posted signs warning women not to enter the neighborhood if they are dressed inappropriately. The ultra-Orthodox Jewish interpretive community has its own ways and does not find the presence of other communities' ways unimportant. This community considers some other groups' performance of self to be obscene if not just an inconvenient imposition.

The obscenity? Women with exposed elbows. Although there are no known interpretive communities that actively contest similar ultraorthodox norms by exposing elbows and getting a thrill out of it, the basis for a potential transgressive community is clear. Please keep in mind that such taboos are not limited to ultra-Orthodox Jews. As Anne Rice candidly reminds readers through the recall of Azriel, who has lived serially for more than two millennia as *Servant of the Bones,* "Vast numbers of the world's women still lived indoors almost entirely and only entered a public street if their face were veiled" (192). Removing a veil is the stuff of the potentially arousing transgressions and yanking a veil from the face without permission or seductively playing with its aerodynamic flotations in dance is highly provocative in cultures that taboo the exposure of a woman's skin.

That is the basis of transgressive community, making certain performances of personhood taboo but then allowing transgression of the taboo under ritualized and unritualized circumstances. The full-fledged ritual formula for acculturating someone in what could reasonably be considered a sadomasochistic cult—a sexualized interpretive community easily identified by its transgressing taboos—runs something like this personal narrative:

> Nuns, priests, devout parents, enforce upon children rigor of self-denial only a hardened ascetic or deadened prude might attain to.
>
> In order to survive this interference, we learned to *appear* to obey—all rules were abided by. We hid whatever pleasures we discovered, for if we did not, and our happiness was observed by our Overseers, we had to support their anger—their at times almost ecstatic displeasure with us. And there was never a punishment without an attendant unbearable humiliation—often performed in public. You would long for the physical attack, just so they might stop saying those terrible things to you, phrases like curses . . . your growth will be stunted . . . you'll go to Hell. . . . God cannot love you if you do that. (*Ritual Sex* 156-157)

That said, the punishers at times display various sorts of pleasure in punishing, and the punished look forward to the physical punishment because that is the sign that the pain and humiliation will soon be over. This sort of situation builds a masochistic habit in children. The moment of pain is anticipated and knowingly preceded by a growing, intense fear that induces pleasurable release at the moment of pain. Of course, this is supposedly not a kinky scene from a movie or novel or from some sexual minority that perpetrates such acts. So too, the S/M activity of this rather sizable cult is not consensual: "*Certainly they* [nuns, priests, devout parents] *have not assured themselves of their victims' full consent*" (156).

That religiosity invites transgression does occur in novels, of course. In Dean R. Koontz's *The Funhouse,* a 17-year-old has recently figured she is pregnant. Amy is quite fearful of her mom and dad finding out because they are devoutly Catholic and because she wants an abortion. Back from prom night, she's quizzed, as usual, by her mom to certify she has remained a "good girl." Her mom dismisses her, reminding her to say her prayers. Upstairs at last in her bedroom, noting the various statuettes and pictures of the Virgin Man, Jesus and His Sacred Heart, and in despair, she thinks, "What could she ask God to do for her? Give her money for the abortion? There wasn't much chance of *that* prayer being answered" (emphasis Koontz's). She strips, examining herself for any signs of pregnancy.

> Gradually the medical nature of her self-inspection changed to a more intimate, stimulating appraisal.
>   She looked at the painting of Jesus.
>   Somehow, by flaunting her body at the image of Christ, she felt she was hurting her mother, deeply wounding her. Amy didn't understand why she felt that way. It didn't make sense. The painting was only a painting; Jesus wasn't really here in the room, watching her. Yet she continued to pose lasciviously in front of the mirror, caressing herself, touching herself obscenely. (81)

Such is the power of icons; in effect, Jesus *is* there watching to her mind. Amy is at a particularly vulnerable moment with no one to turn to, holding resentment about her mother's ways that are so strict that she is the last person in whom Amy feels she could confide. Needless to say, these illustrations, the personal school narrative and the Koontz passage, avidly confirm Bataille's observation that religion invites people to transgress, yielding a pleasurable heightening of their physical awareness.

In contrast, many participants in late modern S/M culture insist that what they do occurs only by mutual consent, and certainly not with minors. Pat Califia reports, "I was taught to dread sex, to fight it off, to provide it under duress or in exchange for romance and security" (161). It is with these sorts of inhibitions Califia works when she performs the role of a dominant top, "I prefer to deny a bottom her inhibitions" (160). Doing so cleanses and releases them both from the oppression of their nonconsensually imposed interpretive strategies and allows them each to explore their sexuality in pleasure, not inhibition.

"Restraint becomes security. She knows I want her. She knows I am in charge" (162). Yet despite the overt roles the two perform, Califia insists the "bottom must be my superior" (163). Indeed, many persons, male and female, who are titularly the passive person in consensual S/M scenarios, report that they are the ones in control of the scenario that often has been elaborately negotiated, discussed, and prepared. Yet in late modern North America, Christian S/M in everyday life is not stigmatized, even when perpetrated upon minors, but S/M between consensually affirmed adults is considered a perverse transgression of the taboos of bondage, pain, humiliation, and dominance.

Perhaps this inversion of values may be explained by observing that easily identifiable transgressors and transgressions are threats to particular interpretive communities, such as women's elbows exposed in some Jerusalem neighborhoods. Nelly behavior by men, butch-appearing women, and leatherbedecked, tattooed, and pierced individuals and groups are all easily interpreted by outsider groups as outré, as well beyond not just the norm but acceptable behavior itself, so much so that proximity is undesirable, laden with the aura of taboo and the dis-ease one normally feels when one gets even close to violating a taboo. Thus, transgression is attributed to these visible communities while the same behaviors incorporated into daily life—but with different sign systems, such as red patches of skin that eventually disappear some time after having been swiped with a yardstick—are not experienced as transgressive, or at least, not transgressive like people who choose to live their transgressions openly.

A fine line weaves between these two experiences of transgression. Some children of late modern, North American culture may be acculturated for the most part yet despite outward conformity, never feel in synch. They may know their true feelings, desires, and motivations are contrary to tabooed norms. They may be aroused by the same sex. They may be quite plain and desire something to make a personal statement about themselves and enhance their looks, such as with a tattoo or body piercing. By taking on transgression, facing it, and incorporating it in their daily performance of self, they and others may interpret their self-performance as personal affirmation and self-empowerment.

Even so-called normal heterosexual performances can serve as the basis of transgression. Fantasies found in men's and women's magazines portray a wife as a little girl, dressed in frilly girl's clothing, innocent, asking permission for everything, and so forth. That may not exactly be considered kinky in comparison with many S/M scenarios, but apparently this sort of little girl-daddy scenario is arousing for some, although, and perhaps because, it involves subordination by gender and age. Perhaps a more extreme example of the same sort of performance inscribes the transgressive qualities of little girl fantasies:

dressing up a sex partner in diapers as a sex scene. Although this fantasy as written in popular periodicals is not as frequent, there are people in everyday life who do it. Taboos enter with pretended soiling of diapers, which requires elaborate, ritualized changing, cleaning, and reasserting cleanliness. Then again, there are those played-out scenarios in which the diapers are actually soiled.

While tattoos and body piercing have been associated recently with "Generation X," other performances among teen to mid-twenty-year-olds in the 1990s also certify the presence of an interpretive community that transgresses sexual norms. Attendees at "raves"—a sort of huge party that moves around and involves new music—are quite familiar with baggy attire, so baggy it is difficult sometimes to tell the sex, gender, or orientation of its wearer. Also familiar are infantilizing logos on T-shirts and ball caps taken from cartoons, candy wrappers, and advertisement logos. The music is often techno or ambient with little or no lyrics, and instead of strenuously dancing, participants may only gently sway, if they dance at all. "Hitting on" behaviors are usually absent or ignored, there being a suspension of normal heterosexual prowling. Finally, ravers may wear many sorts of necklaces, but one of the most popular is a baby pacifier.

What is transgressed at raves? Mainstream, heterosexual culture—the culture from which many, if not most, of them have emerged, an interpretive community that increasingly insists that children cannot fully be adults until they are gainfully employed; yet in many professions, complete competence by training cannot be achieved until well into the third decade of life. Thus, ravers take on their infantilization and wear it to neutralize it in their clothes that make them look like children, that downplay secondary sexual characteristics, and, ultimately, with the pacifier bobbing, useless, on their chests. Fiske would call this "excorporation."

> Excorporation is the process by which the subordinate make their own culture from the resources and commodities provided by the dominant system, and this is central to popular culture, for in an industrial society, the only resources from which the subordinate can make their own subcultures are those provided by the system that subordinates them. (15)

Taking on the bonds that oppress and converting them to liberation may indeed be operative with ravers, although certainly not all opportunities for opposition to culture may be derived from that culture. Again, ravers' "excorporation" may not seem to be sexually transgressive, yet it surely creates a cultural place through which they are not judged by mainstream interpretive strategies nor do they compel each other to do so.

The gay stereotype of the nelly man with the limp wrist, breathy lisp, and mincing step does not inscribe the gay interpretive community as a whole. As a community that has been stereotyped by the nelly image, it is not surprising that any stereotyping would not be taken lightly within that community. For instance, Bawer goes out of his way to deny that ACT UP types, drag queens, and nelly boys represent gay culture (39), and he objects to journalists talking to these three constituencies as if they represented or spoke for gay culture, calling them gay "subculturals" and not really representatives of the vast majority of gays (153-223). Thus, Bawer has received criticism for exclusionary rhetoric that stereotypes and marginalizes many gays as subcultural, something beneath, less.

Drag queens particularly are highly visible targets as a sexualized, transgressive interpretive community. Their status is problematic, as Bawer claims, but not in the way Bawer asserts interpretively. As a drag queen claims in a video documentary, *Queens of Columbus,* "People put drag queens down, but who's there for fund-raisers?" In the context of certain feminist discussions, documentable and in everyday life, drag queens are criticized because they are not women; they have not been born and subsequently acculturated as women; they have not had to live the oppression of women as women; they can always fall back on their male privilege. Claiming that drag queens parody women and by so doing defame and subordinate them, some feminists charge that drag is misogynous and hateful of women (Butler, "Imitation"; Garber; Tyler). To stereotype an already stigmatized minority—in this case, drag queens—as all the same and as all misogynous is at best, incorrect, and at worst, ethically shaky. Drag queens are diverse in their attitude, preparation, and performance.

Many drag queens work carefully to personify women by daily shaving body hair, developing flattering makeup, carrying themselves with poised comportment, and experimenting with various fashions. Some drag entertainers remark that they desire to emulate women because they admire them so much. Their focus is desire—for themselves with the looks of a woman. Of course, it must also be admitted that some drag does mock women by taking the illusion only so far, transparently belittling women. Yet not all drag reflects negatively on women. Some drag highlights stereotypes of women only as hyperfeminine sex objects. Thus, some drag tacitly and often overtly criticizes female stereotypes many feminists find objectionable, in turn sometimes deconstructing and destabilizing received norms for women.

Because some drag queens act and dress flamboyantly and are highly vocal, they attract attention, particularly from journalists and paparazzi. Many drag queens, however, do not see themselves as leaders in the gay community, nor do they feel they represent the gay community despite appearing at charity events, fund-raisers, and pride marches. Unequivocal put-downs of drag queens is a type of verbal bashing, whether the bashers are feminists or gay. Bashing a stigmatized minority of a stigmatized minority is apparently relatively easy. It takes place, however, in a wider context of male bashing that is thousands of years old. Invented by males, male bashing is quixotically untabooed. Gay bashing, however, seems not to be tabooed, although male bashing and gay bashing are intimately connected. The path toward understanding male bashing as gay bashing is paved with tabooed words such as *prick, cock,* and *balls* and common phrases that include them.

Male Bashing as Gay Bashing: Western Culture as a Transgressive Interpretive Community

The Latin term from which both *prick* and *cock* are derived (*praecox*) was used to refer to unruly schoolboys by the ancient Romans. Thus, the ultimate conventions from which the words *prick* and *cock* are derived identify males as out of control, too big for their britches, and, hence, immature. These antisocial images are reinforced by the word *balls,* which further reveals that maleness is fundamentally silly and pretentious. As Willeford maintains in a passage about the characteristics of a fool, clown, or jester, "One could also compare the obscene oath 'ballocks!' or 'balls!'—testicles—meaning 'nonsense!' or 'silly pretension!' . . . in keeping with the exaggerated sexuality of many clowns and fools throughout history" (11). Perhaps Willeford does not take *balls* far enough: Both in meaning and phonotactics, the words *bull* and *baloney* indicate disagreement as put-down.

Twentieth-century, particularly North American, uses are also mostly negative, if not downright derogatory, of males. One can certainly have his dick caught in a wringer; Lyndon Johnson was fond of saying, "I never trust a man unless I got his pecker in my pocket" (Richter 162). American uses of *prick* from 1929 to 1978 listed by the *Oxford English Dictionary* all relay images of abuse and abusiveness by "pricks" (Vol. 12, 456). Some related terms such as *wank* and *wanker* are listed as twentieth-century idioms, and all the examples refer to masturbation as objectionable (Vol. 19, 876).

Almost all citable references to male-coded words for male body parts and male bodily functions derived from the past two thousand years of word use in the West clearly convey the preferential image of men using their penis *with women.* The prevalence of this standard is a sexist norm, with men dominant and in control as enabled by an erect cock. This norm is not merely sexist, however; it is *heterosexist,* meaning all other sexual uses of the penis are not normal, manly, or approved by mainstream culture (Hereck & Berrill 89-107, 149-169; Jung & Smith). Autoeroticism and homosexuality are thus inherently maligned in Western word conventions.

The late twentieth century inherits these traditions and naturally employs them in everyday situations. Common word use not only reflects the heterosexist norm of men preferable for their heterosexual, penile successes, but the same language habits indicate men as boorish, inept, or just plain lacking in social skills. Strikingly, men are linguistically conceived to be inherently deficient in social graces by words and phrases that outnumber linguistic forms that are woman-coded.

Informants in an ethnographic study I conducted that included a survey about "names for persons not good at socializing" consistently perceived boorishness as associated with cockiness, independently affirming the Western traditions of male-bashing terms. The entire list of the survey's responses produced an overwhelming number of male-coded, but few female-coded, words and phrases. Informants suggested that cockiness was far less serious than other accusations in the survey responses, and in turn, they showed me that there is a preferential hierarchy to the words and phrases, with some more serious than others. These categories were suggested and ordered by informants, that is, they are cultural artifacts that reflect cultural norms—they are not my norms. That is why the data are so alarming to me; it confirms just about every queer's fears that indeed mainstream culture stigmatizes queers, especially when mainstream persons do not seem to be aware that they are bashing queers at all, inherently through their language use or overtly through violence. The informants' hierarchy follows, with the initial categories perceived as less negative and the last few highly pejorative:

1. Male body parts
2. Male bodily functions
3. Autoerotic male sexual performance
4. Overzealous male sexual performance
5. Deficient male sexual performance
6. "Deviant" male-male sexual performance

7. Penetrated males

8. Anal words for queer men

Numerous, mostly taboo, words and phrases occurred in each category. Notice that the hierarchy goes from male body parts, which exist naturally, to categories that indicate that the male is out of control (overzealous male sexual performance), to categories clearly labeled as violations of heterosexual norms. I shall focus on the last three domains of attributed meanings.

Male-male sex words such as *dipstick, fag, faggot, fudgepacker (penetrator), gay, homo, inverts, member of the club,* and *queers* were seen by informants as more negative, as more of a put-down of a man than were the first five categories. Worse still, they suggested, are penetrated males. These men received perennial scorn from male respondents and, to a lesser degree, from females. Although an *asshole* could refer to either biological sex to suggest inappropriate behavior, *bumfuck, butthole, chicken, cocksucker, cumbreath, filthy chicken, fudgepacker, penis breath, pud hopper, sucker, twink,* and *twinkie* earned higher negative ratings than *asshole* and for various reasons. *Bumfuck* also set up a paradox of being a lousy fuck but a fuck all the same. *Chicken, twink,* and *twinkie* were deemed to apply most often to gay bottoms. "A chicken is a sweet young thing" predated by *chickenhawks,* who tend to be "older men" although not always. Notice that a chicken is a bottom, young thus immature, and performs the "female" role. This is significant: to bash a male, then accuse him of nonheterosexual sex habits, particularly those that reflect heterosexist images of passive, penetrated femaleness. Sounds like heterosexual dominance to me. A *twink* and its variants also sometimes indicated a male who stereotypically may appear or be perceived as handsome, mostly hairless, maybe effeminate, young, yet perhaps passive and dominatable, which for some informants indicated a spurious male femininity that they found to be "disgusting."

The ultimate cultural domain of meaning to bash males and their performance of their sexuality involved the stigmatization of the anus by assigning queer-coded anal words. *Ass* and *asshole* inscribed the category clearly enough, but other terms further denoted dirtiness, even the brownness of fecal matter with adjectives such as *dirty* and *filthy* and with the noun *fudgepacker,* which evokes fecality paradoxically as chocolate candy. Hocquenghem's observations about a man's butt offered and rapturously played by another man additionally confirms this subdomain as a most taboo realm of meaning (93-112). Clearly, the most stigmatized filth in general was homosexual or gay performance of sexuality. The erection for another man problematizes an already problematic activity of men, even in straight contexts. The penetration of another man furthermore denotes the violation of heterosexist, hegemonic norms.

It is not insignificant that male bashing among men and boys that belittles men and boys as homosexuals and gays *occurs in mainstream, heterosexual contexts* between males who are ostensibly heterosexual. These occurrences present themselves as a premier heterosexist form of communicative dominance because they masquerade gay bashing as straight male bashing. Conversations that include the epithets *chicken* or *asshole* occur frequently then as open lies. They are really queer-coded, in addition to being male bashing-coded. *Chicken* has the native, mainstream meaning of being afraid, yet I can recall the first time, as a boy, I heard this use and tried to figure out why chickens were easily frightened when many of the ones I had seen on farms were ornery, bumptious critters. *Asshole* made more sense to me as a put-down; it is a dirty place, fraught with all sorts of potty training accidents. So, the terms appear to have perfectly good, mainstream meanings.

This sort of closeted put-down enforces heterosexist dominance because these words stigmatize nonheterosexist sexual performance as the most opprobrious status, even to little boys with their playground, ball field humors. "John Reid" shares the irony of such situations.

> I fairly quickly learned that "f—k you" was the single worst thing in the world that could be said by or to anyone. . . . (And I learned how irrational, illogical, impossible, therefore, was the accepted response—I'LL BET YOU'D LIKE TO—when spoken by one boy to another. (13)

Responses such as "kiss my ass," "in your dreams," and "you're not man enough" indicate boys' awareness of the problematics of male sexuality, particularly male homosexuality.

Heterosexist defamation of gayness, even a hint of it, can be a frightening accusation in ostensibly heterosexual contexts. The accusation claims that something fundamental about one's maleness is wrong, deviant, and sick. Defiance to the accusation proves it; acquiescence to the accusation paradoxically certifies one's heterosexual, male status *yet renders the accused submissive to the accuser.*

In sum, male bashing involves a spectrum of meanings shared widely in North American and Western culture. The allegedly less pejorative bashing terms are exclusively heterosexually coded. The most pejorative terms are exclusively homo- and gay-coded. For the least pejorative terms for male bashing to be valorized as less problematic depends on the opposite end of the spectrum that is socially constructed concurrently as highly problematic. In other words, male bashing is at heart, gay bashing. There would be no subtle nuances of heterosexually oriented terms being considered more acceptable without certain homosexually oriented terms that are taken to indicate unacceptable maleness. Thus, my conclusion: Male bashing must inherently assume gay bashing to work in the way it appears to work in everyday life situations. Male bashing, culturally, by males or females against males is intimately bound to queer defamation. Male bashing and queer bashing are engines of heterosexist, mainstream dominance.

Stigmatization

I have used the word *stigmatization* without explaining its importance as a living concept in the West. Its provenance is revealing of the historic undergirding of the gay bashed male situation. Originally, "the stigmata" were the signs of the risen Christ, his wounds. At once a horrifying miracle, it is impossible to separate the holy from the horrible (Ingebretsen). Stigmatized humanness, male or female, works in a similar way. What persons are or appear to be, particularly if marginalized by mainstream, more accepted norms, sets them apart. Any signs of difference may then easily stigmatize persons as horrible, even if, for those individuals, the difference certifies their sense of rightness about themselves and their world. Yet their stigmatization may grant them sacral or sanctionable status. Although sexual minorities are granted shamanic, sacral status among many indigenous peoples (Blackwood; Duberman et al. 106-117; Roscoe; Williams), in Western culture, they are more often demonized for any signs of difference. This happens particularly to persons of minority status, not just sexual minority status, and perhaps is the sine qua non of minority status.

Although many do not seriously consider men as a minority, many men report that lately they feel treated as if they were. Clearly, as both my surveyed database and subsequent informant interpretations suggest, social ineptitude, boorishness, and sexual inappropriateness are overwhelmingly stigmatized as male-coded, thus indicating the treatment of men as a group as a minority, as something less, deplorable, and problematic. If we add to that the realization that these communicative practices closet all males—cover them up, hide them—and even accuse them of gayness if they are out of line, then the minoritizing of men works by minoritizing them as homosexual, gay, queer. Similar to the sadomasochistic experience of some children in some church schools reported earlier, male bashing as gay bashing is not tabooed when clearly it would be in other circumstances, such as the sexual harassment of women that bash them.

Thus, language itself may display taboos and the very structures of taboos without being called taboos in a language's conventional meanings, uses, and rhetorics. Tabooed language may appear in various media, yet it is among fans of specific media where media themselves may be tabooed.

Exit to Eden Versus *Exit to Eden:* Media Taboos

Now, back to the sort of popular culture artifact and event covered in *Forbidden Fruits.* Anne Rice's S/M novel *Exit to Eden* is an explicit portrayal of sex workers and sex clients. The movie inspired by the novel, however, is quite different, scantily clad in the premises of the novel. It is perhaps a common complaint among literary fans that the movie based on the literature is too unlike the novel just as it is a common observation among film buffs that the movie is much better than the novel. These sorts of preferential fan statements may well signify related interpretive communities. Perhaps more interesting, however, is that these sorts of preferential statements are indicative of media taboos, also known as writerly and fan superstitions, avoidances, and embrasures. These media taboos have been acknowledged historically.

Lessing's Laocoön

Gotthold Ephraim Lessing observes a striking difference between the visual impact of a passage in Virgil's *Aeneid* and a later sculpture modeled on the same scene. In the *Aeneid,* Laocoön warns the Trojans not to allow the wooden horse within the city. Neptune, a Greek advocate, sends serpents to silence Laocoön and his sons. Virgil describes horrible, ugly pain. Lessing then compares the literary description with a Hellenistic sculpture depicting the same event. Instead of ghastly pain, Laocoön sighs elegantly. Lessing attributes this crucial difference to a difference between the expressive medium for writing, which may be read in private and which leaves images to the imagination, and how written media work differently from the visual, plastic medium of sculpture, which is a public and civil art. The sculpture, if literal to Virgil, would have been a violation of civility, too horrifying for public sharing. In other words, graphic depiction of pain and horror for some cultures and historical eras is taboo. Lessing's observations about tabooed media are illustrative for under-standing differences between the novel and film of the same name, *Exit to*

Eden—although not necessarily excusing or valorizing either media embodiment. The book and its private experience are far more explicitly graphic than the public movie.

Many of Rice's readers quite honestly expect transgression and explicitness in her stories; that is one ingredient of Rice's fame. Katharine Ramsland observes,

> All of Rice's novels contain erotic elements. Beginning with *Interview with the Vampire*, she brings to the vampire image an engulfing sensory experience of immortality. In her other supernatural series, *Lives of the Mayfair Witches*, Rice develops the powerful sexuality of generations of women associated with an incubus-like spirit.

Although Rice penned other novels, none of them "match the explicit sexuality of the five Rice wrote under two pseudonyms" (ix-x). *Exit to Eden* was originally published under the pen name Anne Rampling.

Pseudonymous publication in itself inscribes the media taboo involved: Writers and their handlers—agents, publishers, and editors—are only too aware that established appeal can be marred by publishing the same author writing in a different style, genre, or even length of story. Indeed, many fans insist that their authors come up with something new but retain the elements that the fans themselves acknowledge as defining characteristics of an author's writing. The fans are, after all, an interpretive community that repeatedly nurtures its participants and the community at large with shared interests. Sex is one thing, and explicit sex and transgressive sex are different for many fans. Thus, Rice published *Exit to Eden* and other, more transgressive novels under pen names. Chronologically, *Interview* came first (1976), then, pseudonymously as A. N. Roquelaure, *The Claiming of Sleeping Beauty* (1983) was immediately followed by *Beauty's Punishment* (1984). Eventually, in one stellar year of publications, *The Vampire Lestat*, *Beauty's Release*, and *Exit to Eden* were released (1985). Clearly, the pseudonyms insulated the Vampire Chronicles from any possible backlash from the more explicit novels. Yet as it all turns out, fans from all three constituencies crossed over and reveled in each. By the mid-1990s, various fans will buy and trade books, attend vampire fairs and soirees, and not be offended by transgression or explicitness in any of the three publishing arenas.

In contrast, the movie version of *Exit to Eden* targets an even different set of interpretive communities, although certainly Rice fans are attracted to screen versions of stories they have read. The filmgoers are just that, filmgoers. They may or may not be readers; some filmgoers may not even be all that familiar with

Rice's corpus. They are also not a narrowly defined audience but a broader conceived market segment, delineated by the headline stars they prefer, if nothing else. There are three mainstream, familiar performers: Rosie O'Donnell, Dan Ackroyd, and Dana Delaney. The first two were spotlighted in television ads for the movie. The sorts of filmic, mythic expectations O'Donnell and Ackroyd invoke in potential audiences are clearly comedic, which are mostly alien expectations to the novel. Dana Delaney's character, Lisa, the female lead of the novel, was not evident in the trailers.

Rice readers, Rampling readers were not attracted to the novel *Exit to Eden* because they knew they would encounter already known characters; the novel's characters were quite unfamiliar to Rice readers—not Lestat, Louis, Armand, or David, not Rowan, Michael, Aaron, or Lasher. Indeed, familiarity of performers is not even part of the novel's warp and weft. Thus, the novel must reveal itself while the movie is prerevealed by its chosen performers.

The style of writing in the novel was different, too, more Spartan than Rice's lush vampire and witch narratives. The film was an exercise in familiarity in comparison. Cloak-and-dagger conventions abound; O'Donnell and Ackroyd are undercover cops who must recover photographic film that Elliott, the male lead of the novel, had taken. The high jinks further insulate the sadomasochistic premises of the two romantic characters by interspersing screen time with levity. Nudity appears in both media expressions, but the nudity in the film is quite brief, limited to various female characters' breasts and one shot of Elliott's butt. Otherwise, film bodies are usually discretely, if not scantily, covered. The scene in which Elliott is called from his stateroom on the boat taking him and others to "Eden" underlines that all of them are to don bikini-style briefs. In the novel, they are all naked from the word go. Of course, in the novel, they are going to The Club, not Eden; they are considered slaves, not "citizens," and so on. Nudity in the novel? Lots.

Sadomasochism in the novel? Lots, but not as much or as explicit as in the *Beauty* trilogy. Sadomasochism in the film is mild, infrequent, and brief, whereas in the novel, it can involve real pain, is frequent, and is often depicted in lengthy passages. One of the remarkable features of the novel concerns Lisa, the professional dominatrix who has experienced absolutely no "normal" sex and romance all her life, only S/M and other transgressive performances. When she falls in love with Elliott, she is unnerved by that love and constantly experiences the sorts of pain and humiliation from "normal" sex and romance that her slaves experience from the rituals and paraphernalia at her command. None of that appears in the film.

In the film, the New Age Aussie man, Elliott—who in the novel is a California boy who unknowingly grew up just down the street from Lisa in Berkeley—fetchingly wins over the dominatrix. In the novel, the pairing is a struggle, but the eventual commitment of Lisa and Elliott to one another is a formulaic constant of love stories common to both the novel and the film. Then again, in the novel, there are no cops, no Ackroyd or O'Donnell, no comedic relief from characters unfamiliar with S/M who can laugh it off.

The media taboos from novel to movie are clear. A novel read in private can be more explicit. A film one sees in the dark—but in public—not only cannot be so explicit, but also it must insulate the audience in various ways, even from the relatively mild suggestions of transgressive sex. Tabooed sex must be managed in mainstream film. Readers of Rice, Rampling, and Roquelaure want it managed all right—managed right into their faces and hearts. Although the movie may be a disappointment to many of Rice's readers, it is palatable for a wider audience.

Actually, these sorts of changes are not unusual for literature-to-screen adaptations. Film is, after all, a visual medium of spectacle, of action in the form of action. Differences should be expected. Yet the media mix is clear: Publishing can reach millions and be explicit; for film to do the same—at least in North America in the late twentieth century—explicitness must be modified, toned down, and cushioned.

"Just Like a Woman"

This sort of transformation of taboo to nontaboo status is not unusual even for adaptations in ostensibly the same medium, such as popular music. Bob Dylan's original song "Just Like a Woman" heaps scorn on the woman not just lyrically but from Dylan's vocal quality. Roberta Flack's cover (the music business term for adaptation of someone else's song) displays empathy for the woman by minor adjustments to the lyrics as well as by Flack's caressing vocals. The two versions seem to contradict each other, yet both are compelling performances.

There may be more than meets the eye about the differences, or, as it were, more than strokes the ear. Music is Sound, not Sight. Dylan wrote in the 1960s and 1970s. Although many of his other lyrics are poetically elliptical, many are quite transparent. "Just Like a Woman" admits to an interpretation that is not far-fetched, namely, that "Queen Mary" is not a woman but perhaps is a gay man. "Queen" is a common appellation for a gay man. "Mary," however, is a gay culture insider word that gay men sometimes employ to refer to other gay men. Thus, the lyrics "She takes just like a woman, yes, she does/She makes love just like a woman. And she aches just like a woman" may indicate that the "woman" who is not a woman is so good at being a woman that she "breaks up just like a little girl," meaning "he" cries, carries on, particularly when the singer leaves "her" or wants to break up with "her." If nothing else, the lyrics seem overtly misogynist. Covertly, they may seem latent with internalized homophobia masquerading poetically as rejection of and distancing from a woman. Perhaps the gay coding of the lyrics also reveals itself in the concluding lines before the final refrain.

> I can't stay in here
> Ain't it clear that—
> I just can't fit
> Yes, I believe it's time for us to quit
> Oh I must admit
> When we meet again
> Introduced as friends
> Please don't let on that you knew me when
> I was hungry and it was your world (Dylan 213)

Thus, Dylan's sometimes puzzling poetry in this case comes out in the wash of gay sensibility freed from the tabooed closeting of the supposedly sexually liberated 1960s. Roberta Flack's version almost miraculously deconstructs the apparent misogyny and reclaims the rejection as a symbol of pride. Then again, a queer reading of Dylan's original can delete the misogyny: "Queen Mary" has taken on the stereotypical—and sexist—accoutrements of womanhood, and Dylan scorns "her" for that.

6

Prehistoric and Historic Texts
from Around the World

Although Immanuel Kant is not a French poststructuralist philosopher, some of his logic still defies easy dismissal, for example, Kant's stated concerns about the conjectural nature of the beginning of human history:

> At least as far as this beginning is made by nature, one may attempt to establish it on the basis of pure conjecture. For here one need not resort to fiction but can rely on experience, if only one presupposes that human actions were in the first beginning no better and no worse than we find them now. (*On History* 53)

In other words, while conjecture may be dicey, there remains a principle by which to proceed for understanding prehistory that mitigates imperfect conjecture: that humans then experience as humans now. Kant articulated what later in geological sciences is the assumption that truly prehistoric geological processes may be logically inferred from current, observable geological processes and what later would be accepted in various social sciences as the principle that knowledge about current folkloric practices can shed light on the customs of ancient peoples. This principle takes on all the more significance when it is realized that millions of people who are alive as of this writing are indigenous peoples whose traditions have existed for thousands of years (Mander). Although undoubtedly there are differences between prehistoric, contemporary indigenous, and so-called civilized peoples, it is common sense to figure that some, if not many, sexual practices derive from prehistoric roots. Thus, once nomenclature about artifacts and texts is presented, the narrative on prehistoric texts will proceed in the accepted manner of referring to observable, document-able artifacts and texts, then inferring interpretations of them.

Prehistoric Artifacts as Texts

Perhaps the most familiar conception of an "artifact" is the sort of material objects archaeologists collect and analyze. A more precise conceptualization is necessary, however—one that also indicates the interpretation of artifacts.

An artifact is something made by human agency. An artifact may be made consciously with some purpose in mind, such as a stack of rocks on a trail to indicate direction. An artifact may also get made accidently or unthinkingly yet remain after its maker leaves its physical presence, such as a footprint. In the case of rocks to show direction, artifacts often are designed to be utilitarian or pragmatic; some artifacts may be tools. In the case of a footprint, artifacts are still the embodiment of human agency, inscriptions that may be read with utilitarian purpose in mind, but well after the fact, such as Pompeian footprint impressions that inscribe flight from the volcanic eruption, left for centuries in Vesuvius' detritus.

Some artifacts persist through time and may be considered more permanent than not, such as pottery shards and metal tools; others disintegrate rapidly and may be considered ephemeral, such as thin paper or garments, graffiti sketched in the sand by the ocean at low tide, or the unrecorded, musical sounds produced by a band. Not all artifacts are material in their embodiment, however. The feelings one experiences in relationship to a piece of music or another person may exist through one's body, but no discernable record may be left by those feelings.

Artifacts reflect the culture(s) from which they emerge. Simultaneously, culture(s) shape artifacts. To describe artifacts, one might look for common patterns and themes among them and try to discern likenesses and differences from cultural patterns and themes. Uncommon patterns may outline idiosyn-cratic or perhaps local cultural trends. Simply stated, to compare artifacts, one searches for common patterns; to contrast them, one searches for uncommon patterns. Once the trajectories of common and uncommon are posed, their development can be tracked spatially, temporally, and conceptually.

Artifacts are also open texts. By "open text," I mean what Umberto Eco means by "open work." An artifact, be it a piece of music, a story, or some other medium, may be crafted with some specific intent in mind, with "a rigid univocality" (*Open* 6), but still may evoke other interpretations to others. Some artifacts may even be crafted to capitalize on this openness, yet that does not mean they are necessarily ambiguous or indefinite. Even then, artifacts may be interpreted variously within the same culture and by outsiders, even by those many years removed from the artifact's origins, some of them who fancy themselves to be experts and experienced in the sign systems of artifacts. In popular culture studies, an artifact such as a lawn ornament may be observed and interpreted as a text. Although the artifact may not have any writing on it at all, for someone it tells a story and generates meaning and values.

The question remains, which artifacts should be selected for research? Sensibly, the answer includes both those artifacts to which a culture subscribes or subscribed as well as those that repeatedly appear in commentaries about the artifacts or the culture. Sexually oriented artifacts that apparently and clearly image sexual scenes and themes (such as some ancient Greek amphorae that show men having sex with one another [Dover]) also indicate artifacts of interest, although of course there is a limitation to this approach. A rather prim or sex-negative culture may hide its sexual interests and activities, particularly those practices that are stigmatized (Duberman, *About*). Other cultures may be rather public about many of their sexual practices, but that still does not mean that oral, written, or artifactual records reflect the warp and weft of everyday life—the records may have been left by persons highly unrepresentative of everyday life. Hence, it becomes wise to pose multiple interpretations of artifacts and their cultures and especially to consider a number of artifacts, not limiting inquiry to one type, place, or time. Sometimes, the scholarly narrowing of research only predisposes narrow observations and conclusions.

Another problem with this sort of inference making occurs when there are no apparent written artifacts contemporaneous to the unwritten artifacts that might serve to guide interpretation. Numerous commentators, however, have demonstrated that an artifact can be interpreted as an inherent sign system; thus, the lack of a written record is not always troubling. With only casual ratiocination on observing an artifact, a stone, for instance, it might be evident that a sharp stone cutting edge may clearly have been fashioned for the left or right hand; furthermore, the artifact's distribution across a wider geographical area than the land that produces that particular type of stone may indicate nomadic or seasonal migrations by the original makers of the tool or even a trade economy.

Sexual Artifacts

Contemporary folktales and contemporary indigenous texts that inscribe sex serve as links to other prehistoric artifacts. As Estes claims, "Collecting stories is a constant paleontologic endeavor" (17). Sexualized myths already discussed in Chapter 3 qualify as prehistoric texts, such as that of the Earth Mother. There are effigies that may be construed as representations of Earth Mother, however, such as the "Venus" of Willendorf. Perhaps the identification of this particular artifact as a "Venus" is unfortunate. The Willendorf effigy and others like it are more likely to personify Earth Mother as nurturer and not as a heavenly goddess: "These highly stylized, ample-bodied figures are today generally understood to be ancient images of the powers that give and nurture life" (17). Noting that there are also numerous male images, Eisler conjectures that Paleolithic peoples undoubtedly performed sexual rites that brought them closer to the Goddess (54-66). Felicitas Goodman argues persuasively that various prehistoric images and effigies underscore ecstatic experience, sexual or not, and the material evidence of gendered communication with the spirit world may be exemplified by artifacts from many cultures that lived on six continents. Even then, it is true that although earth is usually taken to be female and sky to be male by archaic cultures, certain stars in the sky were also attributed sex and gender charac- teristics, some of them female, such as Venus or her counterparts in other cultures.

Yet archaic images of the female defy the modern and late modern exclusive opposition of female and male, feminine and masculine. In a massive and stunningly erudite book that apparently has not been consulted enough yet in culture studies, *Dictionary of Symbols,* Carl Liungman presents ample evidence with regard to the symbols the ancients and preancients used to signify the planet Venus as both the evening and morning star. Significantly, the symbol for the planet Venus is the one many people now use to indicate woman, ♀. But early in prehistory, Venus was taken to be two stars, and apparently no culture pieced together that they were the same. Actually, noting the difference was initially based on simple observation that merely took some temporal patience. The morning star can be seen for 245 days in the east before it disappears into the rising sun's light. Then it disappears for 78 days, paled by the light of the sun and quickly, eventually entirely blocked to the naked eye. "On the 79th evening it appears again in the west immediately after the setting of" the sun (333). The morning star was almost universally taken to be a "goddess of hunt and battle" (336), and its proper "designer-iconic symbol" is a crescent with its points facing to the right (like the waning moon or ☾). The evening star was taken to be the goddess of love and was usually symbolized as a crescent with its points facing left (like the new moon or ☽).

According to Liungman, one version of this goddess tends to influence a culture more than the other.

Throughout history we find that always one of Venus' two aspects has been overemphasized, and this has occurred in nearly all cultural spheres. The planet ♁ as goddess for *hunt, battle,* and *the new day* is symbolized by the sign for the *waning moon* or the *dying snake,* ☡ and the design-iconic ideogram for ♁ namely ⅃ .... No comparable graphic symbol for ♁ that illustrates the divine qualities of *beauty, peace, love making,* and *sexuality* of Venus as the Evening star seems ever to have existed. (336; emphasis in this and subsequent passages Liungman's).

Liungman then shows how the five-pointed star has been taken by many cultures as a war symbol, something to put fear into the hearts of enemies (10; 43-45). "Note that in the United States a rather similar ideogram has been used on fighter jets and tanks" (345). Eventually, he points out, the Virgin Mary was associated with the nonsexual and aloof characteristics of the morning star, bearing a human child without the benefit of sexual intercourse, and she is "a goddess in an ideology that emphasizes suffering, warfare, death, and martyrdom much more than intimate sexual relations, sensuality, and love" (337).

The astronomy-interested priests of some cultures, such as those inhabiting the Euphrates-Tigris region, figured out that the morning and evening stars were the same heavenly body and took a goddess as their main divinity, who was seen as both "the queen of the heavens, goddess of war but also of divine beauty and peace" (335), like Inanna and Ischtar. They figured this fundamental identity of a female who was both what today is conventionally called masculine and feminine through more careful observation of the movement and plotting of the evening and morning stars. Once the ecliptic or basic alignment of most planets was discovered in relation to the horizon, it became "possible to mark the exact place in the 360 degrees of the zodiac where the Morning star first appears shortly before sunrise after a period of invisibility" (333). When this procedure was followed scrupulously, it was discovered that five new sightings of the star bisect the horizon in the pattern of a hand drawing a connected, five-pointed star, hence the five-pointed star as symbol for the morning star. In contrast, although knowing that the two stars were one, the Greek tribes accentuated their differences more than other cultures, and eventually Athena ascended as hunt and war goddess in the cultivation of their culture and its militaristic tendencies. Athena was also a goddess of wisdom and patron of the arts. Aphrodite, in contrast, was goddess of womanly beauty and sensuality and although a lover of Ares, toyed not with the arts or logic or reason.

Notably, the five-pointed star "is sign for both war and pain and their opposites: festivities, favorable opportunities, enjoyment" (10). Examples of five-pointed stars that indicate pain are legion in animated cartoons (Wile E.

Coyote gets clobbered again, and stars circle his head to indicate pain and dizziness) and in comic books (Plastic Man is overcome by being abandoned after having been soaked in a vat of acid, same circling stars). This starry iconography then indicates a pervading sexualization: Pain as emotive is ultimately to be associated with femaleness, either as causing it or receiving it. To cause pain is signified by morning star aggressiveness; to receive it is signified by evening star sensuality. In both cases, pain equals female. Once again, stereotypes of women are not always recent; many are prehistoric in origins and appear in contexts and situations that do not even seem to be sexualized, such as cartoon and comic iconography.

The Power of Place

Many living, as well as prehistoric, indigenous peoples experience particular localities, such as springs, trees, or rocks, as manifesting spirit and energy and even having a personality and gender. For instance, Serpent Mound in southern Ohio is widely recognized as a source of energy for the lowest part of the body at the base of the spine, the part that many cultures identify as the locus of basic energy and sexuality. Many cultures also totemize this particular Earth energy and humans' sexual energy with serpents. Thus, it is no act of merely primitive fancy that the Minoan Earth Goddess, among other Mediterranean Earth Goddesses, was often sculpted and depicted as holding serpents. Serpent Mound, however, does not appear to have been assigned sex or gender.

Other sacred places have. Before Christianity colonized Ireland, one prehistoric tradition for grouping clans and people concerned local geography. In some cases, mounds, either natural, such as a hill, or human made, were the center of their people's fecundity and nurture, functioning as doorways to the "otherworld." The otherworld was inhabited exclusively by women deities, and they and that world energized this world through the contact of the holy mound (Swan 140). The otherworld also is located in the "holy wells of Ireland" in which the well, or spring, itself is regarded as a female deity, and the local clan-lord is her husband, bound to her (Swan 143-145). I observe, at this point, that contrary to the current fashion of dismissing Western cultures as laden with the baggage of violence and domination, the earlier pagan cultures of Europe were quite different—and supplanted by later cultures of dominance.

Among the *Dine* people, those whom the U.S. government calls "Navajo," a creation story also values place and reveals prehistoric, indigenous attitudes about the two sexes.

> Before this world existed, there was a First World far below the world where we are now. . . . There were six beings. Those beings were First Man, the son of Night and the blue sky over the sunset; First Woman, the daughter of Day Break and the Yellow Sky of sunset; Salt Woman; Fire God; Coyote and Begochiddy. Begochiddy, who was the child of the Sun, was both man and woman, and had blue eyes and golden hair. (Caduto & Bruchac 31)

In that world of darkness, Begochiddy makes sacred mountains east, south, west, and north. Things go awry in First World, so Begochiddy leads them all to Second World by means of a Big Reed they could climb inside its hollow. Problems arise in Second World, and once again Begochiddy plants Big Reed, and they escape to Third World. In this world, Begochiddy also created human beings.

> Before long, the men and women began to quarrel with each other. The men said that the women were causing trouble. The women said that it was the men. Coyote came to Begochiddy and told him that men and women were always quarreling. Begochiddy decided to put a stop to it.
> "All of the men," Begochiddy said, "must stay on the right bank of the river. All of the women must stay on the left bank. Neither may cross the river to be with the other." (32)

They lived separately for quite a long time but were unhappy about the situation. Eventually, they implored Begochiddy to be returned to each other. "Some say it was the women who came first, but others say it was the men."

As it turns out, we live in Fourth World, where we can consider this story. Begochiddy is both male and female, a natural state. Eventually, men and women are created but squabble so much they must be separated. Yet they need each other, put together—like Begochiddy. Both sexes are credited with the weakness of first begging Begochiddy to restore them to one another. This almost ritual separation of sexes is not necessarily purely "myth." Many prehistoric and early historical peoples practiced the separation of the sexes except for the quickening of children. Many contemporary indigenous cultures practice similar separation for their various reasons. The Islamic requisite separation of sexes is also highly prevalent. The ancient Celts had their own unabashed reasons. As Arthur Evans translates chronicler Diodorus, concerning Celtic men,

> Although they have good-looking women, they pay very little attention to them, but are really crazy about having sex with men. They are accustomed to sleep on the ground on animal skins and roll around with male bed-mates on both sides. Heedless of their own dignity, they abandon without a qualm the bloom of their bodies to

others. And the most incredible thing is that they don't think this is shameful. But when they proposition someone, they consider it a dishonor if he doesn't accept the offer! (*God* 139-140)

Clearly, Diodorus came from a locale in which heterosexuality was hegemonic, yet the passage clearly attests separation of sexes to the point that Celtic men preferred sex with each other. Keep in mind, even Julius Caesar found subduing these indigenous peoples difficult, which sheds a little light on the U.S. military's policy of "don't ask/don't tell."

Location as sacred both to some deity and to sex may also be found in prehistoric standing stones throughout Asia—phallic and vaginal standing stones that convey male and female energy to their visitors, their pilgrims. These will be interpreted later as they are reported in an historic text by Hirschfeld.

Historic Texts from Around the World

Various records of sexual practices from around the world have vastly influenced popular culture. Some of the records are fictive; some, quite plainly, are sex manuals. Perhaps one of the most widely disseminated narratives that convey exotic techniques as well as sex partners and locales from around the world are Ian Fleming's novels of British secret agent 007, James Bond. Bond is a gentleman's gentleman yet is sexually potent and skilled with the potencies of death regimens, so much so that one aspect is a constant synecdoche for the other. Bond is himself a historic text of sexuality, and his example as a secret agent spawned dozens of other fictive secret agents, all of whom are presumed to be sexually active, potent, and dangerous because they are secret agents. Although Bond may attract more than his fair share of women, that attraction alone signifies his vulnerability. To take him out, to remove him as a player in the Cold War, one needs to attack his genitals.

In the novel *Casino Royale* (and here I emphasize the novel since the movie is only remotely related), Bond has been captured by one Le Chiffre who has taken Bond to a remote country estate in Europe and who is determined to extract secret information from Bond, particularly the whereabouts of a fortune in cash. Unlike the usual tortures (if there is such a thing as a "usual torture") that Bond endures in other tales, this time his sex is directly assaulted and conquered not by a woman but by the extended violence of other men. Bond is bound nude to a chair that has an accommodating hole in the seat. "He was utterly a prisoner, naked and defenceless [*sic*]" (119).

Bond had been bound before, but the sadistic transgression of his person and the entire scene becomes evident as a "cane carpet-beater" is beaten sharply and repeatedly against Bond's exposed genitals. Bond ponders as the torture proceeds,

> He had been told by colleagues who had survived torture for the Germans and the Japanese that towards the end there came a wonderful period of warmth and languor leading into a sort of sexual twilight where pain turned to pleasure and hatred and fear of the tortures turned to a masochistic infatuation. It was the supreme test of will, he had learnt, to avoid showing this form of punch-drunkenness. (119)

As usual, Bond typically calms himself, steels himself, controls himself, this time knowing that the slightest sign of giving in could be his doom. But even Bond has his limits.

> He opened his eyes a fraction.
>   Le Chiffre had been waiting for this, and like a rattlesnake the cane instrument leapt up from the floor. It struck again and again so that Bond screamed and his body jangled in the chair like a marionette. (122)

Although Fleming's prose is quite circumspect in not even mentioning genitals, to witness Bond reduced in this way is rather shocking. The assault on Bond's genitals is a direct assault on his core, his quintessence. Screaming and spasms are also quite the opposite mode of behavior we associate with unflappable, implacable, glib Bond. Later in the novel, it is a serious issue for Bond to see if he can still function in bed after the mangling ordeal. He can, of course.

Although Fleming's Bond generated a series of imitators, perhaps most notable for the purposes of this book is Ted Mark's *Man from O.R.G.Y.,* Steve Victor. Victor is a sex researcher who constantly gets roped into secret intelligence work precisely because he is a sex expert who has earned entrée into all sorts of otherwise secret places. One scene from *My Son, the Double Agent* directly parodies Bond's torture in *Casino Royale,* except the tongue-in-cheek humor and levity of the torture conveys a quite different sense of sexualization.

Victor had been asked to go to the island of Malta to locate the connection between a virulent strain of Malta fever and a group called S.M.U.T. The first cases to contract the fever appeared to have done so in a brothel, and Victor is supposed to be an expert on brothels, and is. The fever itself, however, "is directly traceable to the Micrococcus Melitensis, a microorganism only found present in the milk of Maltese goats. . . . This same goats' milk may have certain aphrodisiac characteristics" (*Double Agent* 28). So, Victor rents a car, cruises into the countryside, and randomly finds a goat farm. After schmoozing his way to witness a goat milking, he gets shot with a heavy stream of goat milk, necessitating that he doff his clothing for cleaning. The goat milker, a woman named Domino, quickly gets him in a compromising position.

> I was standing, but bent over so that my hands were touching my ankles. Each hand was tied to the corresponding ankle. And my legs had been spread wide apart so that the calves could be laced to a pair of bedposts in such a way that I could neither squat nor straighten up.
>
> This particular position served another purpose. It left the most intimate part of my anatomy clearly exposed from the rear. It was this dangling sac which my tormentor had been so delicately stroking with the goose feather. (8)

The novel began in medias res, in the middle of things, Victor laughing until it hurts, constantly threatened by another vicious tickle, with Domino demanding, "Why did you kill our man in Manila, Mr. Victor?" (7). Of course, that she can identify him is surprising to him. Although he thought he had picked just any old goat farm, it turns out that this particular one was owned and operated by S.M.U.T. Of course, he had never been in Manila, which delivers the crux of the novel's plot: Victor had been born with a twin who had died. Then again, maybe not. As the story plays out, Victor is confronted by the same sorts of tortured musings as Bond in *Casino Royale*. For instance, he keeps laughing uncontrollably to dupe Domino into thinking he is still under sway of the tickling, to get her to stop for a while. His sac is not threatened like Bond's, however, and eventually he is saved by a fellow agent, and the two of them then put Domino in the same position to extract information from her. Victor is uncomfortable with that, but the other agent suddenly holds a gun on him to force him to do it. The man may be thoroughly free with his sex, but he has scruples.

The British connection alone is the premise for numerous sexualized texts that have influenced popular culture and was undoubtedly stoked by the British musical invasion of the 1960s and countless infatuations with the Beatles. Eventually hooked up with the Maharishi, the intercultural interests of millions were in many cases permanently incorporated into their lives. The Beatles craze and the Bond craze coincided with the 1960s counterculture movement, and many North Americans acquired a taste for martial arts along with the desire to discover where Bond acquired so much sexual information. Actually, Ted Mark provided the ready answer by generously mentioning numerous foreign sex manuals, from *The Perfumed Garden* to the *Kama Sutra*. These books became sought after and sold well. The most available translations into English, however, had been provided a hundred years earlier by world traveler—and sex expert—Sir Richard Burton, who himself was a model of derring-do for both Bond and Victor.

Thus, the influence of sexual texts from around the world began as early as the Victorian era and was not something to be found only in the mid-twentieth century. The British taste for exotic sex was well informed and helped pique the interest of many individuals in the former colonies. The dispersion of formative ideas—not just about sex, but about many subjects—moved from east to west in Western culture. Although the Renaissance is frequently cited as the impetus of this movement from the Middle East to Europe, the dispersion was already under way in shipping and trade. Boccaccio's sexy *Decameron* eventually moved west into various plays of Shakespeare.

In contrast, for Asian cultures, the dispersion of significant ideas occurred west to east, from what is now called India through the Himalayan Mountains to China and eventually Japan. Neither the Western nor Eastern dispersion of ideas encountered a lack of similar, and in many cases, different ideas in the new geographical areas into which they moved. In each new region of Asia, the original ideas encountered indigenous traditions and eventually assimilated with those traditions. Many of these cultural communities exist in the late modern period, either modified by the west-to-east spread of ideas or relatively intact. Allow me to present a capsule history of cultural norms that are different from but still influence Western popular culture.

India

To this day, large temples standing in various parts of India clearly show pairs and groups of men and women exploring diverse sexual possibilities. These monuments are public and, not so long ago, would have been comparable to a large building down the street in one's locale. Yet to many Westerners, the monumentalizing of explicit, public sex is, perhaps at best, considered strange. Even then, early sculptures of the god Siva sport a male breast and a female breast because the most holy spirits were considered to be both female and male in their ultimate nature. Only later in historical time did the older gods become mostly one sexed. If nothing else, this sculptural convention indicated the otherness of the major deities. A culture that depicts its spirits sexually and its members enjoying monumental sex is a community that demonstrably lives a different sense of body, self, and togetherness than does the sex-negative West.

Although the origins of the Asian enjoyment of body and sex are prehistoric, their later maturation into various Asian traditions and Western popular culture is historic.

Long before any of the Hindu holy books, the *Vedas,* were actually written, they were oral tradition. That oral tradition predates 4800 B.C.E. and may be found in certain ideas and formulas that permeate the ancient texts. Although many gods or spirits were experienced and worshiped in the Indian subcontinent, one spirit was believed to be an oversoul, a soul over and beyond all things that may exist and that permeates them: Brahma. Because each human is part of the oversoul Brahma, an early prayer stated simply, *ta't tvam asi,* or, "that art thou." The various meanings of the prayer resound throughout later spiritual beliefs and customs, particularly with the fundamental recognition that thou art Brahma; Brahma art thou. In other words, a human is fundamentally holy and divine, and one celebrates that joyful communion by living well.

There is a catch, however; humans and other creatures and things may be expressions of Brahma, but they are not perfect. All that humans experience is illusion or Maya. The greatest illusion? That pain is real, that death is real. Pain and the fear of pain, death and the fear of death, motivate humans to commit all sorts of acts, good and bad. Death is an illusion especially because all humans are caught in a cycle of rebirth. In each lifetime of rebirth, or reincarnation, one acquires karma or spiritual matter; karma will accumulate and affect subsequent rebirth and carries over many incarnations. If one causes pain, one accumulates "bad" or negative karma. If one brings enlightenment, one accumulates "good" karma.

Illusion, its resistance, and consequent karma, along with death and rebirth, are all moderated in everyday life in the form of *dharma,* the acquisition of religious merit by performance of social duty. Dharma is largely determined by social class, with brahmins, the high class, having duties or social obligations and roles different from warriors and outcasts. Despite social duty, the joy of Brahma is still available to all, as *kama* or pleasure. Pleasure is good for people because it reflects the joy of and oneness with Brahma.

Fundamentally, then, both the body and sex are sacred. Sexual performance may involve dharma and accumulated karma, but generally speaking, sexual performance is to be engaged in joy. Guilt, sin, and shame are alien to the Hindu experience and culture of sex. Although the basics of sex-favorability are implicit in the *Vedas* and the later *Upanishads,* eventually fairly explicit holy books were written about pleasure and particularly about sex, such as the *Kama Sutra of Vatsayana. Kama sutra* literally means "pleasure aphorisms." Vatsayana is the traditional author of the text. Actually, a Hindu monk, Malanaga, wrote the holy writ as an act of piety and performance of dharma to spread enlightenment. As the conclusion maintains,

> After reading and considering the works of Babhravya and other ancient authors, and thinking over the meaning of the rules given by them, the Kama Sutra was composed, according to the precepts of Holy Writ, for the benefit of the world, by Vatsayana, while leading the life of a religious student, and wholly engaged in the contemplation of the Deity. (220)

The entire work underlines the sacred nature of sexuality, but lest anyone think Vatsayana/Malanaga recommends free sex or uncontrolled promiscuity, one other concluding comment need be kept in mind: "In short, an intelligent and prudent person, attending to Dharma and Artha, and attending to Kama also, without becoming the slave of his passions, obtains success in everything he may undertake."

The *Kama Sutra* is full of sage advice. For instance, one ought to pair considering the size of sex organs—they should match. A man's lingam (penis) determines if he is a hare man, a bull, or a horse, where hare denotes smallness and horse, largeness. Correspondingly, a woman's yoni (vagina) determines if she is a deer woman, a mare, or an elephant. Hares go best with deer, and so on. Malanaga's advice is not limited to a simplistic materiality of size, however; he also observes that there should also be a match of desire between couplers. Males and females both exhibit small, as well as middling and intense, force of passion and carnality. Sensibly, those who match by level ought to get along better (87-88). Unlike the everyday folklore of modern North America, a preferable huge size of a man's penis is not the Indian norm, nor is considering only the man's desire.

Malanaga employs a euphemism for intercourse, *congress*. Thus, fellatio as oral sex becomes "mouth congress," or *auparishtaka*. Administered by either a eunuch, a female, or a male, mouth congress takes place in eight steps, which the *Kama Sutra* describes closely, from "the nominal congress" or first sliding touch of mouth and lingam through "biting the sides," "pressing outside," "pressing inside," "kissing," "rubbing," "sucking a mango fruit" and "swallowing up" (117). Needless to say, the *Kama Sutra*, explicitly provocative as it may be, does not begin to disclose all the mechanics and ritualization involved in actually performing *auparishtaka*. For that, another visit with Ted Mark's *Man from O.R.G.Y.* is instructive.

Hot on the trail of S.M.U.T. agents, Steve Victor meets a Hindu woman at a cocktail party, Samantha, who dallies with him momentarily in another room but confesses she desires to retain her virginity for marriage. Steve retorts from the *Kama Sutra* a passage to the effect that he would not want to be perceived as neglecting her. Thus, they conspire to meet later. Steve's virginity to what Samantha proposes becomes evident when Steve admits he has read about *auparishtaka,* but not experienced it—"Not in its ritualized fashion. No." Samantha begins.

> "The first step is jhúthaméthúna," [nominal congress] she reminded me. Her hands slid up my thigh and grasped me firmly. Her lips encircled only the tip of my lingam and moved in the proscribed [*sic*] circular churning manner. After a moment of this, she paused to look up at me questioningly.
>
> I remembered then that *Auparishtaka* involves a rite of conversational disputation. . . . After each of the eight actions, the one performing them must refuse to go on and "will only finally consent to do so after she has been begged and bribed." I played the game. "Don't stop," I moaned. "Please go on. Please! Please!" (145)

The scene continues through all eight steps, at each level, Steve's begging becoming less feigned and more genuine. So too, Samantha had initially straddled one of his feet with her weight resting just above his ankle. At the climax of step eight, Steve reports "I felt her body moving up and down against my shin" as she pleasured herself while pleasuring him. Both cum simultaneously (148).

While kama may be actively pursued, rebirth also still occurs. It becomes an interest to humans who would be most holy to be released (*moksha*) from the cycle of rebirth (*samsara*). No one seemed to have the knack or acquired knowledge, however, until one Siddhartha Gotama came along, who eventually was called the Buddha. Just as Jesus would have considered himself a Jew, Buddha would have considered himself a Hindu. Siddhartha was a son of privilege, a prince, who grew to early manhood, mostly protected within the walls of a palace his father had given him. "All sorrowful sights, all misery, and all knowledge of misery were kept away from Siddhartha, for the king desired that no troubles should come nigh him; he should not know that there was evil in the world" (*Buddha* 19). Siddhartha eventually convinces his father, the king, to let him see the kingdom. The king relents but has curtains placed over all dwellings to conceal any blight. Siddhartha leaves the palace on a splendid chariot, driven by a charioteer. Reaching the pastoral countryside, they encounter an old man, then a sick man, then a dead man. Siddhartha is rather shocked by what later Buddhist tradition labels "the three woes." On return to the palace, he cannot sleep. Eventually, he renounces his birthright to seek enlightenment and becomes a beggar and religious thinker by profession, a *muni,* joining that name to a family name, becoming Sakyamuni. In repose, Sakyamuni is tempted back to the world by a different king. Sakyamuni persists in seeking deliverance from the evil of the world. He seeks the teachings of brahmin sages and eventually leaves them, dissatisfied. Taking on the ways of asceticism, he becomes emaciated from fasting and is visited by Mara (illusion), lord of the five desires, who could not convince him to eat. Mara then sends three of his daughters to arouse him. They fail. Mara sends evil spirits to assail him. They fail. Returning to meditation, Sakyamuni achieves enlightenment, Buddhahood. Instead of remaining removed from the world, however, in his compassion, he begins to teach the eightfold path to enlightenment. This conversion of Hinduism to Buddhism began to spread, concentrating on the elimination of evil thoughts. Although sex is part of a Buddhist's life, to achieve Buddhahood, even that must be renounced—with detachment, not as shame. Eventually, Buddhism became a missionary religion and its asceticism became modified as it moved into new communities.

Into the Himalayas

Buddhist missionaries in the regions now called the Himalayas, which include Nepal, Tibet, and Bhutan, encountered indigenous traditions that were not wholly alien to them. Spirit and place worship were highly familiar, as were geomancy or shamanic earth magic. Related to geomancy was a practice for managing personal and spiritual health, tantrism. One of the hallmark features of tantric spirituality was its beliefs and practices about sex. One may engage in lots of sex to stimulate the body's naturally good processes, but at the same time there is to be no ejaculative orgasm for the man. Ejaculation was deemed deleterious to health, draining away vital bodily and ethereal fluids. Thus, sex is still sacred, the more the better, and is thus liberating, but on the pragmatic side, male ejaculation is to be avoided. Tantric sexuality is therefore both ecstatic and ascetic, and the ascetic aspect was eminently suitable to Buddhism. Hindu sexuality had been highly ecstatic with Buddhist asceticism an afterthought, mostly dealing with food taboos and meditation. The Buddhist missionaries also discovered that in some mountain communities, men outnumbered women, in many cases so much that it was common for households to develop in which one woman regularly coupled with three or more men. Some missionaries remained, others made it to China, where they found a related indigenous tantrism based on what the Chinese called *chi.*

Figure 6.1. Symbol of the Tao

China

Chi may best be understood in the context of the related indigenous tradition called Taoism. The Tao is the nature of all that is, and all that is is constantly changing, always becoming its opposite. The pictograph of the Tao (Figure 6.1) is the perhaps now familiar model of yin/yan that may be found on T-shirts, ball caps, buttons, and other paraphernalia of popular culture.

Notice that the two sides curve into each other; there is no straight line between them. As Alan Watts has observed, the separation and differentiation abilities of human thinking, particularly symbolized in straight lines, is an imposition on the natural union of nature (51-69), thus the symbol for the Tao does not employ a static borderline depicted by a straight line. Although it may iconographically depict the differentiation of yin and yan, the iconography also clearly indicates both their union and their perpetual tendency of change to the other. The two main parts of the Tao flow into each other, and each side also has the seed of its opposite, the dot that looks to some like an eye. Reality is both aspects together as one, as a whole. One aspect is always moving to become its opposite. Traditionally speaking, the white side is male, bright, and active; the black side is female, dark, and quiescent. The two flowing into each other, balancing, harmonizing, is *the* symbol for *chi* or life force. To the late modern, North American feminist, this may seem all too cozy with male chauvinism. There are two observations that may cast the concern into a more diverse light: (1) Although sexism of various sorts may be found in Asian traditions, in this case, the Chinese norm of action and beauty is to be found in the female images of inaction, waiting, and darkness. Bold action, shining out, and standing out are male characteristics and are often frowned on. (2) In contrast, the ideographs for male and female are perhaps more instructive about the sexist stereotyping of both biological sexes (Figure 6.2).

In the ancient ideographs for female, clearly articulated breasts dominate the figure. In the ancient and modern ideograph for the male, a scythe stands next

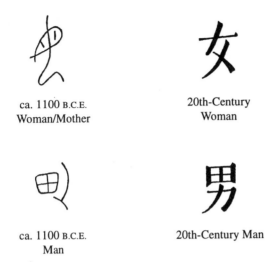

| ca. 1100 B.C.E. | 20th-Century |
| Woman/Mother | Woman |

ca. 1100 B.C.E.   20th-Century Man
Man

Figure 6.2.   Chinese Ideograms for Woman and Man

to a rice paddy, implicating man as his equipment and his labor. Language often is reductionist and stereotypic, and perhaps coincidentally, both biological sexes are depicted in Chinese ideography as if they confirm late modern stereotypes in North America.

Chi. Taoism recognizes that *chi,* energy, flows through human bodies, generating male and female, active and receptive *chi.* If the flow of *chi* is harmonious, in balance yet flowing, like the symbol for the Tao, then the individual human is most likely to be healthy, not just in body but also in mind and spirit. Two other kinds of *chi* influence human bodies, however, which must be taken into account when harmonizing *chi,* air *chi* (wind) and earth *chi* (water). Thus Taoist geomancy focuses on the interaction of all three sorts of *chi* at any given place or time. Too much *chi* flow and its opposite, stagnant *chi,* are physical and psychic killers, called killing *chi.* They must be moderated, or the effects on humans could be disastrous. Lest anyone find this discussion of *chi* irrelevant to the study of popular culture and sex, let alone to Western common sense, it can be confirmed that body *chi* is the basis of acupuncture, the *chi* energy flowing along meridians or *chi* channels and through clusters of energy called *chakras* (to use the term most common for late moderns, the Hindu word). Once thought by the American Medical Association to be quackery, acupuncture works, works consistently, and has as its descriptive context Taoist assumptions of *chi.* If nothing else, acupuncture and the understanding of *chi* have stood the test of time longer than the last three hundred years of Western medicine, by, say, about three thousand years, at least.

Assuming that the time and place are harmonious, a male and a female can also endanger one another by engaging in sex. A man's *chi* can be too strong and hurt, if not kill, the woman. Or, the man's *chi* may be highly weak, as related in the Sui Dynasty's sex manual, *Records of the Bedchamber.*

> The Yellow Emperor addressed the Plain Girl saying: "My spirit is debile and in disharmony. My heart is sad and I am in continuous fear. What should I do about this?"
> The Plain Girl answered: "All debility of man must be attributed to faulty exercise of the sexual act. Woman is superior to man in the same respect as water is superior to fire. Those who are expert in sexual intercourse are like good cooks who know how to blend the five flavors into a tasty broth. Those who know the art of Yin and Yang can blend the five pleasures; those who do not know the art will die an untimely death. (Van Gulik 135)

In a different configuration of *chi,* the woman can be so receptive as to draw all the man's *chi,* thus hurting or killing him. Therefore, men and women engaging in sex must monitor themselves and moderate activity to promote harmonious sharing of *chi,* and it must be kept in mind that sex is both spiritual in nature and healthful physically, for as the Plain Girl later relates to the Yellow Emperor after he has asked about the consequences of total sexual abstinence,

> "This is wrong. Heaven and Earth have their opening and closing. Yin and Yang develop from each other. . . . If one should resolve to abstain from sexual inter-course, one's spirit will not develop. . . . If the Jade Stalk becomes inactive a man will die. But its activity should be controlled and guided." (Van Gulik 137-138)

Notice once again how similar yet different to the Hindu and Buddhist ways the Taoist practice is. It is spiritual as much as physical; sex is good for you. Hindu sex is restrained by caste and dharma, however; Himalayan Buddhist sex is limited by ejaculative orgasm avoidance, and Chinese sex is to be moderated.

Taoism was also cognizant of tantric aspects of *chi* flow. Any number of Chinese sex manuals suggest that by avoidance of ejaculative orgasm and by directing sexual energy through the clusters of energy along one's spine, the chakras, one may induce youthfulness and longevity. The results achievable from ejaculation-free sex were enumerated by the Plain Girl to the Yellow Emperor:

"If a man engages once in the act without emitting semen, then his vital essence will be strong. If he does this twice, his hearing and vision will be acute. If thrice, all diseases will disappear. If four times, his soul will be at peace. If five times, his blood circulation will be improved. If six times, his loins will become strong. If seven times, his buttocks and thighs will increase in power. If eight times, his body will become glossy. If nine times, he will reach longevity. If ten times, he will be like an Immortal." (Van Gulik 145)

The "method" for attaining both orgasm-free sex and then directing the *chi* flow from the act "makes the semen return to enforce the brain" (145).

Tantric sex may be not merely unfamiliar to many Westerners but almost thoroughly alien. Perhaps the goal orientation of Western experiencing is buried in expectations of sexual satisfaction and shrouded in the consequent theatric rituals of ejaculation. Terms such as "scoring," "making it to first base," "hitting a homer," and "Did you get any?" not only inscribe the goal orientation of sex as experiencing orgasm but also associate it with dominance, or, being a winner of sorts. The notion of sex without ejaculative orgasm is thus relatively and literally senseless to many Western men. Western women, perhaps because of several factors, including the acculturation to shun sexual pleasure (L. Rubin), sometimes fake orgasm like Sally (Meg Ryan) in the restaurant scene in *When Harry Met Sally* and as Norma (Lesley Ann Warren) confesses to King (James Garner) in *Victor/Victoria*. They fake orgasm to help the man feel like he's "hit a home run"—for *her.* They may also do so in everyday life to get finished with the personal aerobics.

Not all Westerners are unfamiliar with tantric sex. The suspension of ejaculative, orgasmic norms is the stuff of science fiction and fantasy genres and literally provides suspense. Robert Silverberg conjoins Western, goal-oriented sex and Eastern, tantric sex in *The Book of Skulls*. Four college roommates in their early twenties hear that a monastery constructed of skulls exists in the desert in the southwestern United States where one can learn about immortality and become undying. Novices are taken in as groups of four, and the four decide to try it out. One catch: Before any of the four can achieve the level of monkhood beyond initiate, two of the novices must die. Two of the men are stereotypical jocks, Tim and Oliver. They are fraternity guys who whoop it up and bed at least one woman a day. In New York City, their initial goal is to find a place to sleep for the night, and they begin visiting bars to find pickups. Silverberg describes Tim: "Timothy, all eager, went plunging toward the bar like a musk-ox in rut, his burly body slowing" (13). The other two guys are somewhat nerdy; Eli is the intellectual and also heterosexual, but Ned is gay and knows he is gay; so do the other three. Each lad thinks, at one time or another, that the two to make it to immortality will be Oliver and Tim—because Ned and Eli aren't "real men."

Eventually, they make it to the fabled Arizona monastery, are reminded of the two-must-die rule and that the victims choose death freely. All the same, they enter as novices, a group of four the fraters call a "Receptacle." They begin the rituals, meditations, diet, physical exercise, and working in the fields. After a number of days and spiritual experiences and personal revelations, they realize that the fraters are "instructing us in nothing less than the *tao* of sex." Ned puts it this way: "I know the ancient spiritual significances of these sexual exercises, which are close kin to the various gymnastics and contemplatory exercises we've been practicing. Control, control, control over every bodily function, that's the aim here" (147). Then, one day without preamble, their Trial "moves into a new and raunchier phase" (149). Ned is presented with three women fraters. Being queer, he is immediately perplexed, but with coaching from Frater Leon, he performs the rite.

> Since life everlasting appears to depend on it, I will undergo the ordeal. And I advanced toward the parted thighs. With fraudulent hetero cockiness I sank my sword into the waiting wench. What now? Conserve your *ching,* I told myself, conserve your *ching.* I moved in slow stately thrusts while Frater Leon coached me from the sidelines, advising me that the rhythms of the universe demanded that I bring my partner to orgasm although I myself should endeavor not to get there. (148-149)

Indeed, two of the novices "graduate" from their initiate status, and two die voluntarily. The requisite death is Silverberg's invention; it is not required or even mentioned in tantric texts or practices.

The 1996-1997 best-seller *The Multi-Orgasmic Man* (Chia & Arava) elaborates the specific techniques for separating orgasm from ejaculation as well as for recycling the energy flow to the head and back to the navel, all conscientiously explained as Taoist. Despite the androlocal title, many passages also teach similar techniques for women and for gays. The influence of Asian spiritual sexuality will become all the more sensational with the popularity of this book.

Taoism, its focus on nature and *chi* and its tantric forms, eventually was highly influenced—some may even say supplanted—by a decidedly Chinese source: Confucius. Taoism had been quite popular by the later Chou period (770-222 B.C.E.) but less so among the rulers because they were absorbed by the daily pragmatics of maintaining and enhancing their power (Van Gulik 43).

An itinerant class of diplomatic counselors arose—the beginning of a middle class—and one of these was Confucius, who in direct contrast to Taoism, asserted focus on family and state. Confucianism may be characterized as an optimistic humanism instead of an earth mysticism (Noss & Noss 312-329). "Contrary to Taoism, unworldly and basically matriarchal in orientation, Confucius' teaching was fundamentally a practical philosophy adapted to a patriarchal state, he ignored mysticism and what we would call religious problems" (Van Gulik 44). Although Taoist norms did not vanish, Confucian norms took a different direction. Sexual intercourse retained the notions of stirring vitality for the man and woman, but the first and foremost reason for sex became producing offspring. No lack of ejaculative orgasm there—except to note that tantric *coitus reservatus,* the prevention of ejaculation so *chi* essence will flow (Van Gulik 47), was all the same a common practice for no less than two thousand years without adverse effect on population growth. The Confucian influence of public morality further cast sex as highly private, "not because it was considered as something shameful that ought to be hidden, but only because it was a sacred act, just like other ritual performances such as sacrifice to the ancestors and prayer, not to be engaged in or to be talked about in front of outsiders" (Van Gulik 50-51). Once again, the Asian conception of sex, although practical in Confucian terms, is still sacred, spiritual. As the Empire grew, the three religions or ways of Taoism, Buddhism, and Confucianism grew, sometimes together, sometimes apart. It is a cultural phenomenon that it was—and still is—not uncommon for a Chinese person to practice all three without necessarily thinking or feeling contradictions.

Among numerous sexual customs that may seem curious if not transgressive to Westerners are the practices of foot binding and the eroticization of women's feet, which "played a preponderant role in the sexual life of the Chinese" (Van Gulik 216). Li Yu, ruler of the Southern Tang dynasty from 937 to 978 C.E., is said to be the one who began this practice. Tiny feet for women had already earlier been prized and eroticized as the most tabooed part of the woman's body. Artists did not show bare feet, but showing them being wrapped or unwrapped was carefully iconed because of its pornographic closeness. A man touching the woman's feet became "the traditional preliminary to sexual intercourse" (218). Foot binding itself incapacitated the individual woman, usually deforming her—no small measure of patriarchal dominance—yet at the same time, the foot-bound woman was elevated in Chinese culture. Perhaps the elevation may be read as an inversive sign of dominance, yet it would be incautious to read all Chinese sex customs and texts only with the eyes and sensibilities of the West.

The Story of the Stone. A highly profiled text within Chinese culture is a novel variously named *A Dream of Red Mansions* (Chin 1978), *Dream of the Red Chamber* (Chin 1958), and "Dream of Fair Maidens" (Chin 1958 xii), among other titles and possible translations of the published title *Hung Lou Meng.* "Red mansions" and "chambers" conventionally refer to a woman's bedroom and elliptically imply a visit to her vagina, dream or not.

Different Chinese persons alive at this writing have told me that the tale is more popularly known as "The Story of the Stone." Indeed, *Dream of the Red Chamber* reveals its true name as "The Story of the Stone" in its first chapter, thus, naming itself (6-7). This feature of *Dream* is the frame narrative that explains how the tale originated, such as Chaucer's pilgrimage in *Canterbury Tales,* relief from the plague in Boccaccio's *Decameron,* Tolkien's conceit of Bilbo and Frodo merely reporting their adventures as their journal and recollections in *The Hobbit* and *The Lord of the Rings,* and the spirits of the violently dead's wrath in Barker's "The Book of Blood." More like Barker's version, however, *Dream* purports to originate from the intersection or union of the supernatural and natural worlds, although, as we shall see, it is even more than that.

In the opening of the tale, goddess Nügua repairs Heaven but excludes one and only one Stone from her repair. Even then, "Nügua had touched off a spark of life in the Stone and endowed it with supernatural powers" (*Dream of the Red Chamber* 1). Because the Stone was the only stone she had touched that she did not include in Heaven, it felt rejected, having consciousness, and it therefore continuously sighed over its misfortune.

Two monks, however, one Taoist, the other Buddhist, happen to sit near the Stone, who pesters them to help it enter the world of pleasure—in the Chinese phrase, "the Red Dust." The monks express their reluctance to assist, cautioning the Stone that although the Red Dust has its joys, they are far outweighed by sorrow and sadness. Their objections reiterate the Chinese prioritization of "Quiescence" over "Activity," "Non-Existence yielding to Existence" (2). Eventually, however, they consent to help the Stone, but only after the Stone makes a nuisance of itself, begging. As it turns out, the two monks are immortals, and they use their wisdom to transform the Stone into a translucent piece of jade on which they promise to inscribe the entire doings of the Stone in the Red Dust as the *Dream of the Red Chamber,* much to the Stone's delight. The immortals promise the Stone will live the lives of "a noble and cultured family and all the pleasures that wealth and position can bring" (3). The two immortals summarily disappear with the Stone, but eventually the Stone is discovered to have indeed visited the Red Dust and having its own tale inscribed on it.

> The story was that of the Stone itself. . . . The rise and fall of fortunes, the joys and sorrows of reunion and separation—all these were recorded in detail, together with the trivial affairs of the family, the delicate sentiments of the maidens' chambers. . . . The material appeared eminently suited for the beguilement of idle moments and the relief of boredom. (3-4)

The two immortals pass the Stone in the form of a pendant to a male character named Shih-yin and promise Shih-yin that all manner of spirits will incarnate themselves throughout the story. Thus the story begins in the Red Dust.

The tale weaves numerous themes and spiritual interests of many Asian cultures, and particularly that of Chinese culture that I have already noted: A nature goddess repairs Heaven, and a Taoist and Buddhist interact with deference to each other, without rancor or contradiction. The Stone's "spark" is *chi*, life force. The language of the story is poetically subtle, as in "the Red Dust" indicating the mortal world of pleasure. These themes are all the more remarkable when considering the literary traditions of China, because there were two such traditions, not one.

The two literary traditions in China did not interact until quite recently and, perhaps more precisely, reflect the oppositional categories of high and low, literary and popular, than in most Western modern and late modern writing traditions. What until the twentieth century was taken to be the only "literary" tradition in China was written by "literocrats," governing officials who were literate and familiar with Confucian, Taoist, and other ancient texts. The other tradition had been primarily an unwritten, oral tradition (*Dream of the Red Chamber* xii). Early written versions of oral tradition storytelling were memory aids for storytellers and were essentially collections of different versions of the same tales (xiii). Although one Chin Sheng-t'an in the 17th century extolled this "popular" literature, other than storytellers themselves, the predominant readers of them were "the semi-literate and schoolboys, or read to the totally illiterate by professional storytellers or the village scholar" (xiii-xiv).

Dream, however, broke tradition in that it became "the perennial favorite of sophisticated readers . . . which even the tradition-bound literocrats had to recognize as literature" (xiv). Moreover, unlike any of its predecessors in either the literary or oral traditions, Chin wrote *Dream* about his own life, his family, and its decline (xiv). The Chinese proclivity to emphasize family, group, and society had shown itself in all previous writings and storytellings, but never one's personal family. Thus, it is of no small interest that the most popular tale in China is the one that first defies the conventions of self-effacement and immersion into the greater good. Chin began the novel in 1742, writing 80 chapters; later chapters were added by family and editors (xvi-xvii).

The poetic circumspection of the tale reveals the racy nature of the story, if translated correctly with footnotes for Westerners and others unfamiliar with the subtle language conventions. For instance, a seemingly drunk servant accosts a boy of higher rank, Pao Yu, and the boy is totally clueless about the verbal assault. The servant, however, railed about adultery with his daughter-in-law by calling it "crawling in ashes" (78). The novel's translator, Wang Chi-Chen, at first took this sort of "trivial detail" as unimportant to what could be conceived as "essentially a love story. . . . But I have since come to realize . . . that these 'trivial details' are as important to the book as the story of Pao-yu and Black Jade. I have included, therefore, a great many chapters about the petty jealousies and the squabbles between the maids" (xix-xx). Indeed, young Pao-yu earlier had slept in the "chamber" of a married woman in chapter 5, a passage that intimates this was his first sexual experience, but disguising it as "a dream." "In a dream he seemed to follow Chin-shih to some wondrous place where the halls and chambers were of jade and gold and the gardens were filled with exotic blooms. He thought to himself that he would gladly spend the rest of his life here" but then he hears singing, and the singer is the Goddess of Disillusionment, who leads him to a place with a "stone arch" (53-54). On the one hand, both the chamber and the stone arch are emblems of a female's sex; on the other hand, the identification of them with "jade" and "stone" indicate the presence of the Stone. The Stone—as sex—appears in the suggestive language. Suggestive language may vary between cultures, but the use of language as suggestion in disguise remains a constant.

The tale of the House of Chia was and is so popular that its fame became problematic for a twentieth-century, Marxist government and thus received yet another translation into English but with a Maoist interpretation (*Dream of Red Mansions*). Attributing the novel's thematics to the decadent influence of a feudal culture, the story is cast as a class struggle (ii). "As the Chairman Mao has pointed out: **'The patriarchal-feudal class of local tyrants, evil gentry and lawless landlords has formed the basis of autocratic government for thousands of years'** " (iv; emphasis in 1978 version). Undoubtedly, the People's Republic of China's translation and interpretation of *Dream* are not unfounded in delineating the "patriarchal" oppression that, at least as appearances go, still runs China. More is to be said, however, than dialectical materialism can dictate.

Dream exudes multiple implicature. It folds on itself with soft touch and heavy-handed cognitive complexity. Its aesthetic density speaks and reflects itself in the layering of inert matter to human action, as Heaven and Earth intermediated by the human, social level of the House of Chia, as the hidden and revealed True Nature of All That Is, and, most materially, as grounded in the text's stylistics for storytelling that disguise lurid sexual events in seemingly innocuous turns of speech. The *Dream* is polysemous, and there is no one correct interpretation; the text itself begs for diverse interpretations that mirror and support one another. *Dream* is so highly self-referential, intertextual, and fractal-like in its repetitions that it belies these features as exclusively postmodern in spirit or by date. For that matter, Western, late twentieth-century readers of Lao Tzu would know not to credit their "postmodern" sensibility to poststructuralist criticism, if they allowed themselves to find the "postmodern" in quintessentially nonpostmodern-by-date texts. "Postmodernism" is a convenient and presumptuous Western colonization when its trajectories have been known and actively pursued in Asia for millennia—stylistically and not just substantively. Therefore, the most read novel by the largest population in the world—and presumably therefore, the most talked about novel in history—is no minor cultural phenomenon. The novel's polysemous immaterialism transcends and defies any dialectical materialism or Western indifference that can be imposed on it.

Japan

Eventually, Asian-continental norms reached Japan via missionaries of Kung Fu or the Chuang/Tzuan school. Chuang in Japanese becomes Zen. Once again, although basic spiritual norms and practices moved from West to East, the Chinese-renovated Buddhism found spiritual norms and practices already extant in the new land. Worship at phallic and vaginal standing stones had been incorporated into a yearly festival that celebrated the celestial marriage of two deities, the god Takeinazuminomikoto and the goddess Arata-hime-nominoko.

At the female shrine is a rock in the shape of a vaginal orifice; stalls nearby sell live clams as vulvic symbols, and during a parade a priest carries a banner with a clinical picture of the female genitalia. The male shrine has a large stone phallus at its entrance and houses hundreds of phalli of diverse sizes. The male principle is denoted by a parade of Shinto priests in which a banner of an erect penis is displayed, followed by a litter on which a ten-foot-long carved wooden penis is displayed. (Bullough & Bullough 213)

This fertility festival symbolizes intercourse, whereas other, similar festivals call for either ritualized intercourse or sexual license. Many of these standing stones are ancient and are not merely unshaped erections, raw chunks of rock; they are painstakingly articulated penises and vulvas.

Phallic standing stones still exist in Japan, although few inside cities. But earlier in 1931, in a well-known work on sexual folklore, Magnus Hirschfeld documented the sorts of people who regularly visit phallic shrines or make pilgrimage to them. From observation, interview, and notes left at these shrines by "villagers," Hirschfeld lists pilgrims from most frequent to least: (1) sterile women; (2) women whose children are ill; (3) women suffering from abdominal maladies; (4) impotent men; (5) men infected with sexually transmitted diseases; (6) unhappy lovers; (7) lonely men and women; (8) prostitutes and brothel owners praying for business, and finally, (9) those seeking relief from drought, sometimes whole villages (33-34). If one generally is knowledgeable of Asian beliefs in earth energy—*chi* or *ki,* as the term is borrowed into Japanese—then any sort of remedy expected at a phallic shrine is more understandable because the standing stone pulls earth energy up and distributes it in an umbrella fashion. Nature shrines worldwide are thought to deliver healing earth energy (Swan). This explains the first five categories.

It must be understood, however, that phallic worship in Asia may be linked to ancestor worship and the "creative link between generation and generation" (Hirschfeld 32). This further accounts for mothers seeking assistance for their children at phallic sites. Unhappy lovers may also need healing, but it is interesting that Hirschfeld discovered that "double suicides and individual suicides are consequently not infrequent in the vicinity of phallic stones" (33). Persons in the sex industry—prostitutes and brothel owners—as pilgrims to phallic stones are perhaps humorous, if not odd to some Westerners. But the last group of worshipers who desire rain may be a puzzle. Again, the belief in *chi* may aid understanding. A standing stone pulls *chi* up and distributes it in an umbrella pattern, thus lending sympathetic magic to the desired reality of rain.

Ghost Stories in Japanese Culture. Linkage between the supernatural and the everyday life of sexuality also permeates Japanese culture, particularly in the form of ghost stories and ghost lore. *The Tale of Genji* by Murasaki Shikibu, a Lady of the Emperor's Court near the year 1000 C.E., is a novel that predates Richardson's *Pamela* by almost seven centuries and frequently attributes the death of an illicit lover to vengeful possession. Of course, *Genji* itself is predated by Japanese folk religion that holds that "a vengeful spirit (onryo) is a human being who dies bearing a grudge and appears as a ghost to settle a score." Examples between the sixth and tenth centuries C.E. are widely known in Japanese culture (Barrett 97). Living spirits may also act independently of their embodied counterpart. Thus, in *Genji,*

> Prince Genji does not feel sorry when his girl friend is killed by the *living* spirit of his jealous wife. Still, fear of disgrace, that is, shame, outweighs his guilty feelings and he has the incident covered up. In another passage a wife's jealousy at being replaced by a younger girl is attributed to spirit possession. (Barrett 98; emphasis Barrett's).

Later, Kabuki theater enshrined this concept in the disfigured mask of a poisoned wife, eventually being remade as a film in 1959, the *Yotsuya Ghost Story on the Tokaido,* among other remakes (Barrett 100).

It would be a mistake, however, to conceive of the ghost story tradition as "high" culture not only because it originates in folk culture but because Japanese society is so homogeneous in race and ethnic heritage that what is high culture to outsiders is everyday life and commonly known. For example, perhaps one of the more internationally famous Japanese films of a ghost story that defies easy classification is director Kenji Mizoguchi's *Ugetsu* (1953). Although Mizoguchi wrote the film's screenwriter "how violence disguised as war oppresses and torments the populace both physically and spiritually" is the main theme of the film (McDonald 103), he cast that theme in tales already familiar to the Japanese audience and fused them with elements of a de Maupassant story (Buehrer 72), confabulating a film that appealed to an audience that liked ghost stories, particularly as a summer entertainment.

Couching perhaps a post-World-War-II Japanese sensibility in the sixteenth-century civil wars, the film presents two brothers who figure that the war is a great opportunity for Genjuro, a potter, to sell his wares and make a fortune and for Tobei, a farmer, to become a samurai. They set off to the city of Oziwa by boat to seek their fortune with their families. Along the way, Genjuro sets his wife, Miyagi, and son ashore for safety after being warned of pirates. Later at Oziwa, Tobei's wife, Ohama, gets separated from him when his zeal to purchase a suit of armor carries him to distraction. Ohama searches for him but a lustful samurai detains and rapes her, and she is literally lost, "eventually becoming a prostitute just to survive" (73). Ambition keeps both brothers going. A Lady Wakasa admires Genjuro's pottery and asks him to make a call to her mansion, which he does eagerly, thinking of the wealth he can garner. Once at the mansion, however, Genjuro falls under the Lady's spell, loses track of time, and forgets everything, until one day a Buddhist priest happens by the estate's garden and wises him up that the Lady is a ghost. As Barrett explains, "The ghost of this aristocratic lady . . . is malevolent because she died before she could become a bride, and therefore she eternally tries to entrap an unsuspecting male" (106). With Sanskrit spells inked on his flesh, the duped potter dispatches the Lady with a sword and awakens amid ruins the next day.

In the meantime, Tobei has become a warrior but by falsifying his reputation as a fierce samurai. One day, his retainers and he seek entertainment at a geisha house. To his dismay, he finds his wife there, an "entertainer" for other men, and takes her home to farming, realizing that his dreams are too dear. Genjuro returns home also and finds his wife waiting. Yet the next morning, she has vanished, and he finds that she too is a ghost, but a benevolent one who watches over him. Ugetsu's conclusion embodies what the Japanese call *mono no aware,* or the

> acceptance of the inherent sadness of life and the transience of all things. Genjuro's realization of the folly of his dreams of wealth have led him to the simple but virtuous life which his wife knew all along was best. To flow peacefully with life instead of fighting against it is a basic Zen principle and it is the heart of *mono no aware.* (Buehrer 75)

The film's conclusion also underscores the presumptuousness of male action and the eventual virtue of female yielding—from the Asian perspective. The Lady as ghost also personifies Japanese belief, not in that she never became a bride but in that she would have "no descendants to pacify her with memorial services"; thus she is a malevolent spirit called a *muenbotoke.* In contrast, the potter's wife, Miyagi, is a benevolent ancestral spirit (McDonald 104-105).

A European Interlude

Although Asian popular culture has recently begun to enter the lore of the West, many texts from the West, artifacts and events, have informed Western culture and still do so in late modern North America. For many reasons, Giovanni Boccaccio's *Decameron* is significant not just for its influence on sexualities but also for popular culture in general. At a critical moment in Western culture, the late fourteenth century, Boccaccio chose to write the book in the local vernacular of Florence, Italy—in Tuscan Italian, instead of in Latin. This choice of nonliturgical, common language inscribed a desire to reach an audience either unlearned or disinterested in Latin or removed from arenas of church and theology. Indeed, although the book begins with seven young ladies at a parish church, Santa Maria Novella, discussing their fates concerning the plague, they mutually decide to reprieve themselves from constant death by taking a vacation in the country. Thus, subsequently, all the tales they and three young men tell each other for entertainment are told outdoors; hence the name *Decameron,* which is a foil to the common Italian phrase *da chiesa* (at church)— *da camera* meaning outside church, uninvolved with or not dictated by church, or generally, outdoors. Also helped along with various works by Petrarch and Dante, vernacular Italian became the norm for Italian writing by the height of the Renaissance. In no small way did the choice of common language pave the way for popular culture told and shared in the ways of common folk instead of aristocrats and clergy.

Boccaccio's stated purpose for the book and its stories is quite intriguing, given both the historical context and recent concerns of feminism. In the preface, he wrote,

> In reading them, the aforesaid ladies will be able to derive, not only pleasure from the entertaining matters therein set forth, but also some useful advice. For they will learn to recognize what should be avoided and likewise what should be pursued, and these things can only lead, in my opinion, to the removal of their affliction. (47)

The "affliction" Boccaccio pointedly mentions is being a woman in love, ostensibly. Within the context of his prefacing comments, however, he describes, at length, the many avenues available to men for relieving their own afflictions and, alas, the delicacy of women. Although it seems Boccaccio is merely playing into conventional gender stereotypes, the preface ends, as cited above, with the ambiguous attribution "affliction," which could as well apply to the ladies' low estate. That said, the *Decameron* is a chapbook of various compromising situations in which women may find themselves set on by circumstances or men and how to extricate themselves, if they so desire. Boccaccio's targeting of women as his audience reveals something else important about Florentine culture: Apparently, there were a growing number of women who were literate and who had free time to read to themselves and to each other. Keeping in mind that the *Decameron* was "published" before the invention of the printing press, it is no small measure of the book's initial popularity that handwritten copies circulated avidly, with women as the main audience.

Although the one hundred tales told in *Decameron* are entertaining and at times quite ribald, they also portray commoners, aristocrats, and clergy equitably as venal, avaricious, stupid, and lewd and as sacrificing, prudent, intelligent, and modest. Boccaccio's tales have subsequently been taken as urbane commentaries on human foibles and sexual peccadillos. Ironically, Boccaccio's tales have been accorded canonicity. "Ribald Classics," published in early issues of *Playboy* magazine, were lifted from the *Decameron* both as paragons of Western literature—certifying *Playboy*'s classiness—and because Hugh Hefner could not afford to pay writers for fresh tales early in the publication's history. Brady's biography of Hefner spells it out. "Hefner tried to spend as little money as possible in getting his venture under way" (58). He spent considerable time and effort tracking down potential contributors as well as books and magazines to imitate. "For the most part, however, he searched carefully for material that was in the public domain, which at that time meant anything published before 1900" (66). Even then, Hefner did not begin with a fabled staff, corporate headquarters, and baronial demesnes. "The first three issues of Playboy were laid out and edited from Hefner's Hyde Park apartment" (79). The "Playboy Philosophy" also provided rationales for selecting tales for inclusion as ribald classics: (1) They must have plots; (2) they must be sexual; (3) they "must have an element of humor, or at least of irony"; (4) they must be short; and (5) they must be "briskly readable" (Russell 4). Eventually, other early, "classic" authors' tales were included, those of Guy de Maupassant, Voltaire, Addison, Herodotus, Balzac, and others.

All the initial ribald classics were taken from the *Decameron,* however. Plotting them in their chronological appearance reveals what may be called a marketing design of increasing transgression, considering the mores endemic to the early 1950s in North America. The first ribald classic is Boccaccio's "Day Eight, Tale Eight"; the summary of the tale that Boccaccio provides indicates the nexus of the ribaldry.

> A story concerning two close friends, of whom the first goes to bed with the wife of the second. The second man finds out, and compels his wife to lock the first man in a chest, on which he makes love to his friend's wife whilst he is trapped inside. (16)

The first few stories drawn from the *Decameron* featured similar cuckoldry, sometimes between friends, sometimes strangers, but always with scenarios of wife-swapping that exposed personal foibles of men and women and that posited pleasure as a remedy for them.

With spousal cheating transgressive enough for the times, not until *Playboy*'s seventh issue did Hefner dare to publish what may be considered the most risqué of Boccaccio's tales, at least in its near explicitness—the hilarious tale told by Dioneo at the close of Day Three, "Putting the Devil in Hell." An all too brief synopsis can only begin to convey the clever manner of storytelling that reveals all but actually never is fully explicit.

Alibech, a young woman, a bit simple perhaps, wants to become as holy as possible, and after exhausting all the possibilities in her home town—and exhausting every-one there with her persistence—she is told that out in the desert, she can find a holy man who can help her with her quest. Alibech makes the journey and encounters two hermits who, in their turn, are wisely afraid of Alibech's beauty and fervor as a temptation to their virtue. They are polite to her but send her on her way to the next hermit. Eventually, Alibech is directed to the last desert hovel where she finds youthful Rustico, "a very devout and kindly fellow." Rustico determines that taking Alibech as a spiritual student is exactly the sort of test for his iron will that he needs. Almost immediately on accepting her, however, Rustico is fiercely assailed with carnal desire. He tells her that the Devil has escaped from Hell and God wants them to put the Devil back in Hell. "Where is this devil?" Alibech inquires innocently. Rustico removes his garments, revealing "the resurrection of the flesh." Alibech removes her own garments and questions, "What is this sticking out in front of you that I do not have?" "That would be the Devil—and he's hurting me so much I can hardly endure it—but you have something else instead." "Oh?" "You have Hell." The two proceed to "put the Devil in Hell," and Alibech cannot get enough holiness.

This foray into storytelling raised the stakes of *Playboy*'s publication. The protagonists were single, not married. One was a holy man who apparently cheats on a vow of chastity. A canny reader would readily identify "Devil" and "Hell" as penis and vagina, that "putting the Devil in Hell" was heterosexual intercourse. By this time, *Playboy*'s circulation was not merely dependable but phenomenal and had reached an unquestionable niche in publishing that would be difficult to deter. An even more canny reader might see the inclusion of this particular tale as a new move in the Playboy Philosophy, or at least editorial policy, and that Boccaccio, and by implication, Hefner, was making light of a penis as a "Devil" to deal with and of a vagina as "Hell" with which to live. This was a new move in sexual self-deprecation, whereas it was also a new volley in the increasing popularity of the magazine, its owner, its influence. If nothing else, Alibech and Rustico were shockingly single with the one a holy wanna-be and the other already a successful hermit of sorts. The tale is just about as explicit as one can get without describing penis, vagina, and inter-course. *Playboy*'s circulation was dependable and safe; the new Boccaccio salvo presaged explicitness to come.

Other Historic Texts, Twentieth Century

Although literary fictions of erotica and pornography thrived by the beginning of the twentieth century, sex manuals and self-help books increasingly began to emerge as important historic texts. Earlier, Krafft-Ebing's *Psychopathia Sexualis* had been intended for the smaller audience of medical experts, and although Freud's various works were largely authored for the same sorts of focused audience, Freud's psychoanalytic practices earned a growing cachet, particularly because they seemed to free the sex drive, the libido, from its various oppressions. The notions of sex as a problem, a psychological one, and of sex as something for which one could get help, set the stage for manuals one could read, even if not in therapy. Thus, although the original translations of the *Kama Sutra* and other, Arabian texts into English sold immediately, the taste for more texts about sex increased. Works by Hirschfeld, among others, became good sellers in that on the one hand, they appeared to be scholarly, and thus acceptable as studious and not prurient, but on the other hand, they often seemed to be as much travelogues, merely reporting one's exciting visits overseas, a writing genre already established as popular.

Although a few, more clinical handbooks emerged at midcentury, the late 1960s and the widely acknowledged, heightened sexual revolution called for all manner of texts on sex, including reissues of the *Kama Sutra,* with pictures, and massage books. Reuben's *Everything You Always Wanted to Know About Sex (But Were Afraid to Ask)* and Comfort's *The Joy of Sex* were instant best-sellers, the first as humorous as it was serious, the second explicit in its information and in its encouragement that sex is good for you. Popular psychology received a boost from publication of books such as *Sex in Human Loving* by transactional psychologist Eric Berne. All these works had been written by men. With the women's liberation movement, it was perhaps inevitable that a truly different version of a sex manual would be written. Indeed, the Boston Women's Health Book Collective's *Our Bodies, Ourselves* did just that, being written collaboratively. Various sexual advisers appeared in magazines, such as Pat Califia in the earlier issues of *The Advocate* and Dr. Soothe in *GQ,* along with radio celebrities such as Dr. Ruth and Dr. Judy, both of whom have become widely circulated authors, with Dr. Ruth Westheimer herself a Sight for televisual media and a Sound with her catchy European accent. Manuals particularly geared for same-sex coupling include Hart's *Gay Sex,* Silverstein and Picano's *The New Joy of Gay Sex,* Tatchell's *Safer Sexy,* and Sisley and Harris's *The Joy of Lesbian Sex.*

Historic Publications of Sexual Orientation

Although no one nonfiction publication alone about sexual orientation may lay claim to being historic, a number of enduring writings and their authors deserve mention, particularly because the bulk of Western literature has featured heterosexual love relationships. Thus Gertrude Stein's "writing is both revelatory and secretive, and masks the lesbian subject matter it contains" (Malinowski & Brelin xi), whereas James Baldwin risked his reputation by being more explicit about same-sex love, particularly interracial love, heterosexual, homosexual, and bisexual. Oscar Wilde was imprisoned for his homosexuality. According to Bronski, the more blatant fiction in England and Germany was not available in America, so Horatio Alger's "pull yourself up by your bootstraps" novels "are clearly homoerotic," although not "blatant" (71).

By many accounts, World War II was a watershed in homosexual awareness. Thus, a series of autobiographies captures the problematic nature of realizing oneself as gay in mid-twentieth-century America, having to "come out" to oneself as a major accomplishment in one's life. Paul Monette's *Becoming a Man* relates his own early life resistance to same-sex attraction, his self-loathing, and numerous attempts to conform to heterosexual and dating norms. Monette's description of himself in relation to other men he knew clearly articulates what, in gay culture, is called "being in the closet," or hidden.

> Everybody else had a childhood.
> And every year they leapt further ahead, leaving me in the dust with all my doors closed, and each with a new and better deadbolt. Until I was twenty-five, I was the only man I knew who had no story at all. I'd long since accepted the fact that nothing had ever happened to me and nothing ever would. That's how the closet feels, once you've made your nest in it and learned to call it home. Self-pity becomes your oxygen. (1)

Eventually, Monette came out of that closet permanently, just like many other men of his generation. Martin Duberman reports a similar experience in *Cures,* although his emphasis is on the radical steps he took to "cure" himself of homosexuality, all of which failed. Eventually, he came to the conclusion that the mainstream psychological establishment of mid-twentieth-century North America had it all wrong; homosexuality is natural and can be quite healthy and embraced as a part of some people's lives. Stories such as theirs carry the historic impact of revealing personal triumph in a society largely hostile to them and also increasing visibility of coming to terms with being gay for others with various sexual orientations, letting them know they are not alone, serving as both testimonials and guides.

Later in the century, some texts of "coming out" in the military reflect public policy about sexual orientation while focusing on breakthrough individuals. Joseph Steffan's *Honor Bound* testifies how that meritorious West Point cadet was summarily discharged for acknowledging his homosexuality, just after graduation. Nor does an established, long-term career and distinguished record grant immunity; Margarethe Cammermeyer's *Serving in Silence* documents her experience with the military's "don't ask/don't tell" policy on sexual orientation. Although a U.S. Defense Department spokesperson denied the existence of any participation in the Gulf War by gays, and although various leaders debated the issue, Steven Zeeland reminds us that the arguments used by some detractors of gays in the military are reminiscent of racial discrimination in the armed forces. "Senator Strom Thurmond denounced Clinton with the same speech he used in 1948 to attack Harry Truman for integrating blacks in the military" (16). The mix of public policy and fear of homosexuals that yields potential injustices not just for homosexual individuals but an entire public is not limited to the military. Randy Shilts' *And the Band Played On* also documents the seriousness of dismissing any disease as a "gay" disease and, consequentially, not demonstrating much concern about the disease, letting it become a pandemic through governmental inaction, lack of funding, and lack of research. In the 1980s, it was already known that AIDS had infected numerous heterosexual populations worldwide, yet many Americans still saw it as a gay disease.

The near future undoubtedly will see the publication of numerous texts concerning sexualities and public policy. One particular area of public policy and sexuality has become enmeshed in "the culture wars": pornography. Although the clashes about pornography are themselves historic, the critics and activists rarely place pornography in historical or cultural context. Thus, I set aside the next chapter to focus on a cultural contextualization of pornography.

7

Historic Texts of Beauty: The Problematics of Art, Erotica, and Pornography

Art does not exist without a context. Never. Either it thrives as exciting and fresh or is ignored as commonplace in the culture that generated it, or it becomes reinterpreted when shared with other cultures, stolen by them, or uncovered by them centuries later. In Western cultures, particular conventions about art have been developed as a cultural tradition for centuries, particularly among the privileged. These conventions still influence late moderns and how they interpret art and find beauty or ugliness in art, particularly in art that conveys sexualities. These conventions go relatively unremarked when issues of obscenity and pornography emerge, which is unfortunate because the conventions themselves are formative of what may be taken as obscene or pornographic. The conventions of obscenity and pornography are invisible if all one notes is the obscenity itself; thus, before I discuss obscenity and pornography, I want to delve into their origins in Western philosophy of art and beauty.

Almost any artwork that conveys sexualities has become a contestable battlefield of knowledgeable dominance among culture critics, writers, and pundits. Statements about art that conveys sexualities can be deceptively simplistic and seemingly correct, but even the task of defining art is not so simple, let alone erotic art and its differences from and similarities to pornography. Then again, the lines between the nature of art versus the nature of the erotic and pornographic are themselves blurred.

Literary Art, Literary Beauty

Generally speaking, until quite recently, Western tradition has emphasized literary conceptions of beauty for art, even for nonliterary arts. Literary expression has been deemed the highest form of both art and beauty. The 1759 edition of Edmund Burke's *A Philosophical Enquiry Concerning the Origin of Our Ideas of the Sublime and Beautiful* maintains the aesthetic superiority of words, as used in poetry, oratory, and literature, over other arts—today called other media of communication—on the basis that not merely do superior arts represent images, they excite the mind. Artists such as Joshua Reynolds contested this literary bias by countering that all arts, not just word arts, excite and delight the mind.

> The great end of all arts is to make an impression on the imagination and the feeling. The imitation of nature frequently does this. Sometimes it fails, and something else succeeds. I think therefore the true test of all the arts, is not solely whether the production is a true copy of nature, but whether it answers the end of art, which is to produce pleasing effect upon the mind. (241)

Reynolds' *Discourses* has largely been ignored by literati, perhaps because he was, after all, a painter, thus only reinforcing the superiority of word arts as a latent Western cultural bias.

Although this summary of the Western tradition's spin on art and beauty is all too brief and itself seemingly simple, it displays the transparent, complex net of assumptions that were originally promoted in the classical period and which have been subsequently invented on and varied in various periods. It also displays the relative ease by which many Western literati still can distill the complexities of art and beauty to the alleged superiority of words. It has become an uncritical Western attitude that words hold the greatest potential for art and beauty. This assumption sets up a hierarchy of preferences that belittles other media as lesser in artistic merit. In other words, one type of communication medium has been valorized as the epitome of "high" art; all the rest is less, if not "low." Thus, the twentieth-century culture wars concerning popular and minoritized cultures versus "traditional" and high culture was preformulated in long-standing Western assumptions about art and beauty for thousands of years.

The Western way of understanding art and beauty with words superior is a habitual pastiche of seemingly orderly but all the same wishful thinking that involves (1) the mind and the traditional arts of the mind, (2) the location of the art "in" the artwork, (3) the determination of "good" art, (4) the artist as genius, and (5) beauty preferred over mere persuasion. Art resides in no simple definition; it lives in a series of interrelated, presumptive ratiocinative activities that work as biases for interpreting art.

As for art's connection to the mind, even when someone as incisive as Reynolds contests the assumption that literary arts are the most superior, he still claims that the goal of art in general is *to excite the mind.* In other words, the best art is mental. In this sense, Reynolds' critique of the Western tradition of art and beauty has also largely assumed that art at its best is cognitive and not so much for the emotions and imagination without the correctives of logic, dialectic, and reason.

Many theories of art also involve another material assumption that the work of art itself holds the beauty. The locus of beauty is not to be located in the individual experience of those who listen, read, or generally appreciate arts, nor is art, at base, to titillate the senses. In theory, anyway, because the excitation of the mind by the artwork must surpass emotion and imagination, the ultimate standard for determining if art is "good" concerns whether the artwork is didactic, an edification for the mind. Edification redeems any flaws—such as excitation of the senses or emotions—but cannot work at all without the assumption that the edification resides "in" the artwork, independent of the originating artist or subsequent appreciator.

In turn, the beauty "in" an artwork is deemed not to be caused by accident; it is caused by the work of a genius, someone who is an "artist." The common sort of person cannot instill beauty in an artwork as well or consistently as can an artist. The assumption that only artists can imbue beauty in an artwork is, at best, an elitist assumption. At worst, it prevents everyday people in their everyday lives from valuing the work of their own hands and minds as beautiful, perhaps even as valuable. Hence, except for so-called artful portrayals of sexualities—and particularly those that are literary—other media and formats that communicate sex are not "real" culture. The assumption that art is not supposed to titillate the senses without higher effect, however, is perhaps the most telling bias of all. Arts that arouse the senses and stir the imagination are suspect, potentially outlawable arts, just as Plato ordained about music in *The Republic* and as Aristotle opined in various works. For Aristotle, however, even literary norms of poetics insist on the production of catharsis in an audience for consideration as the best sign of artistic competence. Otherwise, and in general, however, as opposed to literary norms of art and beauty, the art of arousal was and is called *rhetoric.* Rhetoric persuades audiences to take action and is judged by the effect on the audience and not so much by the artwork itself. All of these assumptions about art and beauty that are common to the Western tradition conspire therefore against the erotic, the pornographic, the ugly, and the obscene, precasting them in the mold of the elite intellect as common, mean, demeaning, and, worst of all, literally—literarily—unthinkable.

The conventions about art and beauty are clear enough: Art that appeals to the mind, that expresses in literary fashion, and that certifies the genius of a handful of humans over the rest of humanity is acceptable, even if it portrays sex rather explicitly. Art that appeals to the senses and emotions, that plainly is crafted to arouse an audience's senses and emotions, and that allows that any human can be artful and create beauty is unacceptable, in polite company anyway, especially if it employs the arts of sexual Sounds, Tastes, Aromas, and Touches, even in literary form. In addition, the inclination toward the collective literary norms for art and against persuasive norms permeates Western communities in its formal education; in its legislation, administration, and adjudication of its laws; in its social services; and in the research all these sectors generate.

Arts that arouse with little or no appeal to the mind, as edifications, as pedantic, may easily be considered to display no "redeeming social value" and thus legally be called pornographic in the United States. *Erotic* art, however, which can be claimed to display redeeming social value, occupies a middle ground. If sexual portrayals edify, technically at least, they are not considered as pornographic but as erotic. For instance, Huer considers pictures of a man suckling a woman's breast for milk, which derive from the Western tradition of a Roman woman feeding a starving man, erotic, not pornographic; Huer maintains that sculptures and paintings depicting the act "could not possibly be considered pornographic despite what they show" (186). The question is this: Does the pornographic standard reside in the depictions or in the viewer? Presumably, if viewers are the beneficiaries of traditional Western education and thus know Roman history and mythology by heart, they will automatically process the pictorial data as an act of charity and not as an act of pure sensuality. It seems to be common sense that viewers not steeped in Western culture may process such depictions as pure arousals because they do not provide the needed cultural backstory to render the portrayals as didactic illustrations of charity. To insist that the former, erotic, interpretation is to be assumed and thus valorized in most if not every case of an artwork that is sexually-arousing-but-explainable-by-cultural-convention is sheer cultural imperialism.

Huer furthermore claims that "any object mass produced and distributed with the purpose of marketing it for profit by appealing to our sexual interests" is pornography (189). Huer's definition, coupled with the Roman charity example, underscores the problematics of art, beauty, erotica, and pornography in

Western culture. Until the possibility of mass production, arousing art objects were commissioned by rich, aristocratic men; were owned and displayed privately by the same community and were mostly unavailable to common folk; and were frequently prized as examples of the best of artistry, again, by rich, aristocratic men. Once the same images could be mass-produced, the elitist norm surfaces as the belittling of arousing artworks that could now be purchased by and distributed among common folk, that could be and are owned by many and displayed publicly, and that are prized because they are so arousing. By Huer's standards, postcards of Giorgione's painting, *Lunch on the Grass,* which displays two fully clad men and two nude women, sold by museums, gift shops, stationers, and bookstores, are pornography and not erotica, not that any man or woman was ever purely aroused with no edification by private display of the original painting or by its public display at the Louvre.

Other than the desire to make money, how does one determine the status of appeal? Huer posits appeal as "intentful." Then how much intention is enough to qualify an artwork as porn? Is there a standard scale that may (should) be applied to all cultures and all times that incontestably certifies the plethora of intentful appeal? It would be nice to know that arousal-as-intent could be easily read as a simple mechanism that all individuals and all cultures process identically. This assumption of nice simplicity alone is the origin of numerous sexual misinterpretations. Perhaps the most indiscreet misinterpretation of all is any narrative that maintains that arousal was not intended as sexually provocative in the artwork and that arousal resides "in" an audience, an interpreter. As the saying goes, "You've got a dirty mind" and find arousal where it was never intended. Notice that this attribution places arousal "in" a person, thus verifying the elitist hierarchy of beauty in the artwork that appeals to the mind, not a dirty mind, or a mind given only to the senses and emotions.

Arousing artworks in the possession of the privileged have therefore been valorized as "erotica" because well-educated in the Western tradition that they are, they read the erotica with their minds. The same artworks—originals or mass-produced artifacts—in the possession of the masses are considered pornography by experts paid for and supported by the privileged as well as common folk as tutored by so-called experts. Of course, the historical issues of erotica's male dominance do not seem to matter. Original sculpture and paintings can most certainly be made to arouse and sold for profit to individuals. That is exactly how the Western patronage system worked. Original artworks now, however, can be made to arouse and sold for profit to many persons. It seems moot that an earlier practice was permissible for the privileged but not for everyday people.

Antiporn and the Culture Wars

Allan Bloom presents a different take on pornography, one that apparently includes the more easily observed, usual cultural contexts for discussing it. Taking a modified "history of ideas" approach, he claims that changes in sexual relations in mid-twentieth century were driven by the civil principles of freedom and equality.

> The first was the sexual revolution; the second, feminism. The sexual revolution marched under the banner of freedom; feminism under that of equality. Although they went arm and arm for a while, their differences eventually put them at odds with each other, as Tocqueville said freedom and equality would always be. This is manifest in the squabble over pornography, which pits liberated sexual desire against feminist resentment about stereotyping. (98)

The passage reveals more about Bloom's approach to the situation and its issues than to the situation and issues themselves.

1. Historically, women's liberation, as a movement, preceded the sexual revolution of the 1960s by almost a hundred years, as did the early homosexual rights movement. The sexual revolution itself was as happening in the 1940s and 1950s as it could be, given there was yet no birth control pill; the media of sex that encouraged getting sex was already at work in the marketplace. Queers increasingly found each other in large cities after World War II. Dating patterns in the 1940s and 1950s variously involved "dating around" (a.k.a., sometimes, as sleeping around) and "going steady" (sleeping in a temporarily but continuing exclusive relationship).

2. The images Bloom chooses—"marched under the banner" and "arm and arm"—lends an air of militarism, suggesting perhaps favorably mounting the barricades in the streets, as in the French Revolution, or suggesting pejoratively marching under some ideology, something "commie" or leftist, no doubt, threatening true America. The image also pokes fun: These people take their desire too seriously and go too far in getting militant about it. The word choice immediately after the quoted passage continues the warring metaphor.

3. Perhaps most serious is the rather deceptive rhetorical move that makes it seem that what is happening about pornography and feminism is *only* a matter of freedom versus equality, that there is nothing else involved. So much for the reductive dismissals of the history of ideas approach. Something rarely dis-

cussed and interpreted by any of the players in the controversy is the economic distribution system involved in the porn industry. Perhaps the reason the economics and related features remain undiscussed is because most players buy into the sort of oversimplistic posturing inherent to the freedom versus equality binarism. When people accept a communicative mode of opposition, they usually do not go out of their way to find overlapping factors or arguments that seem not to support their own advocacy. I have interviewed enough porn "stars" to know a little bit about other factors. Typically, new "models" are dashed $1,500 to $2,500 per scene or day of shooting, flat rate. Each movie or video, however, can rake in hundreds of thousands of dollars in profit for the producers or studio that makes the flick. If that particular property sells even better, the money is phenomenal. Most models do not get a profit-sharing share; they just get the flat rate. Once a model becomes famous with fans who want to see more, the model may be able to parlay that into a bigger salary. Few of them earn fabulous salaries. Almost none have employee benefits, unless they too have become producers. In salaries, the class structure in the porn industry is just the opposite of what it appears to be. The models are the lowest class. The invisible, off-screen workers—producers, directors, and technicians—make better money, have more secure careers, and constitute the entrepreneurial class of technicians and artists. The owners, most invisible of all, are the upper class, dispensing minor gigs to their workers, keeping them faithful to the cause. Exploitation is a way of life, although many industry workers claim that the models do indeed get benefits—an intense sex life on- and off-screen, travel, and other variant factors such as hooking up with sugar daddies so they can be kept women or kept boys between films.

Many other factors are involved, but when Bloom does recognize other factors, he aligns them in his tidy diagram of freedom and equality. For instance, he opines that the women's liberation movement is naturally antiporn because it is basically "unerotic" (100). Although indeed, some leading feminists claim that all pornography is violence against women, Bloom's reading of the situation is far from the truth. He is apparently unfamiliar with Camille Paglia, Pat Califia, or early Susie Bright, among others, who are decidedly in favor of pornography, each in her own way. Perhaps he is unfamiliar with their publications and activities because they are mavens of popular culture and, thereby, on his own terms, unacceptable reading. Perhaps works by antiporn feminists such as Andrea Dworkin and Catharine MacKinnon are exempt from this rule, or they have even been admitted to the pantheon of elitism because they frequently consult for monied interests, particularly legal ones. It does seem odd that he is unfamiliar with *Our Bodies, Ourselves* (Boston Women's Health Book Collective), a work by women for women that clearly is not "unerotic" in its assumptions that if women are to have sex, they still can and should on their own informed terms. For Bloom to maintain that women's liberation is "unerotic" by nature is an absurdity that only shows his true mode of thinking: unitary, monolithic, and totalizing. Feminism is not a monolith—what a phallic assumption. And what a great opportunity he had to correct the record and place the controversy over pornography in the context of two thousand years of the literary traditions of art and beauty. One might have expected more that sort of cultural interpretation from an advocate of canonicity than an elitist fantasy masquerading as a cultural critique of sex and feminism.

Dworkin and MacKinnon are also on shaky ground. Their success at the legislated censorship of pornography has also led to the seizure and banning of their own works as obscene (Califia 108). The assumption that all pornography is violence against women is unusual in that it is totalizing: All of something is categorized as the same in all cases. There is no room for variation. That is legalized stereotyping. The assumption also perpetuates an unusual, stereotypical thought process, that violence is perpetrated by men and that women and children are always the victims. Without question, women and children have been victims of violence. Yet the perpetrators have not always been men. Sometimes, men are the victims, particularly of a vastly underreported crime of physical abuse from a spouse, usually, a woman. Ellis Cose refers to his interview with two professionals who know about domestic violence, James Sniechowski and Judith Sherven, who cite statistics that husbands and wives abuse each other in "roughly equal numbers."

> Sniechowski mentioned a male acquaintance of his who, in the midst of a horrible divorce, was beaten by his wife. He knew another man, a former college football player, who was similarly abused. Neither retaliated, he said, because they had been raised not to hit women. He was aware of yet another couple who were "battling it out." . . . Yet, he said, "We do not address the entire dynamic." Instead, society was "characterizing the pathology as a unilateral problem of the man." In focusing merely on brutal men, he said, we were wrongly telling women in such relationships, "There is nothing wrong with what you're doing. Only with what he's done." (204-205)

After many examples, Cose concludes that if we assume that it is only men who routinely whack their wives,

> We may ultimately lose sight of the fact that brutally beating one's spouse is aberrant and pathological behavior, not a gender characteristic, and that batterers are not

troops in some grand war between the sexes, but sick and tormented human beings. (237)

Extremity, Excess, Sublimity

Although intuitive, a judgment leveled against pornography that runs simply, "I know it when I see it," actually has become a legal test. The sex industry counters with lapel buttons that read, "Obscenity is whatever gives a judge an erection." The locus of this clash centers on obscenity as blatant and inarguable—self-evident. The critical and cultural assumptions that undergird this focus are not so simple and self-evident but multivariant, all conspiring pornography to fall into the commonplace argument of extremity and excess.

Extremity and excess are no strangers to the core values of Western culture. Attic Greek *arete* (αρετε) as *kalos k'agathon* (καλοσ κ'αγαθον), virtue as good-looking goodness, not one or the other, but both together, guided the myth of human perfectability early in the historical period. Even for Plato, inspiration and Dionysian frenzy could yield truth as well as logic (Dodds). Plotinus was concerned less with beauty than with sublimity, the very idea of excess incarnate to the degree of awe.

Not until the Romantic period in the West, perhaps, did extremity, excess, and sublimity fire self-articulate artists and become enshrined in common culture. Despite Burke's philosophic interest in the sublime, his contemporaries and he were well-tempered by Neoclassicism and at best can be characterized as preromantics. Barely forty years later, writers such as Goethe, Wordsworth, and Coleridge were keen on strong, personal emotion, unlike the preromantics. Coleridge, however, based his *theory* of poetics in part on the work of Immanuel Kant, "the venerable Sage of Konigsberg" (258), particularly with regard to sublimity and its reflection of the Divine. Fundamentally, as Kant maintained in *Critique of Judgment,* beauty is the representation of quality and the sublime is the representation of quantity with the superadded characteristic of boundlessness (82). Thus, Kant's fundamental conception of the sublime involved size, bigness, infinity, and the awe of infinity. Byron, Shelley, and Mary Wollstonecraft (Mary Shelley) took on themselves the mantle of sublimity, Mary Shelley particularly popularizing sublimity to the masses with *Frankenstein* and other Gothic tales.

Sublimity is perhaps better exemplified than defined: grand scale, striking exoticism and strangeness, the common as intensely emotional, dramatic contrasts of sensibility, and even the ugly and grotesque as sources of feeling. Unquestionably, Mary Shelley's *Frankenstein* embraces all these dimensions.

Please keep in mind here that I refer to the novel, not the Boris Karloff film version, which is vastly different from the novel, having removed the critique of aristocracy and male privilege, if nothing else. Grand scale is shadowed forth in Walton's ambition to discover the Northwest Passage. Striking exoticism may be found in the almost alien ice floes, isolation, and dangers of the frozen north. Walton's yearning for an equal, for friendship, is nothing less than emotionally intense. The "monster" is ugly, as are the soul and overweening ambition of Baron Victor von Frankenstein who created him. As for contrasts of sensibility, Victor is depicted as the privileged male aristocrat, spoiled by friends and family to the core—and he remains remotely insensitive to them—while the "monster" is portrayed as a child shockingly abandoned at birth, a child in psyche who may have adult male genitals but is conventionally female in almost every other way, desirous of affection, caring, learning as well as helpful, who, once born, must learn for himself, usually quite painfully, then becoming a continuous, avenging judgment of Victor's social standing and failed ambition. Mary Shelley's feminism cries the angst of women caught in a male world. The monster resorts to violence only when caring and intelligent empathy are not only ignored but attacked. The monster is a battered person.

In turn, Romanticism stood as oppositional foil to science and its sheer materialism, as the novel *Frankenstein* attests. Science itself was, and is, an extremity of sensibility, steeped in precise description, logic, and testability. In response to both, the elements of relativity predated Einstein's 1905 scientific breakthrough of the special theory of relativity (*Cambridge* 691) among artists, such as Cézanne, who had already honed painting to the sphere, cone, and cube by 1899. Muybridge's multiple exposure photographs of nudes in the late Victorian era (Hooven 12-13) surely inspired Marcel Duchamp's 1912 *Nude Descending a Staircase, No. 2* (Seigel 1) as much as Picasso's multiperspectival *Les Desmoiselles d'Avignon* in 1907 (W. Rubin 73). A new art of abstraction, wildness, and individual feeling played on the precisions of science and technology along with the imaginative capabilities of art. Eventually, by the middle of the twentieth century, hyperrealism challenged abstraction. Norman Rockwell and the Wyeths, among others, set new standards for the photosensuality of the common and the mundane.

While Western cultures imbibed themselves in the foreplays of logic and intuition, science and art interfaced with "maleness" and "femaleness," and new technological media formats developed that grew from and only reinforced extremity as a culturally dominant assumption. Maleness and femaleness became hypermasculinity and hyperfemininity in art, science, and technology. Photography's realism challenged painting with new media capabilities. Film challenged theater as action in the form of action. Sensationalist journalistic reportage, instead of more studied prose, charmed vast populaces. Computers and the World Wide Web have delivered interactivity as well as hyperreal, synaesthetic formats that have only begun to be explored, and, of course, the freedom of expression that went so far as free access to sexual communication, which was bridled by the U.S. Congress and confirmed by the president, mostly under the guise of protecting children. Hence, proof of legal majority—usually being 18 years of age or older—has become commensurate with buying power, because most often now, access to sexual communication on the Net is limited to credit card wielders, usually only gainfully employed adults. This is a capitalized and abridged freedom of communication.

All these trends, and more, inform the preeminent status of pornography as publicly private and as private publication. It would be difficult, perhaps nonsensical, to attribute all these cultural vectors of excess as male or female, heterosexual or homosexual. Although supposedly men are "balanced" and women are "prone" (an interesting word concept of dominance) to excess, these judgments do not hold true in all, or even most, cases.

Thus, the conceptual phenomenon of obscenity as excess is a long-standing cultural habit in the West. The technologies and media may be new, but the tendency and drive for it are not. Although this contextualization does not excuse pornography, it goes a long way toward describing how it is even culturally possible, if not compelling.

Shame Culture

Although I have already argued, in agreement with numerous other culture critics, that Western cultures are sex-negative, it is more accurate to clarify that observation by saying that this sex negativity is largely based in shame. Perhaps then, a fundamental issue of pornography is not that it is bad or exploitive but that it announces and activates our cultural shame so much that we easily impose shame on those who enjoy portrayals of sexualities and on those who create them. Only recently has male frontal nudity appeared at newsstands and, increasingly, in films, revealing the former privilege and protection of male genitals but also exposing the penis as emblem of shameful arousal. Nudity alone may be arousing for some people, with no sexualization portrayed other than the nudity itself. Thus, any mediated portrayal of nude humans becomes suspect as shameful in artistic intent, if not audience interpretation.

In the West, the Urtext of nudity-as-shame is mythically creational: Adam and Eve in the Garden of Eden. I propose, however, that nudity-as-shame is a severe misreading of the Edenic Myth. As the character Toddy maintains in the film *Victor/Victoria,* "Shame is an unhappy emotion invented by pietists to exploit the human race." Please keep in mind, then, that as I remythologize the Edenic Myth, I knowingly shift the onus of exploitation from nudity and its sexual portrayals to the unauthentic hermeneutics of a cultural order of dominance over all bodies, female and male.

The Epistemologies of Shame

Epistemology is the study of knowing and of how humans know. Perhaps one of the most crucial ingredients in misreading the narrative of Adam and Eve centers on the tree from which they eat and their ability to know anything. God tells them that the tree is forbidden (Genesis 2:17, King James Version), information Eve accurately conveys to the serpent later (Gen. 3:3), which, as explicated in Chapter 5, is a taboo, ripe for transgression. Both God and the "serpent" claim the tree's fruit grants knowledge of good and evil. Note well that the tree does not grant knowledge, but a particular type of knowledge. Adam demonstrates the ability to know when he names the beasts (Gen. 2:20). Eve demonstrates the ability to know when she concludes that the tree of knowledge of good and evil is good for food (Gen. 3:6). Thus, Adam and Eve consciously exercised knowledge *prior* to the deed of eating from the forbidden tree. One more observation before continuing: In their state of primordial knowing, "they were both naked, and were not ashamed" (Gen. 2:25). Prior to eating the fruit of the tree of the knowledge of good and evil, they and no one else, including God, knew or said they knew that being naked is shameful.

Once they eat of the tree, however, "they knew that they were naked; and they sewed fig leaves together, and made themselves aprons." On hearing God nearby, taking a walk in the garden, they hide, and God asks them why they are hiding. Adam's answer? "I heard thy voice in the garden, and I was afraid, because I was naked: and I hid myself." God answers immediately, "Who told thee that thou art naked? Hast thou eaten of the tree whereof I commanded thee that thou shouldst not eat?" (Gen. 3:6-11). The development of this conversation is quite plain. God never says being naked is bad. Adam does. God points out that that is a direct result of having eaten the forbidden fruit by asking if they had. The shame that Adam and Eve now experience is their own decision extending their knowing ability to good and evil. They decide good and evil now, not just God, but their judgment may be, and probably is, fallible.

Adam's initial answer is a minor lie. He does not admit that he has eaten of the forbidden fruit; he only mentions fear, because he was naked. Note well that

Adam and Eve are wearing aprons. They are *not* naked. Adam's answer is sheer evasion, which God calls him to confess. They are fearful from disobedience, not nudity. When Adam answers God's direct questions about eating from the tree, instead of evasion, Adam transfers the blame to Eve. Note again that this new knowledge allows Adam to cast blaming judgment on another. God never says Adam is correct in doing so, but he does cast them from the garden, but not before he asks Eve to explain herself. Her answer? The serpent made her do it. This answer too transfers blame and is a knowing judgment. It is not until Adam and Eve are east of Eden that they "know" each other and bear a child (Gen. 4:1). Temporally and spatially removed from Edenic existence is when they have sex, not before. There is nothing to indicate that eating of the tree is sexual at all; eating of the other trees is surely not sexual.

Shame culture begins in hiding nudity and perpetuating that concealment, then evading the shame, then in transferring the shame to someone else—all human judgment, acting as gods. God does not accuse them of nakedness! The mythoplex of Adam and Eve in the Garden of Eden delivers mythic expectation: They live in harmony with only one, simple rule of tabooed avoidance. They violate that taboo. They then cast judgment on themselves that nudity is shameful, something to be hidden, and then they engage in accusing someone else of their shame. Thus, we inherit shame culture from Adam and Eve, not because God wants people to feel ashamed but because Adam and Eve knew shame. Shame is not natural; it is an artificial, social construction of humans, mythically, who are Adam and Eve.

If ours were not a shame culture, portrayals of nudity, let alone sexual activity, would probably not be experienced as transgressive, or at least, not nearly as intensely. Removing shame from everyday life would go a long way to removing the tantalizing edge of nude and sexual communication. The obscenity of pornography is not the depiction itself but the cultural assumption that that depiction is shamefully transgressive at all. Thus, those culture critics who excoriate pornography, its audiences, and its makers, particularly to the point of condemnation and censorship, come close to perpetuating the very shame culture that oppresses women—and others—in the first place. The enemy, if that is really ever an appropriate word, is the elitist proclivity to keep people in place by shaming them. Antipornography activists who employ shame as a tactic perpetuate the dominance they say they decry. By focusing almost exclusively on pornography, these ideological pundits miss the greater reality that shame culture is more all-pervading than pornography; shame culture is present in people's everyday lives when pornography is not. If they would attack shame, then through time, pornography would lose much of its appeal. Attack the symptom, and it will not go away. Shame culture is much more involved than the commodification of smut, much more than the reification of dominant shame exclusively to pornography. Shame culture begins and perpetuates itself in hiding the body. Censoring nudity and pornography perpetuates shame culture.

The Pornography of Everyday Life:
The Plain, the Ugly

If one considers the entire, almost three thousand years of trends that inform the mythoplex of shame culture, including beauty norms and their trajectories into plainness, commonness, or ugliness-as-obscenity, a different matrix of sexualization emerges to the senses, ready for diverse scrutiny. Underneath all those hiding clothes, a man is supposed to be muscular, hard, and strong. His attire should reflect practicality, even at dress occasions, that is, uniforms and their crisp cuts and lines. In contrast—and here I am well aware that the way I am setting this up defines woman in relation to man; I am reporting, not agreeing—a woman is supposed to be soft and enduring. Her attire should reflect the leisure that man's practicality affords—frills, adornments, ornamentation, and cosmetics.

As clothing changed, so did the fashions of body image change during the past century in North America. Both male and female are haunted by sublimity, by bigness and extremity. A big man is a threat; a small man is not much of a man. A woman should bulge correctly, not too much, not too little, but a woman was, well, womanly if she were ample. Some degree of bigness because of fat in either sex indicated prosperity, particularly in older people, but obesity—again the intrusion of sublimity—was, and is, not conventionally acceptable. Only temporarily did the "flapper" seize urban cultural scenes as a desirable, flat-chested, and slender woman—until the anorexic fads of leanness in the late twentieth century. The likelihood that a woman of ample, preferably hourglass figure was a cultural constant until the 1960s may be illustrated by countless voluptuous pinups and the Barbie Doll's impossible measurements of slenderness *and* bigness. In the meantime, what at the end of the nineteenth century was bulgy muscularity for men increasingly became diverse, all preferably lean *and* muscular. Men are to be sleek swimmers and runners or body builders with bulging biceps (but still lean). Women's diversity from amplitude became prizes of petiteness, especially as proved by tiny waists, but women were still expected to have large breasts and perhaps hips.

Anyone who does not come close to these norms of body image may be considered plain, if not ugly. Norms of facial comeliness also create a culture of plainness and ugliness. If one is ugly, even just plain, one is shunned, even though ugliness and grotesqueness may occur at birth, yielding a kind of natural sublimity that is so extreme that it is deemed repugnant. The plainness and ugliness, however, are not inborn; they are culturally born, nurtured by shame culture that worships literary modes of beauty. Thus, in a predominantly light-skinned culture, blackness in and of itself was taken as a sign of the grotesque, stereotypically enshrined in minstrel shows (Engle), in Mandingo warriors, in a "mammie" and her breasts, all to feed the babies for the white woman who culturally was told that breast-feeding itself was gross. Each of these shamed stereotypes, and more, received reeroticization and renewed self-image in the 1960s, initially stirred by the maxim, "Black is beautiful."

Other people whose extremity transcends racial, ethnic, and class boundaries also have been and are shamed, namely, fat people. Obesity is congealed culturally as unnatural, something surely individuals could manage better if they only tried, as if there were only one or two body types that occur in nature. Assumptions such as this only fuel biases against employment and dating. Someone who is fat is either mostly nonsexual or just too "jolly" to care. Oppression of fat people has also required a reeroticization and renewed self-image of obesity. Various magazines have emerged, particularly by women about women. In gay culture, there are such proclivities as "chubby chasers," although certainly they are not limited to gay culture; neither are hairy men or "bears" who many times are slightly older men with a slight amplitude or bigness to obesity. Even then, there are shame norms. Hair on the chest is best but hair on the back is tack(iness), although not for everyone. Once again, hair is something genetically, naturally determined. The cultural norm mitigates against secondary sexual characteristics such as hairy armpits and legs for women in favor of light sprinkles of hair for men. Mostly hairless men, particularly young ones, are "twinks." Shame norms for hair have also called for reeroticization and renewed self-image.

Short people and, particularly, the little people, are also subject to aversion by taller people. They encounter a sense of shame about it, as do otherwise "regular"-looking people who, although they have no physical differences in body and facial proportions as do many little people, are still noticeably less in stature than most. It is no accident that the little Oompah Loompahs in the film version of *Willy Wonka and the Chocolate Factory* are decidedly sexless. Men less than six feet receive less admiration than men taller than six feet; men less than five feet five inches literally expect to be looked down on and are less frequently the object of sexual advance. Women less than five feet may be the objects of desire for many men, yet the less below five feet, the more fragile she is expected to be. Tall people are walking bigness, and North American cultures accord them status and riches. Basketball plays proof to that, so much that Dennis Rodman claims that *the* sport for attracting potential sex couplers is basketball.

> The NBA [National Basketball Association] is the place to go for hot women. If you want your choice of women, this is the place for it. You don't go to football or baseball. . . . Within sports this wasn't a secret, but it started getting more attention after Magic Johnson revealed that he was HIV positive. That put the focus on sex in the NBA. . . . I wasn't prepared for the sex part of NBA when I first got into the league. . . . I'm not the best looking guy around, but people want to fuck Dennis Rodman. It's true for both females and males. (145-146)

It isn't that Rodman is an athlete; he's a *tall* athlete. Sexually, being tall is nothing shameful.

So far, I have considered only naturally occurring features of the human body that earn aversion or attraction, rendering shame on the averted for no other reason than it is a cultural habit, dissociating that it is. These body characteristics are not chosen. Lesbians and gay men face this cultural dissociation in a different manner because many people think that their sexual orientation is chosen, not naturally occurring, and that, consequently, any queerness in their public personae is also chosen. Thus, gays and lesbians are subject not merely to shame and scorn, if not outright hate crimes and physical assault, but also to self-loathing. The following excerpt from a longer interview is rather typical for many gay men. When asked why he chose a military career, "Doug" answered,

> I didn't want to admit the fact that I was gay. It's like everyone else at that age, I guess. Where you know you are, or you're fairly sure that you are, but you don't want to be. Or at least I didn't want to be. And maybe I thought that this was a way to prove I was macho or whatnot. (Zeeland 168)

"Doug" also reported that he is usually taken as straight by his mannerisms. Notice that he feels that his orientation is not a choice, that he would choose heterosexual orientation if he could. The way he appears to others in his case, however, is a choice.

At the turn of the nineteenth to twentieth century in New York City, naturally occurring orientation and chosen public personae were negotiated differently. If a man knew he was gay, he had two options, to pluck his eyebrows and act nelly, even if he was not "feminine" in the first place, or to "act like a man" and socialize with the nelly men anyway, always assuming the dominant, penetrative posture. As George Chauncey reports, this was acceptable for both sorts of men interested in sex with other men, not in the middle classes but the working classes (33-97). The stereotype, then, of a homosexual with a lisp, limp wrist, dandified clothing, and feminine airs eventually then became the iconage of gayness for men. By the end of the twentieth century, there has been no small amount of confusion about the natural occurrence of homosexuality and the later, acculturated assumption that anything that shows, usually some sort of abnormality from the usual gender performance, is a result of the homosexuality, chosen or not. In other words, many people, including some queers, seem to think that appearance is not chosen but follows automatically from the queerness. As one young man wearing Bass Weejuns, Dockers slacks, Izod polo shirt, and a Land's End windbreaker recently volunteered to me,

> I was seventeen, and I heard there was this weekly meeting for young lesbians and gays, a support group. It took me three weeks to get up the gumption to go and was I afraid! I got there, my heart pounding, and I was so surprised. Everyone looked normal!

I asked him to clarify that. "No weird hair or clothes and that night, no pierceage or fagginess."

Fear of finding oneself to be attracted to the same sex in the teen years involves not only shame but also trauma to the point of suicide.

> Gay teenagers are also prone to suicide. The Centers for Disease Control has studied adolescent suicide and come up with a truly gut-wrenching statistic: Fully one third of all teenagers who kill themselves are gay.
>
> It's not difficult to understand the prevalence of gay suicide. Being gay at this age can be traumatic in our society. High-school counselors are generally as homophobic as the general population. Their main aim is getting the teen to conform, i.e., to be less openly gay. (Silverstein & Picano 189)

Shame culture kills, and it keeps gay teen suicide quite secret. Recently, in a Midwest middle school, an eighth grader committed suicide. School was dismissed for twenty-four hours, and on resumption of classes, there were mandatory assemblies that provided information about suicide, its causes, and its signs. More than a dozen psychologists and counselors were made available to students during the next few weeks, ostensibly to help the students through their grieving but also actually to catch any sympathetic suicides before they happened, for such is the epidemiology of teen suicide. When asked about the information, various students reported it all quite well. When I asked any number of them about dealing with sexuality, however, they claimed that yes, that could be a cause, but they reported nothing about orientational issues, which is strange, given the statistics that one third—the largest percentage—of teen suicide is orientationally related. Shame culture, however, appears to be keen on keeping it a secret. That same week, at a Midwest university's counseling center, all flyers on suicide I found made no mention of sexual orientation as a possible cause of suicide or that orientational issues could be dealt with just as easily as any of the others. I discovered similar flyers at five local psychologists' waiting rooms and informed each professional that their free literature was deficient. Some of them corrected the situation. I told my own children about that possible indicator of suicide, and they shared with their friends the information that orientation is nothing to be ashamed of, that there are professionals who can and will support them.

Excorporated Shame

Perhaps some gay and lesbian cultures—as well as rock stars and other musicians and their cultures—have led the way in neutralizing shame culture. They have chosen personae that take what mainstream culture stigmatizes as shamed and then excorporate it, cultivating it into a look of desire, into a series of expectations and habits in their everyday life. Thus, "Generation X-ers" (Gen X) in the United States, as well as diverse ages in other Western countries such as Canada, have taken the excorporation of shame to heart. Whether plain, good-looking, or ugly by nature, they work on it and do not settle for conforming looks. As one T-shirt manufacturer has its mascot JOCKO claim about looks and beauty: "Do the best you can with what you've got, but *remember:* Nothing is more disappointing than a beautifully wrapped package with no gift inside. Cultivate your inner gift" (emphasis JOCKO's).

Thus, what is adamantly taken to be repulsive by generations older than Gen X has been self-chosen *because* it is repulsive or grotesque—sublime. It is not just clothing that may change by the whim of fashion; it is usually more permanent, a self-mutilation, including tattoos, body piercing, scarification, and other body arts. In addition, although candid exploration of sadomasochism is not a requirement of Gen X or gay and lesbian cultures, reports from various participants affirm that by mutually determined scenarios, S/M scenes neutralize shame and resensitize persons to their own bodies and feelings as well as each other's. Leather and latex cultures may or may not overlap with body mutilation and art or Gen X, for that matter, but clearly, the leather look is not acceptable mainstream attire enshrined in John Malloy's *Dress for Success*. Leather, particularly black leather, is associated with delinquency and danger.

The sensation over Robert Mapplethorpe's photography to be displayed in public dramatically announces the play of these sorts of excorporated shame with art and pornography. Many of the photos clearly show what is normatively taken to be obscenity, such as two men engaging in explicit sex. If viewers can get past the alleged obscenity, however, they might see a few other features, that tattoos, piercing, and leather are incorporated in the frame, themselves excorporations of shame culture. If viewers focus on the obscenity exclusively, all they will see is obscenity. They will not see design, chiaroscuro, and so on. They cannot see the art. And any touch of body art, S/M, or leather only adds to the repulsion many viewers might feel. Therefore, Mapplethorpe's true art is not photography but performance art that deconstructs hatred: Viewers who censor it paradoxically validate it. They think they are denying the obscenity, but that is the point; they only prove that that is all they see. Their rejection is stigmatized validation of the photographs' deconstructive impact, not denial of it.

8

The Horror of Sex

Various factors influence the connection of sexualities and horror. Horror fictions in the late twentieth century partake of, continue, and extend a long-standing literary tradition of pity and fear in the West. This literary tradition—elitist, definitely, at its outset—has massaged Western culture with numerous formulas for horror stories for more than two thousand years. It is altogether fitting and proper, then, that a discussion of horror and sex begins with the sketching out of two notions of formula: (1) formulas "in" a story—a typical popular culture studies approach—and (2) how artists employ formulas to evoke formulaic audience appreciation and experience of the horror story. Once these two areas of the critical tradition are addressed, certain other important issues and artifacts will be discussed.

The Ecology of Horror: Aesthetic
Conspiracies Between Artists and Audiences

The use of formulaic patterns in artworks intended to horrify audiences is as new as Clive Barker's animated feature *The Thief of Always* and as old as Sophocles' *Oedipus Rex*. The late modern zeal for popular artistic horror is no more a sign of the decline of culture or public standards of taste than the tragedies of ancient Greece. Certain features of horror fictions in the twentieth century are quite different from ancient horror fictions, particularly spotlighting a common working person such as Sigourney Weaver's role of Ripley in the *Alien* series of films as the protagonist, instead of an aristocrat such as Electra in the play *Electra*. The late modern diversity of media formats for communicating horror and the zeal audiences demonstrate for that variety is as much an indication of what has become of the long-standing human tradition of horror as the changes in the artifacts themselves. Observing both the long history of horror in the arts and its late modern renaissance reveals that the formulas for communicating horror are legion.

Many commentators about horror espouse their favorite observation about horror as a recurring pattern to be found internal to the work of horror, be it a novel, film, or painting. One of the more popular suggestions about the formulas that drive horror is voiced by Stephen King. King maintains there are four major subtexts that reveal the main assumption underlying a horror story. These underlying assumptions deal with real-world concerns and thus reveal that horror is a criticism of our culture and its trends: (1) The economic subtext is revealed in *The Amityville Horror,* which is really a story about making ends meet—the horror of the shrinking bank account; (2) the political subtext of *The Thing* emerges as fear of Russians and their communism in the 1950s; (3) the technological subtext is exemplified by *Them!* which is only a thinly disguised criticism of nuclear testing run amok; and (4) the social subtext of *The Exorcist* is the fear of baby boomers coming of age and taking over during the Vietnam War (*Danse* 131-174).

Although these subtexts and other observations like them (e.g., Walter Evans; Jones; Munster; Underwood & Miller) explain some of the formulas to be found in horror artifacts, they miss one important factor. Horror is also something the audience feels and vividly experiences. If it is located in the artwork at all, it is just as importantly if not more importantly also located in the audience. Scholarly sources miss this rhetorical, audience-oriented dimension; at best, they assume it but do not really discuss its workings. More than that, horror is a way people experience certain facets of life, and therefore horror fictions are mimetic or imitative and evocative of people's everyday life. There is an interface between artists' deployments of horror formulas and audiences' all-too-ubiquitous familiarity with horror, anxiety, pity, and fear in their everyday lives.

David Hume perhaps says it best when he asks why people pay good money to attend theater performances that frighten them or make them cry. How could horror be so pleasurable? Unsatisfied with the answers other philosophers had given (Aristotle and Fontenelle), Hume offers an opinion worth considering. Humans like to be scared *when the scaring is done well.* In other words, yes, humans delight in the safe fright that artistic fictions of horror offer, but the clever crafting of the fright is what we most admire (258-265). Other arts, and not just horror fictions, use formulas to delight audiences (Reynolds 229-244).

Let's talk a little bit more about other horror formulas artists craft into their artworks to generate delight of horror.

As we turn from the artifact alone and also consider the additional effect the artifact is to produce, we move from literary modes of understanding art to rhetorical modes. *Rhetorical* in this case means producing effects in an audience, just as it meant for Aristotle some two thousand years ago (*Art*). His concern, however, entails how an orator might persuade audiences by means of speeches. The concern here is different—how artists produce horror in audiences by means of horror artifacts such as movies, television shows, comic books, video games, novels, and short stories.

Most often, artists produce horror in audiences by presenting information crafted in narrative form. "Narrative form" means that the horror is presented as a story told about characters, and it takes time for the storyteller to tell the story and for an audience to experience it. This temporal feature of narrative is perhaps its most obvious characteristic, yet it is nonetheless central to the crafting of a story. Providing data to an audience to scare them could be as simple as showing someone being slashed by a meat cleaver, taking perhaps far less than a paragraph in writing and less than ten seconds of screen time for a film. Merely telling or showing something gross in an arbitrary manner, however, may not excite an audience nor entice them to admire the presentation of the grotesque. Artists frequently prepare audiences for their most gruesome scenes through many pages in a book or during many minutes in a movie. Thus, horror narratives fluctuate like waves with swells of fright sandwiched in between troughs of recovery. Recovery troughs often involve character development or background.

In addition to the temporal nature of storytelling, narratives also involve a relationship between the story, audience, and storyteller. Most types of storytelling separate the story from both the storyteller and the story's audience. That is, the storyteller provides any number of clues that the audience is to keep a sense of distance from the action. The audience is not "in" the story; the reader is reading and is sometimes reminded of this by the narrator's talking directly to the reader as if separate from the action. Such clues insulate the audience from feeling too ill at ease during painful scenes.

In contrast, many horror narratives, particularly late modern ones, more frequently work at erasing or minimizing the perception of distance between audience and story. Terry Heller refers to this feature of horror stories as decreasing aesthetic distance. Perhaps the materialistic nuance of distance might better be called *difference,* a concept that includes the notion of distance but also signals mental, cognitive, and symbolic separation. Thus, the equally materialistic metaphor of decreasing difference might better be signed as convergence, because the verges, the margins of artistic object and human consciousness, become blurred at the margins conventionally conceived as distinct borders. Thus, "decreasing aesthetic distance"—particularly considering Wolfgang Iser's phenomenology of reading, *The Act of Reading,* on which Heller bases the concepts in the first place—becomes "converging difference," thus erasing materialist ideology from the intentionality of reading. When difference converges, the artwork and reader become one, and in the case of a horror story, the reader *is* the story and vulnerable to its threatening activities. The more the readers feel that the story could happen to them—*is* happening to them—the scarier the story. This leads to any number of strategies for decreasing the audience's sense of distance from the story, or better, for converging story and consciousness, such as describing or presenting physical or psychological pain in vivid detail, such as showing the victim living through mundane experiences the readers have probably undergone, such as getting the readers or viewers to admire the victim so they will identify closely with the victim, and, finally, such as delaying the closure of a horrible situation—not finishing the chase scene but continuing it just when the audience has attained a sense of relief in thinking it is over. In other words, horror artists play with readers' minds. When they do it well, we are delighted.

That horror artifacts so conscientiously manipulate the audience not only sets horror apart from other artistic genres that work at converging difference, it also demonstrates the interactive essence of horror. The basic formula of horror is an ecological formula and is not found "in" the horror artifact alone. Horror is an environment of human experience that exists as the classic communication model in which artists and audiences communicate by means of an artwork that the artist initially creates. The audience, however, must re-create the artist's experience in some manner satisfactory to them as part of their experience (Collingwood; Croce; Dewey). It is not simple to make observations about horror formulas that will be true for all horror stories, on either the ecological or artifactual levels of formulas. For instance, horror found in literature and in film may have similarities, but one must also expect and be able to account for differences. Clive Barker's novel *Cabal* shares the basic plotline of Barker's movie *Night Breed.* Both may be assessed and compared for their narrative structures and for how various artifactual formulas scare audiences. On the other hand, *Night Breed* concretizes the story with a fixed look. Anyone who reads *Cabal* can concoct a different face for each of the main characters, a look that may not agree with another reader's, but persons who see the movie know that most of the decisions about how a character looks are made for them before they ever see the film. On screen, Boone—one of the main characters—may not look like the protagonist fantasized through reading.

Night Breed also adds sound effects and music, both of which enhance the effect of horror and both of which are not part of Barker's novelistic medium. Music itself has acquired special meanings for specific combinations of pitch, instrumentation, and timing. We accept them as formulas of horror. We accept the screaming strings we hear as Janet Leigh is murdered in *Psycho* as a sign of slashing. Similar combinations of sound are used in later films such as *Friday the 13th* at slashing moments and has become what musicians call a *leitmotif,* one of their words for formula (*Harvard*). Equally significant are the silence and quietude just before the slashing begins in *Psycho*. We accept the silence as a formula for being stalked; it means *something bad is about to happen.* Music is used as a gesture to warn of impending danger to the character and to prepare the audience's sensitivity for upcoming fright.

Musical formulas tend to work on a smaller scale than plot development in narratives. Let's say then, that there are two types of artifactual horror formulas, macroformulas and microformulas. Macroformulas tend to work on the plot level, whereas microformulas tend to work on the sequence or passage level of a story. Obviously, they overlap. Musical formulas tend to be microformulas; as they present themselves, they are not the whole narrative in and of themselves. They may, however, enhance crucial moments in the plot's development. Individual scenes and settings in novels and short stories operate on the microformulaic level. Horror microformulas include an ominous descent into a dark basement and Gothic settings such as the Collinwood mansion in the television soap opera *Dark Shadows*.

One of the more frequently used macroformulas for slasher narratives involves an ensemble cast or group of characters. Early in the movie or story, the audience learns about each person and gets a feel for good persons and not so good persons among the ensemble. Characters who are unsavory or peripheral tend to be slashed earlier. The most likable or innocent character is saved for last not just because of a character preference inside the story but because as Dubos maintained almost 250 years ago, the protagonists of tragedies

> should not deserve to be unhappy, or, at least, not so unhappy as they are presented. If their disasters are not merely the effect of the frowns of fortune, but a chastisement for their faults, their demerit ought to be unequal to so heavy a punishment. (92-93)

In other words, the formula of giving a character undeserved punishment by horror or pain has been used for hundreds of years, and conventionally, therefore, the audience's pity and fear are more likely to be heightened when the victim is relatively innocent or undeserving of bloody punishment. Saving a likable character for last heightens the audience's dread for that character's fate. Notice that the camp counselors who slack off their job duties die earlier, not later, in *Friday the 13th*. The character Alice is depicted as helpful and as a good artist. In an early sequence of the film, Alice walks from a cabin through the woods down to the lake and back, being watched by someone nearby. Alice is not an innocent character—she smokes pot like some of the other characters and plays strip Monopoly—but all the same, in contrast to them, Alice does her job conscientiously. The other characters were playing around while Alice kept working; in particular, they were being promiscuous. The stalker, Mrs. Voorhees, saves Alice for last because Mrs. Voorhees' little boy, Jason, had drowned because camp counselors had not been doing their job. Until Mrs. Voorhees actually attacks Alice, it appears Mrs. Voorhees holds no malice for Alice.

The last person to be stalked in the slasher macroformula is usually a woman. Traditional Western values have dictated that women are the weaker of the two genders, and so, stereotypically, these norms additionally cast women in the unenviable role of being stalked last. The gender order of male dominance once again informs both so-called elite and popular culture. This horror convention also perpetuates countless images of woman as victim: bound, gagged, chained, and threatened by weapons (Clover). So many movie posters of horror films buy into this convention of innocent woman as victim that their central, visual focus on a screaming woman approached by a sharp blade of some sort has become an expectable formula, a Sight/site of horror, an eyeful motif to convey fear. On the other hand, the villain, who is usually a male, is most often depicted as righteously punished if not gruesomely killed by the end of a story. In this sense, horror fictions and their most prized formula not only reinforce the victimage of women but also perpetuate the expectation that men by their nature—essentially speaking—are violent and deserve any violence perpetrated back at them. This dual victimage also delineates the conservative nature of horror as a tradition of reinforcing tradition (King).

Sigourney Weaver's role of Ripley in the *Alien* series, however, demonstrates an important alternative microformula to the slasher macroformula that has helpless women stalked last: a woman's transformation into a potent, heroic force. Thus, there are stalker films that conclude with the last character's triumph over the cause of the horror, such as *Alien* and *Aliens*. In contrast, once Alice in *Friday the 13th* knows she is being stalked, she consistently chooses defensive means to save herself, resorting to a machete only when nothing else works. There are stalker macroformulas that involve a protagonist being killed, as in *Psycho,* or that involve the surviving characters also being exiled, as in *The Birds* or *The Forbidden Planet.* Needless to say, beating up the villain while saving the main character's life appears to be the more popular formula.

Other microformulas may be plugged into the larger slasher macroformula just sketched. One microformula usually appears early in a narrative, involving an initial glimpse of some gruesome, heinous act, followed by little or nothing violent for many pages or many minutes. This microformula is one of the most important horror formulas because it is used to solve a number of problems. First of all, people read horror stories or watch horror movies knowing they will be scared. On the one hand, it is difficult to scare persons if they know they are going to be scared; on the other hand, they are more easy to scare because they are primed; they are ready to experience fright. Thus, the horror artist some-times offers the audience a teasing dose of fright because they expect to see it, but then immediately following that teaser, the artist withholds fright for a while. The withholding serves to build excitement.

For an example from a written medium, Dean Koontz begins the novel *Midnight* with a woman taking a night run on a beach.

> Suddenly . . . Janice was sure that she was not alone in the night and fog. She saw no movement, and she was unaware of any sound other than her own footsteps, raspy breathing, and thudding heartbeat; only instinct told her that she had company. (4-5)

She stops, looks around, sees nothing, then continues running. But twenty feet later, she does see something. She looks, then figures it is a trick of the fog. Janice produces all sorts of rationalizations, one by one, but not the idea it was another person or that there was any threat of violence. Running further (this all takes four pages, building in suspense for the reader, converging difference), Janice suddenly does see a human figure. "*Now* fear seized her" (7; emphasis Koontz's). Janice persists in disbelieving her senses however, until the man drops on all fours and runs like an animal at her, and then she literally runs for her life. Then another stalker appears and they take her down, "but she wasn't sure if they wanted to rape or devour her; perhaps neither; what they wanted was, in fact, beyond her comprehension" (10). She dies, rather circumspectly, to keep the nature of the stalkers a mystery to be revealed only incrementally. Then, nothing violent happens or is not witnessed by the reader for almost one hundred pages, while various characters are introduced, some who feel stalked, some who are stalked, some who know about Janice's death, some who have found other bodies. But while the mystery deepens, suspense builds, and when the violence becomes explicit, a reader may almost feel relief at finally facing the source of all the suspense, only then beginning to deal with it as the characters must.

Various microformulas may be conjoined with the early-fright-then-with-holding-fright microformula. When a character is alone for the first time, the audience begins to get the creeps, wondering, when will something happen to that character? Climbing stairs to a half-open door—even having to open a door—is a convention frequently used to build tension in the audience. In films, it is sometimes accompanied by music rising in volume and intensity, a sense of slow motion in getting to the door, putting the hand to the knob, hesitation to turn the knob, turning the knob slowly, opening the door and—nothing there—crashing discord on the soundtrack. Surprise! Sudden silence. Maybe something followed the character up the stairs? After any number of such scenes, the audience is simultaneously encouraged to identify with or to like a character and to be lulled into thinking this story is not so scary after all. That moment of joint identification with a character and lull is the moment aesthetic convergence has been achieved. That's when the slashing starts again. The slashing affects the reader all the more because the artist has maneuvered the reader's feelings so adroitly.

In the film *Friday the 13th,* the basic microformulas just outlined are also used. The movie begins with a brutal murder of a would-be camp counselor who hitchhikes to her death. The murderer remains unseen. As the ensemble cast converges, nothing really deadly happens for almost seventeen minutes. Instead of the protagonist using the stairs, Alice must go into a dark pantry and receives a fright from the town crazy, Ralph, but he is harmless. Then the slashing begins anew. Enter another microformula, keeping one or more characters in the dark about what is happening. Once the horror continues in *Friday the 13th,* none of the camp counselors even know it has happened yet. They do not know it until too late, that is, but the audience does. Recalling that horror is a collaboration between the artist and the audience mediated by the artifact, sometimes an audience of movies such as *Friday the 13th* wants to tell its favorite character to watch out, just like seeing Disney's *Snow White and the Seven Dwarfs* for the first time while the Witch/Queen is handing the poisoned apple to Snow White. "*No! Don't take it!*" Fairy tales often are horror narratives and use similar ecologically motivating horror formulas. They, along with commercial horror tales, encourage us willingly to converge the difference between ourselves and the artifact and its characters. They scare us because we care for the character and wish we could help him or her, as if we were inside the story ourselves. We are inside the story if the storyteller has crafted the telling well enough.

Finally, almost always within the last ten minutes of reading a story or screening a movie, the monster or villain is dead. Enter another highly effective microformula: The monster springs back to life and almost does in the protagonist, after the audience thought the whole ordeal was over. Audiences of the stage play and movie version of *Wait Until Dark* received a heart-stopping dose of this microformula. Every man and woman in the audience who saw this movie along with me for the first time was out of his or her seat, screaming at the top of their lungs—and I mean everyone. As we resumed our seats, muttering excuses and apologies as we comforted a companion, we didn't know for almost two minutes if Audrey Hepburn made it or not. Not knowing was almost as bad as the fright we had just experienced. This was one heroic lady who did not deserve any of the nasty things she experienced.

The next time you read a horror novel or watch a horror movie, you might ask yourself why you enjoy being scared. You might pay attention to and admire the various techniques used to frighten you. If it is a movie, you might want to eat your popcorn first, because you might not feel like eating later; but if it is a book, you might want to check to make sure the lights are on in other rooms, too, especially if it is dark. Horror sneaks up on you. Someone is looking over your shoulder—the artist. Someone is thinking your thoughts, right now. As the teaser on the cover of the U.S. initial paperback publication of Clive Barker's *Books of Blood: Volume One* maintains, "Be thankful if you scream. At least you're still breathing." Even the advertising sneaks up and converges the aesthetic difference between you and the artwork of horror.

The Silence of the Lambs

From the outset, let me affirm that the interpretation of gender horror I am about to present is based solely on Thomas Harris' novel, *The Silence of the Lambs,* and not the movie of the same name by Jonathan Demme. The difference is crucial. As mentioned in Chapter 2, film distills novels while it promotes media features unique to film. In the case of this particular movie, it seems that more changes are going on than only the change of media. A novel may be rich in detail in ways a film is not, and vice versa. The serial killer in the movie, Jame Gumb, appeared to have been some sort of homosexual freak, and the juxtaposition of homosexuality with sociopathy elicited severe criticism from the gay and lesbian communities (Stewart 187). Few homosexuals want to be the opposite biological sex, and even fewer are serial killers. The novel, however, is quite clear in maintaining not only that Jame is *not* a transsexual but that he *thinks* he is a transsexual, not a homosexual, and that in addition, transsexuals are rarely violent at all (164). The novel's more complex characterization of Jame does, however, play an important role in the self-reflexivity of the novel and its central focus on gender horror.

The novel opens with an FBI academy student, Clarice Starling, summoned to the FBI section that deals with serial murders, to Jack Crawford's office, particularly. Crawford runs that section. It turns out there is an investigation of a serial killer they call "Buffalo Bill," and Crawford wants Starling to interview renowned psychiatrist Hannibal Lecter to see what advice about the situation he might have. One problem: Lecter is incarcerated in a maximum security asylum because he himself is a serial killer. One thing Crawford stresses to Starling before she leaves for her assignment, "Tell him no specifics about yourself" (6) because Lecter has a habit of using such information to dupe others into getting hurt, getting killed. So far so good; the relationship between Starling and Crawford is professional, a subordinate and a supervisor.

Before Starling is allowed in Lecter's presence, she must be briefed by the head of the asylum, Dr. Chilton. He immediately calls her "attractive," purposefully calls her "Miss" instead of "Ms." (which she deflects by correcting not the gendered moniker but his mispronunciation of her last name) and then he says, "So the FBI is going to the girls," a clearly patronizing, belittling statement. Again, Starling deflects the gender insult by answering, "The Bureau's improving." Chilton cuts to the chase, blatantly hitting on her, which again Clarice manages professionally without making an issue of it. She has a job to do. Later, complaining about lack of office help as lack of "office girls," he tells her that Lecter is a "pure sociopath, that's obviously what he is," an assessment that should be kept in mind later when Lecter himself has a few choice things to say about it. Chilton then attributes Crawford's choice of Starling as "a young woman to 'turn him [Lecter] on.' " Starling keeps her thoughts to herself ("Well fuck off, Chilton") and merely reminds him that she graduated with honors from the University of Virginia, not a charm school (8-11).

As she enters the locked ward to proceed to Lecter's cell, a voice hisses to her, "I can smell your cunt," to which she makes no visible reaction. At Lecter's cell, she politely introduces herself. He scans her and eventually exchanges pleasantries. He asks to see her credentials, then makes fun of Chilton's credentials. Eventually, Starling presents her ID through a slot mechanism in the wall. He smells it after he looks at it. "A trainee?" he jibes. Starling counters that she's here to discuss psychology, not the FBI. At this point, Lecter negotiates a chair for her to sit, convincing the ward guard with an appeal to courtesy. Once seated, he wants to know what Miggs had said. "He said, 'I can smell your cunt,' " Clarice reports. This is a test, of course, to see if she would be honest with him. He immediately responds with carefully chosen words, "I myself cannot," then proceeds to tell her all he can smell about her. The words are important and ironic: He cannot say the word *cunt* and remain courteous (14-18).

Sparring back and forth, eventually they get around to psychology and his filling out a questionnaire that would produce a profile of himself as a sociopath. Here begins a new level to the novel's gender horror, one that apparently escapes those focused on only feminist issues. He asks her what she thinks of grouping sociopaths into the two groups of "organized" and "disorganized." She claims that it is fundamental, and he corrects her, "Simplistic," and adds that most psychology is "puerile." Again, Lecter's word choice is precise and revealing. *Puerile* is a word derived from Latin that conventionally means childish; precisely, however, it means "boyish." A minute or so later, he follows up this subtle gendrification by belittling the questionnaire, "Oh, Officer Starling, do you think you can dissect me with this blunt little tool?" The implication is wickedly sharp. A "tool" is, in social science, empirical methodology, the means of acquiring and sorting data, frequently called a research "instrument." But a tool is also everyday language for penis. Lecter is making a comparison, that the questionnaire is a little, blunt penis; psychology is, as he maintained, puerile. As put-downs go, he is saying that psychology is an immature toy or penis play by little boys, further implying that psychological research is at best masturbatory. The clincher is that psychologists such as Chilton therefore are incapable of assessing Lecter, who clearly thinks himself unique and unexplainable by puerile tools. Starling suggests he complete the survey to better understand why he is in prison, to which he answers, "Nothing happened to me, Officer Starling. *I* happened. You can't reduce me to a set of influences" (21; emphasis Harris'), again underscoring the "puerile" oversimplification of psychology/psychiatry. Unlike those practitioners, Lecter is not small but big and will not be "reduced."

In contrast to the way Lecter specifically puts down psychology—and implicitly Starling's training in psychology—as childish, male, and penis-centered, Lecter consistently treats her with courtesy, yet always pushing her to assess herself. He had asked why the killer is called Buffalo Bill, and she answers, "because he skins his humps." This honesty produces a startling thought to her, that "she had traded feeling frightened for feeling cheap. Of the two, she preferred feeling frightened." In other words, fear of just being with Lecter was bad enough, but to relay a sexist attribution—centered on the word *hump*, as if that's all women were—not only violates her womanhood but makes her feel less. This is exactly prior to the moments Lecter offers her a male put-down of psychology, as if he is showing her that maleness cheapens itself. The interview concludes with Lecter suggesting not that he will help the investigation, but that he will help her, by giving her a Valentine, as if he would be a lover. But that is all he says; he offers no more information. He ends the interview, and Starling leaves, only to be momentarily distracted by Miggs who flicks semen on her from his cell—another symbolic and demonstrative underscoring of psychology's puerile masturbation and ineffectiveness to cure madness. Lecter is incensed by this treatment, and then he offers the Valentine, a clue to finding a severed head, in a car, in a garage—a head that eventually yields a moth pupa that the killer had placed in the head's mouth, a clue that eventually leads Starling to Jame Gumb (22-25).

After Starling retrieves the head, she interviews Lecter again. The gestural coding of the scene reveals more of Lecter's perceived relationship with her. Just in from the rain, with no chair provided this visit, Clarice puts her wet raincoat on the floor and sits on it. Lecter's cell is totally dark (Chilton is punishing him). At her eye level, after any number of promptings without answer, the exchange slot suddenly pops out; in it is a towel so she may dry her hair and face. His voice issues from her level, and she surmises he must be sitting on the floor too. Barely a minute later, his "voice moved lower. Maybe he was lying on the floor, Starling thought" (59). Another minute or so later, after having only once previously addressed her by her first name, he asks permission to use it—from beneath her level. When she begins to suggest what she might call him, he cuts her off and insists that "Dr. Lecter" is appropriate for the circumstances. This reversal completes a nongendered order between them. Lecter has signified that in some ways he accepts her as an equal, as her subordinate (he's jailed; she's not) and her supervisor of sorts, a mentor.

To emphasize the supervisory capacity, he questions her about Crawford's feelings about her, which he suggests may not be entirely professional. She claims she does not think about it. He reiterates that she has had Crawford's help and his own, that she, apparently, does not know why Crawford helps her but that he would tell her why he, Lecter, helps her. He wants a view; his cell is windowless, and he has been in it for eight years. He gives her another clue and then does not speak again.

The management of gender horror proceeds in the novel—and perhaps not surprisingly as cued by Lecter—with Clarice and Crawford in West Virginia to autopsy another apparent victim of Buffalo Bill's. When they arrive, out of earshot, the local police say lewd things about her, blatant sexual harassment, but not to her face. Yet Crawford needs to assert command over the locals but the way he chooses to do it is to say, in her face, "Sheriff, this kind of sex crime has some aspects that I'd rather say to you just between us men," and the two men enter another room, closing the door, leaving Starling to cool her heels, left to pretend she is not outraged in front of the male deputies (79-80). Later, after the autopsy, Crawford asks her if that burned her. Honest, she answers "sure." He tries to rationalize it, and then, taking a big risk in their supervisor-subordinate relationship, she takes an assertive role, saying, "It matters, Mr. Crawford." She points out that the locals could too easily take him as a role model for proper professional behavior (95-96). As a subordinate, as a woman, for the first time Starling creates the context from which she could be consequentially horrified by gender, career-wise. Crawford, however, accepts her assertions with "Duly noted" and tells her to investigate another bug produced from the autopsy. While the subordination order is maintained, he also accepts learning from a subordinate.

Clarice subsequently visits the Smithsonian, where she finds two male entomologists playing a game with a beetle. They ignore her initially, which may be taken perhaps as sign of a new or at least different gender order. When one of the men begins conversing with her, he does so as she is an FBI agent, not a female agent. Eventually, the other elliptically airs the idea of a date and Clarice says neither yes nor no, but that if it happens, she would treat and all three of them would go together (97-107).

In the meanwhile, a young woman in her late teens or early twenties named Catherine Martin is kidnapped and turns out to be Tennessee Senator Ruth Martin's daughter. Senator Martin chairs a funding committee, and thus Harris images both a woman who is still alive but threatened as a victim and a powerful woman who happens to be her mother. Senator Martin can deliver exactly what Lecter wants, if he helps save the daughter before she is hurt, but Crawford does not want the situation complicated by the senator's involvement. He sends Starling back to Lecter with a strategy allegedly involving the senator, but without her informed consent. Once more a go-between, Starling is confronted by Chilton. His motivation is fear that Starling will publish findings about Lecter and take away his thunder in publishing about Lecter first. With all his huff, he lets it slip that he had a ticket that he couldn't use because of her unplanned appearance—"ticket," singular—for *Holiday on Ice,* and that slip alone speaks more than he intended. Starling sizes him up as a sexual loser, replete with what his domestic scene must look like, the works—just as Lecter does with few clues. This mirroring of Lecter is important in that it implies she is reaching his level of discernment.

The third interview between Clarice and Lecter is pivotal. Lecter clearly has taken her under his wing, both as a student of psychology and as a client. He teaches her about schizophrenia through dialogue. Initially, he sandwiches teaching with offering tidbits of information about Buffalo Bill for Clarice's correct performance of a dialectic, calling it "quid pro quo," this for that (148). He changes gears when he converts the exchange for help in the investigation and her education for an exchange for personal information about her "worst memory of childhood." Although Crawford had warned her never to supply personal information, Starling knows the exchange will go no further without her compliance. With only one prompting, she answers, "The death of my father" (150). The "quid pro quo" formula subsequently weaves intrigue with the expectation of later psychological revelation for the rest of the novel and thus drives the story while it propels the reader into rampant page turning. At this point, Lecter tells her the killer wants "a vest with tits on it" (152), and Clarice leaves his presence to call Crawford to consult.

On her return to Lecter in a few minutes, they continue. Clarice's advanced training in psychology is now intimately commingled with sharing her worst childhood memory. Lecter guides her through the exact data to investigate; Clarice supplies information about being literally farmed out to Montana and about her favorite horse being fattened to be sold for dog food. Unknown to either of them, Chilton had been recording their exchanges, and he reveals all to Senator Martin, who now exerts her considerable power to get Lecter to assist her in finding her daughter—and Chilton cooperates only if Crawford and Starling are circumvented, dismissed from the case. They are, and Lecter is moved to Tennessee where he will meet the senator.

The scene between Lecter and Senator Martin is skillfully styled, beginning with Lecter's gender-laden question about the senator's breast-feeding her daughter and ending with Lecter jibing, "Love your suit," at once a fashion comment and reminder that she is dressed like a man. Clarice takes it on herself to visit Lecter in Tennessee. She is not authorized but says she is and sneaks into the building where Lecter is temporarily imprisoned. He confronts her with her prevarication with him, yet they fall into the pedagogical dialogue for improving Starling's forensic skills as well as the quid pro quo routine. Eventually, it comes out that in childhood, Clarice, after being awakened by the slaughter of lambs and their crying one night, had decided to save her Montana horse by running away with it. Lecter then provides the rationale for the novel's title, "Do you think if you caught Buffalo Bill yourself and if you made Catherine all right, you could make the lambs stop screaming, do you think they'd be all right too and you wouldn't wake up again in the dark and hear the lambs screaming? Clarice?" Clarice admits, "Yes. I don't know. Maybe." Lecter has performed his personal and professional brilliance in providing Clarice both education and therapy. She presses for the name of the killer—her right in the quid pro quo situation—but at that moment, Chilton appears with guards to have her taken away—but not before she retrieves the Buffalo Bill case file from Lecter, later to discover it has a notation by Lecter that indeed leads her to Jame Gumb. Their index fingers touch as he passes the file to her. They both say thank you, and "that is how he remained in Starling's mind. Caught in the instant when he did not mock" (230-231).

The relationship between Clarice and Lecter is remarkable—as Harris, not Demme, portrays it. Arguably, Clarice's only relationship with a male that is nonsexual is with Lecter. They respect one another. He accepts her as an intelligent, apt pupil, as a potential equal. He did not have to, but he had not spoken to Chilton for years. As Lecter puts it at the end of the novel, assuring her of his intentions after his escape in a letter, "I have no plans to call on you, Clarice, the world being more interesting with you in it. Be sure you extend me the same courtesy. . . . Some of our stars are the same" (366-367). He calls on the quid pro quo formula. The "some of our stars are the same" is perhaps peculiar. He credits her uniqueness, but part of his own is his dangerousness. Then again, he has, in his own way, already warned Starling about Crawford's intentions about her. Certainly, the sequel will put the three together again, with Lecter, perhaps, someone who saves Clarice's life.

Back to the novel, however. Although Catherine is initially depicted as a sniveling, panicky female, her quick wit, courage, and resourcefulness—and thus transformation—is shown by her capturing Jame's dog and then feigning its injury for her release—just as Clarice shows up at his door. The ensuing scenario is a chase in the dark between the man-who-would-be-woman and Clarice-who-would-save-the-lamb. Classically speaking, the horror scene pits not one but two endangered women in the dark. Although Clarice is definitely frightened by the darkness, by the unfamiliarity with the turf, with the killer stalking her, she is also empowered.

Vampires and the Kiss of Death

I present an extended interpretation of *Silence of the Lambs* both to display how one might explicate a single text and to demonstrate how gender and sex lie at the core of a nonsupernatural horror tale. I purposefully switch gears to supernatural horror and its now perennial connection to the erotic via the vampire. When a vampire kisses, it may merely kiss, with withdrawn threat of danger or arousal for the reader or viewer. When a vampire kisses, it may drain part of the blood of the victim and thereby enslave him or her until it is done with them. When a vampire kisses, it may slay the victim, draining all blood, all life force. But sometimes, when a vampire kisses, it inverts the supernatural order and by some dark design, the kiss of death transforms death to eternal life. And all the kissing, whether deadly or life giving, quite often involves signs of sexual arousal. Thus, my focus incorporates many tales to indicate the genre of horror and sex, the vampire story, and will not concentrate on only one text.

Perhaps one of the more famous vampire tales is a story written by Joseph Sheridan LeFanu in 1871, "Carmilla." As Carol Senf maintains in *The Vampire in 19th Century English Literature,* Carmilla, a vampire character, not only predates Dracula, but like him, is genteel (18). I add that Carmilla has needle fangs and the tale itself is high Gothic, fraught with female homoeroticism and, as eroticism, also predates Bram Stoker's *Dracula* and its descendants. "Carmilla" sets many features of the vampire dynamic before Dracula, including ruined castles, the visitation of crypts, death by waning away, various characters confusing a naturalistic explanation for the deaths with a supernatural, vampiric one, and a changeling, in "Carmilla's" case, a black cat instead of a bat. The conspicuously unnamed heroine of the story, daughter of an Englishman retired from Austrian service by her nineteenth year, writes the story and recalls "an early fright" from her childhood, sleeping in her nursery. Thinking herself alone, upset that the nurse was not there, she was close to tears,

> when to my surprise, I saw a solemn, but very pretty face looking at me from the side of the bed. It was that of a young lady who was kneeling, with her hands under the coverlet. I looked at her with a kind of pleased wonder, and ceased whimpering. She caressed me with her hands, and lay down beside me on the bed, and drew me towards her, smiling; I felt immediately delightfully soothed, and fell asleep again. I was wakened by a sensation as if two needles ran into my breast very deep. (277)

This fright stayed with the heroine all her life. When a coach unexpectedly appears bearing a woman and an apparently stunned child, the girl's family takes in the stunned girl because she cannot travel further, not knowing that the stunned girl, Carmilla, is the same pretty face that assailed the girl long ago in her nursery. Almost immediately, Carmilla begins to work her power over the nineteen-year-old.

> Sometimes, after an hour of apathy, my strange and beautiful companion would take my hand and hold it with a fond pressure, renewed again and again; blushing softly, gazing in my face with languid and burning eyes, and breathing so fast that her dress rose and fell with the tumultuous respiration. It was like the ardour [*sic*] of a lover; it embarrassed me; it was hateful and yet overpowering; and with gloating eyes she drew me to her, and her hot lips travelled [*sic*] along my cheek in kisses. (292)

By the conclusion of the heroine's tale, she is rather torn, feeling drawn to Carmilla yet relieved that the men in her life saved her from Carmilla. Thus, LeFanu plays on the dread and ecstasy of same-sex desire and its rescue by the male dominant order.

LeFanu's story was published in 1871. Not much more than a hundred years later, homoeroticism and vampires meet anew. Lestat giving Louis the kiss of death/life in both the novel and film version of Anne Rice's *Interview with the Vampire* is not exactly a heterosexual fantasy, nor is Claudia's desire for a female companion. Indeed, many of the vampire characters consistently address the personal desire for a "companion" who is as much a lover, partner, or spouse. The kissing of Louis and the kissing of Claudia, however, are different, and the difference spells itself throughout the Vampire Chronicles. Lestat offers eternal life to Louis; he does not impose it; it is a choice for Louis. Rice has Louis report the sexual ecstasy of the conversion. Its homoeroticism is no source of horror for the "victim," like LeFanu's more veiled threat of same-sex extinction.

> "Listen, keep your eyes wide," Lestat whispered to me, his lips moving against my neck. I remember that the movement of his lips raised the hair all over my body, sent a shock of sensation through my body that was not unlike the pleasure of passion. (17)

Of course, Lestat had wanted a companion, and the young, good-looking Creole man was a welcome foil to his own French, aristocratic, and blond good looks. By Louis' own self-identification, however, Lestat chose a poor companion who feels guilt about taking blood. Yet as Ed Ingebretsen cannily observes, "Louis' passivity and sensitivity accomplish what gender does: confirm and augment the totalizing image of the superior creature, the active male" (in Hoppenstand & Browne 98), and Lestat is nothing if not narcissistically self-absorbed in his superiority.

Finally, however, the lust for human blood seizes Louis, and he winds up in the slums of old New Orleans, sucking blood from a just-orphaned child. Louis tells his interviewer:

For four years I had not savored a human; for four years I hadn't really known; and now I heard her heart in that terrible rhythm, and such a heart—not the heart of a man or an animal, but the rapid, tenacious heart of the child, beating harder and harder, refusing to die, beating like a tiny fist beating a door, crying, "I will not die, I will not die, I cannot die, I cannot die." (Rice, *Interview* 66)

He does not drain her all the way, however, fleeing from his own disgust. Rice herself does not flee from the horror of lusting for a child, not before Louis encounters it for us. Unfortunately, Lestat has followed him and, to his glee, witnesses Louis as he broke his own vow not to take human blood. He teases Louis that he had not finished the job, that maybe they should make her a vampire and have fun with her. So, a day or so later, he surprises Louis with a perversity only Lestat could find amusing. He returns to their home with the girl, Claudia, both to shame Louis and to make her a third companion. In this case, Claudia is given no choice in the matter.

Then, after decades of Claudia's new life, she does not age, she does not grow, but she does learn and experience. Eventually, she resents what they have done to her, particularly Lestat, because she will never experience the world as an adult and know love as they have. She convinces Louis to free themselves from Lestat by killing him; they leave New Orleans and move to Paris, where lonely Louis finally meets someone to love, Armand, someone already a vampire and quite gifted at the ways of compulsion and arousal. Of course, as things turn out in the sequel, *The Vampire Lestat,* Lestat and Armand had already been lovers, a situation depicted quite differently in the movie.

There are also homosocially coded tales in which vampiric eroticism is cold and calculating, like James Tiptree's "Houston, Houston, Do You Read Me?" in the sci-fi fantasy anthology *Worlds Apart.* Basically, some plague has rendered all the men on Earth sterile, and the only form of reproduction becomes cloning. Women ascend to power and then clone only themselves, which spells the end of men, until some astronauts appear by accidental time travel and are rescued. Only incrementally does one of the astronauts begin to realize that there are no other male astronauts. The story ends with the women rather clinically collecting sperm samples from these still potent men, just before their execution, because in that world, it had been determined that men always were violent contaminations of peace. The men are literal sex objects; their only good is the sperm they carry; all else is expendable. So much for essentialism.

"Sex, Death and Starshine" in Barker's *Books of Blood: Volume One* features all sorts of heterosexual suckage of life, from demolishing an old theater so more money can be made with a new building in its replacement, to a director's keeping a star only because he gets sex from her. Yet eventually, she gets revenge when she administers a blow job to the director, and only too late does he realize that she is dead and will not quit until he is dead. The head of a literally undead theater troupe, Litchfield, gives undead life by a kiss of death at need. More in a streetwise, cyberpunk mode that skirts the issue of supernaturality, William Gibson's "The Belonging Kind" from *Burning Chrome* is a pretty scary story of becoming a vampire-like changeling in an urban setting of barhopping. The "creatures" are like everyone else, which is the source of their dread to the protagonist, for they can become any "look" to fit into any bar, club, or situation. The protagonist is initially socially clueless and out of place until he becomes one of them, becomes what he fears, yet desires the most, to fit in, to belong.

The vampire and its play on sexuality are not a tradition limited to mostly Western literature. That would be a grave imposition on other peoples of the world. For instance, many Japanese folktales of ghosts involve vengeful ancestors who were not properly honored, almost literally sucking the life out of their descendants, and others. *The Tale of Genji* involves numerous such occasions, as does *Dream of Red Mansions.* Vampirism has also become a subculture unto itself and is certainly not limited to literature or film; there are fanzines, television, conventions, comic books, role-playing games, and Internet talk groups. If nothing else, during a bad news week, tabloids might punch up their market reach with a vampire story. The "Bat Boy" strikes again! Growing numbers of people, usually but not always teens, appear to take themselves seriously as vampires and blood drinkers. As a sexualized, transgressive interpretive community, vampires combine cosmetics, attire, performance of self, and the play of dominance and passivity with the threat of danger.

Soap Operas, Sex, and Horror

There are different types of horror and ways to contextualize horror, from pure, single-minded screamers to stories that variously instill different levels of fear, terror, dread, and suspense; from the occult and supernatural cause of horror to the natural—sometimes hybridizing horror with other common genres but nevertheless generating horror. In each of these rubrics, there are diverse alternatives. They may be combined. Except for the supernatural, occult element, *Silence of the Lambs* includes the rest. Television soap operas likewise weave the various strands of horror, although they are not conventionally taken to be horror fictions, nor are they regularly analyzed as horror stories. For this section on sexualities and horror, therefore, I propose to explore the media of sex and horror resonant in the televisual medium of soap operas.

Figure 8.1. Marlena and John take time for romance on *Days of Our Lives*
SOURCE: Original photography: John Paschal/JPI; reformatted by David Hampshire

First, some features of soap operas merit mention. Soap operas are serial narratives, meaning the stories told within each soap are not self-contained in one episode. It may take weeks, months, or years to resolve a plot. In part, this serialization caters to viewers who watch only periodically. Serialization also drives regular viewers to stay regular. Serial narrative is a conscientiously continuing, open text. In one of the longest serial narratives in television history, Marlena, John, Roman, and Stefano on *Days of Our Lives* have apparently died, come back to life, and been in various love situations for more than ten years. Thus, serialization and its nature as an open text also retain popular—and hence lucrative—characters (Figure 8.1).

Thematically, at the heart of most, if not all, soap operas is the myth of romantic love. As Mrs. Horton comforts various characters on *Days of Our Lives,* true love always wins out, gets through tough times, and conquers all. Such is the hope of veteran viewers. Yet narrative works by conflict, and the ways of keeping lovers apart are legion. Although certainly not everyone is a fan of soap operas and although their status as artworks may be challenged and disparaged, hard work and careful craft go into soaps. Because of romantic love, perhaps the most perennial central narrative strategy of soaps involves the potential sexual and relational horrors laden in secrets kept by one character, learned by another, then shared by a small but growing coterie, then the secret's revelations and how those revelations spread ramifications throughout the various plots. Television as a medium and soap operas as a televisual format are supernally suited for delivering secrets as horror, threat, dread, and fear, imbuing even simple everyday life situations with terror.

For instance, medially, one mainstay of soap opera camera work is the extreme close-up (Timberg 166-169). Although, until recently, television screens have been small to moderate in size, a character's face and its registration of emotion could cover all or most of the screen when the camera pulled in, rendering a sense of hugeness to the emotional facial gestures, making a spectacle of the tiniest movements. In this regard, Deidre Hall on *Days* can deliver money shots with the ability to shed a real tear from one eye or the other, or both, on cue, depending on camera angle and desired effect. Fake tears are makeup and take time to apply convincingly. Hall's money shots are money savers. Close up, their reality lends a hyperreal verisimilitude to whatever pain, suffering, or fear her character experiences. Extreme close-ups are also used to build tension in viewers. A tell-tale piece of jewelry, a cuff link, or an earring accidently left at the scene of a crime that none of the characters notice cannot escape the audience's attention when the camera work cuts to an extreme close-up of the item. Filling the screen is potentially incriminating evidence or clue that audience members often immediately try to place, empowering the audience with knowledge that the characters do not have. The writers, directors, performers, and the camera work have given the audience a secret. If it could spell trouble for a favored character, tension is created any time a character inhabits the space where the item lies. Any glance in that direction could hurt a character. On the other hand, if it is a villain's piece of jewelry, there is fear generated in canny fans that the item will not be found in time, at all, or worse, that it will be discovered instead by the villain or friend of the villain, thus preventing the disclosure of the secret.

Specific narrative techniques that were incorporated from Saturday matinee film serials have been honed and made another part of the fabric of soap opera sexual horror. Typically featuring a large and varied cast, no soap can regularly feature all the characters on a daily basis. Thus, although most of the main characters will appear at least once a week, their appearances are staggered and sometimes unpredictable. The appearance on-screen of Carrie Brady usually means other Bradys will appear in that episode, building the hope for thousands of fans that Austin Reed will appear and even better, take off his shirt. Of course, that is exactly what happened in 1995 when Carrie's sister, Samantha, spiked

Austin's beer, got him home to bed, and in his stupor, he took her to be Carrie and made love to her. Voilà, Sammie got pregnant, much to the disgust of fans because as the story goes, Austin and Carrie are made for each other—the myth of romantic love strikes again. All sorts of secrets issued from the situation, driving Carrie and Austin apart, pulling them together. Fans will remember, however, that barely a week earlier, Sammie and Austin's half-brother, Lucas, made love. That little secret has not yet made its mark, because the child, Will, is as likely to be his as Austin's. If that secret ever kindles, it will turn all the drift between Austin and Carrie more ironic, making them victims of love and casual sex.

Plot lines and important events can last for days, weeks, months, and years. *Days* is currently entering its second decade of the Marlena-Roman-John-Stefano dynamic. Stefano, evil man that he is, hates Roman, erased John's memory and masqueraded him as Roman whom he supposedly had killed, and loves Marlena but kept her sedated for years, letting her family think she was dead. Byzantine and baroque storytelling can hardly be more convoluted and ornate. This is just the short version, too. As each development seemingly comes to a head, it can be delayed from progressing any further for weeks, thus frustrating closure, building tension, and giving fans opportunities to conjecture outcomes with each other.

This serial redundancy also is suited to the nature of soap opera viewing; many viewers can tune in only serially. Except for diehard fans, many viewers, because of hectic schedules that vary day by day, cannot watch without missing episodes. Thus the soap creators build redundancy into their narrative. This redundancy usually appears on-screen, in industry terms, as backstory, the conceit of having one character talking up other characters to catch them up to current events but really to assist part-time viewers in getting them up to speed. "Backstories help us tune in quickly to who is who if we are new or have not seen the soap opera in a while" (Timberg 171). Backstory has its own signature, even gesturally and situationally. Two characters known by fans to be friends, who are at a restaurant or some other stock situation, who evidence no serious conflict but just talk, frequently are engaging in backstory. I have observed numerous fans who videotape their favorite soap fast-forward during such scenes that have these characteristics because they already know the information and want to get on to some other, more juicy, action scene.

And soap opera creators have become good at delivering televisual action, geared to camera techniques and the social narratives of secrets and their revelation. Triangles, situations with two characters vying for a third character, populate the soap opera landscape. To drive the plot and to keep audiences in a state of expectant, dread suspense, often only two characters meet on-screen, usually potential if not actual lovers. The way these scenes are shot, however, is the camera work of threat and violation of romance. Frequently, a doorway or some entrance is included in the screen frame. An audience cognizant of the conventions cannily wonders, will the third person suddenly appear, overhear something innocent but apparently incriminating nevertheless? Thus the appearance of a doorway is an invitation to dread. The missing other (Timberg 172), the third character in the triangle, is thus endowed with mythic presence, for if he or she shows up, things might go differently. The missing other may show up too soon, too late, or not at all. In every case, the play on absence and presence imbues the scene with emotion. Similarly, a telephone on-screen often suggests threat to a viewer. By ringing, it could interrupt a much longed-for kiss or romance scene. The third in the triangle may make an appearance, of sorts, by calling. The wrong character may absentmindedly pick up the phone and answer, revealing a sense of relationship with the other character whose phone it is.

The momentous return of Marlena on *Days* in 1991 was a day of secrets revealed and secrets set in motion. Almost all the plot lines had erupted into triangles. Marlena, escaped from drugged captivity in the Caribbean, has returned to Salem, dazed, but whole. She goes to the pier and, of course, there's Roman (actually, still John who thinks he's Roman). A few weeks later, the real Roman, not dead at all, but also imprisoned by Stefano, makes his escape. Suddenly, Roman isn't Roman, but who is he? It's taken years to find out the many lives of John Black, with constant revelation of Stefano's diabolic treachery.

The Epistemology of Secrets

Although many critics dismiss soap operas as unrealistic or contrived, they miss that all the same, they mime everyday life. Although the life of secrets is intensified as it is distilled to sound bytes and time parts, secrets and sexualities play in people's lives. Eve Sedgwick's *Epistemology of the Closet* delves into the workings of writers—and by extrapolation, others—who conceal their sexual orientation in a homophobic world and how that affects how and what they can know. I might add, however, that sex in general, in the West anyway, is a dirty little secret for most everyone, and its concealment and subsequent revelations, if any, affect the way we know immensely.

Generally, we protect children from sex, talking about it, teaching it, and most certainly, we, as a culture, strive to keep images of sex from children. Yet with late industrialism and its economy that requires both parents to work gainfully outside their home to make ends meet, children have become freer at an earlier age to learn about sex one way or another. Like Santa Claus or the Easter Bunny, the secrets of sex may seem beneficial for children, but Santa and Peter Cottontail do not abuse children within families or as strangers and do not carry "social" diseases that are not all that social because many people strive not to think about them, let alone talk about them.

What I have called "shame culture" perpetuates itself by concealment. Various media acknowledge secrets in their mimesis of royals and commoners. Oedipus bedded his mother, something the Gods could have revealed to him sooner. More recently, the British royal family has lived more than one *annus horribilis,* or horrible year, of sex secrets disclosed. Early in television history, *Divorce Court* screened private life, although in a veiled manner. No matter, for almost 15 years now, various television talk shows have featured real-world people, paying them to disclose their sex secrets. Although Lucy and Desi had separate, single beds on the *I Love Lucy* show in the 1950s, by the 1980s, soap operas featured near explicit sex during daylight hours while prime-time shows could not dare such sexual feats of mediated derring-do because it is "family hour." Paradoxically, what is secret at night is all right in the daylight. That for a time and to some extent still, evening television is not nearly as explicit as daytime soaps speaks volumes about the perpetuation of shame by secret. The attraction of media explicitness or lack thereof draws audiences. It draws them from their own secrets and reveals to them ways others—not all fictions, either—deal with their sexual secrets. Gender-wise, *My Little Margie* is no more the teacher of women's mysteries than *Rawhide* is of men's mysteries. Nor is *Melrose Place* the chapbook on sexuality with its diversity of orientations, personalities, and bizarre couplings. It is no wonder, perhaps, that thousands of children tuned into the Internet before it was initially censored by the U.S. government, eagerly searching for information about sex because they were not getting it from their parents and certainly were not getting it from most media. Not that children should have free access to sexual information, but a culture that privileges sex without candid discussion, instruction, and access to free information can only initially impair those aging beyond childhood by para-doxically keeping them in the dark and thrusting them into the light of day.

9

Sexual Humors and the Flirtatious
Alchemy of Gaiety and Gravity

In keeping with my attempt to share diversity about sexualities and popular culture, here is a joke I heard in 1995 that I recorded in my ethnographic field notes as soon as I could. Following is a transcript of the field notes, a preliminary, narrative expansion (names changed to protect the guilty):

The party has been happening for over two hours. The various dishes everyone brought stand mostly consumed on the kitchen table and counters. Serious conversation is under way, which is to say, anything goes.

Standing in a mixed group of partiers in a corner of the living room at a neighbor's home, I have listened to Marge, Paul, Dan, and myself trade the latest jokes. Sex and politics seem to be the connection we're making when up walks Joe, beer in hand. Joe listens a bit, waits for a lull, hoists his bottle a bit and jumps into the conversation.

"Did you hear about the spelling bee?"

Of course, none of us had; we told him so with shakes of our heads, shrugged shoulders.

"Yeah, the finalists were Bob Packwood, Ted Kennedy, and Dan Quayle." He paused for a sip and to measure the effect, or so it seemed. We groaned and looked into each other's eyes, winking conspiratorially.

"Guess who won?"

We went for the jugular, "Quayle!"

Joe raised his left hand as if to strike a bell and jibed, "Ding-ding-ding-ding-ding! Very good!" This time he paused for a long swig, and each of us were curious as to why Quayle won.

I prompted, "And?"

Joe smiled, "He was the only one who knew that *harass* was one word!"

We roared and immediately started praising the cleverness of the joke.

Well, now, what happened? How did the joke "work"?

Let's call Joe the Joker, the one telling the joke. The rest of us were the audience. The Joker maneuvered the words so the audience was led to certain lines of thinking. In this case, because Dan Quayle had many times over been publicly lambasted as lacking intelligence, we readily fell into concluding him as the most unlikely winner of a spelling bee. As it turns out, we were right—but we were also wrong in that we had figured out a different reason why he had won. Thus, the Joker provided us with an initial "aha" experience but then surprised us with a different revelation, in this case based on the wordplay of *harass* and *her ass*. Dan Quayle may be attributed to be dumb, but Kennedy and Chappaquiddick and Packwood and allegations of his "harassment" were the other target of the joke.

Such is the nature of humor. It plays on duplicities. In this case, it also plays on images of innocence to the point of dumbness versus images of worldly ways and sexual exploitation as dumb. The audience was led to provide its own information that the Joker had not stated—Quayle's alleged dumbness. This indicates not only that humor operates as an open text (Eco, *Open*)—thrives on it—but also that speakers (Jokers) lead audiences into drawing conclusions without providing them all the information to come to those conclusions.

This speaker strategy can also be called *enthymeme* and was described two thousand years ago by Aristotle in *The Art of Rhetoric*. Technically, enthymeme is a logical procedure or verbal formula for inducing audiences to draw conclusions without providing enough or all information. The setup for the spelling bee joke includes (1) familiarity with a spelling bee; (2) familiarity with the three characters, two of whom are or have been in sex trouble and the other whose trouble is alleged to stem from intelligence, not sex; and (3) the question of the winner. All three ingredients conspire to lead the audience to draw the conclusion of the odd man out, Quayle. As it turns out, there is an entirely different reason he won the fictive spelling bee. Enthymeme is thus an open text and is a formulaic duplicity. Technicalities aside, however, enthymeme is a series of communicative strategies that increases the likelihood an audience will jump to a conclusion favorable to the speaker or initiating communicator by employing minimal data.

One other feature deserves mention. The targets of the joke are three leaders, three rulers. The joke lowers them and makes them the butt of comedy—just as Aristotle implied it would be inappropriate comedy in a different work, *The Poetics*. The mention of Aristotle no doubt evokes consternation both for readers who are generally in favor of popular culture and its study and for that smaller, but no less important, group of persons who consider themselves "postmodernist." Popular culture enthusiasts do not usually find Aristotle and popular culture in the same ball park, as it were. Postmodernists find authors prior to the last thirty years or so to be part of the received tradition and therefore dismissible. Some readers are both enthusiasts and poststructural thinkers.

Before I continue the narrative about sex and humor, therefore, I must affirm that reference to Aristotle is serious and not frivolous. Aristotle's work may be two thousand years old; discrete facts he suggested as observations may have been discredited. As an elitist, his thinking is surely tainted, but how this is so remains debatable; to "dis" all of it is absurd. The age of a critical work is not a reason for rejection; not all observations have been sullied, and Aristotle's approaches to various problems are diverse and often proceeded and concluded in ways contrary to his contemporaries. Aristotle was an observer and reported what he observed, not uncritically, but it should be kept in mind that just because he reports and analyzes something does not mean he endorses it. Otherwise, he must be seen as endorsing fraud (*On Sophistical Refutations*), which clearly he did not. Those who take the time to read Aristotle's Greek find themselves in the labyrinthian sorts of stylistic structures commonly found in postmodernist criticism—rather than the felicitous English to be found in translation. Considering that writing prose was itself a new endeavor in Greece at the time, Aristotle's writing may better be seen as something experimental—like postmodernist writing, and it is amazing how twentieth-century thinkers impose their expectations on that which they do not read. That imposition is as much elitist imperialism as anything they decry.

Elitism does show, however. There is a media hierarchy of dominance embedded in the assumptions of *The Poetics*. Aristotle apparently planned to write at least two parts to *The Poetics*. The first part concerns tragedy; we have that part, or a reasonable version of it. The second part concerns comedy, which we do not have. Tragedy and comedy were already culturally defined by Aristotle's lifetime. He observed their features and reported and incorporated them in *The Poetics*. Tragedy presents protagonists who are aristocrats. Aristocrats' flaws, deserved and undeserved woes, are the kith and kin of tragedy and evoke pity and fear in audiences. Comedy, however, presents protagonists who are common folk. When common folk undergo pain and suffering, deserved or undeserved, the audience laughs and ridicules the commoners' foibles instead of being moved to pity and fear about them. The hierarchy is plain. Tragedy is laden with the aura of seriousness because it portrays blue bloods in serious, life-threatening situations. Comedy is laden with the aura of humor because it portrays commoners in everyday life situations. That is the usual interpretation of Aristotle.

Umberto Eco proposes a different interpretation: Because pain and suffering are the ingredients of both tragedy and comedy, the line between them is not as dauntingly wide an abyss as the simple dichotomy of tragedy/comedy may suggest. One feature of tragedy and comedy, however, seems irrevocably different: Tragedy is serious, and comedy is ridiculous. In Eco's novel *The Name of the Rose,* a historical fiction and murder mystery, two monks confront each other about the second book of *The Poetics.* William of Baskerville, the protagonist-detective, proposes that comedy is born of the peasant villages as an after-meal celebration, that riddles and curious metaphors can be truly instructive by enticing the common to look further into the truth of life (574). William's opponent, Jorge, is most adamant that as long as comedy remained unrefined among "the plebeians," all would be well, but if commoners were to refine comedy, they could all the more easily defend themselves against their rulers—lords and church—and thereby change the human order. Jorge speaks,

> If laughter is the delight of the plebeians, the license of the plebeians must be restrained and humiliated, and intimidated by sternness. And the plebeians have no weapons for refining their laughter until they have made it an instrument against the seriousness of the spiritual shepherds. (579)

This excerpt of Jorge's tirade is instructive. As long as laughter is itself laughable, then the common folk who relish in it will remain common and preoccupied by their demeaned state, relieved of its seriousness by unserious laughter. But if they were to direct laughter as something serious at their rulers, their church, and the holy order it ordains, then suddenly the peasants would have a compelling weapon that could overturn the class system. Notice that the high will be lowered by comedy. Now recall the joke that began this chapter, and one can readily see the truth to Eco's presentation.

Eco outlines arguments that support the study of popular culture, such as those presented in the first chapter of the present book. When the common is taken seriously and directed at all of life, it becomes a potent instrument for understanding inequities. Notice also that Eco's argument is a media argument: Whoever controls the main medium of communication rules. The stakes are high when the common is taken to be uncommon. Eco reverses the situation about tragedy and comedy, blurring their conception. Comedy can be serious, and tragedy can be frivolous. It is no small mark of Eco's own genius that these arguments are written in a fiction instead of a critical work, couching concerns aired in the culture wars as if they were only historical fictions. Eco demonstrates not only that tragedy and comedy have much in common, or could,

:ir class assumptions, but that popular narratives, such as novels, constructively as postmodernist texts.

s chapter explored the relation of horror and sex and, as such, sition of late modern tragedy and its poetics. The present chapter now explores the relation of comedy and sex and considers late modern comedy and its poetics. Humor plays on duplicities, is an open text, and encourages audiences to provide information not supplied by the Joker to make sense of the humor. Then the Joker displays a different connection of the presented data, sometimes called "the punch line," delighting the audience in both the content and the telling of the humor. Finally, comedy often involves pain, the condition of being a victim, and the leveling of the high and the elevation of the low.

Humor as Dominance

That humor involves pain or victimage displays a hierarchy of dominance. Thus, humor could be taken as problematic, as a reflection of the conventional, mainstream order of male dominance. Unquestionably, by Aristotle's example alone, humor was conceived as appropriately lambasting common folk, not rulers. The gendered order of humor is also inscribed by the common, alternative name for the victim of a joke: The victim is the "butt" of the humor. We have already seen in Chapter 5 that the hierarchy of male bashing places the sexualization of the anus as the lowest put-down. Clearly, to be a butt of a joke confirms this hierarchy. The butt of a joke is rendered low and submissive. Legman also confirms the gender dominance implicit in humor.

> One fact strikingly evident in any collection of modern sexual folklore, whether jokes, limericks, ballads, printed "novelties," or whatnot, is that this material has all been created by men, and that there is no place in it for women except as the butt. (217)

Legman immediately emphasizes, however, that no one "conversant with ordinary life today . . . can be ignorant of the fact that women tell dirty jokes, and can listen to them." Legman then presents a series of jokes with men as the butt of the humor. One joke literally derides men and sexual anality:

> A druggist is selling a farmer a French tickler. "Before I sell you this," he says, "do you know what that rubber barb on the end will do to a woman?"
> "No, but I know it'll make a plow-mule jump a ten-foot fence." (268)

Legman opens the monumental *Rationale of the Dirty Joke* by centering on hostility.

> Under the mask of humor, our society allows infinite aggression by everyone and against everyone. In the culminating laugh by the listener or observer—whose position is often really that of victim or butt—the teller of the joke betrays his hidden hostility and shows his victory by being, theoretically at least, the one person present *who does not laugh.* (9; emphasis Legman's)

Hence, jokes are often apprehended as offensive because by their very nature, they offend at least one of the characters in the joke, if not the sensibility of a listener. That victimage and pain—real, imagined, fictive, moral, or physical— cause laughter is itself a clue to the excorporative nature of humor. By *excorporative,* I mean transformative. One takes a trait and incorporates it into one's repertoire of self-presentation and in so doing, changes its meaning. For instance, self-deprecation takes other persons' spoken or unspoken criticisms and applies them to the self in the form of a self-admission. The self-admission deflects criticism. So too, co-optation may deflect pain and suffering. Humor, causing or reporting pain, may relieve pain among the hearers. Slapstick comedy and sight gags portray pain and encourage laughter. In the middle of a serious situation, humor provides "comic relief."

Comic Relief

Although the beginnings of cartooning were steeped in political motivations, highly sexualized cartooning was not readily available to the public until publications such as *Esquire* pioneered their use. *Esquire*'s first editorial statement in its Autumn 1933 issue read like a manifesto, claiming there were no men's magazines that aired topics and issues interesting to men.

> It is our belief, in offering *Esquire* to the American male, that we are only getting around at last to a job that should have been done a long time ago—that of giving the masculine reader a break. The general magazine, in the mad scramble to increase the woman readership that seems to be so highly prized by national advertisers, have bent over backward to cater to the special interests and tastes of the feminine audience. (Table of Contents)

The first two articles were penned by Ernest Hemingway and John Dos Passos, underscoring both the manliness of the magazine and its literary aspirations. As the present interpretation proceeds, this editorial proclivity and the literary

profile must be kept in mind; although it does not excuse *Esquire*'s commodification of women, it supplies a backdrop for the sorts of humor encapsulated
in the cartoons. Beth Bailey identifies the most prevalent shtick.

> Before the sexual revolution of the 1960s provided juicier material, *Esquire* was
> fond of running cartoons featuring a short, elderly, and paunchy millionaire escort-
> ing a tall, enormous-breasted young showgirl through opulent settings. The captions
> didn't really matter. The cartoons worked best subtextually, and all contained
> variations of the same theme: money and sex; the coupling of wallet and bosom.
> (57)

Bailey extends this summary by admitting that the system portrayed commodified the man as "interchangeable with any other well-stuffed wallet" and also
by highlighting the stereotype of the showgirl as her "essentials: legs, breasts,
and greed."

That said, however, not all the women depicted are showgirls; not all the men
are millionaires, and sometimes captions did matter. Many of the cartoons in
the early issues do indeed feature the iconage of a rich, older man and his
seduction of a young, pretty woman. The millionaire eventually became the
bald, pop-eyed icon for *Esquire* and appeared on the second cover (January
1934). But more is going on, culturally speaking, than objectification of
maleness and femaleness—although such objectification deserves deeper investigation than Bailey can supply in the confines of a monograph on courtship.

One cartoon clearly shows an older, balding, mustachioed man in tuxedo
taking a young lady's wrap. In the background is an Asian wearing a white serving
jacket and carrying a tray of drinks. The lady looks at an artwork on the wall.
She says, "It was so nice of you to drive me way out here just to show me this
picture" (January 1934, 33). The young woman is trapped: trapped in the
assumption that the rich man's intentions are exclusively benign and artistic;
trapped in that there is no sure ride home when she wants it.

In the same issue on the next page, the millionaire clone stands in an elevator
with a young, almost flapper-like woman (34). He advises her to "just drive up
and down," which is suggestive enough, but the request is more devious than
that. It helps to know how elevators actually operated in the 1930s. The woman's
left hand rests on a handle on a wheel situated at the side of the elevator car;
her right hand touches the middle of the closed elevator door. Anyone familiar
with this gestural array and with 1930s elevators would be an informed reader
who could read more into the caption than whimsy. The young lady is quite
likely to be the elevator's operator. More than twenty years ago, it was custom-

ary for elevators to have a resident operator assigned, mainly because not all elevators had push-button systems with which we are familiar today. Even with push buttons, an operator was formerly common. Her right hand on the door signals she had just closed the door, part of the operator's job. Her head turned back to the man signifies that she is waiting to hear what floor he desires, part of the job. But the caption delivers the humor: To operate the lift system, the operator must turn the wheel clockwise or counterclockwise, and by so doing, the young woman will, in effect, perform a bump-and-grind.

Another cartoon displays a *young* man and an *older* woman in a sports car convertible. She may be older, but she is attractive, even to the point of being quite vampish and sultry. The lad's face, however, is covered with kisses and appears to be in the throes of dizziness (43). Caption? The woman says, "I suppose I'll have to marry him now." In this scenario, the woman is in the driver's seat, and the man is the one who is dizzy. This is not the in-control millionaire with the ditsy showgirl. Other interpretations flag themselves: The lad is so virginal he may expect a commitment, just from overpowering kisses. Ergo, men are weak. The woman is sulking, perhaps because the boy isn't man enough.

Marriage gets barbed, too (Figure 9.1). In a store selling firearms, a male sales clerk appears to extol the virtues of a shotgun to a male customer wearing a fedora, long overcoat, and slacks. Behind the counter, a male clerk's face reveals surprise at a woman's request (she wears tasteful high heels, a long overcoat with a fur draped over the shoulders, a hat, and gloves; her back is turned on the cartoon viewer who therefore cannot monitor her looks or age): "I don't know what calibre I should get, but my husband is about that size—" she says, pointing at the male customer.

Is the woman merely acting ditsy (bad enough for female stereotyping) in that she is selecting a gun by the size of a man instead of more practical, technical requirements? Is she buying the gun for her husband, and if so, why isn't he buying it? Or is it perhaps a respectable reading that she wants to shoot her husband? Perhaps a clue to the last interpretation may be found in the issue of size that also enters the picture. Are "calibre" and "size" elliptical references to penis size and girth? If so, her husband has a huge penis, judging by the size of the shotgun, which, in turn, lends more credence to the interpretation of the woman wanting to shoot her husband because the stereotypical convention appears to be invoked that holds that the larger the penis, the more insatiable the man. In turn, he may wear her out, he's so insatiable—or cheat on her because he's so sexed. In this final nuance, the caption is a polysemous and subtle concision that speaks a thousand words.

"I don't know what calibre I should get,
but my husband is about that size—"

Figure 9.1.   *Esquire* Cartoon
SOURCE: David Hampshire, *Esquire,* Vol. 1, Autumn 1933, p. 26.

Even then, not all the cartoons feature a male-female pairing. One of the more insinuating cartoons shows a corncob-smoking cook at a chuck wagon, working on a meal, listening to a radio. The caption reads, "Now lightly sprinkle in three teeny pinches of spice—" and the cook is plainly bewildered by the instructions (Autumn 1933, 21). Keeping *Esquire*'s editorial policy in mind, the cartoon plainly shows how woman-oriented mass communications can be and that there was no cooking show for a man in a man's language—conventionally speaking.

Later issues presented a wide array of circumstances, but on the advent of the United States' entry into World War II, some changes were made to suit the times. Some cartoons had sexual yet war-oriented intrigue: A man just arrives home to find his wife—his woman?—in the arms of another man (October 1943, 49). The caption spells it out for those familiar with the rationing of commodities crucial for the war effort: "Hello dear," the woman says, "this is the gentleman who sells us our fuel oil." The play is on sexual commodification in trade for heat, and the man—husband?—smiles.

The majority of World War II-era cartoons featured sailors and soldiers, sometimes with women, sometimes without. Changing norms of women "dating around" (Bailey) are confirmed by a cartoon that shows a sailor and a woman at her place in a clinch on the couch. The sailor says, "Is that so—and how did you find out that sailors are all alike?" (November 1943, 39). Having been caught out, the woman looks slightly startled.

An intriguing cartoon shows three young Wacs shooting dice outside their barracks. Just stepping out of the barracks is their sergeant, a big, stern-looking woman. With no caption, the reader must parse the visual cues. Two of the dice players do not yet see the sergeant. One does, her eyes popping, the dice more dropped than thrown, signifying that they have been caught doing something illegal. The three dice players are slender in appearance, compared with the sarge, who is full-figured. Unlike the other three women, her hair is decidedly short. The subtext of the sergeant's mannishness—and probably a career woman—may suggest to some that her sexual orientation may not be completely heterosexual. Perhaps, again for some, that adds some humor; others may well find it homophobically offensive. But suffice it to say, there are no bald millionaires and no pretty showgirls.

Perhaps changes in editorial policy were inevitable. The war ended, and America was moving on. The 1950s were perhaps not the nuclear family and chicken-in-every-pot myth many people apparently recall or believe. It was a time when the lines on the sexual battlefield were drawn. Hugh Hefner, formerly an *Esquire* executive, left his job, produced the first issue of *Playboy* on a song, and the rest is history. Hefner became the millionaire with the bevy of showgirls. But something else happened.

The more cartoons *Playboy* published, the fewer *Esquire* published. As *Playboy*'s cartoons became increasingly racier, *Esquire*'s became more tame. By the late 1960s, the few cartoons that appeared in *Esquire* did not even have a sexual subtext whatsoever. One cartoon shows a news anchor introducing a reporter who was covering a riot; the reporter is all beat up (October 1969, 208). That's the humor, a sight gag. Another cartoon is scatological: A clown, having walked past the dog act, realizes he's picked up something on his shoe (October 1969, 213). That's it—fecal matters.

Two of *Esquire*'s later cartoons do demonstrate a sexual subtext but quite different from those from the 1930s through early 1950s. The first depicts a city sidewalk. Down the walk at a distance is a nicely dressed mom, dad, son, and daughter. In the foreground is a beatnik couple, the man pointing at the family, saying, "This is just the sort of thing I'm against!" For the first time in print (November 1959, 124), with humor, perhaps, the restrictive norms of hetero-sexual family values are lambasted. As the saying in the 1960s went, part of the problem, not part of the solution. *Esquire* clearly picked up on the times.

These later cartoons also suggested alternative sexualizations. The second cartoon shows a man holding a dog leash with a spiked collar on his neck, facing off with a woman. He says to her, "I thought I'd wear it as long as you're making me lead that kind of life!" (October 1959, 74). The role reversal of gender stereotypes is clear enough, but the employment of a dog leash not only suggests that she treats him like a dog but also permits the interpretation that the two of them may engage in some form of dominance/submission in their relationship, consensual or not, perhaps more correctly called sadomasochistic. Just as transgressive to mainstream norms of sexuality, the man's eyes are dreamy although stern, sometimes iconage for gay homosexuality. The woman's close-cropped, tightly curled hair may also be taken as iconage of homosexuality. Neither interpretation—of sadomasochism or homosexuality—is necessary for humor to be evoked by the cartoon, but the three levels demonstrate how cartoons and humor often work as open texts while providing minimal data to go on—and that *Esquire*'s desire to feign elitism showed in a far different way than in the 1930s.

Since the 1950s, more mainstream, newspaper comics adapted to changing times too. Beetle Bailey showed the General's (bald with moustache) sexual harassment of his voluptuous secretary, Miss Buxley—reminiscent of *Esquire*'s dirty old man plus showgirl. The initial inclusion of Miss Buxley and her treatment by the entire male Army staff raised a furor in the early 1970s. The *Minneapolis Tribune,* among other newspapers, deleted Miss Buxley's appear-ances with statements such as, "Editor's note: Beetle Bailey does not appear on today's comic page because the subject matter was considered by the editors to be sexist" (*Miss* 1). Editorials and articles about the situation spawned fre-quently. Perhaps most indicative of the nerves struck were the hundreds of letters to the editor submitted to various newspapers. Many persons did indeed find the depiction of Ms. Buxley and her harassment to be repugnant as blatant sexism. Some defended the comic strip, its artist Mort Walker, and its freedom of speech.

Others, such as Mr. F. B. from New York City, saw things perhaps more perceptively.

> Some of your critics claim that your portrayal of sexism "trivializes" it. Isn't that what cartoons are supposed to do? When you ridicule military blunders aren't you trivializing the whole United States Army? Is that so bad? If you are going to have humor in any sense you are going to have trivialization because that is the nature of the beast. (*Miss* 11)

Mr. F. B. affirms that humor works by lowering its target, although not necessarily in a male-dominant way. He also recognizes that the Army is made to look bad, that sexism is not promoted, in one sense, but lambasted. As signs of the times, one of the characters in *Doonesbury* turned out to be gay, and *Cathy* has more of a relationship with her toaster than with any man. Although mainstream newspaper publishing does not pick them up, strips such as *Dykes to Watch Out For* may be found in various underground publishing venues.

Rationale of the Dirty Joke (Second Series)

In this chapter, I have maintained that humor serves to elevate the low and level the high and that it often highlights pain and can promote group solidarity. Of course, humor can do more than that, and it can often get out of control. Legman's *Rationale of the Dirty Joke* (Second Series) is proof of that. Although Legman's work is an invaluable source not just of particular jokes but also of commentary about how humor functions, outdated conceptualizations may be found. The section on homosexuality and jokes is particularly objectionable. The "cause" of homosexuality, Legman claims, "is a form of neurotic sexual impotence, *or flight from normality*" (55; emphasis Legman's). Furthermore, "the homosexual or lesbian is incapable of pleasurably fulfilling his or her proper biologically normal sexual goal." Legman's heterosexism is essentialistic and leaves no room for either a sane, healthy homosexual (" 'Gay' here is obviously the equivalent of *sick*" [64]) or for a socially constructed one. Thus, Legman's commentary is fraught with the assumptions that all homosexual jokes are told by people who hate homosexuals or by homosexuals who want to dirty themselves (70). Of course, this was 1975, and Scott Thompson of the

Canadian television show *The Kids in the Hall* and Sandra Bernhardt, stand-up comic and lesbian character on television's *Roseanne,* were not part of Legman's experience. Both comics are self-identified gay or lesbian, do not hate homosexuals, and do not "dirty" themselves. Legman stereotypes all gay men as lispers, and although lisping may conventionally be a source of comedy, not all gay men are lispers. Hence, both Legman's choice of homosexual jokes and the provided commentary about them are flawed—at their face value.

I append "at their face value" because Legman's choice and commentary themselves reveal the true nature of jokes about homosexuals. Not only is there a gendered hierarchy of male dominance, there is a heterosexist order. The heterosexist order seeks to perpetuate itself; one way this is accomplished is by telling jokes that place homosexual orientation literally so beneath the heterosexist order that heterosexuality is bolstered and constructed as normal, righteous, and preferable. In other words, Legman assumes heterosexist normality and then selects jokes to reinforce that severely limited, socially constructed assumption. Heterosexist jokes about homosexuals indeed put homosexuals in their place—*outside* the social order, closeted away from having to think about them seriously or to recognize that their sexuality is only one factor of their existence, just as it is for so-called normal people.

For that matter, a number of changes have taken place in North American culture since 1975 that admit to an order to sexual humors different from Legman's. The night of the last *Cheers* episode, the show immediately following was the Seinfeld episode that has come to be known as "the masturbation episode," although officially the title is "The Contest" (Fretts 93). The word *masturbation,* however, was never used. Three of the four friends—Jerry, Kramer, and Elaine—are seated at a booth at their regular diner when George walks in and sits. He confesses that his mother caught him. At first they don't know what he means, to which he replies meaningfully, "You know, *it.*" It turns out that he was checking out a *Glamour* magazine and became sexually aroused. The other three are variously shocked and amused. When they discuss it, they decide on a bet: Whoever can go the longest without doing "it" wins. At first, the three men balk at the idea of Elaine getting in on the bet, Jerry claiming that it's a way of life with men, but they relent and make the deal. Because of the nature of the bet, they agree to participate on the honor system, meaning, they trust each other to report themselves if they should fall from the path of autoerotic chastity. Of course, all sorts of arousing situations happen to each of them, but they refrain from doing "it" to win the bet, aroused or not, frustrated or not. George's mom had hurt her back when she discovered George doing "it" in her living room and winds up in the hospital. When George visits her, her roommate gets a sponge bath behind a curtain, giving George an arresting magic lantern show. John F. Kennedy Jr. happens to take aerobics during Elaine's class, right in front of her. Jerry is dating a virgin, and across the street, a woman walks around her apartment nude, driving Jerry and Kramer nuts. Before cutting to commercial, viewers see each of the four, three of them restless in bed—but not Kramer; he's sleeping like a baby, having succumbed first. The way the show works through each of the character's dilemmas is funny enough, and the closest they ever get to actually saying the word *masturbation* occurs during their ritual questioning of one another with the title: "Master of Your Domain," "George's variation is 'King of the County'; Jerry's is 'Lord of the Manor,' and Elaine's is 'Queen of the Castle' " (Fretts 53).

Circumspection gets called for about sexual orientation, yet orientation gets excorporated to deny its dishmissal or avoidance. In 1996, rumor circulated that Ellen DeGeneres' character "Ellen" on that sitcom would reveal herself to be a lesbian. Ellen appears on Rosie O'Donnell's talk show, and they skirt the issue, Ellen hemming and hawing, pausing at the end of her sentence before saying the "L" word, which, eventually Rosie supplies: Lebanese. The word is close enough and absurd because neither Ellen nor her character have much in the way of Lebanese ethnicity. Of course, Ellen then goes on to say to Rosie, "I've thought you might be Lebanese for a long time." The audience laughs at the wordplay, transforming the conventionally serious disclosure of orientation to gaiety.

The Alchemy of Gaiety and Gravity

I call the transformative nature of humor *alchemy,* the magical science of converting lead to gold, heaviness to levity, gravity to gaiety. Generically, however, humor means any mood, temperament, or attitude, not just capricious jocularity; in the old physiology, it referred to the four humors or body fluids of blood, black bile, yellow bile, and phlegm. The relative proportions of the four humors were believed to influence a person's physical and mental constitution. A preponderance of blood yields a sanguine nature, which is hopeful, optimistic, ruddy, and florid. Yellow bile is choleric, irritable, and angry. Black bile produces the melancholic persons who are sad and lack cheerfulness. Phlegm yields a phlegmatic, slow, not easily roused personality. Humors are psychic but intertwined with physical causes. Thus our later, more specific meaning for humor—something that permits, invites, or encourages smiles and laughter—transforms humors of more serious or indifferent vein. In contemporary times, the sexual seriousness of leaders and opinion mongers model pretensions of gravity.

Yet *gravity* has also come to mean the force that holds one down to earth. In contrast, humor lets one fly; it levitates and defies gravity. The two together inscribe a dominant epistemological hierarchy of up as heaven and joy, which is good, and down as earth or worse, Hell, which is the mundane, the not so good and unjoyful, even the bad. Gravity is the grave, the solemnity of our slice of eternity, because according to Western culture, one lives only once and is not reincarnated—with only one touch of incarnation, things are indeed quite serious. For other cultures, although this life is one of many, life is still serious. Yet humor incarnates as the sacred clown who, by divine vocation, transforms the pretensions of life's seriousness to joy, the echo of the divine (Duberman, *About* 121-132; Hillerman). Sexual humors also transform overindulgence of sex and its pretension of superior performance of humanness.

Gravity is an intensely *oriented* conception. Set as an opposite to gaiety, levity, it clearly inscribes a cultural domain of meaning that is hegemonically heterosexual. To be grave is to be solemn, sober, serious, and thoughtful. These attributes are the stereotypical attributes of the remote, controlled male in Western cultures. In contrast, to be "gay" once denoted lightheartedness, caprice, whim, and giving in to and demonstrably showing feelings. Conventionally, socially constructed, these attributes were and are the stereotypical attributes of the close, uncontrolled female in Western cultures. Victims of this binarism, lesbians are supposed to be stereotypically grave, whereas male homosexuals are stereotypically supposed to be *gay,* unserious, unreal. Both heterosexual impositions are inversions of the heterosexual stereotypes. Thus, as this cultural logic goes, not only are gays not serious but also they are not to be taken seriously. The more precise stereotype of the flighty, easily panicked homosexual male personifies unseriousness—but also personifies the less-regarded femaleness, gaiety. Because gay men are literally, by dominant cultural conception, not down to earth (not grave) when they are supposed to be (as male), they are the easy, ready butt—literally and figuratively—of humor that perpetuates heterosexual male dominance.

Heterosexist compulsion aside, gravity is still a serious attraction, attraction that dispels all other movement and is too serious and too grave to warrant unacceptance. Thus obsessive-seeming attractions are themselves the fodder of humor because only gaiety can relieve the compulsive attraction, lighten it up, and make it face its own self-absorption. Situations themselves—social occasions, meetings, greetings, and chance encounters—may bury affection in the solemnities of the moment or squander seriousness on the rocks of flirtation.

Flirtation is itself a regnant humor in that it arrests attention and diverts it, transforms it to levity if the situation is serious or to gravity if the situation is capricious. Flirting is the humor that opposes situational norms and converts them to interpersonal conspiracies that violate those situational norms. Flirtation variously inspires enthusiasm between communicators or quells the hunger of adventuresome joy. Flirtation is a mood alterer, a controlled substance. And time is now due to enter a flirtational mode of writing.

Wink Upon Wink Upon Wink: On the Interpretive Implicatures of Flirting

I now switch into a different discursive mode and style: I propose an exploratory style to mime the kith and kin of the inquiry itself. I'm in good company, or so I tell myself; Aristotle made a similar move in *The Art of Rhetoric*. Instead of defining rhetoric—speaking, communicating—in the painstaking precision of most of the rest of his logical procedures, Aristotle did not define rhetoric at all. He said in Greek, "Rhetoric *may be* defined as . . ." and not *is*. The entire opening to the point of this so-called definition was rhetorical from the word go, full of humor, wordplay, and inferential leaps of logic.

I plan to look at the sphere of flirtation and strip it, layer by layer, to its core, if I can get there at all. If the layers reflect each other, fine. If not, oh well. I choose flirting as a topic for many reasons, not least of which is my interest in it—my successes, my shortcomings. I suppose other people may have similar interests. I also suppose another title for this particular section of the chapter might be "The Art of Flirting." And like Aristotle's comment about the nature and nurture of communication skills in general, I recognize that some people seem to have an inborn talent or knack for flirtation. They can still learn and improve, just as those with apparently less natural talent at it can learn and improve. But how does it work?

Wink Upon Wink Upon Wink

Clifford Geertz presents us with a humorous—for academics, anyway—mul-tilayered metaphor for studying culture when he discusses, at length, Gilbert Ryle's notion of "thick description." Ryle illustrates the notion of description with boys contracting their right eyes at one another. One boy twitches; the other winks; although, empirically, both performances appear to be identical, "as anyone unfortunate enough to have had the first taken for the second knows," there is a vast difference between them. Geertz then notes five characteristics of the wink as opposed to the twitch. It (1) is deliberate, (2) is aimed at someone in particular, (3) imparts a particular message, (4) works according to a cultural code, and (5) works without others' awareness of its occurrence (*Interpretation* 6). At its simplest level, a wink is not simple. It looks like a twitch but is not a twitch. It may be taken as a twitch and ignored or interpreted as some sort of nerve disorder. For that matter, a twitch may be taken as a flirtation when it is not. Thus is cultural interpretation laden with multiplicities, not merely for anthropologists and ethnographers, but for people in daily life, as well as for people as they are depicted in stories, theater, films, and music. A wink, and by extension, flirtation, is a communicative conspiracy, reliant on communicators consciously performing and interpreting while others remain oblivious to it. A wink is an open text and works by the principle that it indeed was not a wink but a mere twitch. Nothing intended. Really.

Geertz and Ryle do not leave it there. What if, they confer, a third boy catches out the wink and then parodies a wink—performs the basic gestures but does so in an obvious, amateurish manner? All five characteristics of a wink still attain but with the added nuance that the communication by wink is no longer just a conspiracy; it is ridicule or commentary on the previous wink. Of course, the other boys may interpret the parody as a twitch, themselves oblivious to the criticism involved. In addition, the third boy, caught up in a splendid, critical glee, goes home, stands in front of a mirror, and practices the wink to discover what factors might make it more unmistakably a parody, a fake-wink—or further, practicing the fake-wink to use it, not a wink, out in public, with a friend to make third parties think there's a conspiracy when indeed there is not, other than the fake-winking, of course.

Thin description? "Rapidly contracting the right eyelid."

Thick description? "Practicing a burlesque of a friend faking a wink to deceive an innocent into thinking a conspiracy is in motion" (7).

Thus, Geertz and Ryle leave out an important ingredient of winking, of flirtation: It must be learned as to its significance, and one may practice how to signify by winking, thus improving its signification. At its critical—fake—level, the irony of winking or flirtation is most evident, yet a simple wink is also ironic because it can be taken at least two ways. Something else neither mentions is the equally present cultural feature that their illustration involves all boys. The illustration, taken only at face value, suggests that the boys are not really flirting but either playing at it from the first, or just plain playing. In any case, play is a central feature of their conspiracy. All the same, the illustration is homosocial. What if the initial wink means "I think you're terrific *because* you're a boy," and the subsequent parody by the third boy is a homophobic criticism? It has been known to happen. That the issues of play and homosociality are not commented on by Geertz and Ryle further underlines how flirting is an open text in which all sorts of diverse cultural nuances may be embedded without all people being aware of them, much to the advantage of oppressed minorities.

So let's take this winking illustration one step further. The actors have practiced their parts, and now they are on stage, on-screen, or in an opera, and they must convey flirtatious conspiracies in such a manner that the audience is pretty much aware of the various interpretive levels while one or more of the characters is clueless to the conspiracies. The play *Charley's Aunt* by Brandon Thomas is a comedy of errors that works exactly in this manner. Charley and Jack are buddies at Oxford. Charley is in love with Amy Spettigue, and Jack loves her friend Kitty. Amy and Kitty are to leave on a trip the next day, and Charley's aunt, whom he's never met, a fabulous millionaire, is due any moment. The two men resolve that the aunt's visit could not be better timed; they could invite Amy and Kitty to lunch to meet the old girl, who, in turn, would chaperone them. They also invite their friend, the Lord Fancourt Babberly (Babbs) as a luncheon partner to entertain the aunt while they make time with the girls. Babbs begs off because he is about to do some theatrical rehearsing for the first time, coincidentally, an old lady role. Jack and Charley connive him to stay, having a servant fetch Babbs's costume. Just as the girls arrive, offstage Babbs is donning the old woman's outfit. Because the aunt has not yet arrived, Kitty and Amy excuse themselves discretely, after which Charley receives word that his aunt will be delayed. Now they're in a fix. The aunt cannot show. By the time the girls return, Babbs is in costume, and the lads commandeer him into playing Charley's aunt.

The premises are set. Babbs has never acted before. He walks like a man. Although he initially tries a high voice, it keeps cracking, so he settles for almost his normal voice, avoiding deep tones. Amy and Kitty accept her as the aunt. Jack and Charley make progress with them. Unfortunately, Amy's father shows up and is immediately smitten by the "aunt." Because Charley and his roomie do not want to get into any trouble with Spettigue, they encourage Babberly to continue the charade as Charley's aunt. To do so, Babbs must walk the line of accepting Spettigue's flirtations, deflecting them but giving the impression "she" is flirting back, but not really. It just so happens that Charley's aunt, the Countess Donna Lucia D'Alvadorez, hails from Brazil, or at least was once married to a Portuguese count, and therefore it seems only natural for Babbs to employ a fan to hide his face so Spettigue can't see his face so well. Of course, Spettigue takes the fan wielding as flirtation, with long periods of Babbs hiding behind the fan interspersed with tantalizing and brief glimpses when the fan slips, gets involved in a hand gesture for emphasis, or is temporarily forgotten by Babbs as a most important prop to his dissimulation.

Add one more level: Charley's real aunt eventually appears with a lovely young woman as her protégée, Ela, a woman Babbs had met in Monte Carlo and had fallen in love with. Babbs immediately recognizes Ela and starts to flirt with her until he remembers he's supposed to be a woman. All the while, the humor is based on the ironies of Spettigue's ignorance of the true situation, the fiction of it; then, the table turns, and Babbs is desperate for the fiction to end so he can come on to the young woman and declare his undying love. But alas, he cannot because he's a woman, and he must perform even more carefully than before because the real aunt must not be revealed to Spettigue.

This sort of flirtatious, problematic, and thus humorous high jinks with men dressed as women but who lust for women was regular fare on the television show *Bosom Buddies.* Henry (Peter Scolari) and Kip (Tom Hanks) are roommates and happen to work together in a New York City advertising agency. When their apartment house is unexpectedly demolished, they are left without digs until their friend suggests they move into her building—but with one catch: the Susan B. Anthony Hotel is strictly an all-women residence. Henry becomes Hildegarde and Kip becomes Buffy, leading dual lives as men and women, generating all sorts of dilemmas, particularly such as finding women attractive when they are in drag. Hence the humor reaffirms heterosexuality while premising itself on the forbidden nature of same-sex coupling.

The more complex levels of flirting that involve obvious, overstated performance, either as a commentary or as a theatrical ploy so audiences will not mistake it as a throwaway gesture, may be considered as "camp," the cultural set of performances of exaggeration as irony. Perhaps the most complex version of flirtation of all, camp is "the re-imagining of the material world into ways and forms which transform and comment upon the original. It changes the 'natural' and 'normal' into style and artifice" (Bronski 42). Notice how well Bronski's definition of camp inscribes Geertz's wink upon wink upon wink. Camp is a commentary and criticism. Camp involves creative transformation of twitches—and even cultural performances—into something else. For Bronski, camp is a primary manifestation of gay culture, a culture that is powerless but must make mainstream culture "represent and respond to their lives. Refusing to accept the oppressive world as it is, gay sensibility has often imagined it as it could be" (41-42). This continuing act of imagination is camp. Camp is thus what Fiske would call an excorporation of mainstream culture, making it one's own to oppose it. Bronski adds that camp not merely is protective but also can be aggressive as wit, as performance that is at once funny but also incisive and truthful.

Charley's Aunt, thus, pokes fun at the wiles and ways in which men and women try to win one another for pairing. The feature that Babbs is a man playing a woman does not automatically mean Babbs is gay, or even close, but for some audience members, it may well raise that interpretive set of values as interesting or as problematic, or perhaps, both. Certainly, the play is funny, incisive, and through fiction, truthful about human relationships of a particular, British social class and time. To say that *Charley's Aunt* is campy is not to say that camp and flirtation are entirely the same. They are not, yet on a number of levels, campiness is a sort of flirtation, and flirtation is a sort of campiness. Therefore, although camp is highly manifest in gay culture, it is not limited to it. In addition, exaggeration itself is complex. Exaggeration does not always mean "over the top" obvious. It can be quite meticulous and subtle and yet obvious to an insider, someone aware that the camp, the flirtation, is likely to happen.

The Pulses of Flirting

Flirtation may be interpreted not only for its symbolic action and strategies but also for its psychological motivation. Noting that one condition that accompanies sex in all forms is "some degree of resistance" and that "sexual interest is whetted by stress and by barriers that have to be surmounted," Tripp observes flirting as always involving "stimulating attentions that are interrupted by momentary withdrawals. The meaningful wink is a cameo example" (108-109). From this psychologist's perspective, flirtation is a series of attention stimulations alternated with withdrawal, superattentiveness whetting and whetted by obliviousness. The aforementioned examples from *Charley's Aunt* concur.

Culture, religion, morality, and various taboos inhibit feeling and action and therefore provide the cultural assumptions and everyday life contexts both for expressing the inhibition and for releasing it. In other words, flirtation may be described as the social catharsis of ritually acknowledging inhibitions to create a place through which one may release the inhibition. Therefore, flirtation that between the two communicators violates civility, politeness, or custom may often take place without others present, except the intended audience, catching on to the flirtation. In that way, inhibitions may be broached publicly while at the same time privately, adding a frisson of breaking resistance to the interaction. In no small sense, then, flirting is a persuasive course of action and is rhetorical in that its symbolic cuing works to convince someone to interact, perhaps eventually to have a sexual interaction, except the symbolic nexus of flirtation takes advantage of the psychological pulse of resistance and release of usually acknowledged and conformed norms. Symbolically playing with resistance, inhibition—a sense of taboos and trespassing their bounds—is taking the pulse of give-and-take as an available means of flirtation.

Numerous books that style themselves as self-help manuals in flirtation focus on the sort of pulse of the interaction that Tripp mentions. For instance, claiming that flirtation is a formula that can be found in large urban centers and remote jungle villages, Money isolates the steps in flirtation as alternations of contact and disruption of contact, particularly as ways of escalating the flirtatious encounter into something more than flirtation, perhaps courtship and/or coitus. First is the mutual holding of the visual gaze between the flirters. "Next, one of the two tests the other by demurely drooping the eyelids so as to avert the gaze," which is a test to see if the other person will continue the encounter and if so, in which of various ways. The opening gambit leads to conversation, usually trivial at first. If the talk continues, it becomes accelerated, louder, perhaps with heavier breathing, with vocal exaggeration of all sorts. By now the two are physically closer, have adjusted clothing, and find opportunities to touch one another, usually feigned as an accidental brushing of skin by means of a natural gesture appropriate to the situation. If the communication continues, if the initial "accidental" touching produces no withdrawal or recoil, "the two people begin mirroring each the other's gestures and their bodies move in synchrony" (45).

Because flirtation willfully tests the other, withdraws with the possibility of no further significant contact, Adam Phillips suggests that flirtation is sadomasochistic at its core.

It is inevitable that flirtation—the . . . calculated production of uncertainty—will be experienced at best as superficial and at worst as cruel. Flirtation as sadomasochism with a light touch is a modest exposé of excitement as inextricable from tantalization; of desire as desire for a certain kind of torture, an enlivening torture, so to speak. . . . The generosity of flirtation is in its implicit wish to sustain the life of desire; and often by blurring, or putting into question, the boundary between sex and sexualization. Flirting creates the uncertainty it is also trying to control; and so can make us wonder which ways of knowing, or being known, sustain our interest, our excitement, in other people. (xvii-xviii)

Without question, the instigator of flirtation puts the person of interest on the spot and may indeed make the person uncomfortable. The discomfort may become factored as something rather nice or as something horrible. In the first case, the flirtation reaches another person and alchemically generates enthusiasm. In the second case, it may meet disfavorable inclination to the point of generating perceived harassment.

Goffman and Contextual Variation

Harassment is no small consequence of flirting where angels fear to tread. Some persons, for whatever reason, be it mood, temperament, or social stricture, reject advances of a nature that require their personal disclosures. The classic case involves work. At one's place of employment, one may rightly expect there to be a suspension of flirtation because it might corrupt the seriousness of getting work done. Yet that is exactly when humor, pure and simple, is called for to deflect seriousness, tension, or fatigue. The border between humor and harassment is touchy and will not vanish with sexual harassment rules because the border itself begs for transgression, articulating a new taboo of the later twentieth century. Thus, another feature of flirting that is no less significant than the other factors is its risk-taking nature, which has acquired even legal consequences. It may lead nowhere. It may wind one up in bed. It can buy one a ticket to court. Hence, the stakes are high, at least for some people. Even outside the workplace, the risk of rejection drives some to avoid social situations as much as possible. Others, able to cope with possible and real rejection, thrive on the excitement that putting oneself in a position of rejection entails. Others, cast in the stone of seriousness, flirt with danger and seek to lend an air of levity to working relationships and address the pretensions of the moment with personal violations and transformations to other enthusiasms, just for a little comic relief.

Erving Goffman has observed that certain social situations and terrains, such as bars and parties, are more likely to permit risky, flirtatious behavior because these situations invite the active violation of polite, public norms (*Behavior*). Certain locations, however, invite what Goffman calls a high degree of "consequentiality." Consequentiality involves a high number of outcomes to one's behavior, with the taking of risk perceived as an opportunity of winning a prize but usually with a strong likelihood of losing. One can lose money, as in a bet (*Interaction* 149-270). One can lose a game, as in pool. One can lose the pool game and lose money, and betting is illegal in many places, thus raising the stakes by possible legal ramifications. One may make a play for another person for sexual pairing with similar sorts of dynamics and outcomes. Indeed, the issue of making bets about whether one can "make" a possible lay occurs in enough popular fictions that it speaks excitement for some readers and audiences, whereas others—usually the ones treated as commodifications of consequentiality as depicted in the fiction—find such stories horrifying, if not demeaning.

Therefore, social occasions are relatively predictable sets of inventories for the levels of consequentiality a participant might expect for flirtation to happen. The likelihood of flirtation is predictable, yet open, with chance and initiative not completely controllable factors that influence outcomes. Flirtation is itself a way to increase the likelihood of sexual consequentiality and also may build sexual tension. Hence, the script of one beer ad, Bud Light: The voice-over runs, "Tonight I'm not gonna think about work or the usual but I'm going to flirt with the most dangerous woman I can find." The shots are a montage of clubbing, significant eye contact, and physical closeness between the man and various women. Both going to a club and the open invitation to flirt at such venues as a suspension of the everyday life norm of "civil inattention" (Goffman, *Behavior* 84) offer the sort of "attitude adjustment" inscribed in the voice-over, as many late modern, North American constituencies call it.

In *Like Water for Chocolate,* a man marries the older daughter in a family only because as eldest, she is offered in marriage, but he is in love with one of the younger daughters, and she with him. The only way she can communicate with him without upsetting the family arrangement is through her cooking. She prepares tasty, provocative foods instead of the regular, bland fare. She makes everyone uncomfortable with her cooking, however, although he is delighted with this flirting. Although the flirtation makes the whole situation problematic, their relationship is confirmed through the sign system of their flirtation, which is open to all family members. She's just improving her cooking skills.

Flirting Enthusiasm

Flirting operates by the employment of ambiguous signs that may be read variously, optimally with innocent, nonsexualized readings as possible as goal-oriented, sexualized readings. The trick of flirting involves contextual cues melded with timing to evoke a continuing interaction. Thus, strategies of using ambiguous signs to catch and guide an audience's attention have been known, theorized, and artfully methodized for hundreds of years as "rhetoric," but most particularly, the device that employs few signs ambiguously was named *en-*

thymeme by Aristotle. The term *enthymeme* is itself ambiguous as a polysemous pun that indicates that communicating by few, ambiguous signs involves lots more than stock devices. With our modern and late modern experience of language, we have been habitualized to look for singular, correct meanings. It is easy to ignore the facticities of language for Aristotle and contemporaries for whom writing in prose was a new medium, immediately preceded by archaic orality and its poetic norms (DeRomilly). In other words, Aristotle's conception of enthymeme, a device for getting an audience to draw a conclusion or conclusions with little data offered to convince them to do so, could well have been playfully presented, indicating what phenomenologists might call a word field of meaning. Looking into words with the same linguistic structure as *enthymeme* not only suggests that the term *enthymeme* means more than the word device itself but also suggests the way enthymeme was conceived to work, both in the common sense explanation we may well expect from Aristotle and in a prehistoric, spiritual explanation. Let's explore this word field of enthymeme and see if it would be so easy to dismiss the spiritual from the practical in Aristotle.

A series of words share the same phonotactic of sounds as does enthymeme. *Phonotactic* literally means sound deployment, the order of the sounds, a term linguistics researchers employ to indicate sound arrangements or the order of sounds in naturally occurring languages and situations. The phonotactic of the Greek word *enthymeme* initially involves *en* + *th*[*e, u,* or *y*] to yield words such as *entheos* (Liddell & Scott 566), indicating being full of the god, inspired, possessed—notions fully supported in Evans' *God of Ecstasy* as he discusses possession of a god in relation to the term *entheos* (58). *Enthesis* means putting into the mouth, insertion, a mouthful, as in "putting words in my mouth," whereas *enthousia* similarly means to be inspired or possessed by a god or to be in ecstasy or state of enthusiasm, inspiration, or frenzy. The verb *enthumeo-mai,* when employed in passive voice, signifies to be in a person's thoughts, to be desired. Thus the word *enthymeme* involves no less than two senses, the first like those immediately above—generating enthusiasm or spirit in an audience. Literally, this sort of enthymeme is an in-spiriting, that is, a putting inside of someone else's spirit, stirring the spirit, giving the person spirit, arousal. The second sense, however, denotes the symbolic form that generates the in-spiriting, usually by supplying two pieces of information that may have many logical connections, but the initial communicator or flirter leaves the connection unsaid, as in telling a joke, perhaps leading the audience down one line of thought, later yielding surprise or delight as endearments of the arousal. Thus the audience must supply the connection to make sense.

Before proceeding to some concluding examples of flirting, I must take this opportunity to affirm that enthymeme, the production of enthusiasm in an audience, is at the core of rhetoric and persuasion for Aristotle. The complete "definition" of rhetoric runs something like this: "Rhetoric may be called the ways available for connecting up with others." Enthymeme and the generation of enthusiasm are clearly ways to connect people, or connect with them, to get them to commit, to bond. A communicator, journalist, or entertainer who learns to generate plausible connection in an audience through supplying insufficient data is a star because they deliver a community of fans who desire to relate about those enthusiasms repeatedly, the very definition of popular culture. Thus, flirting is a sort of enthymeme in both senses, generating enthusiasm and a set of symbolic strategies for evoking and directing sense making in an audience.

Flirtation may be defined as observing the available ways of connecting up with others. Clearly, connecting up may include enthusiasm, enthymeme, and flirting but may include other strategies. Goffman presents some ideas about flirtation, particularly on appearing not to flirt. Although Goffman's commentary may well be construed as homophobic (Goffman attributes men's distance from one another as caused by fear of homosexuals approaching them, but barely fifteen years of the men's movement has observed that there are plenty of *heterosexual* causes of emotional and physical distance between men in many, but not all, Western societies), it is all the same instructive of the rules and taboos governing beginning flirtation with another man.

Homosexuals, "when 'cruising' for pickups, will utilize casual contacts involving innocuous requests or innocuous sociable comments as a cover" (Goffman, *Behavior* 141). Basically, that confirms the multilayered description of flirting earlier established from Geertz and Tripp. Because there is often the possibility another man might approach a man for sex, the initial interaction is ambiguous or calculatedly so, and either man or both men may need to monitor the signs they convey to the other. But even when a homosexual is in a homosexual bar, he may be reluctant to use certain words or phrases because they are stock inventories for flirting. Goffman's example from Rodney Garland's 1956 novel, *The Heart in Exile,* clearly indicates the dilemma of not being able to use words and phrases common to the club scene because they are so flirtatious. A gay man wants to light his cigarette but is matchless. Although there are any number of men in the bar to approach for a light, the cultural and insider knowledge dictates another course of action: "The legitimate phrase, 'Could you please give me a light?' was, in these surroundings, a recognized approach and a too obvious one at that. I walked up to the counter and bought a box of matches" (47).

In the movie of Paul Rudnick's off-Broadway comedy, *Jeffrey,* Jeffrey has already decided not to have sex with anyone because of the possibility of getting AIDS. Although self-identified as gay, apparently he buys into the notion that AIDS is a gay disease. Without question, he determines that love is just not going to be possible for him in the age of AIDS, gay or not. So he joins a new gym to work out and forget about it all, jumps into the weight room, and airs a general request for someone to "spot me" for a set of bench presses. But a hot, buff, hunky man answers his request for someone to "spot him" with "How much do you want?" The ramifications of the wordplay are priceless. "Spot me" yields a play on spotting, which is in one sense getting physically close to assist someone doing a weight drill, but in a different sense, it can also mean the effect such closeness might have for a man, an autonomic reaction of arousal, precum spotting one's pants. Hence, the innocent request to "spot me" is returned with an equally duplicitous "How much do you want?" The question at once asks how much weight Jeffrey wants to lift, but it also alerts the audience and him to issues of size, force, length, time, or even relational commitment. Jeffrey turns to see who's offered to help, only to find a really handsome, extremely well-built man. Clearly, the "line" and the man arouse him immediately. One person says something perfectly innocent for the occasion, but something that also has other meanings, particularly sexual innuendo. The other person has a choice to go along with the subterfuge or not. In this case, the second communicator takes it and runs with it, continuing the fiction of the innocent surface, but flirting back with innocuous innuendo that indicates acceptance of the original contact possibly on more than the surface level. As the scene plays, Jeffrey lays down to position himself for the presses but the man stands at his head near the barbell to "spot" or assist if the weight gets to be too much. Underscoring the flirtation on size and crotch problematics, Jeffrey is directly looking into the guy's crotch. His encouragements to Jeffrey are fairly orgasmic in their pacing, building, growling. This situation is just the sort of situation Jeffrey had hoped to avoid. Of course, he falls for the man, Steve, and to his dismay, Steve is HIV positive. Thus, while the film is a comedy, it alchemically explores the issue of falling in love with someone with a contagious disease and tries the limits of gravity in determining one's life.

10

After the Beat: Popular Music

The Western art music tradition undoubtedly has been in no small way formative of Western popular music; so, too, have "folk" music and popular music itself. Although one approach to popular music could involve detailing prior influences to a popular song, group of songs, or type of song (such as country and rock), I will take a different approach. First, I readily acknowledge that culture commentators have known for a long time that music affects audiences. Both Aristotle and Plato noted that Doric mode elicited discipline and was good for troops marching off to war. On the other hand, the Phrygian mode allegedly evokes licentiousness and therefore ought to be avoided, as should virtuoso flute playing, at least according to Aristotle, because both tend to make poor citizens. Plato and Aristotle, however, provide their comments in works on government and ethics, whereas the traditional Western discipline for understanding both how effects are produced in audiences and how to produce those effects was and is called rhetoric. Commonly defined as persuasion, rhetoric has been applied to speech, writing, and word-mediated human communication.

Thus, there are literally hundreds of publications on the lyrics of popular song and their persuasiveness but few that address music at all at length (Holmberg, "Toward"). Analyzing lyrics analyzes poetry, not music. When interpretations of music-as-persuasion have been offered, they have been mostly disregarded because the suggested interpretive treatments do not limit themselves to words, sometimes with the rather weak excuse that music is not a particular researcher's specialty. It is indeed an odd argument that a particular researcher's lack ordains that the musical research cannot be rhetorical or valid. This dismissal of seriously engaging the rhetoric of music without providing an alternative for understanding how music works persuasively is narrow, if not myopic. Admittedly, researchers lack as common a critical vocabulary for assessing music and its effects as we do poetry and literature, but that does not excuse ignoring the music. Perhaps in too many circles of rhetorical and communication studies researchers, rhetoric remains relegated only to the usual semantic systems of words. This calcification is all the more strange because, now more than thirty-five years ago, the "Wingspan Conference" and its capstone "National Conference on Rhetoric" recommended that " 'rhetorical studies' be understood to include any human transaction in which symbols and/or systems of symbols influence values, attitudes, beliefs, and actions" (*Prospect* 214), that interdisciplinary work should be promoted "to look at the same rhetorical transaction from different perspectives" (216-217), and that research of "theory and function of language *and other symbol systems* which influence man" [*sic*] be expanded (217; emphasis mine). The elite, scholarly tradition in rhetorical studies still does not speak much to persuasion beyond words and language, and the "prospect of rhetoric" remains largely unfulfilled.

Even without words, music still may clearly be construed as a semantic system, with cultural conventions such as rising melodic lines signifying ascent and falling ones indicating descent (Winn). At base, however, music is—or may be interpreted as—a nonsemantic sign system, a series of open texts that suggest not one and one only "correct" interpretation but numerous trajectories of interpretation and use. With lyrics superadded, the musical complexities may be variously interpreted as a fabric the lyrics reflect, defer, or oppose. The criticism of popular song is in no way as simplistic as some commentators ordain—but it should focus on the music.

The remaining variety of approaches for studying popular music reveal more about the studiers and the reasons why they conduct research about popular music than they do about popular music. In the radio broadcasting and recording industry, it is customary to conduct audience response research to determine the likelihood a particular market segment will remember a new song before a song's release. The research is not so much about the music or the audience but whether the musical artifact has a strong likelihood to sell. Arbitron ratings of radio listeners quantify audience reach and market share and also do not really interpret music or how people use music in their everyday lives. Marxist-derived approaches seem to focus on everyday lives yet focus more on processes or praxes about which common folk are unaware, disinterested, or unable to influence directly.

For a few stolen moments, therefore, I would like to sidestep the controversy over just what is the proper manner for researching popular music by providing different approaches for understanding the persuasiveness and pervasiveness of popular music, ways that any rhetorician can understand because I shall employ words and not musical theory. Instead of taking any of the typical tacks on interpreting popular music by measuring audience response; discussing its commodification, production, and distribution; or analyzing the lyrics; and instead of taking the lowly and polemicized interpretation of the music itself, let me first suggest an alternative: the ethnographic collection of data concerning how popular songs and music are used in everyday life.

None of the other, traditional approaches for interpreting popular music and culture address how music in and of itself galvanizes audiences not just to listen to it but to congregate in groups or wear clothing deemed appropriate to certain styles of music and dance. Thus, researchers have overlooked popular music as it is played at many venues, particularly informal gatherings: (1) at parties, particularly those that air cassette tapes produced solely for use at parties from the wide range of songs available; (2) at clubs, particularly those that on different nights play a limited range or type of music; and (3) during sports activities. To get at party songs and party tapes and their sexual significances, I shall share some findings of an ethnography I conducted. Then, to get at what is happening with popular music and sexualities at clubs, I shall present a brief history of disco, its musical characteristics and its origins, and how these were later transformed by suggesting a second and novel approach for getting at the persuasiveness of music: Referring to Andrew Holleran's novel *Dancer from the Dance,* I shall demonstrate an inversion of the preference for literature over music. *Dancer*'s various micro and macrostructures are musical, not literary, in their mimesis of the early disco scene. Finally, I shall discuss connections between popular music and sports observed in everyday life. These connections reveal the bases of what I shall call "physical mysticism," the ecstatic—and sexualized—immersion into the direct experience of the body as cued by rhythmic auspices. These connections will then also link to the next chapter, which concerns gesture and body image.

Party Songs and Party Tapes: An Ethnography

Popular music is social (Fornas 298) and is ubiquitous for many cultures and their social gatherings. Most persons readily acknowledge the use of music at large, ritualistic, and public events. It is omnipresent and formative of both individual consciousness and group collectivity on occasions such as commemorations, dedications, graduations, weddings, funerals, and memorials. On these occasions, special music may be brought forth, music not often performed at other times, such as Elgar's "Pomp and Circumstance" and Wagner's "Wedding March." Specific musical compositions used only for special occasions underline the liminal nature of the events and often define or help to define the events (Turner, *Forest* 93-101; Van Gennep 177-188).

Naturally, music occurs at times other than culturally sanctioned events, but these more informal occasions are often conceived as mostly for enjoyment, for passing the time. All the same, everyday life (Douglas, *Understanding*) situations are no less interesting for cultural interpretation than are formal and elite cultural events that call for music. Indeed, understanding what Glassie calls concrete "situations" is perhaps as important as the artifacts that are employed in or emerge from the situations (33). Although music may appear to be just a way of passing time, in some cases, there are deeply resounding features of the uses to which music is put; these uses may even supplant the more public and formal uses if for no other reason than that they are performed frequently or on a daily basis. In North American cultures, the apparently capricious and idiosyncratic uses of music at parties acquire greater significance because although many public rituals with music are publicly attended but may be privately scorned, parties among friends are events most people anticipate with pleasure.

Getting together with friends certainly receives little social censure and is often encouraged. Nevertheless, although beer busts and wild parties are admired by some, they are also scorned and vilified publicly, even to the point of legislating ordinances against loud music as a means for controlling parties. Most important, however, both the more tame, friendly get-togethers and the more deviant social gatherings often include music.

Sound and culture obviously involve music. The audeographic study of sound and culture as a type of ethnography helps locate music in the cultural landscape differently than does the study of lyrics or musical form. Ethnographers are fond of studying human interaction in particular locales, as well as the types of social roles enacted on different occasions. The locales for parties are many; the role of music presents itself as a cultural domain of meaning.

Research Context

I observed hundreds of parties during an ethnographic study of communication at social gatherings from 1985 to 1991. Not all gatherings were classified as parties by informants, but music was heard at no less than eighty-two percent of gatherings that informants considered to be a party. Early in the data collection, it became evident that music was used consciously and unconsciously to solve all manner of social problems, particularly with regard to the etiquette and ease of meeting strangers. Data were collected by participant observation (Spradley, *Participant*) in many geographical areas of North America, including Canada. Field notes were transcribed as preliminary expansions. Preliminary expansions suggested directions for formal and informal ethnographic interviews. Initial discovery of cultural domains (Spradley, *Ethnographic* 185-203) of semantic meaning for party participants was verified by interviewing 130 participants and planners of various types of parties and gatherings. Interviews yielded subdomains that are characteristics of music at parties, at least in North America. Analysis of these characteristics yielded conclusions that suggest that music at parties is a use category of culture that enhances social situations, particularly the reaffirmation of friendship, sexual pairing, and a sense of community support of backstage (Goffman, *Presentation* 106-135) expressions of personhood apart from regular daily activity.

Establishing Cultural Domains of Meaning

On the basis of a list of songs most frequently recorded in my field notes, I interviewed informants about their conceptions of "party music": What other songs or types of music should be considered? Why? What was the nature of a piece of popular music that rendered it appropriate—or even mandatory—for a party setting? Naturally, the song list was biased by the types of parties I attended. It was also biased in that the field of data initially to be discussed between the informant and myself was limited to examples of rock and roll. Beginning an individual interview with rock and roll titles was planned in part as a control measure to assess honesty and validity of the informants' data. Would they suggest other types of music that the informants might have heard at parties? Would they report the types of variation of party characteristics that I had already observed? Asking appropriate follow-up questions was also planned to mitigate the rock and roll bias of song titles initially presented to informants. I eventually asked each informant to supply added song title data or to delete data that had been initially presented them by me. Many did indeed supply new data for consideration, thus mollifying the bias.

Establishing the Domain of Party Music

I placed one song title per individual note card and presented various sets of cards to informants and instructed them to conduct a card sort. Informants were asked to sort the cards in any way they desired—but they were directed that there had to be no less than two groups of cards when their sort was finished. All but six informants grouped the cards by musical style that they perceived to be significant. The remaining six grouped them by songs they liked and disliked. After I asked informants to look over their groupings and titles and then characterize the songs, usually they came up with a name for each pile of cards, such as "classic rock," "progressive," "hard rock," and so on. I encouraged informants to suggest names that might apply to more than one pile. "Rock and roll" was the most frequent answer. Words and phrases such as "upbeat," "fun," "danceable," "sexy," "party," "party songs," and "easily sung to" were mentioned with no less than fifty percent frequency. Informants were then asked to supply names of other rock and roll songs they knew that they thought belonged among the cards; any new title was immediately printed on a fresh card, and informants were asked either to put it in one of the piles they had already sorted or to begin a new pile. They were also asked to delete any title they thought did not belong. This procedure usually began a more interactive phase of the interview especially because some informants professed they did not yet know how all the titles were supposed to fit into one category, if at all.

If "party" or the phrase "party song" had not yet been used by the informant at the end of adding and deleting song titles, I asked them to think of the times they had heard any or all the songs on the cards. Informants supplied terms such as "bars with a live band," "parties," "beer busts," "having friends over," and "cover bands"—cover bands being local rock and roll bands that perform songs made popular by famous or Top 40 bands. Some informants volunteered that the song titles were limited in scope; they had perceived the party orientation of the titles and maintained there were other types of parties and appropriate music to go with them. Informants were then asked to discuss what made songs suitable for "having friends over." If they had employed the phrase "party songs," they were asked to discuss what made songs suitable to be called party songs and which, if any, of the songs they had listed were good, representative party songs. The congruence of their lists with the lists originally generated from field notes was strong verification of the field observation.

Subdomains

Characteristics most often suggested by informants as definitive of party songs were (1) the beat, (2) lyrics, and (3) danceability. On further questioning, some informants offered that lyrics and danceability also included a fourth characteristic, participation.

The Beat. Informants ascribed the range of this subdomain variously as "upbeat," "driving," "good driving beat," "good beat," "sexy beat," "fast," "rapid tempo," "very strong beat," "constantly punctuated with the beat of a bass drum," and "listen to those drums." The primary factor was speed, and speed delineated a realm of preference among party songs. Fast songs were considered to have more the quality of a party song; slow songs could still be party songs but were usually ranked lower in card sorts of most representative party songs, if they made individual lists at all.

Lyrics. Many informants claimed that the lyrics of a good party song had to be singable and easily remembered. When describing lyrics, some used the industry term, "hook" (Burns 1987), saying, "A song has to have a good hook," or "There is a part of every good party song that most everyone will join in and sing the words." The meaning of the lyrics was also mentioned frequently as an important characteristic of party songs. Lyrics were often directly or indirectly sexually provocative. Singing them in mixed groups provided opportunities for individuals to look into each other's eyes and monitor interest in later sexual pairing while seemingly just having fun and innocently singing along. Even rebellious lyrics such as Twisted Sister's "We're Not Gonna Take It" allowed partiers to express feelings they felt were inappropriate to voice among family, at school, or on the job.

Some songs offered groups opportunities to demonstrate group solidarity. For instance, the song "And She Was" was performed at any number of undergraduate Greek fraternity and sorority parties at colleges and universities; when the refrain occurred, the women would shout "She was a" (insert their sorority's Greek letters) and the men would counter antiphonally, "She did a" (insert their fraternity's Greek letters). I observed this behavior not only at various Greek chapter parties but also when groups happened to be on the same dance floor at bars in Bowling Green, Ohio; East Lansing, Michigan; and State College, Pennsylvania. On these occasions, women from various sororities would vie to see who could shout their letters the loudest, as did the men for their respective fraternities. This example illustrates a common phenomenon, that popular music is used and adapted by people in specific situations for specific purposes.

Danceability. Danceability was a characteristic of party songs that some informants mentioned first because, as they claimed, it was important that a song make them want to move. I observed that at one party, AC/DC's "You Shook Me All Night Long" got partiers to sway their hips when previously few persons had demonstrated any interest in moving to the beat of a song. Another person began jumping up and down. Asked later what he was doing, he said, "That song gets me into a party mood." Dancing was not observed at all parties, but the eurhythmic mime of the beat was. At parties at which there was dancing, men and women used music to relay nonverbal messages through their dance movements such as hand gestures, smiles, eye contact, and physical contact, particularly brief or lingering touch with the fingers. Music was often played loudly at parties, and these nonverbals were all the more important because it was almost impossible to talk and be heard adequately. One informant liked to include Def Leopard's "Pour Some Sugar on Me" on a tape for parties because he knew people would dance around seductively, grab other partiers, and fondle one another as the lyrics declared "shake it up, break the bedroom and have some fun."

Participation. Most informants claimed that the type of party at which they played party songs was usually attended by friends who brought along guests who were strangers to the hosts. Between fifty and two hundred persons or more might appear at this type of party. Hosts chose songs such as party songs to get people unfamiliar with one another to raise their spirits, move around, forget their troubles, and mingle to meet new people.

Party planners—or the persons inhabiting the social role of host—had as one of their goals the creation of a party mood. A "party mood" was a release from formal norms of etiquette. Creating a party mood was considered to be mostly the responsibility of the person or persons who held the party. Goffman might say that creating a party mood may be accomplished by sending signals that all guests are in a backstage area where public norms of sociability may be discarded (*Presentation* 106-135), whereas Turner might say that a party mood is accomplished by sending signals that all guests are in a liminal situation in which regular social rules and roles are suspended, thus allowing for more informal and impolite behaviors (*Celebration* 19-41), particularly yelling, clapping, stomping the feet, whistling, and making loud smacks of the lips. Without these loud sounds, party planners and their guests would often claim a party to be "a dud." Thus, party planners played certain songs to let their guests know they could let down their hair with relative impunity.

Naturally, loud behavior is disapproved of by some neighbors. Most communities have noise laws for the purpose of legally inhibiting party behavior. Audeographically, the party norm for certain types of parties to be considered a success is to make as much noise as possible. Ritual release received comment the next day in the form of "Wow, I sound like a frog! Some party, hunh?" The community's audeographic norm moves in the opposite direction: A successful party is one that is not noticed or, at worst, is merely a minor disturbance of the peace.

Party planners reported they take both audeographic norms into account. In college towns, however, hosts most often leaned in favor of the party norm. Thus, they looked for signs of success during their parties. Planners knew inhibitions were more relaxed when partiers started to play "air guitars" or "air drums" in synchronization with a song. Planners knew inhibitions were discarded when songs such as "Mony, Mony" elicited stock, ribald responses or when the lead singer sang "Here she comes moanin' Mony, Mony," and most if not all partiers responded in time to the music by shouting "Hey! Get laid! Get fucked!" Raising the roof with shouting was an important sign of party success. Shouting was observed at most parties, naturally, because the noise level of people talking and loud music required shouting just to communicate simple information. As a subdomain of party song characteristics, however, shouting was a ritual form of participation, signifying a party mood. Songs such as "Why Don't We Get Drunk and Screw?" by Jimmy Buffet and the Coral Reefer Band almost always prompted hearty vocal participation during the hook, accompanied by the hoisting of beer glasses and swinging them back and forth to the beat.

Each of the four characteristics of party songs is a subdomain of the more generic cultural domain, party song. When I attempted to verify if party songs had to be perceived as having one or more of these characteristics, however, informant answers suggested on the one hand that this assumption was correct but on the other hand that there were other types of parties with different types of music played at them. In essence, "party song" was a subdomain of a more universal cultural domain, namely, party music.

Music as Background and Foreground Sound:
Promoting Interaction among Friends

One informant, a former heavy metal guitarist from a cover band, said, "Most of the songs you showed me are beer bash songs. When I have friends over nowadays I put jazz or New Age music on my stereo so we can talk and kick back." When asked to supply examples of the types of music he might play for friends for this quieter kind of party (but not at a beer bash), he supplied me with five tapes. He identified two as tapes for playing when friends come over to talk and spend time. The other three tapes he had made in high school and college and had been played at big parties where lots of beer was served. He called both kinds of tapes "mixed tapes," although he claimed it was more correct to call tapes to be played at bigger parties "party tapes" although they were still "mixed" in styles and performers.

Because the whole phenomenon of making mixed tapes had also escaped scholarly attention, I then began to collect "mixed" or "party" tapes as well as data about them in much the same fashion as about party songs. Further data verification was warranted as another sort of artifactual verification of characteristics or subdomains of party music. It was also warranted because I had rarely observed party hosts changing discs or tapes for individual songs while a rock and roll or beer bust party was in progress. Most of the time, songs had already been copied onto a fresh tape or series of them for the express purpose of playing at that party. Informants also verified what I had observed, that not all North Americans conceived of party music as solely for wild and crazy parties that produce drunkenness.

Party Tape Characteristics

People who live in mass culture environments are always interacting with mass culture, consciously or unconsciously. When they consciously make tapes for parties, they are in essence making their own album or performing the function of a disc jockey or station manager who determines the playlist of music. For the purposes of the present report, a party tape is defined as a recording of many different performers on cassette format that was actually compiled for and subsequently played at one or more parties by a person or persons who desire to convey a particular party mood for the gathering. Party tapes have redundant characteristics: (1) the predominant musical style on the tape and (2) the order of music on the tape. These two characteristics in turn suggest the domains of tapes' cultural uses.

Predominant Musical Style. Tapes either included the types of rock and roll songs already mentioned along with other rock and roll or were compilations of quieter, often slower, music. These latter tapes usually included musical styles such as soft rock, light jazz, New Age, light classical, or even show tunes, but the music was almost exclusively instrumental, not vocal. When I played a tape of the latter music for informants, they almost always described the social gathering at which it would be played as having a small number of people in attendance. They characterized the guests as probably knowing each other well with only a few less familiar guests, if any. They conjectured that a less familiar guest would have been invited to get to know them better. The informants expected the music would be more in the background to allow for conversation, also figuring that if alcoholic beverages were involved at all, they would consist of wine or mixed drinks; if beer was drunk, the quantities were low. Many also said that unless the get-together was for a couple with the express purpose of intimacy, the sexual innuendo would be at a minimum. One woman said, "Parties with this kind of music are for talk, and people feel more free to talk if they're not overly concerned about being hit on." Naturally, the sound level was low. In sum, the relation of sound and culture for the quiet, friendly get-together may be characterized as low, respectful of personhood, nonprovocative, and relatively hidden during discourse. This last point is important. The music was a backdrop, not something at the forefront of attention. A third type of musical tape was a hybrid of the other two but was still used as a tape for a quieter party. It consisted of rock and roll played quietly in the background. Individual titles might be party songs, but there were less of them, and as a whole, the titles were more idiosyncratically chosen.

Order of Music. The order of music was more important for people who made the louder rock and roll tapes. The order was also idiosyncratic to what they expected or wanted to happen at their parties. Most said that they would intermingle party songs with other songs. In other words, they would rarely make a tape exclusively with party songs on it; variety was important for maintaining a spirited party mood. The other songs that hosts put on a party tape usually reflected their personal interest or favorite performer. Hosts felt that if a song they chose by personal preference might be less popular at a party, most guests knew that a favorite would probably happen next on the tape; thus they placed one or two stronger, more familiar songs after personal preferences.

Some tape makers agreed, however, that they tended to play their own preferences earlier in a party than later. Later, they would play more party songs with universal appeal. Naturally, this meant that they had more than one tape in mind for a party, and tapes to be played later in the evening would have more upbeat and familiar songs, except within the last half hour or so of a long party. Then a host might play more slow songs to signify the party was shutting down.

Rock and roll tapes usually began with two to six fast songs, followed by one or more slow songs. Tape makers said they wanted to establish a party mood right away with the music. Slow songs allowed guests to rest if they had been dancing; they also allowed them to fill up on drinks before another party song was played. Slow songs also allowed for consolidation of paired relationships after dancing because they encouraged romantic and seductive moods. Most tapes followed the slow song or songs with faster songs and ended with an upbeat song. The most frequent tempo formula for tapes involved the alternation of fast and slow songs with a tape side ending with one or more fast songs.

The order of music on tapes made for the smaller and quieter parties with friends had little to do with tempo or with creating and sustaining a frenetic party mood. Creating a mood was still important, but the mood most often had nothing to do with wildness or sexual behavior. An observation made many times was most telling: Hosts wanted to give their guests a novel experience with the music; they often made sure that some, if not all, of the music on the tape was something their guests had not heard previously. Conversation occurred more at smaller gatherings, and thus the host was more likely to interrupt a tape and select one or more individual pieces of music so particular guests could hear a piece or performer the host had learned was unfamiliar to them.

The host would bring out albums and pass them around, both for tapes and individually played music. Sometimes, guests would write down the album title and performer's name. In contrast to rock and roll tapes that elicited participation in the song by loud singing or acting it out, the quiet music tape only infrequently elicited conversation about the music. Because quiet music tapes had far more instrumental pieces on them than rock and roll tapes, it was only natural that singing along was less likely. I observed, however, that partiers at larger, more raucous parties did not talk about rock and roll party songs, whereas the same persons did talk about music when they attended the quieter, more intimate, friendly get-togethers.

Prevalence of Norms as Insider Knowledge

Music was observed to create specific effects at parties. Even when tape makers professed no plan in putting together a mixed tape other than "I just like these songs; that's all," they chose songs consistently in congruence with those who consciously chose particular songs, ordering them in particular ways with the effect of producing rowdiness or conversation. When they themselves lacked the stereo equipment or records, they would ask friends to bring tapes; invariably, the friends supplied tapes that were appropriate for the type of party the host had in mind.

Party Moods

In general, hosts wanted their guests to have fun and enjoy themselves. They knew that the wrong type of music might drive away and annoy their guests or kill the party mood they most desired. Beer bash music invited rowdiness and the relaxation of sexual mores, so guests could easily invent ways to meet and perhaps pair with persons of their gender orientation. The music accomplished this effect by creating stock opportunities that called on partiers to pursue various social exigencies of their choosing, such as meeting strangers, acting crazy, achieving some level of catharsis, or pairing sexually. The music was a rhetorical artifact (Holmberg, "Toward") for enhancing social interaction. Partiers had a clear expectation of themselves and others that they must use their communication skills. Music strategically supplied by their hosts facilitated their communication. In essence, the beer bash mood was an obvious dramatistic scene to the participants although their conscious recognition of it as such was no doubt in most cases inchoate. The music itself was an agency of their interaction. Both the scene and the agency encouraged partiers to be actors who might perform parts pursuing varying interests, even the invention of fictive biographies similar to those Cavan observed in bars. Fictive or genuine, the roles or their entertainment value to other partiers were seemingly invented on the spot, with some actors more successful than others. Hosts were admired for how well they generated a "pumped" mood by means of music and other artifacts. Guests appreciated the various opportunities provided and the consequent freedom to socialize.

These major calculated effects were expected by most partiers. They had anticipated that the party would involve chemical intoxication with beer or liquor; they also knew that the party would allow them to shout, act wild, and do things they did not do during the rest of their everyday lives. They knew but were not always able to express that the rock and roll beer bust had ritualistic qualities; that earlier in the evening, social interaction was more awkward than later because of music and other party ingredients; and that sexual pairing started to occur the moment one arrived but that most decisions about it usually did not occur until later in the evening, especially during well-chosen songs that encouraged sexual innuendo and gestures.

Partiers also knew they were expected to participate in all sorts of activities with ritual overtones. Some rituals were relatively similar to those found in daily life, such as meeting friends and being introduced to strangers. Some activities, however, reflected the party mood, such as acting humorously (e.g., talking softly to someone's gender orientation during a loud party so the individual would have to lean closer to the speaker), singing boldly along with lyrics, gesturing wildly to songs, touching people, drinking in time to the music, and playing drinking games, much as various ethnographers report about bar behavior (Cavan; Spradley & Mann). Although participation appeared to be spontaneous, the behavior was *de rigueur* and learned at previous party attendance. Most of all, partiers appreciated parties as occasions during which they could "be themselves" with the tacit support of others like themselves—not the artificial selves they felt they had to be during daily life. The music reinforced their sense of community support of their individuality.

Parties that had been intended as bashes but that frustrated the guests' expectations tended to have fewer party songs and loud noise as well as more idiosyncratic recordings. The popular maxim about parties—"out of beer, out of luck"—was not the only norm operative for determining whether to stay or leave, whether the party was a good one or not. Guests wanted stock situations in which they could maneuver; too many idiosyncratically chosen songs required them to have more of a unique identity that made it difficult to behave in a more generic, "wild" way. They had no lyrics, license for wildness, or participation gestures to act out a stock social role. Even worse, they felt they might even get stuck not knowing songs and thus feeling or looking "out of it." Hosts who were acknowledged as throwing good parties were rhetorically canny; they made sure not only that there were large quantities of drink and food available but also that the musical mix provided many and varied chances to "act crazy." Because most of the songs lasted for three to five minutes, opportunities for changing persons with whom to interact occurred frequently. In sum, hosts provided for the etiquette norms expected of rowdy parties. A bad host violated the etiquette norms of rowdiness and ritual mood elevation by not supplying artifacts that encouraged rowdiness and mood elevation.

Hosts who wanted guests to interact more through conversation played quieter music and avoided music commonly accepted as signifying license for wild behavior. The quiet party mood could be recognized by guests from the music alone, especially because the absence of particular songs or styles was conspicuous. In addition, the appearance of any specific piece was difficult to predict because the host had chosen pieces as novelties to enjoy. The taped artifacts were intended to encourage delight in the novelty as opposed to providing stereotypical opportunities to act wild.

Although sexual interest may have been aroused during the quiet conversation, sexual behaviors, especially gestures, were far more subtle than those observed at bashes. Hosts still wanted to offer guests opportunities for interaction but without sexual expression as the main focus. Hosts at the smaller gatherings often steered conversational topics away from sex at signs of discomfort from one or more guests. The music currently played was frequently used by hosts as a diversion from provocative talk. Although the music could become a topic for conversation, it was usually in the background and apparently not in the fore of guests' attention.

Pieces tended to last longer than five minutes, as did individual threads of conversation. Sometimes, all the guests discussed the same topic, taking turns; sometimes they would informally break into groups. The changing of a mixed tape provided a space in which they would move to the kitchen or table for refreshments; when they returned to their original seating or standing spot, they might find different persons there, or they themselves might opt for a new configuration for conversation.

Guests at bashes often left without thanking the host. Even if they knew the host well, they were invested with anonymity by virtue of the number of guests and the loudness of music, both of which covered or masked their individuality. Guests at smaller gatherings almost always expressed personal thanks for the hospitality; some had even brought food and drink with them as a form of thanks. They arrived expecting to be individuals and treated the host more formally.

Hosts and guests at both types of parties realized that parties are rites of reversal (Jewett & Laurence; Norbeck). Parties are events that reverse the day-to-day norms and allow partiers to escape from mundane concerns. Bashes dramatically reverse norms, which hosts must be prepared for because purposefully getting guests intoxicated invites possible community sanction (Holmberg & MacDonald). Friendly gatherings also reverse norms. Daily life and the workplace do not always allow for lingering, in-depth conversation. The additional suspension of sexual innuendo is also a type of reversal that friends give to one another. Both types of parties used music as a symbolic sound system that signified the reversals. The music provided a nurturing environment for anticipated behavior.

Party music is thus perhaps the most important guest for interaction at social gatherings. At times, its voice is the only voice heard. At times, it helps us speak.

Disco: The Musical Stylistics
of *Dancer from the Dance*

Perhaps one of the more daunting roadblocks in interpreting music is the familiarity about particular pieces and types of music that may or may not be shared between the critical-interpreter and a reader—between me and you. It is relatively easy to quote a literary passage and go at it with aplomb, all the while the audience able to focus on the referred text. Music—in prose form—is not so easy to work. On the other hand, sometimes familiarity breeds contempt: Disco became so laden with aversive baggage by the late 1970s that the music taken as the most familiar and representative disco—certain tunes by the BeeGees with John Travolta practicing semaphore code on a disco dance floor—is not representative of disco music, let alone the club culture that spawned it in the late 1960s and early 1970s. One novel provides a neat solution to the familiarity issue: Andrew Holleran's *Dancer from the Dance* mimics the disco music it relates in its stylistics and also provides glimpses into that music and the club culture from which it emerged.

Holleran contextualizes the scene. It is autumn 1972, long before discotheques had become "another possession of the middle class" (29). The club in question, the Twelfth Floor, is situated in the fashion district, which at night is otherwise deserted. This contextualization is no mere convenient fiction; the location inscribes some of the margins of New York City culture of the time. The middle class does not go there. Fashion for the world issues from it. The people who visit it nightly are "bound together by a common love of a certain kind of music, physical beauty, and style" (30).

After describing some of the clubbers in their seriousness and their other habits, Holleran sets the beat of the rest of Chapter 2 by locating the moment

> when their faces blossomed into the sweetest happiness, . . . when everyone came together in single lovely communion that was the reason they did all they did; and that occurred around six-thirty in the morning, when they took off their sweat-soaked T-shirts and screamed because Patty Jo had begun to sing: "Make me believe in you, show me that love can be true". . . and the others rising from the couches where they had been sprawled like martyrs who have given up their souls to Christ pushed onto the dance floor and united in the cries of animal joy because Patty Jo had begun to sing in her metallic, unreal voice those signal words: "Make me believe in you, show me that love can be true." (31)

The passage speaks the minimalistic musicality and club culture of early disco. The repetition of the name Patty Jo and her lyrics suggests the repetitive nature of disco music. The reaction to her is predictable yet ecstatic. It is six thirty a.m., and the dancers have apparently been dancing for quite a long time to have worked up a sweat. They are not wearing polyester leisure suits; they wear jeans and T-shirts. At this point, as described, they remove their soaked shirts, and now, on the dance floor, is the rocking, thriving vision of communion and martyrdom of sweating men, naked to the waist, gyring to the beat. The spiritual, even mystical nature of the dance is subsequently leitmotifed as "baptized into a deeper faith . . . brought to life by miraculous immersion" (35) and a mystic prescience, an archaic, polysynthetic, all-is-one knowing signified by sexual revelations of knowing what other men "like to do in bed. But then so did everyone else in the room" (36).

The passage and its subsequent playing out are carefully coded. The club is a gay dance club. Holleran had already established that women were present (Egyptian heiresses, during this scene; 37), but most of the persons present were men and gay, except for the singer. The preferred singer is a black woman, herself an oppressed performer. The dancers are mostly fit men, whom Holleran's narrator describes variously as "athletes after a long and sweaty game of soccer" or "athletes coming from a game" (32). The minimalism of the Twelfth Floor and its habitués is further remarked as Holleran introduces his cast of major and minor characters. He does this adroitly by having the narrator sit on the end of a couch that sits opposite the main entry to the club, monitoring the men who seize that particularly convenient spot for scoping the others. As the narrator watches another group of men talk, he also keeps an eye on the two men in plaid shirts and moustaches next to him.

> In the midst of their deliberations, Zulema's "Giving Up" suddenly burst out of the recapitulations of Deodato, and the two woodsmen got up to dance; at their rising, two other boys in black with tired, beautiful eyes, sat down immediately and began discussing the men who had just left. (37)

This brief passage conveys a then unique feature of music at gay clubs of the time: what now is called "mix," or beginning a new song long before the previous song is finished, sometimes, as in this case, doing so suddenly, sometimes doing so with such finesse that it may be difficult to figure the conclusion of one and the start of the other. Again, this inclusion further demonstrates another important feature of the music, signified by Holleran's use of the word *recapitulations,* namely, that the music is relatively simple, or at least the chosen songs are similar enough in key, beat, and harmony that overlapping them is not terribly problematic.

The two lads watch the two woodsmen approach a man in drag on the dance floor—one of the two main characters, Sutherland—and the narrator watches all, until,

> At that moment, "Needing You" began, buried still in the diminishing chords of "You've Got Me Waiting for the Rain to Fall," and the two boys on the sofa—with hearing sharper than a coyote's, and without even needing to ask each other— bounded up off the sofa and headed for the dance floor. Instantly their seats were taken by an older, gray-haired man and his friend, an even older fellow who because of his hearing aid, toupee, and back brace was known among the younger queens as Spare Parts. (38)

On this recapitulation of Holleran's stylistics, the "mix" of songs is subtle, signified further by the two "boys" who picked up on it with a coyote's hearing and who, mystics that they are, stood and entered the dance floor with no visible communication to do so. A mix occurs, the sofa-transients leave to dance, and new sitters appear. These particular sitters are well-known among the club's clientele, having being given names. Eventually, a new recapitulation occurs. The gray-haired man speaks to "Spare Parts,"

> "My dear, whole *lives* have been wasted chasing dick." He sat up suddenly. "Oh!" he said. "There's that song!"
> At that moment, "One Night Affair" was beginning to rise from the ruins of "Needing You," and they both put down their plastic cups of apple juice and started toward the dance floor. (39; emphasis Holleran's)

The narrator hears a "rustle of silk and distinctive voice," and Sutherland and a young, shy millionaire take the sofa. What ensues is the first of many hilarious conversations with Sutherland. Like the former sofa occupants, they discuss men as they watch the dance floor. Eventually, one man enters who instantly rivets the young millionaire. " 'That is Malone,' said Sutherland in his lowest, most dramatic voice, 'and his only flaw is that he is still searching for love' " (47-48). Indeed, after Malone's appearance, no further reference to the music or dance occurs in the rest of the chapter, as if a timelessness has entered with a sacred being. The narrator confirms, "I looked at Malone and thought: His eyes are like Jesus Christ's" (50).

Notably, the origins of disco, as reported by Holleran, are not the heterosexual, macho-proving ground of *Saturday Night Fever.* As Lori Tomlinson interprets, early disco emphasized the beat, vigorous body movement, songs sung by black women, songs with few words, songs with little or no chord progression—songs extremely unlike Top 40 hits or Western "art song." The choice of dance music in early disco was decidedly oppositional to mainstream culture. Gay men chose music largely generated by black people, favored by them and the Latin communities. Taken as a group, they were all marginalized by the middle class. Holleran gives sign to this marginalization concisely as discos "before they became another possession of the middle class" (29), which they did after *Saturday Night Fever* slowed the beat and added many words, chord progressions, and references to heterosexual love (Tomlinson).

It is intriguing to note that Holleran's observation about disco being initially subcultural is not so fictive. It presages Fiske's discussions of "excorporation" by ten years. Gay, black, and Hispanic cultures contributed to the early formation of disco music and its culture; they excorporated songs produced by mainstream culture and made them oppositional. Later, mainstream culture took over disco, although in so doing, mainstream culture rejected the minimalism, the faster beat, the lack of lyrics, and the gayness, what Fiske calls "incorporation," a phenomenon that Holleran also documents.

In addition, not all gay men succumbed to AIDS during the interim between the birth of disco and the late 1990s. The assumption that AIDS is only a gay disease is another elitist fantasy. Although acknowledging that Holleran's "Twelfth Floor" does not capture the diversity of all discotheques, many gay men who embraced early gay disco affirm the accuracy of detail as well as the feel of Holleran's prose. I have also interviewed eleven heterosexual women who actively patronized early disco clubs, each of whom finds Holleran's depiction accurate and genuine in feel. When I asked why they went to gay clubs, their answer is a minimalist leitmotif itself: Because I could go out and dance, have fun, and not get felt up constantly.

Disco did not disappear, even with the "I Hate Disco" or "Dump Disco" movement. It went back underground, surfacing in the early 1980s as "progressive" and "alternative" music, both highly subscribed by gay culture. The first alternative rock song to hit the charts was REM's "Melt with You," and once again, the beat was incorporated into mainstream culture. Even then, it did not disappear. Disco's latter-day descendants include "industrial," "techno," and "ambient," each marginalized or certainly not considered to be mainstream popular music. They have yet to be "incorporated."

Sports and Music

The physicality of gay disco suggests another context for popular music that is overlooked so often that the oversight begs for an explanation: the linkage of music and sports. Both gay disco and sports deal with athletic performance, sometimes individually, sometimes in dyads and groups. Both may be practiced (Malone "was a terrible dancer at first: stiff and unhappy" [Halloran 103]). Both may be coached (Sutherland coached Malone).

Yet it may seem strange, initially, that a section on sports appears in a chapter about popular music. Perhaps the connection seems tenuous because everyday perceptions have been acculturated to compartmentalize interpretation of everyday experience, deleting difference and diversity while highlighting sameness in disciplinary, narrower ranges of interest. Certainly, sports themselves create a place for action and intensity apparently unlike everyday experience. All sorts of intense physical, muscular, and endurance skills, however, are as central for musicians as athletes. Yet sports experts—coaches, players, and researchers—are not immune to the common compartmentalization that habitually dissociates music and sports, nor are many musicians. Literally, the professionals rarely see athletics and music in the same ballpark. The connection is not tenuous but strong, even in the sorts of research in both areas that concentrates more on structures and motion than everyday life.

Other than physiology and other science-based research, sport research focuses on situations and performances that conventionally repeat among a wide distribution of the populace, such as games and matches; strategies and drills; practices; relationships between players and coaches; and formal behaviors, such as tournaments, special calendrical events such as memorial relays and annual marathons. The topics and issues studied are particularly interesting to coaches, policymakers, and other administrators who fund athletics, fully knowing that even amateur sports draw considerable money to schools and civic programs. The research methods to drive sports research are therefore modeled by business and are mostly quantitative.

The emphasis on coaching and administrative interests misses the point of view of the players—everyday life—as well as the novel events that may repeat but only for small groups. Likewise, there is little research on informal gatherings that are more like get-togethers among friends than formal contests between organizations. This point of view that is relatively ignored centers on topics and issues of interest to participants and calls for interpretive research. During the past seven years, I have taught an annual course on media and popular culture, and one of the units has covered various aspects of popular music. One project reported the use of "party songs" and "party tapes" that precipitated the study of a novel series of events limited to a hometown small group that has met regularly for eleven years at the printing of this book. The informants told me all about their "dunk parties," during which they played mostly "rap" music as loud as neighbors allowed.

The research design involved interviews with the participants of these dunk parties along with actual observation. The goal was to write their subcultural values in a form they agreed captures their togetherness.

The scene is a small town in northwest Ohio. I'll call the two starting agents Buddy and Phil, ages eleven and twelve just as this all began. They live on the same street and have older brothers who regularly get together to play basketball in their homes' driveways, usually with a hoop attached to a garage, over the door. Buddy and Phil were really tired of not being able to dunk, both because their brothers rarely let them play and because they were still too short. Yet they admired the professionals they saw on television, particularly dunk competitions during National Basketball Association (NBA) halftimes. So, Buddy builds a ramp to help them jump higher, make the rim, and more easily dunk. More of their friends their own age get involved. The ramp is great but is not enough. Phil lowers the rim. They use a regular-sized ball at first, but about the time Buddy improves the ramp—by putting logs under it, thus increasing height and riskiness—they start using a mini ball. Their get-togethers become frequent enough that they are told to be quieter because of neighbors.

In summer, they meet just about every day, from eleven a.m. to one p.m. Then, off to the local pool. When it gets cooler in the evening, they play again. This all got a head of steam in sixth grade when Buddy was twelve (1985). They went through seven or eight rims, all retired to Phil's room at home as trophies for his bedroom wall. Later, when some of them are in college (early 1990s), the originals get together only on breaks and weekends.

They started to use music while they played, early on, because the NBA dunk contests had music. They had a strong sense of tune selection. "I made this tape when I would hold dunk-ball festivals at my house," one said, call him Joe. "They couldn't be radio hits. They had to be underground hits, street music. The songs had to be hard rap instead of dance rap. The songs had to be rebellious or violent with an upbeat, hard drums, and a harsh, rap, street voice." The party tape Joe made included Special Ed, "I'm the Magnificent"; Eazy E, "Still Talkin Shit"; Ice T, "Power"; Eric B & Rekim, "Lyrics of Fury"; Above the Law, "Murder Rap"; and TERMINATOR X, "Back to THE SCENE OF THE BASS," among others.

As to the function of the hard-driving songs, Joe offered, "A good dunk-ball tape has to get the dunkers pumped up. The music has to transfer a surge of adrenaline to the dunker." If the guys liked a song in particular, "their performance would increase along with their creativity. For instance, when an LL COOL J song was played, people would start dunking harder with more aggression." Girls were rarely present at these dunk fests; hence, "none of the songs' themes dealt with sex or getting girls. The themes mostly dealt with social issues or boasting oneself."

The aggressive nature of rap and its place within the African American community may be both applauded and maligned (*Emergency*), but these are young, European American males, modeling their athletic prowess in small-town America as an amalgam of rapsters and NBA star players. While the song pumped them up, they also played the amalgam further: Each guy's driveway and hoop was his favorite NBAer's home arena. Phil was Walter Kareem at the Los Angeles Forum. Buddy was Charles Barkley at the Chrysler Arena; Joe, Bernard King at the Boston Gardens, and so on. Moreover, each NBA star had his own, personal style of dunking, which each boy mastered. Yet Michael Jordan's ability to vary dunk style inspired them to imitate numerous styles. According to "Drew," another of the boys, they had a Dr. J. Dunk, the Drew Berry Jam, a Dominic Wilkins Tomahawk, and a Kenny Smith Dunk Dunk.

As time passed and they moved into junior high and high school, most of them turned out to be rather short, necessitating a redoubled effort at play to have a closer chance to make the team. They videotaped themselves, mimicking professional analysis. The videotapes reveal rituals. There was a big tree by Phil's hoop. If the ball got stuck in the tree, play ceased immediately as they scrambled to try and get it. They tackled each other getting to it. The winner variously could start a new game or series of dunks. Buddy's hoop sported a Martini Glass, and although most of them had figured out how to move their hoops from one locale to another, Buddy wouldn't share it. They all thought it was cool; it made them feel big.

The last six paragraphs served as one of the ways I used to write their subcultural values in a form they agreed captures their togetherness. I retained their everyday language and verified their activities and their interpretation of them by having them read the narrative and suggest additions, deletions, and corrections. This particular grouping of paragraphs was their final word on their novel subculture.

Their conflation of rap music with vigorous basketball dunking and the concomitant social rituals they developed through time speak volumes about music and sports. They were in a liminal or in-between state. Initially, they were not old enough; eventually, most of them were not tall enough, either. They established their own in-group, and only two of them ever played varsity basketball. With virtually no adult or coach supervision, the emphasis was on fun and personhood. There were group norms, yes, but individuality was not only allowed but also encouraged.

The individuality shows in the music some of them chose; it was not the same as the others' choices in groups and particular songs. One thing their tapes and athletic performance inspired by the tapes had in common was the perfection of imitating NBA stars and each other, with emphasis on the personal feeling of success, seeing oneself as a hero. In no small way was music used as an avenue to hero worship, solidarity with each other, and the personification of self-esteem.

I should add, too, that the dunk party is thoroughly coded as male, or at least, conventional masculinity and its toughness, goal orientation, and competition. Their choice of aggressive music with violent lyrics further affirms their rituals as what Pronger calls "the arena of masculinity." Not needless to say because it cannot be said enough, only now in the late twentieth century with girls and women freer to pursue athletics can such novel groupings occur, let alone be studied. Informal sports activities between females will most likely be different in some ways, and their study is something to be anticipated. Whether music would be involved remains to be heard.

The informants—the dunkers—also suggested other connections between sports and music that deserve study: dance music for aerobics, hard, driving

rock and roll to pump one up during a weight workout, mellower music for relaxation and cooling down, the use of a portable tape or CD player with headphones to push out environmental distractions to enhance concentration, and so on. Clearly, the connection of music and sports is vastly unplumbed.

Love, Sex, and the Music of the Spheres

In common among the party songs interpreted at the outset of this chapter, gay disco, and music at dunk parties is "the beat," a fast, thumping, driving beat. Music is nothing, if not fundamentally rhythm. There may be pitch, harmony, and sometimes lyrics, but pitch and harmony may also be characterized as rhythm, the alternation of action and inaction (and, to be clear, not the alternation of presence and lack, which is a heterosexist construction that mimics penis and vagina). "The beat" audially mimes the thrusting and clasping of diverse sexual encounters, however.

Sex is also rhythmic not merely in coupling and perhaps eventual waves of orgasm but also in flirting and its phases of action/inaction and in the afterglow of having performed sex. Even visual images of afterglow may be rhythmic: In the dark, one or two cigarettes glow, subside, glow, subside, mimicking slowing orgasmic contractions, smoking cigarettes a ritualized Sight leitmotif of the moments immediately following sex.

In turn, sexual rhythms are influenced by the alternation of season(s), an earthbound sense of rhythm. Yet sexual rhythms are also influenced by the phases of the moon, both an earthbound influence and a sky influence. Other heavenly bodies influence the actions or fate of coupling bodies, or so the folklore of various cultures ordains whether astrology is "true" or not. Planets and stars vibrate and sing, and their celestial music is the original version of universal gravitation, the music of the spheres. This cosmic sort of influence is often captured by sentiments such as "It's in the stars." Romeo and Juliet were "star-crossed lovers," and these days, maleness and femaleness are still essentialized as *Men Are from Mars, Women Are from Venus.* C. S. Lewis' novel *That Hideous Strength* also essentializes heterosexual marriage roles as influenced by the stars, and although Jane and Mark Studdock may have their problems, they are cosmic soul mates when all is said and done.

Thus, love stories may be construed and even interpreted as musical artifacts instead of as literary or quasi-literary artifacts. We have already seen this in Holleran's stylistic handling of Chapter 2 in *Dancer from the Dance. The Princess Bride* flows with narrative rhythm in the alternation of Grandfather and Grandson telling the story with the story itself. There is a rhythm of the plot twists, often in quanta of threes, there being three villains, two of whom become good guys. Inigo Montoya's sword duel of revenge plays reversal as rhythmic. He's on the attack, and the man who killed his father is going to be vanquished. Then he gets the drop on Inigo. Now under attack, Inigo fades fast—until he remembers his long burning revenge. Three times he says "Hello, my name is Inigo Montoya. Twenty years ago you killed my father. Prepare to die." The statements themselves come in three. Then, revenge is counted sweetest, because the myth of number in the Western tradition ordains that three is blessing, a sign of holy favor, in this case valorizing the revenge as sacred.

Not surprisingly, many fairy tales work in the rhythm of threes, from Hans Christian Anderson's "Little Match Girl" who lights matches to warm herself three times and three times has visions, to latter-day retelling of fairy tale classics such as Peter Cashorali's gay-themed "The Fisherman and His Lover." The Fisherman catches a fish, who offers to grant a wish if the Fisherman lets him go. The Fisherman agrees, but each time it is his lover who wants more. Each time the Fisherman later catches the fish, it grows to horrible proportions. Still the lover is not satisfied. Only after the third wish does the Fisherman realize how truly miserable he is. As frequently happens in fairy tales, a fourth wish cancels the first three. In Cashorali's tale, however, by being true to himself, the Fisherman's life does not return to normal but winds up a little better than before.

The musicality of storytelling—the rhythmic pacing, the surges, the reversals, the melodic semantics with open and sometimes mythic, harmonic over- and undertones, is usually described in language and words alone, thus, perhaps, slighting significant features of storytelling that appeal intrinsically, inchoately to audiences as musical. Although popular audiences may not have the critical vocabulary—as indeed most literary and rhetorical critics do not—they know what reaches into the heart and soul by means of embodied dance in tandem with enlivening musical fabric, and they know enjoyment, uplift, and transport. It should not be forgotten, then, that the origins of song and music have often also been the origin of storytelling. It is no wonder, then, that storytelling should retain musical characteristics, long after Western culture has abandoned sheer audiality, so many times removed by alphabets, diacritics, and dietitians of the mind. Dietitians of the mind are starved souls.

After the Beat: Physical Mysticism

The religious fervor and hysterias in Western culture's history have given way to a different order, one liberating yet just as enslaving. The ecstatic mysticism of loving god has given over to a new mysticism, one that emphasizes the body, its rhythms, its beat. The theme of enslavement will be taken up in the next chapter; for now, I concentrate on the liberating. This mystic fancy of moderns and late moderns exhibits itself with the desire for music, music that is intimately linked with sexuality—pursuing it, having it, and even side-stepping it. Mysticism is ecstatic; sex and the dance of sex are ecstatic. Both set and follow "the beat." Therefore, sex is physical mysticism. Sex and its linkage to music speak the metaphysics or ontology of social prioritizing for many late modern North Americans. Sex, in one way or another, is their ultimate concern. The further linkage to sports and emphasis on ecstatic immersion into the physical underscore this ultimate concern, Paul Tillich's catch phrase that he uses to define religion (*Ultimate*).

Unlike prior religious mysticisms in the West, physical mysticism/ecstasy is achievable in this life, by many, not the few. Physical mysticism is quite congruent with DeRomilly's interpretation of Attic Greek incantations of poetry and Georgianic prose that create illusion, if not reality. Physical mysticism is also congruent with E. R. Dodds' major, groundbreaking interpretation of Plato's divine madnesses, an interpretation that belies the notion of the Greeks as thoroughly rational folk. Along with Evans' later interpretation of Euripides' *The Bacchae,* it may now be divined that the Greeks were not as culturally committed to "reason" and rationality as Edith Hamilton's popular *The Greek Way* once led many to believe. In fact, Evans' newer interpretation demonstrates that physical mysticism—the divine madness of Dionysus' celebrants through frenzied dance, again musical—was once a norm, one alien to male dominant, militaristic masculinity (*God*).

I add, then, that the late modern physical mysticism may or may not be a return to that earlier norm. Some of it appears to occur through the auspices of religion and otherworldly spirituality, but to assume that mysticism occurs only that way is presumptuously narrow. Some, but not all, late modern physical mysticism is inspired in neopagan contexts, as the foregoing studies in this chapter suggest. Bataille is now dated in this regard.

The trances, the states of rapture and the theopathic states prolifically described by mystics of every religious discipline—Hindu, Buddhist, Moslem or Christian, *not to mention the rarer ones who have no religion*—all have the same significance: non-attachment to ordinary life, indifference to its needs, anguish felt in the midst of this until the being reels, and the way left open to a spontaneous surge of life that is usually kept under control but which bursts forth in freedom and infinite bliss. (246-247; emphasis mine)

Bataille, writing in the early 1950s, did or could not foresee physical mysticism as a cultural phenomenon more frequent than rarity, and he did not consider that the vast majority of the human race—in his lifetime and in the history of the world—were pagan and unknowing of revealed religions, or disinterested in them.

Spiritually connected or not, many party goers report music as enabling an "attitude adjustment," a transformation and break from the mundane. Persons from both biological sexes, various sexual orientations, ages, ethnicities, races, and regional/national origins have told me they love to have music playing while they have sex, that they frequently choose music that has "the beat" at the speed that pleases them most to match. Holleran reports the nature of disco in its simultaneous abandonment of gay personhood and its ultimate presence. Some athletes report music "pumps them up" and helps them achieve a burn. Clearly, late moderns are *after the beat.* Call it a burn, the beat, personal effacement, communion, *le petit mort* (the little death of shattering orgasm), abandonment, or engagement, the experienced garnered in the physical exertions cued through music and dance appeals directly to human interest without resorting to words and their semantically entrenched, cognitive coding. Music and sex are a true break from the tyrannies of words. So, too, scholarship about music must eschew words and face the music.

11

Gesture, Body Image, and
the Fashion of Sex Toys

Dance and sports involve gesture and exercise. In turn, exercise tones the body, either by design or without it. Again, with or without conscious design, people write their gendrification with their gestures and on their bodies. The reflection of body and gesture conveys both self-image and the acculturation of self. In popular culture, gesture speaks louder than words, and it may be hotly contested as to its meanings. The body—how it looks and makes oneself feel—is also hotly contested, and gesture and body image are considered as related in this chapter. Body as naturally given may be developed. In turn, gesture, fashion as gesture, and sex toys as physical enhancement are an artful extension of the naturally given body.

A caveat before continuing: When I say *gesture,* I include what is commonly called nonverbal communication, but I am not limited either to that term or to its related communicological study.

The Gendrification of Gesture

The stakes for performing gesture deemed appropriate for one's apparent biological sex are high. In the real world, an effeminate man is a target for violence to "straighten him out." In the film world, particularly comedy, an effeminate man and the training to act like a man are the source of laughter and all sorts of high jinks. *The Birdcage* (1996), the latest film based on the original

French stage play _La Cage Aux Folles,_ shares the dilemmas of a gay couple when one of them needs to butch it up and act like a man.

Armand manages a popular drag club in South Beach, Florida ("half the audience is Kennedys"). Albert is the club's featured performer, "Starina." They are partners. Yet Armand had a fling some twenty years previously, had a son, Val, and basically, Albert has been Val's mother all that time. Now Val wants to marry a senator's daughter and is afraid the domestic partnership will ruin the marriage plans because the parents are so conservative. Worse, the senator, his wife, and the intended bride are on their way to South Beach to meet Val's parents. When Albert discovers that Val and Armand have conspired not only to change their apartment's decor from gay to severely monastic ("We've been robbed") but also for him to be absent from the visit, Albert is understandably upset. He says reservedly, "I'm leaving. The monster, the freak is leaving. You're safe." He leaves like a martyr, and when Armand catches up with him, Albert swoons, and they enter a restaurant where they are regulars.

Now seated at a patio table, they discuss options. Albert finally says it wouldn't do to introduce him as Val's mother "on the first visit," and then a bright idea hits him.

Albert:	Could you tell him I was a relative who dropped in? Val's Uncle. Uncle Al!
Armand:	Oh, what's the point? You'd be Val's _gay_ Uncle Al.
Albert:	Oh, I could play it straight.
Armand:	Oh please. Look at you, look at the way you hold your glass. Look at your pinkie; look at your posture.

After a bit of a fuss, they decide to coach Albert to behave in a manly fashion. Armand chides, "First, get your pinkie down; it's up again," and on touching Albert to adjust Albert's posture, Albert turns hysteric, "What are you doing?" Armand retorts, "I'm teaching you to act like a man!"

What ensues is a comedic version of what some men, gay or not, face daily in living up to restricted norms of comportment. They begin by practicing putting mustard on toast. Albert immediately uses a spoon to dribble little dots of mustard on a point of toast. "No," scolds Armand, "you take your knife and you smear. Men _smear._" Albert tries again, but with his pinkie up. Corrected, he persists but is so tense, he breaks the toast and goes to pieces. Armand coaches him that this reaction is inappropriate, "You have to react like a man—calmly." So, they switch gears and try walking. Albert stands, minces around the restaurant's patio with his fingers prissily elevated out from the hips, and returns to their table where he monitors Armand's disbelief. "Too swishy?" he inquires. Armand coaches, "Let me give you an image—it's a cliché, but it's an image: John Wayne." Miraculously, Albert walks like John Wayne—the exaggerated John Wayne to be sure—but the walk is no longer swishy.

The dilemma of an effeminate man—or a man who does not appear manly, who doesn't do "guy" things—is not always the source of comedy; sometimes, it is the basis of drama. In the 1956 movie *Tea and Sympathy,* Tom Lee (John Kerr) is a gender anomaly. He does not play touch football with the other lads. He "likes Bach more than baseball and prefers the company of the housemaster's wife, Laura (Deborah Kerr)" (Russo 112). The screenplay carefully poses Tom as heterosexual, in love with the older Laura. Thus, his effeminacy is pathologized as something to be avoided, something to be redeemed by full heterosexuality. A friend coaches him how to "walk like a man," among other behaviors, but still Tom is the scapegoat sissy. "The film pleads tolerance, therefore, not for sexual deviation but for unfortunate heterosexuals who happen to be less than 'masculine' " (Russo 113). Eventually, Laura and Tom sleep together, thus assuring Tom that he is heterosexual, sissy or not.

Both Albert in *The Birdcage* and Tom in *Tea and Sympathy* are faced with what Judith Butler has described as "normative sexual positions that are intrinsically impossible to embody" (122), and they are always potentially comedic, serious or not, and thus heterosexual maleness in particular is a constant parody of itself. The gestures are an act, totally constructed. Whether gesture is totally constructed or not, acting like a man may be problematic for a shy, heterosexual man; for a gay man, conforming may be fraught with terror. Then again, terror may be prevented if one's act is convincing enough as Ann Rice so readily recommends.

For a woman to "walk like a man" from an essentialist perspective is not natural, yet a woman, fictive or real, may need or desire to imitate a man's walk. Precarious plot twists place Julie Stratford in a situation in which she must rendezvous with her lover on the lam, Ramses/Mr. Ramsey, in Anne Rice's *The Mummy.* Samir, a mutual friend, has purchased Bedouin men's clothing for her to wear for her to go unnoticed on the streets of Cairo. Yet one detail belies the whole look, prompting Samir to coach Julie to walk like a man.

Two Arabs left the rear of Shepheard's, one slightly taller than the other, both striding very fast.

"Remember," Samir said under his breath, "take very big steps. You are a man. Men do not take small steps, and swing your arms naturally."

"I should have learned this trick a long time ago," Julie answered. (284)

Julie's word choice is telling. Imitating a man's walk is a "trick," an artifice, theatrics.

From a purely constructionist point of view, what if a man wants to walk like a woman, like a drag queen, or more convolutedly, a woman acting like a man who does drag? Such is the premise of the movie *Victor/Victoria*. Victoria Grant, coloratura soprano touring with the Bath Touring Light Opera Company in Paris, is jobless because the company went out of business. By chance, she meets Toddy, a nightclub entertainer who himself had just been fired. Through mutual commiseration, they become friends. Because she has been kicked out of her hotel room, because her clothing has been ruined in a rainstorm, and because Toddy tells her he's a homosexual, she's "safe" to stay over for the night. The next morning, Toddy's lover, Richard, shows up to claim his clothing, but Victoria already wears some of those clothes. Richard mistakes Victoria as a man, and Victoria doesn't like the way Richard treats Toddy, so, she smacks him, roughs him up, kicks him out. Voilà, Toddy realizes the dream of a lifetime. He tells Victoria she's convincing as a man. After a haircut, a little training, and an audition with the most influential talent agent in Paris, Victoria will debut as Count Victor Grazinski, a drag entertainer from Poland, in six weeks. Victoria's training thus intensifies. It is not easy. Although she manages most of the grueling schedules of dance routines, vocal coaching, and the like, she may be convincing as a man, but not as a drag queen. Back in the privacy of their apartment, Victoria despairs that she'll never be able to pull it off. Rushing her off to yet another rehearsal, Toddy reassures her, ending his comforting by broadly swiveling his shoulders, saying in a breathless, campy voice, "Now, when you're dancing, remember, make it broader with tons of shoulder! Remember you're a Drag Queen!" Trooper that Victoria is, she successfully incorporates the "drag" gestures of excess into her stage acts.

Perhaps the most extreme constructionist perspective on gender maintains that all male gesture, comportment, and movement are an act, a pure construction. On the one hand, masculine, muscular, "butch" bodies, fashion, and action are suspect because they are the results of hundreds of years of conditioning, from ancient Rome to the present. Arthur Evans states it categorically.

> All American men have been conditioned throughout their lives to think of disciplined aggressiveness as masculine; to look down on effeminacy, playfulness, passivity, and open emotionalism; to admire hardness in other men; to dread above all things being called a sissy; to enjoy relations of domination and obedience; to get a thrill out of seeing pain inflicted on others; to get turned on by uniforms; and to be able to accommodate themselves to functioning in large, impersonal, hierarchical institutions. (*Witchcraft* 121)

In another scholarly work, Evans bemoans that although at one time it seemed that the norm for gay men was the nelly queen, a whole new generation of gays has embraced masculinity.

> The great majority of American gay men are acutely anxiety-ridden about their masculinity, just like their heterosexual counterparts. An evidence of this anxiety is the extreme lengths to which many American gay men now feel they have to go in order not to be taken for "sissies" . . . compulsive body building, wearing denim and leather uniforms with Armylike short-cropped hair, deliberately adopting stiff body postures and lumbering styles of walking. (*God* 178-179)

Notice how Evans puts it: The masculinity of gay men, at least so many of them, is an act, artificial. As an "anxiety," it is couched as a psychological reaction to internalized homophobia. It is odd, however, that commenting on the constructed nature of masculinity, Evans seems to believe that effeminacy is natural, essentialistically speaking, to being gay. That's debatable.

George Chauncey would certainly agree that at the turn of the nineteenth to the twentieth century, gay men wore foppish clothing and sported limp wrists, lisps, and other so-called effeminate manners and gestures, whereas "real" men did not, even if they had sex with the effeminate men. Most important and to reiterate, Chauncey spells a different interpretation than Evans. The men that *acted* like men were taken to be men, not gay, *even if they had sex with another man*. The difference between them and "gay" men was gesture, attire, comportment, and the presumed gender roles of active versus passive, penetrator/penetrating, and so forth (*Gay New York* 44-97). I add here that ethnographic interviews I have conducted concerning human rights organizations in northwest Ohio confirm the status of effeminacy among many homosexual men as socially constructed and not necessarily a given set of behaviors because one is gay. Speaking about coming out in the 1960s and 1970s, one informant, Art, told me, "You know, in those days we didn't know if we were men or women, so a lot acted femme." I asked him how he acted. "Just like now," he said, "I didn't buy if you're a queer, you're really a female."

Advertising increasingly has featured naked men, and the same sorts of critiques feminists have stated about the exploitation of female bodies may be argued about the depersonalizing of maleness, its dismemberment, and its disfiguration (Simpson 104-107). While these sorts of new moves in late modern imaging of males threaten many and diverse folk (Simpson 13), I note, from my field notes and everyday experience, if nothing else, that something else interesting concerning male image has been happening among many North American males, aged variously from sixteen or so to mid-twenties during the past five years. I do not claim that advertising has fueled the change, especially because this particular set of observations involves men fully clad. Perhaps it has happened the other way around—everyday life has fueled advertising: Gestures, body image, fashion, and comportment once easily assigned to either male or female have become blurred—not to say androgynously, but merged, fused in the excorporation of commodities and social performances manufactured in late modern culture, fused into oppositional stances and actions that deny and defy that late industrial complex of things and images. Ten years ago, in many dance clubs I visited, two guys would never step on a dance floor without at least one gal with them, unless it was a gay club or a gay night at a straight club. In the past five years, however, an increasing number of guys dance together, just as formerly only gals did.

Let's take this new male ritual as a cue; indeed, there's more going on, too. Guys and gals cultivate themselves as walking paradoxes of the traditional gender roles received from late modern culture. Transvestism is not something uncommon, if its concept is not limited to full drag. There are more subtle ways of dressing and imaging oneself paradoxically. Even then, the milder forms may threaten "vested interests," or the male, dominant mainstream, as Garber describes it. For instance, about four years ago, I first noticed that young guys would strip their flannel shirts and tie them around their waists when a cool day turned warm, but it wasn't until the dead of winter three years ago that I began to realize that stripping down to the last shirt, usually a T-shirt, to cool off is perhaps a convenient excuse for altering the masculine look of a plaid or work shirt into a skirt. When most everyone has layered their clothing for extra warmth, guys or gals, even after they may have checked their coats, the longer they dance the more likely it becomes that they have to wrap the extra layers around their waists. Guys and gals of diverse ethnicities and orientations in the late Deco bloom of ball cap, T-shirt, jeans, and jack boots, hiking shoes, or Doc Martens have at least one or more flannel, plaid shirts stripped from their torsos and tied below the waist. These temporary, multiple layers swish about and, on many guys, accentuate their broad shoulders and narrow hips by adding a bustle, rendering their body an hourglass so they can tick time in butch threads. It's not really feminine, technically. It's *men's* clothes, usually blue work shirts or plaid flannels, which, as skirts, produce the effect of *macho frou frou,* macho transformed to manly frill. *Macho frou frou,* however, has other manifestations.

The Dangles. Drawcords hang down from sweat pants, swimming trunks and tanks, leisure pants, and the like. They hang down, sometimes further than the crotch, swaying back and forth as the male body enacts its various missions, as if to say, "Hey, baby, I got it, I want it." The dangles appear in other ways: Guys wear belts that are overlong so the tip can dangle from the waist like a phallus, like sympathetic magic, waving on top of or near the crotch. Even better are the woven, braided sorts of belts: raised pleasure dots. Leather men and bikers capitalize on this when they wear black belts with metal studs of various sorts. Bikers also dangle various chains from their leathers and harnesses and arm-bands—butch, yet precious. Construction workers' belts sport various tools, sometimes the largest and longest immediately over or beside the crotch.

Playing with Caps. I know someone who derides the wearing of ball caps by men, saying, "I twist it around, I turn off my brain." The visor, especially the bill, is the ubiquitous sign of maleness, a symbolic erection. The majority of men who wear ball caps alter the bill to some desired shape. Some like a peak in the middle; some like the sides rounded; some just accentuate the curvature. If a guy, het or gay, touches the bill to modify it, it's as if he's playing with himself, figuratively speaking, and in public. Whacking back the bill like a Little Rascal could be like slapping his cock to his belly. Naturally, some wear the ball cap turned around. Twisting the bill to the back is literally a sign that the wearer is a catcher—he'll take anything thrown at him. Woman certainly wear ball caps at times, sometimes often, something rarely seen in the 1930s.

Scarfing Up. Men can wear bandanas to advertise their sexual interests or wear them innocently as an accessory. They can work like the dangles from pockets, but they can also be twisted around necks, arms, and legs. When using bandanas as sweatbands, some guys shove the bandana up the forehead to make a poofy fountain out of the front of the hairline.

Signs of Wear. Old buckskin coats and moccasins with frills, worn jeans with holes in various places, and threads flopping around like scrota and breasts and dicks are enshrined in popular culture as a sign of wear. This woman or man, boy or girl, works hard enough to wear out his or her clothing. Thus, tattered clothing dresses up the person as a glorification of blue-collar vigor. Wear and tatter signify toughness.

Men typically wear old clothes for working out. While holes and tears show toughness, men identify the discipline of working out with work, and they feel they won't soil new clothes. Yet some athletes actually claim what they consider to be pragmatic uses for tattered old gear. Male swimmers in the midst of training for competition wear two Speedos. The outer Speedo is old, threadbare, and falling to pieces, which creates friction with the water or an extra feeling of pull, drag. The swimmers eventually transform these tatters paradoxically into tatters' opposite, sleekness—for their major swim meet they only wear one, brand-new Speedo to decrease drag. In addition, to psych themselves, they will shave their bodies for an even sleeker feel in the water, creating the enhanced illusion and perception of sliding through the water like a snake. They are hairless yet toughened by their former tatters, which include their body hair, and thus do they become undeniably seasoned, hardened males, but without the secondary characteristic of hair that is conventionally taken to signify manliness.

Hair Today. To shave or not to shave—the armpits (fewer rashes), upper body (weight lifters *never* do this), the back, the pubic areas? These are questions that Wildroot Creamoil Charlie did not ask in the 1950s. Yet it is still the hairdo that constantly and publicly shows a self-concept. "Big hair" on women is often associated with country culture. Short hair was the norm for men in the late 1950s into the 1960s, something Archie Bunker could needle his son-in-law, Michael, about because Michael had long hair. In the 1990s, there appears to be no fixed norm. Diversity, from sculpted hair and razored racing strips to Dennis Rodman's dyed and scripted hair, is not as unusual as it once was. Then again, the butch look of short hair competes with the ultrashort, velvet touch and with shaved heads. The moppy soupbowl look once considered cheap now may cost plenty to acquire at a hairstylist, and many, boys and girls, men and women, sport the bowl cut. Cinches in the back or on the sides render tails and ears of hair, spilling a chiaroscuro of frills and no-frills about the seat of thought, the head. All one needs is a Ted Turner to colorize the affair, and a guy can remake what he thought was completed long ago.

In North America, the received norm for males is toughness, silent conformity, and hard work. Many men and women, particularly in traditional business professions, perform the open deception of conforming to mainstream heterosexual appearance while perhaps violating some of the heterosexual norms. Colorful, skimpy underwear and body piercing may be physically masked by outer clothing, but the individual still knows they are there. Even then, the gay community's strong identification with white briefs that sport the logo "Calvin Klein" maintains the appearance of conformity potentially to both heterosexual and homosexual norms.

Although I have observed these various paradoxes of gesture, fashion, and body image conventionally taken as female but now on male bodies as something happening in the past five years or so, if literature reflects reality, then these sorts of paradoxes have been around for a longer time, for at least thirty years. Puerto Rican boys with white T-shirts dangling from their waists are a leitmotif in Holleran's *Dancer from the Dance* (late 1960s, early 1970s). When Harlan Brown sees Vince Matti for the first time in Warren's *The Front Runner,* Vince wears "wavy black hair down to his collar . . . faded Levis, a torn Air Force jacket and mountain boots" (4). Billy Sive, Harlan's future lover and partner, wears "goldrimmed glasses . . . faded, tattered blue-quilted Mao jacket. His brown leather pants must have been expensive—they were bagged and worn now, but they still displayed his long racehorse legs. . . . On his feet he had worn-out blue Tiger racing flats" (5).

When Michael Mouse goes cruising in San Francisco's Castro district in Maupin's *Tales of the City,* he finds a man at the bar "wearing Levi's, a rugby shirt and red-white-and-blue Tigers" (113). Michael discerns right away that the guy likes him, although he confesses to himself, "What *was* it with this butch number?" (114). The man, Chuck, has a shoe fetish and had singled out Michael almost immediately because he wore Bass Weejuns. Naturally, the Tigers he wears are "just like Billy Sive's. In *The Front Runner*" (early 1970s).

In *The Fancy Dancer* (Warren; mid-1970s), a priest falls in love with a dark, half Native American named Vidal, who on their first contact in the confessional has "dark young fingers with broken nails and smudges of black motor grease" (18). Vidal happens to be a mechanic. When Father Tom steps out of the confessional "in the flickering red half-light from the votive candles," Vidal was a "strange sight."

> He was wearing faded, tattered Lee Riders with a wide tarnished silver belt cinched around his narrow hips. His old walking boots were spattered with mud. His shirt was bright red satin, also worn and stained. His wavy black hair came down to his collar. Around his neck he had a couple of tarnished silver necklaces. . . . The hat he twisted in his hands was a black high-crowned thing, very Indian-looking, with a band of silver conchos around the crown.
>
> Pushing aside the black leather motorcycle jacket in the pew, he sat down slowly and made room for [Tom]. (20)

Literature, however, is not alone in exemplifying paradoxical gesture, attire, and body image.

The Village People dress in various costumes that exhibit *macho frou frou:* a cowboy and a worker wearing their equipment close to the groin; a motorcycle cop wearing black leather boots and carrying a big stick. A jockstrap can be seen under the construction worker's torn jeans. For that matter, athletes and sports gear speak masculinity and its paradoxes (Pronger), and Jane Fonda sorts of aerobic leotards speak a vigorous femininity in the thousands of aerobics classes now to be found all over North America.

Crotch Grabbing by Stars and in Everyday Life

Popular singers are no longer singers such as Giselle McKenzie on *The Hit Parade*. They are crotch grabbers. Andrew Holleran indicates this change in the music scene by having his main character, Lark, in *The Beauty of Men* ponder, "how his country went from 'Some Enchanted Evening' to 'Me So Horny' in less than fifty years" (173). Perhaps the most instant answer to the question is the move from music to MTV music, from audial music to visual music. It's not as simple as that, however. Although music videos are themselves advertisements for music, the advertising industry has paid attention to the crotch and its main crotch grabbers, Michael Jackson, Marky Mark, and Madonna. Simpson puts it bluntly.

> Here's white rapper Marky Mark, on stage, stripped to his Calvin Kleins . . . gripping the mike in one hand and his packet in the other. And here's Madonna in her *Express Yourself* video also grabbing her crotch. Superficially similar—but what a difference in symbolic meaning! Maddy's stylized crotch-grabbing, dressed in a parody of a man's suit, pulses with power while Marky Mark's groin-gripping pulses with pathos. No matter how many times that boy grabs himself, he still only possesses a mere cock, whereas Maddy wields a *phallus* which grows bigger with every press launch. (150)

Simpson has a point; there's a difference between Madonna's doing it and Marky Mark's doing; whether the difference between them is only as Simpson says is moot. If nothing else, Marky Mark's obsessive crotch grabbing could be interpreted not as a marketing ploy that renders him passive to female fans but instead as hysterical heterosexuality, constantly proving he's straight, not gay. After all, Marky's "autobiography" is dedicated to his dick, along with a picture of himself fully clad, once again grabbing his crotch.

Michael Jackson's crotch grabbing may also be construed as hysterical heterosexuality, but until recent lawsuit threats concerning his friendships with boys, his image was rather squeaky clean. In that former context, crotch grabbing was an easy gesture to incorporate in his stylized dance moves to show he has a wild side. Madonna's grabbing is, indeed, a seizure of power, but of male power? If nothing else, the notion of sex, let alone masturbatory gestures, is no longer something kept from kids. The very act of calling attention to the crotch by a performer considered by many to be a sexual transgressor is a self-reference to the erotic crux Madonna wears. Her crotch grabbing is not merely stealing male privilege and pumping it out of proportion for money but a deconstruction of what was once secret—a woman's nether sex, emblazoned in many two-dimensional centerfolds, but now, being stroked, live, on stage, canned in video.

Crotch grabbing is not just for the stars, however, and certainly does not "mean" the same way in all contexts, particularly everyday life in situ. In rural Andalusia, a region of Spain, crotch grabbing occurs between men in a complex or inventory of gestures and social performances. Unlike gatherings in larger cities, which may tend to stratify by class, men of various backgrounds interact in Andalusia, particularly at cafés and bars. Their physical performance is "direct and obtrusive" in that they hit and strike each other forcefully, slap dominoes on the table while playing, and so on, displaying their strength, testing each other's toughness. Virility is "thought to reside in the testicles" and thus "they play an important part in the body language of bars." To assert themselves, either on entering a bar or during a debate, they lift their own balls to support a point. Another gesture literally comes from the heart, a hand extended from the chest, the palm up, wiggling around to mime the weighing of balls, the gesture meaning "huge, powerful and enormous," again a mode of emphasis. Between friends, testicles are also the targets of pranks; if a buddy is lost in his own talking, another bud will sneak up behind him and grab his nuts from behind, which produces amusement among their drinking partners who saw it coming (Driessen 244-245). Thus, crotch grabbing may at times be not a staged, calculated way of capturing the public's attention to garner more money but a paralinguistic mode of emphasis, virility display, or joking. Both the crotch grabbing of stars and that by Andalusian men in their everyday lives suggest dominance as part of the meaning. Yet for the Andalusians, grabbing a friend's nuts lowers him, brings him back down to earth when he's too full of himself.

Hyperreal Body Image

Prior to the "Twiggy" look of the late 1960s and its resurrection in waifish Kate Moss and look-alikes, the positive image of woman in the West tended to be full-figured. Perhaps a result of seeing women only or mostly as child bearers—and hence married, living in a domestic, family scene—a woman's body seemed naturally to call for a look that bespoke not only easy birth (wide pelvis) but also someone not prone to exertion outside the home, someone who would be a dependable child rearer, someone whose body shows good cookery.

During the twentieth century, this body image for women began to diversify, if not change. Pinups featured narrow waists and nonmatronly looks. Slender models and film stars eventually superseded the more voluptuous models and stars such as Jane Russell. Once the fitness craze worked up a head of steam, women, and not just men, began to flock to gyms and YWCAs for aerobics and the promised slimming that could provide. In the last two decades of the twentieth century, an increasing number of women body builders abandoned "feminine" strength and went for the musculature and definition previously sought only by men.

In the meantime, women who did not fit the positive body imaging—particularly, those identified as "fat"—were constantly put on the spot: to diet, to exercise, to do anything that would work, because their size just could not be "natural" or healthy. Susan Bordo maintains that fat is perceived as "indicative of laziness, lack of discipline, unwillingness to conform, and absence of all those 'managerial' abilities that, according to the dominant ideology, confer upward mobility" (in Tuana & Tong 475). Bordo then reads movies such as *Flashdance* and *Vision Quest* as literally embodying the athletic and mental control over the body to "render the hero's or heroine's commitment, will, and spiritual integrity through the metaphors of weight loss, exercise, and tolerance of and ability to conquer physical pain and exhaustion" (475). Culturally predicated norms of goal-oriented sleekness spawn anorexia (avoidance of food to the point of starvation) and bulimia (eating as much as desired but regurgitating it so little could metabolize). It also spawned all sorts of cruel jokes, perhaps some of the more famous ones told by Joan Rivers about Elizabeth Taylor, demanding if starving Africans have no problem losing weight, why can't Liz? The play on unwilling starvation, race, and national origin against Taylor's privileged and therefore presumed willing starvation is quite wicked.

Facing low self-esteem and a documented greater difficulty in landing a job when compared with slim women with the same credentials because size is an emblem of laziness, some fat women currently vocally oppose their oppression. Roseanne, stand-up comic and television star, is fond of saying, "The sexiest thing I can do is be this fat." Oprah Winfrey persistently airs problems concerning body imaging and fitness yet affirms that first and foremost, be healthy, not slim. Some recent studies also confirm that some excess weight is statistically more healthy than being underweight or exactly on target.

A growing number of women share their personal experience with their bodies, particularly being overweight. An entire recent issue of the periodical

SageWoman explored body image issues in the context of various spiritual paths, particularly Earth-centered spiritualities. The editor, Anne Newkirk Niven, relates childhood ambivalence about her body and how later as an adult she regarded the good-looking women who "got men" with disdain. Still, she herself did not have a favorable body image of herself. Reporting a spiritual breakthrough, Niven says, "I feel that by coming to love my body I am learning to let go of the past and be open to the future" (4). Lisa Sarasohn's narrative confirms Bordo's critique of slenderness. "When I first started dieting, I finally felt a sense of control in my life that I never had before," but dieting and bingeing alternated, sometimes five or six times a year. "I obsessed about food, my weight, and my shape. I was lonely, directionless, and unhappy because I was too busy being preoccupied with 'trimming my tummy' to cultivate a sense of identity and purpose or any intimate relationships" (7). Indeed, the motivations to trim to make oneself desirable defeated that goal. Claiming that the belly is the site of feminine sensibility, North American culture targets it through "rape, unnecessary hysterectomies and Cesarians, reproductive technology, legal restrictions on women's authority in pregnancy and childbirth, and belly-belittling fashions, exercise regimens, and diet schemes" (9).

Overweight men, however, are also subjected to cultural norms and discriminations. The body image for males in the West may have undergone some diversification in the last century, yet the late Victorian image was the he-man body builder. To this day, weight-trained, male musculature tops the box office with the likes of Arnold Schwarzenegger and Jean-Claude Van Damme, among others. Even Harrison Ford in his role as Indiana Jones sports a "Body by Jake." Then again, Sidney Greenstreet never played a romantic lead, nor did Peter Lorre.

The muscular norm for male image was undoubtedly informed initially by the Western traditions of painting and sculpture, originally inspired by beefy Greeks and Romans. Early photographs of male nudes that served as studies for artists indeed posed muscular men like Greek and Roman statues (Cooper 14-19). Not surprisingly, interest in physique can appear to be a "sexless pursuit of the 'healthy' male body" (Pronger 169) and yet allow homosocial admiration (Sedgwick, *Between Men*) if not homoerotic appeal. Pronger claims that the first professional body builder was "the nineteenth century Russian strongman Eugene Sandow whose photos appeared in private collections" (Pronger's Figure 15) and the early physique magazine *The Strong Man* (Figure 16), inspiring similar posing (Figure 17). Apparently Sandow was more than a pinup. Hooven claims, "Florenz Ziegfeld started both his career and the modern commercial exploitation of muscular males when he made the German strongman Eugene Sandow a household name as 'Sandow the Magnificent!' " Vaudeville strength exhibitions led eventually to the increasing popularity of serious weight training as well as physique competitions that showed the results of weight training and not the actual lifting of weights (22-23).

Bordo maintains, in contrast, "Muscularity has had a variety of cultural meanings." Muscles symbolize masculine power and yet are also associated "with manual labor and chain gangs . . . suffused with racial meaning . . . the body as material, unconscious, or animalistic" (474-475). Yet recently, muscularity has become a sign of upward mobility.

Not that the muscled look is all pervasive: Edweard Muybridge's landmark movement photographs from the mid-1880s feature trim men, but not overly muscular ones (Cooper 30; Hooven 12-13). There are no fat men, however. Other, lesser-known photographers abound, and many of their subjects were slim and apparently not weight lifters.

Because it was and is culturally permitted for men to doff their shirts in public—and on screen and in photographs—broadcasters knew in the 1950s that Clint Walker's *Cheyenne* with his shirt off translated into a larger viewing audience. Nude men, however, were not a Western cultural norm, as were nude women. Yet advertisements since *Playgirl*'s publication of George Maharis' *Route 66* have increasingly shown beefcake and as much male skin as possible. Calvin Klein's first advertising coup featured a gay porn star on a billboard in Times Square, wearing only CK briefs. Subsequently, a series of underwear and jeans ads featured buff "Marky Mark" Wahlberg. Wahlberg snapped his waistband and frequently dropped his pants during concerts with his rap group, the Funky Bunch (Mark & Goldsmith).

Thus are men who do not fit the trim or muscular athletic body image beset to conform to the norm or suffer the same sorts of stigmatization and prejudice as do women who did not fit the image of thinness. Certainly, however, perhaps, a wider range of women find chunky men acceptable if not preferable as romance or sex partners, more so than men who find chunky women preferable. Yet in gay culture, except for men called "chubby chasers," slim is in, and as the saying goes—even to be found on T-shirts—"No Pecs, No Sex!"

In an era of what I call physical mysticism, body focus derails many possibilities for getting to know someone as other than the surface of his or her skin. The emphasis on skin and good body looks conventionally appropriate to either sex is so extreme, the expectation so perfect, and late modern bodies so perfectible, that body image has become what Baudrillard and others call "hyperreal," more than real. "America is neither dream nor reality. It is a hyperreality" (28). Baudrillard notes that what appears to be reality is actually transferred from the dream reality of movies. The facile screen images—the seemingly natural beauty of the made-up actress, the handsome looks of the actor who effortlessly performs breathtaking stunts that actually are done over many takes of the scene or sequence with a stand-in stuntman—lend a sense that normal, everyday folk can replicate the beauty, the ruggedness, the dash. "It is not the least of America's charms that even outside the movie theaters the whole country is cinematic" (56). Thus, Americans are obsessed with perfecting their looks, their bodies, from cosmetics and rampant exercise to dieting to plastic surgery. Americans are hyperreal; they are real dreams that would not exist naturally. Hence, on Baudrillard's terms, rugged and muscular men are literally hypermasculine, real dreams. Likewise, slim and waifish women are literally hyperfeminine, real dreams.

I note here that Baudrillard maintains that Europeans are not caught up in this hyped perfection (73), yet Umberto Eco seems to think otherwise. In *Travels in Hyperreality,* Eco claims he visited the same places Baudrillard visited and had, essentially, the same reactions. Eco's replication—as a fellow European—is a wicked satire of Baudrillard, and it is instructive. Cultures replicate themselves reflexively, like a fractal moving over the face of chaos. Body image works in similar fashion. Regardless of national origin, body image reaches beyond mapped boundaries and waves into new lands. North American body norms now reach a good deal of the rest of the world in various sorts of exports. With the Internet, the export of body image can now progress in the hyperreality of cyberspace.

Body image incestuously feeds on cultural conventions, monitoring others' bodies and their regard of self and personal self-regard. The dynamic is undoubtedly more complex, but incestuous it is. Body image allows one to have sex with oneself through perceived intimacy with others, or it curtails the self-esteem of self-pleasure by lack of identification with desired others. Not so much how one would get along with another person, body image seduces the self and other into how one will look with this person in public. Hanging out with someone perceived conventionally as less attractive than oneself can be taken any number of ways. The company makes one more attractive? One has low standards, is settling? The relationship is based on something other than looks? What would that basis be?

Although The Look is enshrined in Hollywood and cosmetically sealed by Madison Avenue, not everyone buys it. While any number of heterosexual women do not buy it (Bordo in Tuana & Tong 480), as a group, lesbians often choose partners who do not have The Look, including the look of slender. Gay men, however, are peculiarly taken by surfaces, and their regard and frequent insistence on men with The Look of slender muscularity speaks homophobi-cally. Thus there is a heterosexual, male dominant dynamic also operative for gays and straights. A man's fat body is censorially equated with the female body, but as something less without the possibility of fecundity. Then again, untrue of all gays, bears who are gay do not always go for slim, hairless twinks. Bears are hairy, but some, not all, are husky, do not suit themselves to fashion, and cultivate their personhood—and their friendships—with other attractions in mind.

Disabled Interpretive Communities

Body awareness and self-esteem are intricate intimates to each other, and they both vary by interpretive community. Depending on how it is viewed, one interpretive community is either sizable or minuscule—and is popularly per-ceived as unsexualized. The legal status for having sex is ambiguous for some of this interpretive community. Others are sheltered from the public and may not avail themselves to popular—or much of any—culture. Some were once "normal" but are no longer and, technically by convention, never will be again. Taken as the diverse group that they are, they have been endowed with mythic forbearance, in that they are believed they can't have sex, don't have sex, and shouldn't have sex. I am speaking about persons who are disabled.

Visible disability claims stares or avoidance in many North American cul-tures. The intensity of gaze and the literal ignorance of persons who are disabled set the stage of their invisibility. "They" make people uneasy, an easy attribution that people actually supply themselves and actually persuade themselves to believe. Unthinkable though the disabled are, their having sex is perhaps even more unthinkable to so-called normal people. Born impaired or later becoming impaired by age, accident, disease, or malice, disabled persons suffer the egregious fortune of being treated like freaks, but freaks no carnival sideshow would feature. That they are not freaks does not matter to mainstream culture.

The myth that persons who are disabled do not have sex is what convention-ally impairs the reality that they desire and have sex despite imposed norms: beliefs of alleged immaturity, that sex would cause the already pained more pain, of apparent dependency, that only married people can have sex, that para- and quadriplegics cannot possibly have a sex life, and so on (Blum & Blum 33) all delimit options to those who never chose options in the first place. Thus various teachers and social workers need specialized training in bolstering self-esteem, as well as materials for facilitating the needs of disabled individuals. Regardless of demanding morals and ethics, some learning-disabled persons are affectionate, and for the affectionally deprived, affection can easily be read as sexual. Even for "normal" persons, this can often be so. Although issues of reproducing the learning disability abound for the families, handlers, and government agencies—in behalf of the learning disabled—persons who are learning disabled still may encounter desire, untrammeled by the heterosexual surveillance of the gene pool. The real-world Forrest Gumps get ignored on the Net with all sorts of ancillary issues about a filmic confabulation. How convenient that a learning-disabled protagonist is not perceived by culture critics as representing the disabled—reluctantly, unconspiring, not on the make but all the same protective of a friend who becomes sexualized. Disability was taken as a motif of marginality—accurate—but therefore as a leitmotif of the film's unreality—not so good, as if film were always thoroughly mimetic.

Learning Disabilities

Three initial concerns for sex education of persons who are educable mentally retarded and trainable mentally retarded are called for: (1) alerting that they can be taken advantage of, (2) training about "appropriate" public behavior, and (3) educating about safer sex. Unwanted sexual advances may easily be misread by persons who are mentally retarded because their response to gestures normatively read as neutral may be disproportionate; the affection shown may be quite strong and persistent. They may also do whatever is asked of them without hesitation (Kempton 15). Blum and Blum recommend a series of training units that initially focus on learning the differences between public and private. Photos from magazines, newspapers, and other sources are collected and then shown to groups one at a time for them to identify the scene and then decide if it is public or private. With the learning that certain types of touching of others and self are appropriate for private, not public, the groups then learn how to say "No." Once individuals and the group are practiced in these awarenesses and strategies, they learn ways to deal with unwanted sex (20-29).

Most specialists in the field argue that parents, however, are the primary source of sex education for children with mental retardation, but that they too may need special training (Craft 23-49). Raising the awareness of parents and allaying and directing their concerns about their children as sexual beings are problematic, but intervention strategies abound. Although "some parents reinforce, some do not become involved, and still others interfere. . . . Parents of handicapped children are generally more interested in the subject than parents of normal children" (Kempton & Forman 81). Yet educating children with mental retardation themselves is a daunting task because several characteristics make it difficult for them to acquire information as well as develop attitudes about their own sexuality, including (1) not knowing how to ask for help, (2) reading levels that limit "access to accurate information," (3) lack of friends or friends who provide them with inaccurate information, and (4) social skills that never had opportunities to be practiced (Kempton 14).

Individuals who are learning disabled, however, can pantomime and act out various scenarios in dramatic play (Kempton & Forman 68-72). Other ways of instruction have been developed. Because learning "appropriate" behavior becomes highly problematic if the teacher trains one way but a movie or television show images just the opposite, films, videos, and slide shows have been produced to instruct basics in sexual mechanics, feelings, and self-esteem, whereas others graphically portray sex. Persons who do not process verbal information all that easily often can process visual information. Others need tactile learning; hence anatomically correct dolls and genitalia have been produced as educational materiel that are most frequently employed in small group and therapeutic situations (Kempton 130-133; Kempton & Forman 74, 132).

Disability as Limitation: Reclaiming the Body

Disabilities acquired after "normal" acculturalization and personhood formation may feel different both to persons who are newly disabled and their intimates, but they are treated in a similar manner as are those who are learning disabled. Conventions and myths ordain that they are dis-abled and limited. Overcoming the myths is no easy task. On the one hand, sexual difficulties affect personally, and their enabling may be perceived as individually oriented. Thus, intervention strategies may be suggested by particular disability, from back and neck pain to urinary leakage and vision problems, as well as specially made devices—manufactured, medical, or made by the therapist—for solving all sorts of needs (Neistadt & Freda 41-59). On the other hand, sexual difficulties affect interpersonally, socially, in "privacy, dating, marriage, and childrearing" (vii; 61-76).

Even then, the loss of favorable body image, even if previously only marginally enjoyed, can be devastating. In a most remarkable book directed "to the average quadriplegic and paraplegic" (x), Mooney, Cole, and Chilgren provide explicit photography and candid advice about how various persons with spinal cord injury may still have sex. They recognize that the "able-bodied majority of our culture" could also learn from the example of disabled persons.

> Consider those who sit conspicuously in their wheelchairs with numb and paralyzed extremities. . . . Then consider those who have other physical problems—the fat or thin, the tall or short, the deformed or weak, the bald, those with false teeth or acne, those who are too tired, too busy, or in too much discomfort to try for sexual fulfillment. If the spinal-cord-injured person can become sexually successful through a process of reassessment of goals, attitudes, and abilities, others can do the same. (xi)

The photographs show "average" spinal-cord-injured persons in various scenarios, often with expressions of ecstasy and often showing catheters and other devices most people would not find sexual, that indeed might well inhibit their sense of sexuality.

Mooney, Cole, and Chilgren's book was published in 1975, immediately after the Vietnam War. It is perhaps no accident that spinal injuries and amputations needed attention as to self-esteem—another issue screened in *Forrest Gump,* regarding Gump's lieutenant whose legs had been amputated. The issues Mooney and colleagues discuss are all the more stunning as they consider other sorts of disability that in our culture automatically are perceived as inhibiting, if not prohibiting, sex. Disability as limitation of sex inscribes the bounds of cultural normalcy and its impossibility.

Because the status of disability is conventionally taken as less than standard, its possibilities for transgression in art will vary with the cleverness of the artist and the Sights, Sounds, Smells, Tastes, and Touches chosen to be fused in the work of art. The hue and cry over some of Robert Mapplethorpe's photography was perhaps a vindication of the transgression of disability. The photos are stunningly aesthetic, yet they depict not just actual sex acts but subcultural, apparently gay but butch men as if they were disabled. Some viewers could point to explicit sex to dismiss the art as not art; they did not see the art that was there: arraying transgression artistically. Melody Davis' study on the male nude in photography includes numerous photos of disabled men. The cover photo shows an African American man, left arm amputated, staring with a serious look directly at the viewer. For that matter, some folks find disability arousing, not as a lack or something less. On April 7, 1995, rangers from the National Park Service raided a private home at which various computer components allegedly stolen from the Park Service had been assembled to serve up an Internet site for profit. As reported in the National Park Service Morning Report dated 4 November 1996, "The service catered to individuals with a sexual fetish clinically known as acrotomophilia; the service provided graphic images of and information about physically impaired individuals."

Numerous issues clamor together in this event, a late modern fusion of desires, freedoms, and illegalities. The seizure and thus eventual closing down of this Web site had nothing to do with the nature of the images per se; many of the computer components had been specially tagged and had not been sold, hence the rationale to warrant the search in the first place. Who was accessing the site is another matter. Nothing in the National Park Service's report indicated anything perverse, although the use of the words *fetish* and *acrotomophilia* indicate some sort of psychological pathology. Someone with disability who cannot find a copy of any of the sorts of books already mentioned here may well want such information out of no pathological desire. Internet access is certainly more facile for many disabled persons if they have a computer and e-mail address from which to surf the Net. Although there may be those persons in whom the arousal by images of disability is certifiably pathological, it would be difficult to maintain that all arousal by images of disability is pathological. Clearly, many of the writers mentioned here state just the opposite, that disabled persons need self-esteem to find themselves desirable.

The Limits of Disability

Arousing disability raises a whole series of questions, but the one most fascinating, to myself at least, may be put simply: What are the limits of disability? With mass media and folklore washing our daily thoughts constantly with Sights, Sounds, Touches, Tastes, and Aromas of normalcy, we live in a state of compulsive normalcy. Normalcy is norm. Normalcy is heavily laden with the diaphanies of handsomeness and beauty. Yet few people fulfill these norms. The rest must scramble to alleviate their perceived lack of this normalcy and achieve some greater, hyperreal self in a hysteria of acquisitional transformation.

So many images, stereotypes, and myths are imposed on particular persons and groups that it is surprising there are many "normal" people at all. Andrew Holleran's latest novel, *The Beauty of Men,* brings together numerous societally perceived disabilities. Lark, a gay man in middle age bemoans his aging, his increasing invisibility. He has fled New York City and the numerous deaths by HIV-related causes among his friends and acquaintances and has moved near Gainesville, Florida. There he obsesses about his loneliness and his few and now limited connections to other men who might be sexually interested in himself. Small-town America and the obsession with looks, physical perfection, and the need for personal affiliation all conspire against Lark. Or so he thinks. His mother, paralyzed from the neck down, lives in a nearby nursing home. Their relationship, although not sexual, is perhaps the novel's signal, most satisfying human relationship—bright among the blight. The paradoxes of satisfaction and dissatisfaction play throughout the novel as the taken and missed opportunities of socially sanctioned and personally stolen moments of ecstasy. Finally, that the novel will most likely be taken as a "gay" novel and therefore invisible to mainstream culture only underlines the stigmatization of gays as disabled to speak concerns of interest to nongays. The book is much like some of Mapplethorpe's photographs; it explores disability as an act of life. Horrifying though it may be, disability resides in "normal" persons, too.

The disability attributed commonly to aging in North American culture brings a fictive sense of disability to those who uncritically "buy" popular culture, although many "seniors" report more satisfying sex after forty or fifty than ever before in their lives. "It seems as they grow older, some people become better at being intimate. Although society tends to think that sex among the elderly is unlikely, those who live to older ages may be the group that has the best sex" (Tallmer 2). Children are also credited legally as disabled, particularly sexually, thus sex with children by adults is highly tabooed. The margins of this disability get foggy when the "children" in the situation are persons with learning disabilities who are legally old enough and of legal capacity to make decisions for themselves. Yet society feels a necessity to monitor them along the entire spectrum of aging, like societal surveillance (Foucault).

A fat, nonstandard body look is taken to mean one is disabled. Acting faggy or dykish is taken to mean one is disabled. If one is not handsome, not conventionally pretty, then one is disabled. It occurs to me, then, that normalcy is rare and that by the way we believe and act, disability is the norm—not beauty, not handsomeness, not a svelte body or one that is properly toned, tanned, tucked, or cosmeticized. Susan Bordo presents convincing observations about the play of alleged normalcy and weight; although her examples of fitness and hair coloring ads apply to women, her basic argument about the misleading mixture of elements of resistance to imposed norms and acceptance of them applies to men, too.

> One might argue that an adequate analysis of advertisements such as those I've been discussing would take into account both their resistant element and their normalizing messages . . . (weight-training and exercise often do have socially empowering results for women). . . . We need to recognize, in connection with this, that the most obvious symbols of resistance in these ads are included by the advertisers in the profoundest of cynical bad faith; they pretend to reject the sexualization of women

("I believe 'babe' is a four-letter word") and value female assertiveness ("Coloring my hair with Nice and Easy made me feel more powerful") while attempting to convince women who *fail* to embody dominant ideals of (slender, youthful) beauty that they need to bring themselves into line. (*Unbearable* 287-298; emphasis Bordo's)

Thus are we trained to monitor the flaw and judge ourselves and ignore any favorable feature or talent, particularly in ourselves, thus attributing normalcy or favorability to Other, as something one does not "have" but should acquire. The commodification of normalcy thus ordains that normalcy is desirable but scarce and that all else is undesirable although available.

The trick for defeating this stunning turn of logic is finding oneself sexual, if that is one's desire, or perhaps estimable, desirable, favorable, OK, despite the tyrannical norms that only a narrow range of body image and gestures are "sexy." One can start to monitor one's favors and let monitoring flaw atrophy. Not easy—perhaps, for many of us, constant and lifelong work. After a mastectomy, Deena Metzger, a "goddess activist poet," had a vine tattooed over the scar, reclaiming the loss as chosen, as beautiful, so the body for her once again becomes erotic (Gadon 302). Body reclamation is personal empowerment despite the face of culture. Yet in this regard, Gloria Steinem and I are in complete agreement: revolution is from *within*. It is not going to be legislated and certainly is not going to be brought to us by entrepreneurs such as Calvin Klein, vested interests such as the tobacco industry and their pocketed politicians, or smug lookers with attitude who someday will awaken to find themselves disabled by age, if nothing else, the targets of the ostracism they perpetuated in their quest for personal satisfaction. Although many may have thought this latter group—the lookers—to be highly self-centered, they were and are not. They are centered in the economics that sell commodities that purport to enhance one to the rare, vacuous state of hyperreal normalcy.

The Fashion of Sex Toys

Ever ingenious, humans invent enhancements for overcoming perceived imperfections and bodily distance between each other in a variety of ways. Consider this narrative of field observations gathered during Spring Break in Fort Lauderdale, 1985.

Spring Break in Fort Lauderdale brings hundreds to the beach. The empty sand gets crowded by noon and then the high jinks begin.

Scores of mostly exposed bodies lay in the sun on beach towels, blankets, and the like. The smell of coconut oil catches on the breeze.

Two guys, looking fit in their clamdiggers, are tossing a Frisbee on that breeze, but suddenly, the Frisbee dips and lands right on a pretty girl's bikini top.

"Sorry," says the guy, walking over.

She smiles and makes him come get it.

This brief narrative account includes a toy used sexually. The term *sex toy* is recent; as Bullough and Bullough maintain, "The moniker 'sex toy' has been in use less than two decades and even today is not in wide circulation. Broadly defined, it includes any object used to enhance sexual activity, whether or not the item was specifically designed or marketed for that purpose" (587). I think the use of a Frisbee as reported in the narrative account qualifies under this definition, particularly in the light of some of the responses to the narrative account I gathered in 1985 and subsequently. Consider them a sample of everyday language.

Twenty-two-year-old male:	He's coming on to her.
Twenty-year-old male:	Yep, works pretty good for me too.
Twenty-year-old female:	Hey, I got hit by a football once, right in the boobs and I jumped up and tackled the guy, then joined them.

Indeed, this sort of use is not limited to Frisbees. But the commonality among all collected examples was the use of some toy for first contact with an interesting, potential sex partner. For instance, just after the last respondent finished her sentence, she paused, thinking, so I prompted, "And?" She smiled, "We had a good time later, if that's what you mean." I said, innocently, "Oh?" "Yah, sometimes it pays to have a few older brothers. Knew how to play football pretty rough and the more I played with those guys on the beach, the hotter we got for each other."

So much for personal accounts and everyday language. Naturally, culture critics may have different spins on the narrative account, "thick" description.

Rhetorical studies language: The Frisbee is a rhetorical artifact (Holmberg, "Stray") in that it creates a rhetorical situation (Bitzer) that calls for further communication. Furthermore, the particular use generates an immediate audience response and suggests inventories of words, gestures, and eye contact appropriate to the situation, familiar from prior experience or invented on the spot.

The language of semiotics: The circle is a sign system of revolving. The Frisbee revolves and lands on breasts, also circles. It is as if circle is drawn to circle in the confirmation of the circle's field of signification. Then, the two signers take turns and revolve to each other.

Mythic interpretation: The Frisbee is a symbol of wholeness, a mandala of fun (Jung). It brings people together in celebration of sun, sand, ocean, and play. Fetching the Frisbee is an heroic journey fraught with loss, rejection, reversals, restoration, and salvation.

Postmodernist jargon: The Frisbee's intentional trajectory confines the expression of heterosexuality to a symbolic economy of male literally hitting a female. Her submissive response is flirtation, and the bricolage of seduction inscribes the received, mainstream gender stereotype of womanhood. Even play at the beach involves violence and dominance.

So much for the language of culture critics. Of course, each version is true and does not falsify the other. They enrich each other but employ language alien to everyday life and to the lived experience of actually being on a beach, scoping and cruising for possible sex.

Deeper into the Scene

A recent issue of *GQ* (*Gentleman's Quarterly*) included under one of its regular features called "The Single Guy" a brief commentary about dogs as objects of attraction for women.

> A lick on the face from the right furry mongrel is more thrilling than, say, mere alcohol if the beast is presently being woman-handled by a lovely lady.
> That women are attracted to men with dogs is an undisputed fact. But why? . . . I believe that women are attracted to the persona that only the right kind of dog can bring out in a man. (Moritz 91-92)

The author, Robert Moritz, then proceeds to figure which breed of dog "would get me the most action?" by actually experimenting by walking a variety of dogs. Answer? It will vary, of course, but Moritz found that a male Jack Russell terrier works best for him.

The advice is clear, and it appears to issue from a modified rhetorical studies perspective: A dog is a communication instigator that provides opportunities to meet people of one's sexual orientation, whether the others are walking a dog themselves or not. Rhetoricians consider this persuasive tactic as a way of getting an audience's attention, then directing it. The dog is a rhetorical artifact (Holmberg, "Stray") in that its breed, leash, walking route, and more are all premeditated to increase the likelihood of communication effectiveness. Communication effectiveness in this case is meeting people and possibly then continuing to relate with them, perhaps under more intimate circumstances. Moritz seems to infuse the whole strategy with wit and stylistic cuteness, however, instead of cookie cutting a five-part research design.

Although the phrase "sex toy" does not usually conjure up an image of a dog, let alone taking it for a walk or a spin around the local research design, the *GQ* illustration suggests that there is more to the concepts of sex toy and sex play than the sorts of apparatus one can purchase at a condom shop, an XXX-rated video store, or GayMart (N. Halstead Ave., Chicago). Seemingly innocent possessions and toys invest an individual conventionally "closed" to approach with public approach protocols—permission to ignore the usual ritual that Goffman calls "civil inattention" (*Behavior* 83-88; 124-139). The Frisbee example involved the purposeful targeting of an individual. The dog-walking example is slightly different in that one walks the dog, waiting for an approach. It is still calculated. A potential sex partner is more likely to talk if some sort of investitive goods that invite interaction is present. Investitive goods also provide the circumstances for someone to look longer without discomfort for either person. He or she may voice a desire to touch the animal, looking for permission and leading to a negotiated interchange. Thus, various activities may invite attention or at least permit an initial communication between people.

In this sense, we *wear* toys, pets, and material culture artifacts to advertise our *fashion* of being in the world. Fashion is not limited to threads but may very well be chosen to attract others, if not open the universe of discourse with them. Premeditated or not, everything beyond bare skin is an accessory or access to self, access to others by fashioned signification. A hot-looking guy in clamdiggers on a beach is one sort of fashion. A hot-looking guy in clamdiggers on a beach who's playing Frisbee is a different sort of fashion. The muscular activity alone is an immaterial feature of the material culture of fashion. Boots on a shelf hold immaterial potential. On a body, on feet, they *move* and inscribe arcs of work and play.

Toys, pets, accessories, and possessions promise media impact on one's self-concept and self-image and on others' attention and assessment. Conscious and unconscious selection of fashion that sexualizes oneself underscores that almost all human commodities—manufactured or handmade, excorporated from the mainstream or incorporated by it—hold potential as sexual enhancements, as sex toys. If, as McLuhan says, the wheel is an extension of the foot, if clothes are an extension of the skin, if electronic media are an extension of the central nervous system (26-41), then sex toys are extensive simulacra of the imagination itself. Hence fashion in the regular sense may show style and wit as well as buying power. Fashion in the sense of sex toys may show styles of desire and the intellect for passion.

Gendered and Oriented Toys

Employing playthings and pets as come-ons circumscribes a use category in material culture studies. There are toys, however, that have been specifically fashioned to cue the performance of sexual roles. Dolls in general have been commodified for little girls, prompting fantasy play most often correctly characterized as acculturation to the traditional mainstream gender role of woman as nurturer, homemaker, and mother. The Barbie doll in particular has received close attention as furthermore promoting impossible body measurements and thus poor self-image for thousands, as well as a sense of fashion that further entraps females into desire for only the best clothing, particularly, dress-up attire (Lord). Yet not everyone attracted to dolls is female. The film *The Adventures of Priscilla, Queen of the Desert* plays nicely on the conventionally gendered roles of dolls for girls and trucks for boys. One brief flashback sequence depicts young Ralph and family at Christmas. His sister is opening a present, accompanied by the expectant cooing of Mother. When the package is unwrapped, the girl is rather disappointed. It's a truck. Mother quickly sizes up the situation. Ralph had switched tags on Christmas presents so he would get his sister's toys such as dolls and she would get his toys such as trucks. Indeed, Ralph is sheepishly smiling, holding the doll dearly.

Other toys create expectations of performing gender roles. Ostensibly, the Ouija board is a divination party game device that requires one or two people to place their fingers on a movable planchette that spells out answers to questions, variously explained as spirit communication or the energy of the person(s) speaking. In reality, "Two people using the device are supposed to touch knees in order for their body energy to help propel the planchette around until it spells out some answers" (Sann 141). Two additional, folkloristic parameters apply: (1) The fingers above board are not allowed to touch; and (2) preferably, when two persons play Ouija, one is male, the other female. Ouija boards inscribe the nature of party games as mixing sexes and in allowing them ritualistic opportunities to touch when normally they would avoid it. Interestingly enough, the public and visible placement of fingers allows no Touch. Under a card table, however, knees Touch, further inscribing the hidden nature of Touching and the polite qualities of nontouching, a hierarchy of values, another example of the Western cultural bias against Touch in favor of Sight.

And such is the paradoxical frisson of sex in everyday life: Two people are in full view of others, but hidden out of sight, they are at the same time rubbing knees. Another popular party entertainment involves the levitation of one person by four others. In this case, optimal efficacy will be achieved by the alternate placement of male and female, two each around the person seated on a chair to be levitated (Childress 55-57). Thus some party entertainments permit the license to Touch, even caress, when usually such performance is not allowed.

Sex Toys and Sex Machines

Of course, there are also toys that have been specifically fashioned to incorporate during sex, but there have also been contraptions specifically designed to prevent sex. Part of medieval sexual lore includes a device called a chastity belt, a metal contraption with lock that prevents other men from having sex with a particular woman. Such a device appears in Mel Brooks' film *Robin Hood, Men in Tights;* of course, Robin has the key to Maid Marion's lock, but Prince John wants it first. In quite a different cultural setting, no physical entrapment was used, and public decency alone ordained the relation of men and women. By the time of the Ming Dynasty in China, 1368-1644 C.E., the Confucianist recommendations of keeping the sexes separate and secluding women began to be "practised [*sic*] in earnest" (Van Gulik 264), even to the point of forbidding physicians to see female patients. With the patient behind numerous curtains, the physician employed a figurine of a nude female (see Figure 11.1).

> However, in order to explain to him the exact location of the woman's complaints, the husband or a female relative could point out those spots on the ivory model of a naked woman that a doctor always carried on him. These "medical ivories" usually measure about 10 cm. in length, and represent the woman lying on her back with her hands behind her head. (319)

Of course, this use of "medical ivories" is hotly debated, with some sources claiming the artifacts were erotic, if not porographic, hand-held items of arousal that could easily be hidden (Watson 42-43). One of the possibilities that seems not to be considered is that *both* uses actually occurred—to what extent, the jury is still out.

Emerging from a shame culture, modern Americans proved keen on inventing devices to prevent sex. Although the U.S. Patent Office's first award to a sexual device was for vaginal contraception in 1846 (Levins 8), the vast majority of sex patents were not for preventing conception; they were for preventing male

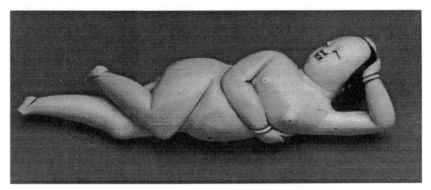

Figure 11.1. Medical or Erotic Chinese Figurine
SOURCE: Used by permission of Royal Ontario Museum, Toronto, Canada. Reformatted by David Hampshire.

masturbation and employed strategies such as pins, electricity, and just plain entrapment to limit erection (14-25). Eventually, body suit models were also adapted for women. Contraptions for preventing wet dreams employed the same range of mechanical remedies (27-42). Devices for preventing prolapsed or fallen wombs eventually led to various contraceptive devices (44-67). While other potential maladies received inventive attention (rubbers for contraception and disease control, erection problems, and supporting breasts with bras), in 1911, the first vaginal vibrator was patented (214). Although phalluses made of wood, stone, bone, or hide had been popular for centuries, and although massage and methods of vibration had also been known and popular, this was the first time the two were combined. At the end of the twentieth century, vibrators sell by the hundreds of thousands per year at various types of stores, not just XXX-rated ones, as well as by mail order.

Cock rings that enhance hardness and time endurance of an erection are not a twentieth-century afterthought of inventors. Wrapping a band of silk around a "member" is "often mentioned in Ming erotic novels," as are white bands boiled in aphrodisiacs, jade rings, and the like. Perhaps a prize in itself, one carved ivory cock ring conjoins Chinese spirituality with erotic practicality. It features two dragons along the perimeter, their tongues entwined, making a spiraled sun image, the "pearl that shines in the dark," a symbol of fertility and potency, but "the spiral doubtless had at the same time the practical function of stimulating the woman's clitoris during the movement" (Van Gulik 281 referring to Plate XV between 280 & 281). Even sex toys bespeak heaven and earth in Chinese tradition.

Although many of the sex toys already mentioned may well be perceived as transgressive by various interpretive communities—for instance, any form of contraception is "unnatural" and therefore stigmatized by some right-to-life, antiabortion communities—certain sex toys perhaps have attained a greater notoriety as transgressive. Leather and latex wear alone signals transgression for some people, yet whips, chains, and other accoutrements of leather culture that are signs of S/M activity even more clearly signify the transgression of pain as arousal. Various harness devices were originally patented to assist sex, particularly for holding on to one another or not slipping off a bed (Levins 225-229). Slings, usually leather and metal devices hung from a ceiling, are not necessarily S/M modes of entrapment but may simply be used for greater ease of sexual interaction with less exertion.

Purchasing Power

A visit to a Victoria's Secret shop is not exactly the same as ordering something racy from Frederick's of Hollywood by mail order. Victoria's Secret populates the controlled domains of malls. In no small way, the items offered for purchase are sex toys: peignoirs and scents, baby dolls and nightgowns, bras that skimp and lift, and cosmetics that presumably render a woman cosmic in allure. While there is no mistake that the artifacts enhance a woman for another person, they also permit her to address herself, to let imagination play on her surface and soul, to, in fact, encourage it. The toys are frequently as much for her self-esteem and self-image as for attractiveness to another. Thus one may purchase an erotic self at the mall, something previously accomplished at more generic stores or by catalog, yet now unabashedly packaged as such, in places that are taken to be classy, with tasteful, old-fashioned decor and sold by oh-so-polite sales personnel. The entire coding makes self-eroticization of women acceptable to certain types of women and their lovers, be they men or women. A mall is safe; everything's out in the open. The secret is plain as day.

In contrast, a visit to the local XXX-rated store is more like a walk on the wild side, although even then, commodification rules. XXX-rated stores are rarely found in malls. They usually are situated in smaller buildings set off from other small buildings. Their parking lots are not anonymous like a mall's; hence, many lots are sheltered from direct sight from the street. Thus, parking in the lot is tinged with a sense of transgression, surmounted by walking through the blinded door with its red-lettered warnings of adult-oriented goods, then confirmed by the sorts of displays and sales personnel one will not find at Victoria's Secret. The person at the cash register behind the generic counter display case is usually a man, usually older. He may be helpful but often in a laconic sort of way. While numerous periodicals and videos with explicit covers and jackets populate the inner terrain of XXX-rated stores—along with the video arcade yawning through a simple door or archway—prominently displayed are sex toys of all sorts. There may actually be lace and femme outfits, but there may also be leatherware for men or women, dildos, and condoms. One particular area is definitely male-coded: penis enlargement devices. Even if a man is not "hung like a hamster," he may feel a need to be "more of a man" and consider the purchase of such an apparatus. Ostensibly, the item's use will enhance sexual confidence and prowess, but that's not all that's happening. Like a purchase at Victoria's Secret, buying something is in itself a form of empowerment. In the case of penis enlargement devices, however, the purchase is a commodification of the penis, something to expect in a business-oriented, consumer culture. The purchase may be an erotic event, similar to one at Victoria's, not just in the use of the product. Like a bra that creates the illusion that a woman's breasts are actually bigger than they really are, the penis enlarger enhances deficiency, even when, perhaps, there is no real deficiency. Yet only temporarily, while wearing it, does a bra increase breast size; a penis enlarger does increase penis size for a while, even when it's nowhere near the actual penis. One more secret event also factors in the purchase and use of a penis enlargement device that is similar to and different from a purchase at Victoria's Secret. Potency, hardness, and self-concept/self-esteem mask what are, by and large (pun intended), masturbation tools and experiences. While a guy may use the device with the assistance and encouragement of a partner, or, may use it solo to better please a partner, that layering of bigness to turn on someone else is a denial of self-pleasuring as a viable sexual performance in and of itself, a convenient fiction that makes the operation of a penis enlarger potentially or actually masturbatory.

When one purchases what may be specifically marketed as a sex toy or what by imagination can turn into a sex toy, one purchases power. The power is not necessarily a power of dominance; it is a perceived enhancement of one's personal power, for others, for oneself. Although the potential for fashion or sex toys to overpower someone else, to become so compelling and irresistible for them, is present, the potential may or may not play out as dominance. For that matter, natural ability and one's natural body may or may not fit one's community's image of personhood and performance of sexuality. One may thus diet, work out, work on the body and its abilities themselves as artful enhancements of one's nature to interface it, to adjust it to the norms one finds imposed by culture. Further, one may employ fashion and artifacts—inventions separate from humans but concretized desire all the same—in an attempt, sometimes successful, to modify one's erotic appeal to others and to oneself. Thus sexual potential becomes activated in cultural context, nature to personal erotic art, and although not all persons in North American cultures ascribe to the whole notion of sex toys, they usually are able to verbalize a sense of fashion, and that fashion bears on their self-image, the way they comport themselves in everyday life, how they feel, or how they resist sexualization. Ultimately, everyone invents his or her sexuality, perhaps mostly guided by received norms, perhaps in opposition to them. Sexuality is itself an ultimate physical, emotional, and spiritual interaction that is inventive by nature, persuading ourselves and others to communicate in ways that satisfy us, pursuing various communities' available inventories for affirmation and ecstasy of the body, mind, and spirit. Sexualities and popular culture limit, exonerate, and release the inventories in their play through our consciousness, musculature, and constant reinvention of desire.

Works Cited

Abbott, Franklin, ed. *Boyhood, Growing Up Male: A Multicultural Anthology.* Freedom, CA: Crossing Press, 1993.

Aristotle. *The Art of Rhetoric.* Just about any translation is superior to the Lane Cooper translation. I use John Henry Freese, trans. Cambridge, MA: Harvard University Press, 1967, because it includes both a version of the Greek and its translation.

Asante, Molefi Kete. *The Afrocentric Idea.* Philadelphia: Temple University Press, 1987.

Bailey, Beth L. *From Front Porch to Back Seat: Courtship in Twentieth-Century America.* Baltimore: Johns Hopkins University Press, 1988.

Baldwin, Charles Sears. *Medieval Rhetoric and Poetic (to 1400), Interpreted from Representative Works.* New York: Macmillan, 1928.

Barker, Clive. *Books of Blood: Volume One.* New York: Berkley, 1986.

———. *Books of Blood: Volume Three.* New York: Berkley, 1986.

———. *Cabal.* New York: Pocket, 1989.

Barrett, Gregory. *Archetypes in Japanese Film: The Sociopolitical and Religious Significance of the Principal Heroes and Heroines.* Selinsgrove, PA: Susquehanna University Press, 1989.

Bataille, Georges. *Erotism: Death and Sensuality.* Trans. Mary Dalwood. San Francisco: City Lights Books, 1986.

Baudrillard, Jean. *America.* Trans. Chris Turner. London: Verso, 1989.

Bawer, Bruce. *A Place at the Table: The Gay Individual in American Society.* New York: Poseidon, 1993.

Berne, Eric. *Sex in Human Loving.* New York: Simon & Schuster, 1970.

Berry, Thomas. *The Dream of the Earth.* San Francisco: Sierra Club Books, 1990.

Bitzer, Lloyd. "The Rhetorical Situation." *Philosophy and Rhetoric* 1 (1968): 1-14.

Blackwood, Evelyn. "Sexuality and Gender in Certain Native American Tribes: The Case of Cross-Gender Females." *Signs* 10 (1984): 27-42.

Bloom, Allan. *The Closing of the American Mind: How Higher Education Has Failed Democracy and Impoverished the Souls of Today's Students.* New York: Simon & Schuster, 1987.

Blum, Gloria, and Barry Blum. *Feeling Good about Yourself: A Guide for People Working with People Who Have Disabilities.* Mill Valley, CA: Feeling Good Associates, 1981.

Bly, Robert. *Iron John: A Book about Men.* New York: Vintage, 1992.

Boccaccio, Giovanni. *The Decameron.* Trans. G. H. McWilliam. London: Penguin, 1972.

269

Bogle, Donald. *Toms, Coons, Mulattoes, Mammies and Bucks: An Interpretive History of Blacks in American Films.* New York: Continuum, 1989.

Bordo, Susan. *Unbearable Weight: Feminism, Western Culture, and the Body.* Berkeley: University of California Press, 1993.

Boston Women's Health Book Collective. *Our Bodies, Ourselves: A Book by and for Women.* New York: Simon & Schuster, 1973.

Brady, Frank. *Hefner.* New York: MacMillan, 1974.

Bronski, Michael. *Culture Clash: The Making of Gay Sensibility.* Boston: South End, 1984.

Brown, Helen Gurley. *Sex and the Single Girl.* 1962. New York: Pocket, 1963.

Buddha: His Life and Teachings. New York: Crescent, 1973.

Buehrer, Beverley Bare. *Japanese Films: A Filmography and Commentary, 1921-1989.* Jefferson, NC: McFarland, 1990.

Bullough, Vern L., and Bonnie Bullough, eds. *Human Sexuality: An Encyclopedia.* New York: Garland, 1994.

Bunch, Charlotte. *Passionate Politics: Feminist Theory in Action.* New York: St. Martin's, 1987.

Burke, Edmund. *A Philosophical Enquiry Concerning the Origin of Our Ideas of the Sublime and Beautiful.* Facsimile of 1759 ed. New York: Garland, 1971.

Burke, Kenneth. *A Grammar of Motives.* Berkeley: University of California Press, 1969.

Burns, G. "A Typology of 'Hooks' in Popular Records." *Popular Music* 6 (1987): 1-20.

Butler, Judith. *Gender Trouble: Feminism and the Subversion of Identity.* London: Routledge & Kegan Paul, 1990.

———. "Imitation and Gender Insubordination." *Inside/Out.* Ed. Diana Fuss. New York: Routledge, 1991. 13-31.

Caduto, Michael J., and Joseph Bruchac. *Keepers of the Earth: Native Stories and Environmental Activities for Children.* Saskatoon, Saskatchewan, Canada: Fifth House, 1989.

Califia, Pat. *Public Sex: The Culture of Radical Sex.* San Francisco: Cleis, 1994.

Cambridge Dictionary of Philosophy. Ed. Robert Audi. Cambridge, UK: Cambridge University Press, 1995.

Cammermeyer, Margarethe, and Chris Fisher. *Serving in Silence.* New York: Viking, 1994.

Campanelli, Pauline. *Wheel of the Year: Living the Magical Life.* St. Paul, MN: Llewellyn, 1989.

Carpenter, Edmund. "The New Languages." *The New Languages: A Rhetorical Approach to Mass Media and Popular Culture.* Eds. Thomas H. Ohlgren and Lynn M. Berk. Englewood Cliffs, NJ: Prentice Hall, 1977. 4-12.

Cashorali, Peter. *Fairy Tales: Traditional Stories Retold for Gay Men.* San Francisco: Harper, 1995.

Cavan, Sheri. *Liquor License: An Ethnography of Bar Behavior.* Chicago: Aldine, 1966.

Chauncey, George. *Gay New York: Gender, Urban Culture, and the Making of the Gay Male World, 1890-1940.* New York: Basic Books, 1994.

Cheney, Lynne V. *Telling the Truth: Why Our Culture and Our Country Have Stopped Making Sense—and What We Can Do about It.* New York: Simon & Schuster, 1995.

Chia, Mantak, and Douglas Abrams Arava. *The Multi-Orgasmic Man: Sexual Secrets Every Man Should Know.* San Francisco: Harper, 1996.

Childress, David Hatcher. *Anti-Gravity and the World Grid.* Stelle, IL: Adventures Unlimited, 1987.

Chin, Tsao Hsueh. *Dream of the Red Chamber.* Trans. Chi-Chen Wang. New York: Twayne, 1958.

———. *A Dream of Red Mansions.* Trans. Yang Hsien-Yi and Gladys Yang. Peking, People's Republic of China: Foreign Languages Press, 1978.

Clark, Donald Lemen. *Rhetoric in Greco-Roman Education.* Westport, CT: Greenwood, 1977.

Clover, Carol J. *Men, Women and Chainsaws: Gender in the Modern Horror Film.* Princeton, NJ: Princeton University Press, 1992.

Coleridge, Samuel Taylor. *Selected Poetry and Prose of Coleridge.* New York: Random House, 1951.

Collingwood, R. G. *The Principles of Art.* New York: Oxford University Press, 1969.

Collins, Patricia Hill. *Black Feminist Thought: Knowledge, Consciousness, and the Politics of Empowerment.* New York: Routledge, Chapman & Hall, 1991.

Comfort, Alex. *The Joy of Sex: A Cordon Bleu Guide to Lovemaking.* New York: Crown, 1972.

Cooper, Emmanuel. *Fully Exposed: The Male Nude in Photography.* 2nd ed. London: Routledge, 1995.

Cose, Ellis. *A Man's World: How Real Is Male Privilege—and How High Is the Price?* New York: HarperCollins, 1995.

Craft, Ann, ed. *Practice Issues in Sexuality and Learning Disabilities.* New York: Routledge, 1994.

Croce, Benedetto. *Aesthetic.* Trans. Douglas Ainslie. New York: Noonday, 1970.

Davis, Melody D. *The Male Nude in Contemporary Photography.* Philadelphia: Temple University Press, 1991.

Deleuze, Gilles, and Felix Guattari. *Anti-Oedipus: Capitalism and Schizophrenia.* Trans. Robert Hurley, Mark Seem, and Helen R. Lane. Minneapolis: University of Minnesota Press, 1983.

D'Emilio, John. *Sexual Politics, Sexual Communities: The Making of a Homosexual Minority in the United States, 1940-1970.* Chicago: University of Chicago Press, 1983.

DeRomilly, Jacqueline. *Magic and Rhetoric in Ancient Greece.* Cambridge, MA: Harvard University Press, 1975.

Dewey, John. *Art as Experience.* New York: Capricorn, 1958.

DiLallo, Kevin, and Jack Krumholtz. *The Unofficial Gay Manual: Living the Lifestyle (Or at Least Appearing To).* New York: Main Street Books, 1994.

Dodds, E. R. *The Greeks and the Irrational.* Berkeley: University of California Press, 1951.

Dolce, Joe. "The Warrior, the Wound and Woman-Hate: The Politics of Softfear." *Changing Men* 26 (1993): 6-12.

Douglas, Ann. "Soft-Porn Culture." *New Republic* 30 (August 1980): 25-29.

Douglas, J. D. *Understanding Everyday Life: Toward the Reconstruction of Sociological Knowledge.* Chicago: Aldine, 1970.

Dover, Kenneth James. *Greek Homosexuality.* Cambridge, MA: Harvard University Press, 1978.

Dowling, Colette. *The Cinderella Complex: Women's Hidden Fear of Independence.* New York: Pocket, 1981.

Driessen, Henk. "Gestured Masculinity: Body and Sociability in Rural Andalusia." *A Cultural History of Gesture.* Eds. Jan Bremmer and Herman Roodenburg. Ithaca, NY: Cornell University Press, 1991. 237-252.

Duberman, Martin. *About Time: Exploring the Gay Past.* New York: Meridian, 1991.

———. *Cures: A Gay Man's Odyssey.* New York: Plume, 1992.

———. *Stonewall.* New York: Penguin, 1993.

Duberman, Martin, Martha Vicinus, and George Chauncey, Jr., eds. *Hidden from History: Reclaiming the Gay and Lesbian Past.* New York: Meridian, 1989.

Dubos, Jean Baptiste. *Critical Reflections on Poetry, Painting and Music.* Facsimile of 1748 ed. Trans. Thomas Nugent. New York: AMS, 1978.

Duggan, Lisa, and Nan D. Hunter. *Sex Wars: Sexual Dissent and Political Culture.* New York: Routledge, 1995.

Dundes, Alan, ed. *Cinderella: A Casebook.* Madison: University of Wisconsin Press, 1988.

Dylan, Bob. *Writings and Drawings.* New York: Random House, 1973.

Eco, Umberto. *The Name of the Rose.* Trans. William Weaver. New York: Warner Books, 1984.

———. *The Open Work.* Trans. Anna Cancogni. Cambridge, MA: Harvard University Press, 1989.

———. *Travels in Hyperreality.* Trans. William Weaver. San Diego, CA: Harcourt, Brace, Jovanovich, 1986.

Eisler, Riane. *Sacred Pleasure: Sex, Myth, and the Politics of the Body.* San Francisco: HarperCollins, 1995.

The Emergency of Black and the Emergence of Rap. Ed. Jon Michael Spencer. Durham, NC: Duke University Press, 1991.

Engle, Gary. *This Grotesque Essence: Plays from the American Minstrel Stage.* Baton Rouge: Louisiana State University Press, 1978.

Estes, Clarissa Pinkola. *Women Who Run with the Wolves: Myths and Stories of the Wild Woman Archetype.* New York: Ballantine, 1992.

Evans, Arthur. *The God of Ecstasy: Sex Roles and the Madness of Dionysus.* New York: St. Martin's, 1988.

———. *Witchcraft and the Gay Counterculture.* Boston: Fag Rag Books, 1978.

Evans, Walter. "Monster Movies: A Sexual Theory." *Journal of Popular Film* 4 (1975): 124-142.

Farmer, Steven. *The Wounded Male.* Los Angeles: Lowell House, 1991.

Fish, Stanley. *Is There a Text in This Class? The Authority of Interpretive Communities.* Cambridge, MA: Harvard University Press, 1980.

Fiske, John. *Understanding Popular Culture.* Boston: Unwin Hyman, 1989.

Fleming, Ian. *Casino Royale.* New York: MacMillan, 1953.

Forbidden Fruits: Taboos and Tabooism in Culture. Ed. Ray B. Browne. Bowling Green, OH: Bowling Green University Popular Press, 1984.

Fornas, J. "Moving Rock: Youth and Pop in Late Modernity." *Popular Music* 9 (1990): 291-306.

Foucault, Michel. *Discipline and Punish: The Birth of the Prison.* Trans. Alan Sheridan. New York: Pantheon, 1977.

Frank, Robert. "Women Want the Whole Package: For Some, UPS Delivery Men Are Sex Symbols for the '90s." *Toledo Blade* 19 Feb. 1995: C12.

Frazer, James G. *The Golden Bough: A Study in Magic and Religion.* 1911. 12 vols. Edinburgh, Scotland: R. & R. Clark, 1935.

Fretts, Bruce. *The Entertainment Weekly Seinfeld Companion, Atomic Wedgies to Zipper Jobs: An Unofficial Guide to TV's Funniest Show.* New York: Warner Books, 1993.

Freud, Sigmund. *Three Essays on the Theory of Sexuality.* 1905. Trans. James Strachey. New York: Basic Books, 1962.

Friedan, Betty. *The Feminine Mystique.* New York: Norton, 1963.

Gadon, Elinor W. *The Once and Future Goddess.* San Francisco: Harper, 1989.

Garber, Marjorie. *Vested Interests: Cross Dressing and Cultural Anxiety.* New York: Routledge, 1992.

Geertz, Clifford. *After the Fact: Two Countries, Four Decades, One Anthropologist.* Cambridge, MA: Harvard University Press, 1995.

———. *The Interpretation of Cultures.* New York: Basic Books, 1973.

Gibson, William. *Burning Chrome.* New York: Ace, 1987.

Gilligan, Carol. *In a Different Voice: Psychological Theory and Women's Development.* Cambridge, MA: Harvard University Press, 1982.

Glassie, Henry. *Passing the Time in Ballymenone: Culture and History of an Ulster Community.* Philadelphia: University of Pennsylvania Press, 1982.

Goffman, Erving. *Behavior in Public Places: Notes on the Social Organization of Gatherings.* New York: Free Press, 1966.

———. *Gender Advertisements.* New York: Harper & Row, 1976.

———. *Interaction Ritual: Essays on Face-to-Face Behavior.* New York: Pantheon, 1982.

———. *The Presentation of Self in Everyday Life.* Garden City, NY: Doubleday, 1959.

Goldstein, Laurence, ed. *The Female Body: Figures, Styles, Speculations.* Ann Arbor: University of Michigan Press, 1991.

Goodman, Felicitas D. *Where the Spirits Ride the Wind: Trance Journeys and Other Ecstatic Experiences.* Bloomington: Indiana University Press, 1990.

Goodwin, Marjorie Harness. *He-Said-She-Said: Talk as Social Organization among Black Children.* Bloomington: Indiana University Press, 1990.

Groneman, Carol. "Nymphomania: The Historical Construction of Female Sexuality." *Signs* 19, 2 (Winter 1994): 337-360.

Halperin, David M. *One Hundred Years of Homosexuality: And Other Essays on Greek Love.* New York: Routledge, 1990.

Hamilton, Edith. *The Greek Way.* New York: Modern Library, 1942.

Harding, Christopher, ed. *Wingspan: Inside the Men's Movement.* New York: St. Martin's, 1992.

Harner, Michael. *The Way of the Shaman: A Guide to Power and Healing.* New York: Bantam, 1982.

Harris, Thomas. *The Silence of the Lambs.* New York: St. Martin's, 1989.

Hart, Jack. *Gay Sex: A Manual for Men Who Love Men.* Boston: Alyson, 1991.

Harvard Dictionary of Music. Cambridge, MA: Harvard University Press.

Heller, Terry. *The Delights of Terror: An Aesthetics of the Tale of Terror.* Urbana: University of Illinois Press, 1987.

Helprin, Mark. *Winter's Tale.* New York: Pocket, 1983.

Herdt, Gilbert, ed. *Gay Culture in America: Essays from the Field.* Boston: Beacon, 1992.

Hereck, Gregory M., and Kevin T. Berrill, eds. *Hate Crimes.* Newbury Park, CA: Sage, 1992.

Hillerman, Tony. *Sacred Clowns.* New York: HarperCollins, 1993.

Hirsch, E. D., Jr. *Cultural Literacy: What Every American Needs to Know.* Boston: Houghton Mifflin, 1987.

Hirschfeld, Magnus. *Curious Sex Customs in the Far East: The World Journey of a Sexologist.* New York: Capricorn, 1965.

Hocquenghem, Guy. *Homosexual Desire.* Trans. Daniella Dangoor. Durham, NC: Duke University Press, 1993.

Holleran, Andrew. *The Beauty of Men.* New York: William Morrow, 1996.

———. *Dancer from the Dance.* New York: Bantam, 1979.

Holmberg, Carl Bryan. "Dialectical Rhetoric and Rhetorical Rhetoric." *Philosophy and Rhetoric* 10 (1977): 232-243.

———. "Hey Butch, Your Slip(page) Is Showing! The New Language of Self-Presentation and the Paradoxes of the He/art." *Harvard Gay and Lesbian Review* 3, 3 (1996): 25-27.

———. "The Rhetoric of Media and Popular Culture as the Basis of Culture Studies: A Postmodern Critique." *Popular Culture in the Twenty-First Century: Essays in Honor of Ray Browne.* Eds. Marilyn Motz, Jack Nachbar, et al. Bowling Green, OH: Bowling Green University Popular Press, 1994. 171-189.

———. "Stray the Course: Technology's Impact upon the Representative-Elector Artifact." *Communication Quarterly* 32 (1984): 84-90.

———. "Toward the Rhetoric of Music: 'Dixie.' " *Southern Speech Communication Journal* 51 (1985): 71-82.

Holmberg, Carl, and William MacDonald. "Student Perceptions of Assault and Date Rape: A Qualitative and Quantitative Study." *Campus Law Enforcement Journal* 20 (1990): 16-19.

hooks, bell. *A'int I a Woman: Black Women and Feminism.* Boston: South End, 1981.

———. *Talking Back: Thinking Feminist, Thinking Black.* Boston: South End, 1989.

Hooven, F. Valentine, III. *Beefcake: The Muscle Magazines of America 1950-1970.* Cologne, Germany: Benedikt Taschen, 1992.

Hoppenstand, Gary, and Ray B. Browne, eds. *The Gothic World of Anne Rice.* Bowling Green, OH: Bowling Green State University Popular Press, 1996.

Huer, Jon. *Art, Beauty and Pornography: A Journey through American Culture.* Buffalo, NY: Prometheus, 1987.

Hume, David. "Of Tragedy." *The Philosophical Works.* By David Hume. Vol. 3. Eds. Thomas Green and Thomas Grose. Darmstadt, Germany: Scientia Verlag Aalen, 1964. 258-265.

Ingebretsen, S. J., ed. *Maps of Heaven, Maps of Hell: Religious Terror as Memory from the Puritans to Stephen King.* New York: M. E. Sharpe, 1996.

Iser, Wolfgang. *The Act of Reading.* Baltimore: Johns Hopkins University Press, 1978.

Jewett, R., and J. Laurence. "Norm Demolition Derbies: Rites of Reversal in Popular Culture." *Journal of Popular Culture* 9 (1976): 976-982.

Jones, Stephen, ed. *Clive Barker's Shadows of Eden*. Lancaster, PA: Underwood-Miller, 1991. 202-208.

Jung, Carl. "The Archetypes and the Collective Unconscious." *The Collected Works of C. G. Jung.* Vol. 9, part 1. Trans. R. F. C. Hull. Princeton, NJ: Princeton University Press, 1970.

Jung, Patricia Beattie, and Ralph F. Smith. *Heterosexism: An Ethical Challenge.* Albany: State University of New York Press, 1993.

Juno, Andrea, and V. Vale. *Angry Women.* San Francisco: Re/Search Publications, 1991.

Kalweit, Holger. *Dreamtime and Inner Space: The World of the Shaman.* Trans. Werner Wunsche. Boston: Shambhala, 1988.

Kammer, Jack. " 'Male' is not a Four-Letter Word." *Wingspan: Inside the Men's Movement.* Ed. Christopher Harding. New York: St. Martin's, 1992. 63-71.

Kant, Immanuel. *Critique of Judgment.* Trans. J. H. Bernard. New York: Hafner, 1968.

———. *On History.* Trans. Lewis White Beck, Robert E. Anchor, and Emil L. Fackenheim. Indianapolis, IN: Bobbs-Merrill, 1963.

Karlen, Arno. *Sexuality and Homosexuality.* New York: Norton, 1971.

Katz, Jonathan Ned. *Gay/Lesbian Almanac: A New Documentary.* New York: Carroll & Graf, 1994.

———. *The Invention of Heterosexuality.* New York: Dutton/Penguin, 1995.

Keen, Sam. *Fire in the Belly: On Being a Man.* New York: Bantam, 1991.

Kempton, Winifred. *Techniques for Leading Group Discussions on Human Sexuality.* 2nd ed. Philadelphia: Planned Parenthood of Southeastern Pennsylvania, 1973.

Kempton, Winifred, and Rose Forman. *Guidelines for Training in Sexuality and the Mentally Handicapped.* Philadelphia: Planned Parenthood, 1976.

Kinder, Marsha. "Music Video and the Spectator: Television, Ideology, and Dream." *Television: The Critical View.* Ed. Horace Newcomb. 4th ed. New York: Oxford University Press, 1987.

King, Stephen. *Danse Macabre.* New York: Berkley, 1983.

Kinsman, Gary. *The Regulation of Desire: Sexuality in Canada.* Montréal, Quebec, Canada: Black Rose, 1987.

Kirk, Marshall, and Hunter Madsen. *After the Ball: How America Will Conquer Its Fear and Hatred of Gays in the 90s.* New York: Plume, 1990.

Koontz, Dean R. *The Funhouse.* New York: Berkley, 1994.

———. *Midnight.* New York: Berkley, 1989.

Krafft-Ebing, Richard Von. *Psychopathia Sexualis.* 1894. Trans. Harry E. Wedeck. New York: G. P. Putnam, 1965.

Kramarae, Cheris, and Dale Spender, eds. *The Knowledge Explosion: Generations of Feminist Scholarship.* New York: Teachers College Press, 1992.

LaDuke, Winona. "War of the Rices." *State of the Peoples: A Global Human Rights Report and Societies in Danger.* Ed. Marc S. Miller. Boston: Beacon, 1993. 40-45.

Lauritsen, John, and David Thorstad. *The Early Homosexual Rights Movement (1864-1935).* New York: Times Change Press, 1974.

LeFanu, Joseph Sheridan. *Best Ghost Stories of J. S. LeFanu.* New York: Dover, 1964.

Legman, G. *Rationale of the Dirty Joke: An Analysis of Sexual Humor.* First Series. New York: Grove, 1968.

———. *Rationale of the Dirty Joke: An Analysis of Sexual Humor.* Second Series. New York: Breaking Point, 1975.

Lessing, Gotthold Ephraim. *Laocoön: An Essay in the Limits of Painting and Poetry.* Trans. Edward Allen McCormick. Indianapolis, IN: Bobbs-Merrill, 1962.

Levins, Hoag. *American Sex Machines: The Hidden History of Sex at the U.S. Patent Office.* Holbrook, MA: Adams Media Corporation, 1996.

Lévi-Strauss, Claude. *Structural Anthropology.* Trans. Claire Jacobson and Brooke Grundfest Schoepf. New York: Basic Books, 1963.

Liddell, Henry George, and Robert Scott. *Unabridged Greek Lexicon.* 1843. 61st reprint of 9th ed. Oxford, UK: Clarendon, 1940.

Liungman, Carl G. *Dictionary of Symbols.* Trans. Carl G. Liungman of 1974 *Symboler—västerländska ideogram.* New York: Norton, 1991.

Lord, M. G. *Forever Barbie: The Unauthorized Biography of a Real Doll.* New York: William Morrow, 1994.

Lovett-Graff, Bennett. "Culture Wars II: A Review Essay." *Modern Language Studies* 24, 3 (1995): 99-124.

Malanaga. *The Kama Sutra of Vatsayana.* Trans. Richard Burton and F. F. Arbuthnot. New York: G. P. Putnam/Berkley, 1963.

Malinowski, Sharon, and Christa Brelin. *The Gay and Lesbian Literary Companion.* Detroit, MI: Visible Ink Press, 1995.

Mander, Jerry. *In the Absence of the Sacred: The Failure of Technology and the Survival of the Indian Nations.* San Francisco: Sierra Club Books, 1991.

Mann, Nicholas R. *His Story: Masculinity in the Post-Patriarchal World.* St. Paul, MN: Llewellyn, 1995.

Mark, Marky, and Lynn Goldsmith. *Marky Mark.* New York: HarperCollins, 1992.

Mark, Ted. *The Man from O.R.G.Y.* New York, Lancer, 1965.

———. *My Son, the Double Agent.* New York: Lancer, 1966.

Maupin, Armistead. *Tales of the City.* New York: HarperPerennial, 1994.

Mazis, Glen A. *The Trickster, Magician and Grieving Man: Reconnecting Men with Earth.* Santa Fe, NM: Bear, 1993.

McDonald, Keiko I. *Cinema East: A Critical Study of Major Japanese Films.* New Brunswick, NJ: Associated University Presses, 1983.

McLuhan, Marshall (with Quentin Fiore). *The Medium Is the Massage: An Inventory of Effects.* New York: Bantam, 1967.

Mei, Huang. *Transforming the Cinderella Dream: From Frances Burney to Charlotte Brontë.* New Brunswick, NJ: Rutgers University Press, 1990.

Messner, Michael A., and Donald F. Sabo. *Sex, Violence and Power in Sports: Rethinking Masculinity.* Freedom, CA: Crossing Press, 1994.

Minard, Rosemary. *Womenfolk and Fairy Tales.* Boston: Houghton Mifflin, 1975.

Miss Buxley: Sexism in Beetle Bailey? Bedford, NY: n.p., 1982.

Monette, Paul. *Becoming a Man: Half a Life Story.* San Francisco: HarperCollins, 1993.

Money, John. *Gendermaps: Social Constructionism, Feminism, and Sexosophical History.* New York: Continuum, 1995.

Mooney, Thomas O., Theodore M. Cole, and Richard A. Chilgren. *Sexual Options for Paraplegics and Quadriplegics.* Boston: Little, Brown, 1975.

Moritz, Robert. "The Single Guy." *Gentlemen's Quarterly* 8 Aug. 1996: 91-92.

Munster, Bill, ed. *Sudden Fear: The Horror and Dark Suspense Fiction of Dean R. Koontz.* Mercer Island, WA: Starmont, 1988.

Murasaki, Shikibu. *The Tale of Genji.* Trans. Arthur Waley. New York: Anchor, 1955.

Nachbar, Jack, Deborah Weiser, and John L. Wright, eds. *The Popular Culture Reader.* Bowling Green, OH: Bowling Green University Popular Press, 1978.

Nash, Elizabeth. *Plaisirs d'Amour: An Erotic Guide to the Senses.* San Francisco: Harper, 1995.

Neistadt, Maureen, and Maureen Freda. *Choices: A Guide to Sex Counseling with Physically Disabled Adults.* Malabar, FL: Krieger, 1987.

Nelson, James B. *Embodiment: An Approach to Sexuality and Christian Theology.* Minneapolis, MN: Augsburg, 1978.

Nietzsche, Friedrich. *The Birth of Tragedy.* Trans. William A. Haussmann. New York: Russell & Russell, 1964.

Niven, Anne Newkirk. "Living the Dream." *SageWoman* 33 (Spring 1996): 3-4.

Norbeck, E. *Religion in Human Life: Anthropological Views.* New York: Holt, Rinehart & Winston, 1974.

Noss, David S., and John B. Noss. *A History of the World's Religions.* 9th ed. New York: Macmillan, 1994.

Nye, Russell. *The Unembarrassed Muse: The Popular Arts in America.* New York: Dial, 1970.

Ong, Walter. *The Presence of the Word: Some Prolegomena for Cultural and Religious History.* New Haven, CT: Yale University Press, 1967.

Oxford English Dictionary. Eds. J. A. Simpson and E. S. C. Weiner. 2nd ed. 20 vols. Oxford, UK: Clarendon, 1989.

Paglia, Camille. *Vamps and Tramps: New Essays.* New York: Vintage, 1994.

Peper, Karen. "Female Athlete = Lesbian: A Myth Constructed from Gendex Role Expectations and Lesbiphobia." *Queer Words, Queer Images: Communication and the Construction of Homosexuality.* Ed. R. Jeffrey Ringer. New York: New York University Press, 1994. 193-208.

Phillips, Adam. *On Flirtation.* Cambridge, MA: Harvard University Press, 1994.

Popper, Karl R. *The Open Society and Its Enemies.* 2 vols. Princeton, NJ: Princeton University Press, 1966.

Pronger, Brian. *The Arena of Masculinity: Sports, Homosexuality and the Meaning of Sex.* New York: St. Martin's, 1990.

The Prospect of Rhetoric: Report on the National Development Project. Eds. Lloyd F. Bitzer and Edwin Black. Englewood Cliffs, NJ: Prentice Hall, 1971.

Radway, Janice A. *Reading the Romance: Women, Patriarchy and Popular Literature.* Chapel Hill: University of North Carolina Press, 1984.

Ramsland, Katherine. *The Roquelaure Reader: A Companion to Anne Rice's Erotica.* New York: Plume, 1996.

Reid, John (pen name). *The Best Little Boy in the World.* New York: Ballantine, 1993.

Reuben, David R. *Everything You Always Wanted to Know about Sex (But Were Afraid to Ask).* New York: McKay, 1969.

Reynolds, Joshua. *Discourses on Art.* Ed. Robert R. Wark. New Haven, CT: Yale University Press, 1975.

Rice, Anne. *Interview with the Vampire.* New York: Knopf, 1976.

———. *Memnoch the Devil.* The Vampire Chronicles. New York: Knopf, 1995.

———. *The Mummy or Ramses the Damned.* New York: Ballantine, 1989.

———. *Servant of the Bones.* New York: Knopf, 1996.

Rice, Anne, as Anne Rampling. *Exit to Eden.* New York: Ballantine, 1985.

Richter, Alan. *Dictionary of Sexual Slang: Words, Phrases and Idioms from AC/DC to Zig-Zig.* New York: John Wiley, 1993.

Ritual Sex. Eds. David Aaron Clark and Tristan Taormino. New York: Masquerade, 1996.

Rodman, Dennis, and Tim Keown. *Bad as I Wanna Be.* New York: Delacorte/Bantam Doubleday Dell, 1996.

Rogers, Carl. *On Becoming a Person: A Therapist's View of Psychotherapy.* Boston: Houghton Mifflin, 1961.

Roman, Camille, Suzanne Juhasz, and Critanne Miller, eds. *The Women and Language Debate: A Sourcebook.* New Brunswick, NJ: Rutgers University Press, 1994.

Roscoe, Will, ed. *Living the Spirit: A Gay American Indian Anthology.* New York: St. Martin's, 1988.

Roszak, Betty, and Theodore Roszak. *Masculine/Feminine: Readings in Sexual Mythology and the Liberation of Women.* New York: Harper & Row, 1969.

Rubin, Gayle. "The Traffic in Women: Notes on the 'Political Economy' of Sex." *Toward an Anthropology of Women.* Ed. Rayna R. Reiter. New York: Monthly Review Press, 1975. 157-210.

Rubin, Lillian B. *Erotic Wars: What Happened to the Sexual Revolution?* New York: Farrar, Straus & Giroux, 1990.

Rubin, William. *Picasso and Braque: Pioneering Cubism.* Boston: Little, Brown, 1989.

Russell, Ray. *Playboy's Ribald Classics.* New York: Waldorf, 1957.

Russo, Vito. *The Celluloid Closet: Homosexuality in the Movies.* Rev. ed. New York: Harper & Row, 1987.

Sann, Paul. *Fads, Follies and Delusions of the American People.* New York: Crown, 1967.

Santino, Jack. "Popular Culture: A Socio-Aesthetic Approach." *Studies in Latin American Popular Culture* 15 (1996): 31-41.

Sarasohn, Lisa. "Goddess Ungirdled." *SageWoman* 33 (Spring 1996): 6-10.

Schlafly, Phyllis. *The Power of the Positive Woman.* New Rochelle, NY: Arlington House, 1977.

Schramm, Wilbur. *The Process and Effects of Mass Communication.* Urbana: University of Illinois Press, 1955.

Sedgwick, Eve Kosofsky. *Between Men: English Literature and Male Homosocial Desire.* New York: Columbia University Press, 1985.

———. *Epistemology of the Closet.* Berkeley: University of California Press, 1990.

Seigel, Jerrold. *The Private Worlds of Marcel Duchamp: Desire, Liberation and the Self in Modern Culture.* Berkeley: University of California Press, 1995.

Senf, Carol A. *The Vampire in 19th Century English Literature.* Bowling Green, OH: Bowling Green State University Popular Press, 1988.

Shelley, Mary Wollstonecraft. *Frankenstein or the Modern Prometheus.* New York: Collier/Macmillan, 1961.

Shilts, Randy. *And the Band Played On: Politics, People and the AIDS Epidemic.* New York: St. Martin's, 1987.

Silverberg, Robert. *The Book of Skulls.* New York: Berkley, 1972.

Silverstein, Charles, and Felice Picano. *The New Joy of Gay Sex.* San Francisco: HarperCollins, 1993.

Simpson, Mark, ed. *Male Impersonators: Men Performing Masculinity.* New York: Routledge, 1994.

Sisley, Emily L., and Bertha Harris. *The Joy of Lesbian Sex: A Tender and Liberated Guide to the Pleasures and Problems of a Lesbian Lifestyle.* New York: Crown, 1977.

Spradley, James. *The Ethnographic Interview.* New York: Holt, Rinehart & Winston, 1979.

———. *Participant Observation.* New York: Holt, Rinehart & Winston, 1980.

Spradley, James P., and Brenda Mann. *The Cocktail Waitress: Woman's Work in a Man's World.* New York: John Wiley, 1985.

Steffan, Joseph. *Honor Bound: A Gay American Fights for the Right to Serve His Country.* New York: Villard, 1992.

Steinem, Gloria. *Revolution from Within.* Boston: Little, Brown, 1992.

Stewart, Steve. *Gay Hollywood Film and Video Guide.* Laguna, CA: Companion, 1994.

Swan, James A. *The Power of Place: Sacred Ground in Natural and Human Environments.* Wheaton, IL: Quest, 1991.

Tallmer, Margot. *Questions and Answers about Sex in Later Life.* Philadelphia: Charles Press, 1996.

Tatchell, Peter. *Safer Sexy: The Guide to Gay Sex Safely.* London: Freedom Editions, 1994.

Thomas, Brandon. *Charley's Aunt: A Play in Three Acts.* New York: Samuel French, 1965.

Tillich, Paul. *Systematic Theology.* 3 vols. Chicago: University of Chicago Press, 1951-1963.

———. *Ultimate Concern: Tillich in Dialogue.* Ed. D. MacKenzie Brown. New York: Harper & Row, 1965.

Timberg, Bernard. "The Rhetoric of the Camera in Television Soap Opera." *Television: The Critical View.* Ed. Horace Newcomb. 4th ed. New York: Oxford University Press, 1987. 164-178.

Tiptree, James, Jr. "Houston, Houston, Do You Read Me?" *Worlds Apart: An Anthology of Lesbian and Gay Science Fiction and Fantasy.* Eds. Camilla Decarnin, Eric Garber, and Lyn Paleo. Boston: Alyson, 1986. 37-94.

Tomlinson, Lori. "This A'int No Disco, or Is It? Youth Culture and Rave Phenomenon." *Youth Culture: Identity in a Postmodern World*. Ed. Jonathon S. Epstein. Cambridge, MA: Blackwell, 1997.

Tripp, C. A. *The Homosexual Matrix*. 2nd ed. New York: Meridian, 1987.

Tuana, Nancy, and Rosemarie Tong. *Feminism and Philosophy: Essential Readings in Theory, Reinterpretation and Application*. Boulder, CO: Westview, 1995.

Turner, Victor, ed. *Celebration: Studies in Festivity and Ritual*. Washington, DC: Smithsonian Institution, 1982.

———. *The Forest of Symbols: Aspects of Ndembu Ritual*. Ithaca, NY: Cornell University Press, 1967.

Tyler, Carole-Anne. "Boys Will Be Girls: The Politics of Gay Drag." *Inside/Out*. Ed. Diana Fuss. New York City: Routledge, 1991. 32-70.

Tyler, Mick. "A Matter of Survival." *Advocate Men* May 1994: 17-20.

Underwood, Tim, and Chuck Miller, eds. *Fear Itself: The Horror Fiction of Stephen King*. New York: New American Library, 1982.

Valdivia, Angharad N. *Feminism, Multiculturalism and the Media and Global Diversities*. Thousand Oaks, CA: Sage, 1995.

Van Gennep, Arnold. *The Rites of Passage*. Chicago: University of Chicago Press, 1960.

Van Gulik, R. H. *Sexual Life in Ancient China: A Preliminary Survey of Chinese Sex and Society from ca 1500 B.C. till 1644 A.D.* Leiden, Netherlands: E. J. Brill, 1961.

Warren, Patricia Nell. *The Fancy Dancer*. New York: Plume, 1976.

———. *The Front Runner*. New York: Plume, 1974.

Watson, William. *Chinese Ivories from the Shang to the Qing*. London: British Museum Publications, 1984.

Watts, Alan W. *Nature, Man, and Woman*. New York: Vintage, 1970.

Watzlawick, Paul. *The Language of Change: Elements of Therapeutic Communication*. New York: Basic Books, 1978.

Watzlawick, Paul, Janet Beavin, and Donald Jackson. *The Pragmatics of Human Communication: A Study of Interactional Patterns, Pathologies and Paradoxes*. New York: Norton, 1974.

Wiener, Norbert. *Cybernetics, or Control and Communication in the Animal and the Machine*. New York: John Wiley, 1948.

Willeford, William. *The Fool and His Scepter: A Study of Clowns and Jesters and Their Audience*. Evanston, IL: Northwestern University Press, 1969.

Williams, Walter L. *The Spirit and the Flesh: Sexual Diversity in American Indian Culture*. Boston: Beacon, 1986.

Winn, James Anderson. *Unsuspected Eloquence*. New Haven, CT: Yale University Press, 1981.

Wymard, Ellie. *Men on Divorce: Conversations with Ex-husbands*. Carson, CA: Hay House, 1994.

Yolen, Jane. "America's Cinderella." *Cinderella: A Casebook*. Ed. Alan Dundes. Madison: University of Wisconsin Press, 1988. 294-306.

Zeeland, Steven. *Barrack Buddies and Soldier Lovers: Dialogues with Gay Young Men in the U.S. Military*. New York: Harrington Park/Haworth, 1993.

Index

About the Author

Carl B. Holmberg is Associate Professor of Popular Culture at Bowling Green State University. He studied music and interdisciplinary and Asian studies at Heidelberg College, Tiffin, Ohio; philosophy at The University of Innsbruck; interdisciplinary studies and classics at The University of Chicago; and communication studies, field methods, and Attic Greek at Ohio University. He enjoys media studies, gender studies, and figuring out how horror fictions work. He has published interdisciplinary research in journals as diverse as *Philosophy and Rhetoric, Communication Education, Popular Music and Society,* and *Campus Law Enforcement Journal.* Other scholarly projects include anthology, dictionary, and encyclopedia entries with separate studies of horror music, audeography, gay and lesbian human rights groups, and men's mysteries forthcoming. A brace of poetry, *Split Rails,* was released in November 1997, and a novel and other fictions are on their way. When he is not playing racquetball or working out, he is continuing a longitudinal ethnographic study of parties and social gatherings begun in 1983.